Group F

and

Public Policy

Group Politics

and

Public Policy

Second Edition

A. PAUL PROSS

Toronto   OXFORD UNIVERSITY PRESS   1992

Oxford University Press, 70 Wynford Drive, Don Mills, Ontario M3C 1J9

Toronto   Oxford   New York
Delhi   Bombay   Calcutta   Madras   Karachi   Kuala Lumpur
Singapore   Hong Kong   Tokyo   Nairobi   Dar es Salaam
Cape Town   Melbourne   Auckland

and associated companies in
Berlin   Ibadan

CANADIAN CATALOGUING IN PUBLICATION DATA

Pross, A. Paul, 1939-
Group politics and public policy

2nd ed.
Includes bibliographical references and index.
ISBN 0-19-540892-6

1. Pressure groups–Canada. 2. Canada–Politics and
government. 3. Political planning–Canada. I. Title.

JL148.5.P76 1992   322.4'3'0971   C92-093017-4

This book is printed on permanent (acid-free) paper.

FOR CATHERINE

Contents

Figures and Tables

Preface

In 1986, when *Group Politics and Public Policy* was first published, Canadians were beginning to realize that pressure groups had become prominent political actors. In the six years since, the significance of their role was brought home to us time and time again. In the Meech Lake dispute, the bitter abortion debate, the wrangles over Free Trade and the GST, and on many other occasions pressure groups have been forces to reckon with.

One purpose of this second edition is to keep pace with these events and the changes they have brought with them. It is too soon to reach definitive conclusions or even, in some cases, to discern a trend. Yet we must take note that pressure groups have had an unprecedented impact on constitutional politics; that they have become more litigious; and that their financial relations with government are becoming contentious.

A second edition should also, at least in part, reflect the expansion of the literature. The extent of this expansion can be measured in the select bibliography. Coleman and his colleagues have given an empirical base to some aspects of Canadian pressure group studies. Forster and other historians have enriched our understanding of their past performance. There have been numerous case studies and group 'autobiographies' and some examinations of the ideas presented in the first edition of this book.

The latter have helped me to review those ideas and to push them on a little. In particular, in chapter 4, I have tackled once again the difficult business of categorizing groups. I regret that this discussion is couched in technical language but typologies are by their nature technical and their development demands a more precise, and sometimes alien, terminology.

Much of the evidence that underpins my argument is presented in footnotes and endnotes, but there is a limit to every publisher's bank account and a good deal has had to be excluded. The historical survey offered in chapters 2 and 3 is intended, both in the text and notes, to supply evidence to support the argument developed in the rest of the book. The evidence itself is largely drawn from secondary materials, as is only to be expected in a study that looks at the whole gamut of pressure politics in a country. Where possible I have drawn on my own research and on the many opportunities I have had during my years as a lecturer in a school of public administration to observe at first hand pressure groups and their members.

I should like to thank Phyllis Wilson and Greg Ioannou for the excellent advice they have given me as the book went to press and for their help in seeing it through the process.

A. PAUL PROSS
January, 1992

CHAPTER 1

Introduction:
Groups and Politics

In 1946, pressure groups were of so little moment in Canadian politics that R. MacGregor Dawson did not mention them in his pioneering and highly respected text, *The Government of Canada*.[1] They were a minor feature of federal and provincial politics, insignificant in comparison with such major policy actors as political parties, members of various élites, senior public servants, provincial leaders and, above all, members of the federal Cabinet.

By 1977, however, Robert Stanfield voiced a concern that was shared by many who were familiar with the way policy is made in the federal and provincial capitals. 'It is one thing,' Stanfield declared, 'for individuals to pursue their own interests as they always have: it becomes a qualitatively different kind of society when individuals organize to pursue their individual interests collectively. National life has become a struggle for advantage among large and powerful organizations — not simply trade unions and corporations. Organized pressure groups abound.'[2]

Jeffrey Simpson echoed that same concern in September 1990, when he commented that modern politics is interest-group politics, 'a giant bazaar where parties try with increasing desperation to satisfy interest groups which, by definition, have a stake in being dissatisfied.'[3]

Stanfield, Simpson, and other observers of Canadian politics were worried by the declining influence of political parties; the diminished role of Parliament; the growing power of the Prime Minister and his isolation from traditional influences in the Cabinet and the country; and the extent to which policy-making authority was being delegated to the public service. In the shadowed areas of politics where these changes were taking place, observers could make out more and more prominently the influence of pressure groups. As early as 1965, John Meisel had linked their rise to the decline of political parties, warning that 'their numbers and means permit them to become rivals of political parties' by taking over parties' role as mediators between 'individual and group interests and the state'.[4]

A series of academic publications in the early 1970s helped delineate the activities of pressure groups and seemed to confirm the worst fears of observers.[5] Between 1969 and 1985, private members proposed to the

1

House of Commons no less than nineteen bills providing for the registration and regulation of lobbies, ultimately persuading the Mulroney government in 1987 to secure the passage of an act to register lobbyists.[6] Politicians and journalists criticized retired civil servants who had taken positions with consulting firms and other representatives of special interests.[7] To many this trend smacked of 'influence peddling'. An eminent observer, J.A. Corry, warned that Canada was well on the way to becoming a 'special interest state'.[8] More recently, as the constitutional crisis has developed, the role of the so-called 'Charter groups', particularly groups representing women and the aboriginal peoples, has come under scrutiny.[9] Alan Cairns in his on-going diagnosis of the decline of Canadian federalism has repeatedly drawn attention to the part played by organized interests in the evolution of fragmentation politics.[10]

While these concerns express the widespread fear that the activities of pressure groups threaten democratic government, they also raise other fundamental questions. Why do we have pressure groups? What develop-ments have made them so prominent? Are they now essential institutions? If so, is it sufficient to point to the dangers they pose for Canadian democracy, or should we go further and try to devise ways to safely absorb them into our political system? This book addresses these questions.

WHY DO WE NEED PRESSURE GROUPS?

I will argue that pressure groups are essential in any modern state, and that Canada is no exception to this rule. Furthermore, the ability of pressure groups to channel information to and from policy-makers can work to the advantage of society without jeopardizing traditional democratic institu-tions. I will even suggest that the proliferation of pressure groups has enhanced Canadian democracy, not undermined it.

This argument is not easy to make. Anyone who has studied the policy process in industrialized states knows that while it is a simple matter to demonstrate the functional importance of interest groups, it is much harder to show how they can live in harmony with the institutions of representative government. Nevertheless, we believe that with an understanding of why pressure groups exist, what they do and how they do it, and how and why they relate to other political institutions, the problems they create can be addressed optimistically.

Two parts of this book are especially concerned with these questions. The following three chapters assess our experience with pressure groups, look at their historic origins, and show how their roles have developed as those of other institutions have changed. Pressure groups are seen as 'adaptive' instruments of political communication, equipped with sensitive antennae for locating power. As other political institutions — political parties, cabinets, legislatures, and bureaucratic agencies — have gained and lost power and influence, pressure groups have adjusted their relations with them, expanding their contacts or letting them dry up. As Robert Stanfield and others have done, we will find they have indeed proliferated and their influence has swollen. The historical survey will develop an explanation for their expansion that will be used in the last chapters of the book to give us insight into the meaning of today's trends and to guide our evaluation of the measures that have been proposed, and occasionally implemented, to harness pressure groups' political power.

WHAT ARE PRESSURE GROUPS?

Pressure groups are *organizations whose members act together to influence public policy in order to promote their common interest*.

The chief characteristic of the pressure group is that it tries to persuade governments to pursue the policies it advocates. Persuasion takes many forms, nearly all of them intended to exert political pressure. Most groups hope that the force of logical and well-prepared arguments will be sufficient to convince reluctant ministers and sceptical bureaucrats to adopt their proposals. Failing that, many groups look to an aroused public to persuade government of the error of its ways, as pensioners did when the 1985 budget proposed reducing their incomes. They may imitate the response of the unions to the Trudeau government's wage and price controls and withdraw from advisory boards and other joint activities, actions that can not only embarrass government but deny it access to information. They may threaten economic sanctions. Some observers consider the threat by Native organizations to boycott Expo '86 as a means of forcing the British Columbia government to discuss Haida land claims to be more effective than the demonstrations that had marked the first part of the campaign. The choice of tactics of persuasion can be as extensive as the relationship between government and the society it serves.

Persuasion depends on organization. Modern governments are not easily convinced. Persistence, extensive knowledge of substantive issues and policy processes, and the financial resources necessary to communicate with the public and with government are all essential ingredients in a lobbying campaign. Common objectives must be identified, strategies worked out, procedures adopted, responsibilities assigned, and consistent positions formulated if a group is to persuade government to take specific action and if it is to watch over the development and implementation of supporting policies. Above all, pressure group activity must have continuity if it is to have lasting effect.

These activities require organization, and it is the quality of organization that distinguishes the pressure group from the mob and the movement. The mob is an ephemeral thing, a product of chance. It may win clearly stated and immediately realizable goals. It cannot provide for the future because it cannot provide for its own continued existence. It lacks organizational capacity. In contrast, movements do exist over time, but they represent generalized progressions of public opinion. Organized groups participate in the progression, but the movement consists of too many distinct elements to be described as a coherent unit such as a pressure group. For this reason nationalist movements, for example, are not treated by most writers as pressure groups, though we recognize that pressure groups take part in them.[11] Organization — the association of individuals within a formal structure — is, then, the second defining characteristic of pressure groups.

Organizational capacity facilitates a third characteristic: the articulation and aggregation of common interests. Formal structures and constitutional procedures enable group members to identify the demands they wish to make upon government and to explore the conflicts that arise when the objectives of some members clash with those of others. Debate, though it may entail disaffection and secession, brings these demands together and eventually achieves agreement and support.

Other Types of Groups

Other groups beside pressure groups are formally organized, able to articulate and aggregate common interests, and willing to act in the political system. Political parties are notable examples. The fourth characteristic of pressure groups — the desire to influence those who hold power rather than to exercise the responsibility of government — distinguishes them from these other organizations. Pressure groups focus on the special interests of a few, a restricted role that permits them to complement rather than to rival political parties in the process of political communication.*[12] Any power pressure groups do exert is delegated to them by government and is narrowly defined. By delegating to professional associations the power to regulate their members, for example, the state acknowledges 'the political need to afford a measure of autonomy to those whose activities have been brought within the scope of the law', and admits that the state lacks the administrative capacity to 'fine tune' the relations between a professional group and the public.[13] Even so, the state can always change the powers delegated or even withdraw them.

Having defined what pressure groups are, it is necessary to draw

*Lyon argues that though parties seek direct control of state power directly and the interest groups want only to influence it, and though there are significant organizational and tactical differences between the two, we tend to ignore 'the essential fact that both parties and interest groups want to gain preferential treatment from the state for the core interests which are the *raison d'être*' of each.

distinctions between some of the terms commonly associated with pressure group activity. For example, the terms 'pressure groups' and 'interest groups' are often used interchangeably. To speak of 'interest groups' conveys a sense of general, non-political activities. It, more than the term 'pressure groups', helps us remember that for most of these organizations political activity — activity carried on in relation to the political system — is often a minor and unwelcome addition to the concerns that have brought the group together.

Unfortunately, both terms are frequently used to refer to other aspects of political life. Observers of élite behaviour may speak of governments responding to pressure from 'the interests', without meaning to suggest that these interests have engaged in the type of organized behaviour under study here. Even though pressure group politics may have been a part of the activity to which these observers refer, the more important part probably has been an unorchestrated but compelling expression of individual opinion and the exertion of personal political power by those who stand to gain or lose through changes in government policy. Sometimes these 'interests' are grouped together by the observer because they behave in a certain way or share a common purpose, not because they have developed the organizational structures we associate with formal pressure groups. Simply because consumers are said to want a particular policy, we should not assume that consumers' associations have lobbied for that policy. Organizations that claim to speak for specific interests may take positions quite different from those adopted by the interests themselves. Our terminology has to be precise enough to enable us to recognize such distinctions.

Faced with a choice between using 'interest group' (which is apt to be used imprecisely) and 'pressure group', I prefer the latter, even though it focuses on a narrow aspect of the behaviour I am concerned with, and although some feel it emphasizes a part of the relationship between groups and government that they find distasteful.*

---

*Such objections are nonsensical. Pressure — whether from groups, parties, élites, or from government agencies themselves — is essential to political life, which after all is sometimes referred to as the routinization of conflict. The term 'pressure group' merely recognizes that reality.

S.E. Finer considers the term 'pressure group' too narrow to describe the activities of what he calls 'the lobby'. It is a mistake, he argues, to use a nomenclature that suggests that these organizations constantly apply pressure to government or that they exist solely to influence government. 'Most groups, most of the time, simply make requests or put up a case; they reason and they argue, but they do not threaten' (*Anonymous Empire* [London, 1966], 3). This is true, but it overlooks the possibility that the threat of sanctions, whether explicit or not, is the ultimate weapon of any lobbying group; it suggests that groups are indifferent to the outcome of their interventions, which seems unlikely. It is more realistic to assume that groups do in fact calculate the costs and benefits of applying the sanctions that lie within their power, and in general refrain from exerting the full extent of the leverage available to them. Their restraint is a product of the institutionalization discussed more fully

Nevertheless, the literature refers so frequently to 'interest groups' that we must find a way to clarify the term's various uses. I do this by dividing the entire spectrum of interests associated with any given public policy into three categories: formal interest groups, solidary groups, and latent interests.[14] I prefer to call formal interest groups 'pressure groups'.

Solidarity

A solidary group is 'made up of individuals with common characteristics who also share some sense of identity'.[15] What these individuals have in common may be sufficient to encourage them to vote for one another, or act in one another's interest. It may foster enough group feeling to elicit a common reaction to public events, which may register in individual interventions in public debate (letters to politicians, for example) or in a clustering of group opinion in the polls. But in a solidary group, the recognition of common interest does not bring about a formal organization that can mobilize group effort to achieve policy goals. The composition of the group remains vaguely defined and its political power and influence indeterminate.

Latent

Latent interests are even harder to define — both theoretically and in actual political life — than solidary groups. As the word 'latent' suggests, these interests have not yet been mobilized to recognize shared interests, much less act upon them. Nevertheless, they have political significance. Policy-makers are aware that latent interests are potentially able to achieve self-consciousness and eventual mobilization, and that once they are set in motion their political impact is incalculable. Consequently, politicians and civil servants are often anxious to identify the attitudes of those they judge to be latent interests. Opinion surveys are carried out, experts consulted, and media reports analysed so that policies that are sensitive to the needs of latent interests are developed.

Mobilizing Interests

These categories of interests can be related to one another in a funnel of mobilization, as shown in Figure 1-1. Individuals and corporations with

---

in Chapter 5. For political scientists, who are concerned with the study of power, it makes great sense to characterize a political institution by the feature that best exemplifies its relationship to the state. Nor does use of the term suggest that the political scientist is unaware of the non-political qualities of all groups. Though political scientists must take those qualities into account in assessing the political capacities and activities of groups, these are generally outside their domain.

The term 'lobby' has connotations that are equally difficult to deal with. It is often associated with venal aspects of influencing government. The noun 'lobbyist' can refer to an individual who is part of a group, either as a member or as a full-time employee, but it can also refer to someone who, for a fee, temporarily lobbies on behalf of a group. Generally we will try to avoid confusing these two activities — which have very different implications for behaviour — by referring only to temporary, paid spokesmen as lobbyists.

Figure 1-1: A Funnel of Mobilization

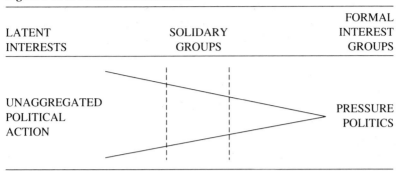

latent interests in common have no sense of solidarity with one another. They may energetically protect their individual interests, but do not feel the need to recognize their mutual interest and promote it collectively. In the centre of the funnel are solidary groups, whose heightened awareness of their common interests has moved them to support one another informally. Their sense of political power has not yet inspired them to establish formal associations to take political action. This occurs in the last stage, when interest groups are formed and carry out campaigns designed to promote the common interest.

Do not assume that because some people with shared interests have been mobilized into pressure groups, the entire interest community — all those who share, or are likely to share, a specific interest — is equally alert and prepared to engage in pressure politics. Many people never recognize their shared interest, others are indifferent, some oppose the use of pressure tactics, and a few would rather act individualistically than join interest groups.

Recent history has given us many examples of interests mobilizing. Native people, while clearly a solidary group, for many years paid scant attention to their potential power. Since the Second World War, however, their awareness has grown apace and in the last two decades it has given birth to various Native pressure groups, and their loose confederation in the National Indian Brotherhood and the Assembly of First Nations.[16] Ronald Manzer's account of the 1960s debate over bilingualism and biculturalism illustrates the way in which Native groups, along with other language and cultural groups, became more and more conscious of their political interests and the need to articulate them:

> During the 1960s two rival perceptions of Canada became the subject of political debate. These were 'The Two Nations Theory' and the 'Mosaic Theory'. The first was expressed most frequently by French Canadians who saw Canada as a partnership between two relatively monolithic language groups.

The second prevailed outside French Canada (and especially outside Quebec) and saw Canada as the home of peoples of many different origins working to form a new nation.

Articulation of these perspectives during the 1960s debate over Confederation, and particularly during the hearings of the Royal Commission on Bilingualism and Biculturalism aroused the concern of two other segments of the Canadian community: the aboriginal peoples and Canadians who were neither of native origin nor English, nor French Canadian. The Indians asked 'Why is the Indian always forgotten? This was the first culture and this was the first language in Canada.' As for others: 'the Royal Commission found that the idea of Canada having a dual culture aroused particular fears among members of European and Asian ethnic groups. They saw themselves and their part in the development of Canada being forgotten in a dialogue defined as being between Canadians of French and British origin, and wanted more emphasis on the multi-cultural character or "mosaic" of Canadian society. For them, "in the complex ethnic situation existing in Canada, the only kind of unity which can reasonably be striven for and achieved is unity in diversity: the harmonious co-operation of all ethnic groups in the Canadian country as a whole."'[17]

The major middle-class social movements of the 1970s — the women's movement, consumerism, and environmentalism — went through similar processes of mobilization, with vanguard groups, like the Consumers' Association of Canada and the Canadian Wildlife Federation, anticipating the change and doing much to bring it about.[18] Sometimes mobilization has occurred within unsuspected latent interests. The Rusty Ford Owners' Association came into being because one disgruntled owner of a rusty Ford was angry enough, energetic enough, and sufficiently persevering to identify a latent interest, whip it into self-consciousness, and organize it into legal and political action.[19] This group made legal history and initiated improvements in consumer protection for automobile owners. Another latent interest to mobilize during the last two decades is the English-speaking population of Quebec. Perhaps because English Quebeckers had for many years held a recognized place in provincial politics, they slowly developed a well-defined sense of solidarity and gave substantial support to pressure groups that aspired to speak for them only after their traditional economic and cultural position had been significantly eroded by legislation intended to enhance that of the French Canadian community.[20] Property owners constitute another interest whose mobilization has been sporadic and, until recently, dependent on local conditions. Ratepayers' associations were a part of local politics in some cities for many years, but were virtually unknown in others. The trend to city planning and the intrusion of large apartment buildings into areas dominated by single-family homes accelerated the formation of such groups, just as the introduction of rent controls and rental commissions fostered a sense of solidarity amongst landlords and prompted the creation of organizations designed to promote their interests.[21] As a result of the mobilization of these latent and solidary interests, political life in Canadian cities has become increasingly vibrant and dynamic.

Because the chief concern of this book is the behaviour of formally organized groups as they work within the political system, latent interests and solidary groups will not be discussed at length. Nevertheless, we should keep them in mind, for the essence of pressure group influence is the sense in the minds of group representatives and policy-makers that pressure groups speak for a part of the public that can be mobilized into political action should its interests not be accommodated in public policy. Yet the variety and indefiniteness of individuals' concern for their interests means that group leaders cannot be sure that their members are fully committed to a cause or represent significant portions of the community. Policy-makers confront the other side of the same conundrum. They want to know whether the group truly reflects the views of a significant proportion of the public and have to assess whether group members are committed enough to take actions that demand a policy response. Such assessments are useful in group-government bargaining, and also protect governments from adopting policies that lack real public support.

Pressure Group or Government Agency?

As governments expanded their activities and came into contact with wider, more diverse segments of the public, they developed a warm regard for the diverse skills of pressure groups. Many government responsibilities could not be met if these organizations did not exist. Consequently, governments not only encouraged many groups, they often created so-called 'pressure groups' and bodies that some observers consider to be interest groups. This raises a difficult question: When is an apparent pressure group really a government agency?

We have already used our definition of a pressure group to differentiate among political parties, solidary groups, and latent interests. To distinguish between genuine pressure groups and government agencies, we must incorporate three other concepts into the definition: the concepts of membership, collective action, and promotion of common interest.

Membership — the willingness of supporters to list themselves as dues-paying participants in an organization — is central to the legitimacy of any pressure group. An association derives legitimacy from membership by showing that it speaks for all those it claims to represent.[22] Ideally groups aspire to include everyone in the relevant interest community. A good deal of the authority of trade unions and inclusive associations, such as the provincial colleges of physicians and surgeons, comes from the fact that they *do* represent everyone in their potential membership. Groups whose potential members do not have equivalent economic and legal incentive to join are less fortunate. They must be content with some form of voluntary association. These organizations try to recruit as many of the potential members as possible, and to demonstrate that the group's actions have the support of the larger interest community. To demonstrate such support, groups often take out newspaper advertisements that urge like-minded citizens to send postcards, telegrams, and prepared coupons to MPs and Cabinet ministers. Policy-makers particularly dislike this form of pressure politics and claim that it makes no impression on them. Nevertheless, its repeated use suggests that group leaders believe that a heavy volume of mail does convince officials that the group represents the views of a much larger public. In summary, a legitimate pressure group must be able to show that it speaks for an entire interest community or that it can elicit the support of a significant part of that community. Membership statistics are an important aspect of its claim.

Government-affiliated organizations cannot readily meet these conditions, since they are frequently appointed bodies. If membership is neither inclusive nor voluntary, the group leadership cannot plausibly claim to have a mandate from the interest community.

Collective action also presents criteria that cannot readily be met by government-affiliated groups. Can the group, and particularly its leadership, use its resources autonomously? No group is entirely free to use its resources completely independently. Most have some patron or revenue source whose sensitivities must be consulted. Nevertheless, a genuine pressure group should be substantially autonomous in choosing methods for promoting its goals. Resource allocation by a true pressure group cannot be overruled by an outside actor.

Similarly, the quality of the staff available to most pressure groups and how they are deployed are critical factors. Many groups with extremely limited financial resources have been able to make a disproportionate impression on public policy because of the great ability and dedication of their employees and their members. It is important for the group membership, and particularly its leadership, to have complete freedom to hire, fire, and manage its employees. Many government-affiliated organizations lack this freedom, depending on secondments from the public service for their staff. Because their careers are oriented towards success in government service, not to achievement in the organization where they are temporarily working, seconded employees cannot be expected to be as whole-heartedly committed to the organization as employees of more independent groups are.

The Economic Council of Canada offers an example. Its administrative leaders and employees are appointed from the public service of Canada. The Council has been chaired by people who came from, or went to, deputy ministers' positions elsewhere in the service. Many of its research staff have been associated with various economic ministries of the federal government. It would be naïve to expect such people to vigorously criticize policies they helped to develop, or agencies with which they might hope to be associated. Yet these are the people who prepare studies for the Council members, who use them to tender 'independent' advice to the Government of Canada.* For these reasons, we cannot call the ECC a true pressure group.

Our last criterion for distinguishing a pressure group from a government agency is that of 'common interest'. Who determines the common interest of the group—the membership or some external agency? Common interest includes not only the day-to-day determination of the group's needs and goals, but its basic, long-term goal. If some external agency determines the group's common interest, we cannot consider that group a true pressure group. Only if its goals are established by the membership—or can be changed only at the instigation and with the concurrence of the membership—can we classify a group as a genuine pressure group.

Applying the Test

We have defined pressure groups as 'organizations whose members act together to influence public policy in order to promote their common interest'. In the interests of systematic inquiry and practical politics, we devised a method for using this definition to distinguish pressure groups from some of the other elements in the political system—latent interests, solidary groups, social movements, political parties, and government-affiliated organizations—that sometimes act like pressure groups and can be confused with them. Table 1-1 combines these individual tests to help us determine whether any specific group is a full-fledged pressure group.

There are two important reasons for distinguishing between pressure groups and other types of interest groups. First, people engaged in political life must be able to determine the source of policy advice and weigh that information against their sense of the public interest. The legitimacy of policy advice depends on its source, or its quality, or both. The legitimacy of pressure group advice derives first from its source, and only secondarily

---

*While the Economic Council of Canada is not a genuine pressure group, it does very often act like a pressure group and is often treated like one. For example, its reports are made to the government *and the public*, not simply to the government, as are those of conventional agencies. They are frequently intended to excite public demands for changes in government policy. The government's regular advisers are formally prohibited from appealing to the public. Again, though the Council is appointed by the government, an attempt is made to ensure that it is genuinely representative of regional and sectoral interests. It can, therefore, make a modest claim to speak for the interest community. For all these reasons we cannot treat the advice it gives as pure 'withinput', like the advice of a regular government department.

Table 1-1: A Test to Determine if an Organization Is a Pressure Group

TEST	CRITERION: A FULL-FLEDGED PRESSURE GROUP WILL:
ORGANIZATION: Does the group possess a formal organization?	possess a formal organization;
MEMBERSHIP: Is membership inclusive of the interest community; self-elected from that community; or selected from that community by the existing membership?	derive its membership in one of these ways;
POWER: Does the group seek power or simply influence?	seek only influence;
RESOURCE USE: Is the group free to deploy and manage its resources as its members see fit?	substantially determine its use of resources autonomously;
COMMON INTEREST: Is the common interest determined internally?	determine its own common interest and its own long-term goals.

from its quality. A group that is known to speak for its interest community is listened to by government, regardless of the quality of the advice it tenders. When good advice comes from a group that is totally a creature of government, the quality of the advice gives it legitimacy, not its source. Such advice, however sound, is not useful if it fails to win the support either of the interest community or the public at large. A government that fails to appreciate the difference is at best running the risk of misunderstanding public opinion, and at worst trying to manipulate that opinion.

A second reason for clarifying the status of pressure groups stems from our need as social scientists to strive for clarity of analysis. A clear understanding of the relationship between pressure groups and governments has important implications for political theory and political philosophy. Some scholars have remarked on the blurred distinctions between agencies and groups, suggesting that because groups may exercise power on behalf of government or come close to exercising a veto over government policy, they in effect share power with government. Others point to the fact that government financial assistance and positional politics* allows the state to manage groups and blurs the distinction between groups and governments. These scholars believe that groups and the state work together in a

---

*Positional politics is the term used to describe the efforts of groups (and their allies) to secure positions of influence, and the efforts of their enemies to keep them out of such positions.

'corporatist' system by sharing the power and responsibility of govern-ment.[23] Their arguments will be discussed in Chapter 9. Although it is often extremely difficult to disentangle the respective roles of groups and agen-cies, the approach these scholars advocate is not adopted here. This study assumes that ultimately the state alone has the authority to impose its will on the interest community. It may delegate that authority, but does not relin-quish it. Pressure groups may exercise delegated authority and they may be extremely influential, but their power is held on sufferance from the state, which may withdraw it at any time.

ANALYSING PRESSURE GROUPS

A great deal has been written about pressure groups. Some of these writings have helped to create the philosophical underpinnings of modern American ideology. Bentley's *The Process of Government* and Truman's *The Govern-mental Process*, for example, articulated an understanding of democratic processes that is still potent, despite being subjected to vigorous criticism.[24] Although case studies abound, very few of them systematically apply existing theoretical perspectives to the pressure groups described. As Grant Jordan has put it, the student of pressure groups has 'a temperamental disinclination to define' and, not coincidentally, 'is less likely to start with a conspectus of political theory, than with a file of press clippings'.[25]

   Canadian pressure group studies have shared this poverty-stricken analyt-ical approach. There have been three basic difficulties. First, with a few important exceptions, scholars did not until the early 1970s move beyond descriptive, historically oriented case studies. Second, scholars have not worked within the context of a conceptual framework for the analysis of the Canadian policy process as a whole. The third problem stems from the early uncritical adoption of the pluralist analytical perceptions of US scholars. While the majority of studies explain how Canadian interest groups carry on their activities, very few explain why pressure groups exist in Canadian politics, or why some methods of organization are functional in this setting, but others are not. Only in the last few years have Canadian scholars, goaded by concerned politicians like Robert Stanfield, tackled important theoretical issues. In short, there has been little probing analysis of the roots and consequences of pressure group behaviour.

   By the early 1970s, only two attempts had been made to tackle the analytical problem. Engelmann and Schwartz, studying party/pressure group relations, approached their analysis from a communications and organization perspective: 'The aim of interest articulation is to affect government outputs. Any interest system must, therefore, be oriented toward the maximization of access to governmental structure and, therefore, be adapted to this structure.'[26] Their brief review concluded with the significant observation that there was 'a tendency among organized interest groups to transmit their demands directly to the governmental structure, and not to parties'.[27] In other words, the form of pressure group adaptation in Canada had tended to exclude the political party from the pressure groups' area of interest. Schwartz and Engelmann thus gave an early indication of Canada's susceptibility to the problems that concerned Robert Stanfield.

In 1973 and 1974, Robert Presthus published an important comparative study of élite accommodation in Canada and the United States.[28] Since Presthus defined élites in terms of the leadership of organized interest groups, this research shed a great deal of light on the groups' activities in their interactions with the federal government and three provincial regimes. Presthus confirmed the strength of the relationship between highly organized groups and administrative agencies and challenged the widely held view that pressure group interaction with Parliament is limited and relatively insignificant. His was, however, a partial discussion of pressure group behaviour in Canada, since it dealt only with élite groups and not with the many lesser groups whose influence, though individually minuscule, is collectively as significant. These aspects were tackled by the present writer in a series of papers whose argument will be expanded here.[29] Several later studies and papers also pursued these issues. In a pioneering systematic study, a team of scholars at McMaster University, in conjunction with a European group, conducted an elaborate and exhaustive compilation of data about Canadian business interest groups with a view to estimating the extent to which this country has developed the corporatist state-group relationships widely noted in Europe.[30] Our study contributes to this growing body of systematic observation by building a conceptual framework for understanding relationships between Canadian pressure groups and the political system.

In order to do this, we must ask four basic questions: What are pressure groups? What do they do? Why do they do it? In what circumstances — how, when, and where — do they do it? These questions revolve around a central one: What roles do pressure groups play in the Canadian political system? To answer that, we must first go through the exercise we have just completed and decide how to describe pressure groups. Many actors in the political system are skilled in using 'pressure tactics' to gain power and influence. It is not easy to distinguish one from another, but it is important to do so, for their behaviour grows out of different capacities and roles whose differences must be understood if groups are to be channelled into directions that are in the public interest. Definition, then — the first concern of the scholar — should also be the first concern of the activist and policy-maker.

Clear definitions are also needed to sort out the roles groups play. Our first impression of pressure groups is that they play communications roles in politics. They transmit demands from sectoral constituencies to public authorities and they carry messages, including demands, from the authorities to their members. Close examination reveals that they fill other roles as well. They help build public support for programs and policies. They even administer some programs for government, and they often engage in regulatory activities.

This is not all, however. Critics of pressure group studies point out that because most writers in the field are interested in the political influence of groups, they forget that few groups participate in policy formation out of an altruistic desire to shape the goals of the community at large.[31] Rather, their activity is demanded by the interests of members: their first concern — their primary role — is to serve their members' needs, only some of which have anything to do with public policy. Canoeists form clubs so that they can share their sport with others. By working together, they can arrange ambitious canoeing trips and learn from one another. They can also obtain discounts from suppliers. Organized involvement in public policy is not likely to be one of their objectives. Participation lurks in waiting, as it does for every voluntary organization — perhaps taking the relatively passive form of signing petitions for new public parks, or even lobbying vigorously to preserve or extend amenities — but it is seldom welcomed by members. Analysts, preoccupied with the influence of groups on public policy, often forget that the particular concerns of the membership figure more prominently than public policy in the lives of most groups. It is essential that we do bear that in mind, because it helps us understand the variations in the efforts that groups will make to influence public policies. To meet the primary demands of members many groups ration the energies they devote to policy causes. Their role in policy formation is consequently diminished and that of groups single-mindedly concerned with policy issues is enhanced.

Once pressure groups and their roles are defined as precisely as possible, we can examine how, when, and where they play these roles and, most significantly, why they play them. The fact that most groups play public roles to promote their members' interests does not explain why the political system grants them participation. We need to understand the reciprocal benefits involved in order to discover why some groups are so much more influential than others; why policy-makers accommodate some groups but not others. By studying how, when, and where groups exert pressure on the system, we learn a great deal not only about groups, but about the system as well.

Case studies teach us, for example, that the policy process is highly bureaucratic and that the most successful groups are those that know whom to talk to — and when — and are able to communicate in a bureaucratic fashion, with briefs, working papers, and professional consultations, rather than with placards and demonstrations. By classifying the information of case studies, we discover that different types of groups tend to follow

predictable behaviour patterns — patterns related to what the political system expects of groups, and to the resources that groups bring to the process.
Case studies give us information to classify; typologies help us find out why
groups play the roles they do. By applying the analysis thus achieved to
historical data, we can see how the roles of Canadian groups have changed
over time and observe current trends. We can also learn a good deal about
our own system, and we gain valuable practical information as well, by
comparing group politics in other countries. Concern that our pressure
groups are becoming 'Americanized' has brought much discussion and
some inappropriate policies.* Comparison not only helps us understand that
Canadian behaviour, while it is similar to that of US groups, has different,
indigenous roots. Comparison also suggests more temperate and constructive methods of containing and utilizing the immense energies generated by
pressure group politics.

Governments encourage pressure groups because they provide policy-
makers with essential information. Once we understand that, we stop calling
for the elimination of pressure groups because they compete with political
parties. Instead, we begin asking how more representative institutions — our
legislatures, in particular — might play a larger role in the communications
process. We realize, in effect, that group/party competition is a symptom of a
decline in the policy role of political parties and of our elected representatives, and not the problem itself. These and other examples will help us to
see how a systematic, as opposed to anecdotal, approach to the study of
Canadian pressure groups will help us address the criticisms of them raised
by Robert Stanfield and others.

THE PATTERN OF THE BOOK

We will be asking two types of questions: clinical and normative. Clinical
questions are purely factual; they look for explanations of events and try to
fit many different observations into a coherent pattern. Normative questions
ask whether certain types of pressure group behaviour should be permitted,
whether they promote or undermine democratic institutions. This book is
divided into three parts, the first two clinical in orientation and the third
normative.

In the first two parts, we will investigate the environment in which
pressure groups flourish. We explore why they develop in one way in some
settings and differently in others. We review the part groups play in policy
formation and look at some of the trends suggested by pressure group
development. These discussions try to establish the facts about Canadian

---

*The misapplication of others' experience is illustrated by the 1983 amendments to the
Canada Elections Act, discussed in Chapter 7.

pressure groups: how they work; what functions they perform; who joins them; who runs them; how they differ from one another; how these differences lead them to behave differently in the political system; and so on. The chapters that follow will be concerned with the evolution of pressure groups in Canada. Our account will be descriptive, showing how early groups developed, the forces that influenced them, and their gradual assumption of a significant voice in politics. Though largely historical and descriptive, these discussions will lead us to make several more theoretical observations that will become pertinent when we deal with conceptual and normative issues in the later chapters. We will be especially interested in the tension that has always existed in Canadian politics between the need to represent geographic communities and concern for the representation of specialized, or sectoral, interests. This tension is one of the most difficult problems facing all representative industrialized democracies, but it is particularly compelling for Canadians.

Part II will focus on the groups themselves rather than on the larger system that houses, feeds, and uses them. In the course of this discussion we will define the functions of pressure groups; develop an analytical framework; and build a typology of interest groups on the basis of their functional relationships to their members and to the policy systems in which they find themselves. We will move towards the global picture we are seeking of the relationship between group politics and public policy. This discussion will not be exclusively theoretical. It will look at the practical problems faced by pressure groups and those who organize them, especially the problems of 'groups in action' and those associated with the internal operations of groups. A prominent pressure group leader has said that good management is the key to pressure group success. Much of our discussion will demonstrate the importance of his observation, though we will also point out some other significant ingredients. Part II will also elaborate further our functional typology, demonstrating how groups of different types vary their internal behaviour as they adapt to their specific resources and to their opportunities to relate to the political system.

In asking why pressure groups develop here but are retarded there, we expect that determining the dependent relationships between groups and their environment will guide us to a better understanding. In this way, our clinical investigation will help us respond to the weighty, value-laden questions about the impact of pressure group politics on democratic government that are taken up in the last portion of the book. There we look at pressure groups from the perspective of the policy system as a whole: What do pressure groups contribute to policy formation? Are they necessary to the modern industrialized state? How are they related to other elements in the political system — such as political parties, the media, and administrative agencies — that are also involved in policy communication?

We conclude that they are necessary, that in an era of highly diffused power, the political system depends on special publics — we call them policy communities — to articulate, implement, and monitor the general will.

Pressure groups contribute vitally to the life of policy communities. They perform functions that other institutions cannot perform. They are necessary. At the same time, they create a major problem in democratic representation, threatening to substitute sectoral representation for the geographically based representation upon which our legislative system depends. These two systems of representation can co-exist, but not as equals. History has determined that in Canada the state's legitimacy depends on maintaining legislative representation that is geographically based. Sectoral representation, through pressure groups, must take second place to the representation of territory that is organized through political parties and manifested in our legislatures. Pressure groups must therefore be contained, and other institutions strengthened.

In Part III, we will explore some of the available means of accomplishing this. Our dilemma, however, remains. We must contain and channel the energies of pressure groups without destroying the vitality and creativity they contribute to modern democracy.

Part I

The Evolution of a Policy Actor

CHAPTER 2

Beginnings:
Space versus Sector

Pressure groups have never been strangers to Canadian politics. In colonial days it was common for groups to lobby authorities in the mother country — whether France or England — for public policy concessions that would advance their interests.[1]

In 1804, a group of Nova Scotia merchants organized themselves into a committee to lobby for measures to protect them from American competitors in the West Indies trade. For several years the committee focused its attention on the Governor and Council, but by 1811 it had decided to take its appeals directly to London. There the group's members encountered 'very great difficulties in promoting their applications . . . , the same being frequently neglected or misrepresented by persons interested in opposing them'. They soon learned the business of lobbying. Informed that 'the West India Planters were accustomed on particular occasions, to employ Special Agents in London to solicit their interests — being Gentlemen intimately conversant in the object of their immediate pursuit', the Halifax committee followed suit and was soon able to report, with satisfaction, that 'their success has . . . been answerable to their expectations'.[2] As long as dominion status fell short of complete independence, a number of groups continued to make the trek to Westminster. The intensive lobbying of British parliamentarians before the patriation of the constitution in 1982 was the extravagant finale to this custom.[3] For the most part, though, following Confederation these delegations turned increasingly to Ottawa and the provincial capitals, rather than London.

By the end of the First World War pressure groups were becoming numerous. The Canadian Manufacturers' Association (CMA) was by then well established and others, like the Canadian Construction Association, were being encouraged by government.[4] In 1932, when federal trade negotiators were preparing for that year's Ottawa conference of Commonwealth leaders, pressure groups were clearly a part of the policy process, as this comment by one of the officials demonstrates:

If it can weather this summer's meeting I think we can say that the

Commonwealth has come thro' its most critical stage. I'm not sure it will but prospects are more propitious than some months ago: . . . Bennett to do him justice is as ready to bully the CMA as any other organization — and has already read them the riot act. They have not taken his orders with very good grace but have at least abandoned their first . . . impertinence of asking for further all-round increases on the [tariffs applied against British goods] as a preparatory 'bargaining measure' for the coming Conference. The export industries — notably lumber and mining — have organized their own influential lobbies and are busy looking for concessions on manufactured goods to be offered in return for preferences in the British market.[5]

Despite the patronizing tone of these remarks, they indicate that interest groups had established a bridgehead in some aspects of policy-making at least and that their views — though unwelcome — carried some weight. The expanded role of interest groups following the Second World War, particularly during the 1960s and 1970s, has often been described in terms as dramatic as those used by Kayyam Z. Paltiel:

The 1960s were characterized by an explosion of self-awareness among consumers, students, women and native groups and in Canada by Quebecois nationalism and ethnic group self-consciousness. These social movements were accompanied by a bursting forth of clientelist groups created in response to the elaboration of the welfare state during the same period. In turn, the emergence of these new formations galvanized established institutional groups into renewed action to protect themselves against the demands of the newly conscious and to restore a shattered equilibrium which had previously operated in their favour.[6]

It was this proliferation of activity that prompted Robert Stanfield and others to worry about the effects of pressure groups on the operation of democratic institutions. Although it is interesting to note the extent to which Canadian groups have sought to influence public affairs for many generations, it is more important here to appreciate how much the development of interest groups has mirrored the evolution of the Canadian state, and particularly the evolution of its policy systems. This chapter will focus on this relationship as we trace the historic development of pressure groups and build a factual base for later analytical discussions.

This chapter will also consider some of the underlying factors affecting the evolution of the policy process and pressure group behaviour. Economic development has been the factor with the greatest impact on political life, particularly on the roles of key institutions such as Parliament, parties, Cabinet, and bureaucracy. The evolution of pressure group behaviour reflects the shift of power among these institutions. As an aid to understanding these complex interrelationships, Table 2-1 presents a summary of the historical processes to be discussed in this chapter and the next.

Table 2-1: Historical Development of Canadian Policy Institutions

PERIOD	ECONOMIC STRUCTURE	CABINET	PARLIAMENT
Confederation 1867	Interdependent but decentralized.	Principle of ministerial responsibility established. Cabinet dominance developing unevenly across country.	MPs have considerable personal influence. In some provinces 'parties' are analogous to late 18th-century British factions, but party system developing.
Late 1800s to Depression ('Executive dominance')	Development of joint stock company ushers in process of corporate and economic concentration.	Cabinet dominance established. PM and key ministers in turn dominate Cabinet and bureaucracy.	Party discipline tightens. Pork-barrel politics becomes a major preoccupation. Role in policy formation is more and more limited.
Mid-1930s to early 1960s ('Age of the Mandarins')	Considerable concentration. The 'planning system' (Galbraith's term) becomes central as multinationals develop.	Political leadership continues to dominate Cabinet and Parliament, but control of civil service only secured through close co-operation of senior civil service.	Debates banal. Parliament is increasingly seen as ineffectual.
Mid-1960s to present ('Diffusion of Power')	Concentration in economy increasingly seen as threatening, though necessary.	Cabinet and mandarin control broken. Cabinet reorganization and reform to re-establish coordinative control, but not fully successful.	Reform of committee system, creation of Parliamentary 'task forces' gives MPs opportunities to develop sector knowledge, encourages group attention to Parliament. Diffusion of power undermines legitimacy of Cabinet and bureaucracy but benefits Parliament.

BUREAUCRACY	INTERGOVERNMENTAL RELATIONS	PARTY SYSTEM	PRESSURE GROUPS
Plays almost no policy role	No institutionalized co-ordination between governments. Ottawa seeks to regulate provinces through disallowance, guidance of Lt. Gov. Period of constitutional challenge in courts.	Decentralized Local party organization competent to transmit sectoral and spatial concerns to centre.	Little institutionalization. Chiefly voluntary groups, active at local or provincial level.
Develops expertise, but decision-making is still centred in political leadership. Decision-making tends to be *ad hoc.*	Some specialized intergovernmental agreements. Meetings of leaders becoming institutionalized by end of period.	Power shifts to leadership. Loss of local influence. Grass roots organization becomes primarily a 'fighting machine' for elections; dispenses petty patronage	Begin to develop institutionalized structure (e.g., Canadian Manufacturers Association) but still predominantly local in orientation. Lobbyists prominent.
Run by the 'mandarins'. A small group of senior officials and key ministers has extensive control.	Responses to Depression and WW II accentuate growing federal role. Co-operative federalism major feature of '50s and '60s. Provinces become concerned at diminution of sovereignty. Intergovernmental conferences (executive federalism) a growing part of policy process.	Party has virtually no policy influence. Below Cabinet and senior levels main function is to dispense petty patronage, win elections.	More influential, but in tutelary relationship with bureaucracy. Some publicity-conscious issue-oriented groups, but most group influence exercised privately through sub-governments, contained government agencies, and institutionalized groups.
Bureaucratic pluralism — centre and line agencies tussle over policy dominance via policy communities, corporate structures. Lessened legitimacy forces more attentive relationship to Parliament.	Major policy increasingly made through intergovernmental conferences, which — as growing disputes suggest — may have reached limits of effectiveness. Relations beset by much tension as federal and provincial governments each seek key role in demand and supply management.	Attempts to revive policy role make little headway.	Increasingly active and numerous. Considerably freer of agency tutelage. Tendency to form policy communities. More publicity-conscious and more attentive to Parliament.

The table divides our time frame into four periods. Each is distinguished from its predecessor and its successor by a major shift in the relations between the institutions of public policy-making and those governing the economy. Table 2-1 characterizes the principal features of policy institutions during these development epochs. On paper these distinctions seem to be clear-cut, but in actuality they merged into one another. The table provides a simple summary of a complex pattern of development.

A good part of this historical overview will be concerned with such issues as the contribution pressure groups have made to the decline of the policy role of political parties, the rise of bureaucratic influence, and the diffusion of power — which is one of the most important difficulties currently facing Canadian governments.

A feature of the evolution of Canadian groups that will be explored more fully in Chapter 10 is the tension between the sectoral representation of interests through pressure groups, and the spatial representation of interests through legislatures and political parties.[7] Our legislatures are organized around the selection of representatives from geographically defined constituencies. Neither they, nor the party system upon which they depend, are effective vehicles for considering the needs of those whose interests cut across geographic barriers. These, whether they be hand-loom weavers or bankers, electricians or academics, have found it necessary to express their needs through pressure groups concerned solely with their special or sectoral interests. These groups ally themselves easily and naturally with the bureaucracies that advise the political executive — so much so that many public agencies treat the pressure groups as constituencies as significant and as influential as the geographical constituencies represented in the legislatures. Inevitably, the struggle between representatives of territory and the representatives of sector to gain their respective objectives excites the criticism of pressure groups cited earlier. Because the tension caused by this struggle is of great importance to Canadian government, it is a central concern of the last two chapters of the book. This chapter and the next, with their focus on the evolution of pressure groups, permit us to see when, and to some extent how, this problem developed.

COLONIAL INTERESTS AND LOCAL DEVELOPMENT

A colony may have the institutions needed for full statehood — legislatures, executives, and judicial systems — but the power to make key political decisions resides elsewhere. Early pressure group activity in Canada reflected this reality. In the most settled regions, groups pivoted around issues of colonialism: trading relations between the colonies, the powers of colonial officials, and so on. Such issues mobilized colonial élites, which —

as the history of the Family Compact, the Château Clique, and similar groups suggests — were by no means unsophisticated in the use of influence.

Because the British imperial system made no provision for the parliamentary representation of colonial territory, these élites turned to sectoral representation and became adept at sending delegations to London. While much of this lobbying promoted personal interests, some petitions did come from groups we could call formal interest groups, even though they were seldom more than convenient extensions of colonial élites. The Halifax delegation that sought to maintain the navigation laws was clearly an interest group of this sort. It and many similar bodies were issue-oriented groups. They developed from the constant need of local interests to petition authorities in the mother country about specific sectoral issues.

Colonial ties brought attitudes and institutions that encouraged pressure group development. Robert Presthus says of our British heritage that 'the activities of such groups are so deeply integrated into the policy-making system that no question of their legitimacy has arisen among observers.'[8] While we may not entirely accept this view, there is no doubt that during the years when our political institutions were forming and were most susceptible to outside influence, Britain was herself experiencing a vigorous and lively flowering of interest groups. The crusade against the slave trade, the long and tortuous struggle to reform working conditions, and the campaigns to improve public health, to give the poor access to education, to promote free trade, and to reform Parliament and public administration were all spearheaded by pressure groups. The leaders of the Committee for the Abolition of the Slave Trade, the Chartists, the Anti-Corn Law League, and many other associations believed that it was necessary to 'raise an agitation through the length and breadth of the land' in order to influence Parliament.[9]

Their activities were watched with interest by colonial politicians, and though their concerns were often different, their example was followed in a variety of ways.[10] Robert Gourlay, for example, whose campaign for reform riveted Upper Canada in 1818 and influenced the rebellion of 1837, was a British emigrant who began 'his plague of petitions against the tyranny of the poor laws' as early as 1815, two years before he emigrated to Canada.[11]

Less dramatic imitations of the British tendency to form associations could be found in every town and village across British North America. Although intellectual concerns and governmental reform excited some groups, the majority were created to meet more prosaic needs. In Kingston, Ontario, which for several decades saw the trek of destitute immigrants from the British Isles to the frontier, the need for 'philanthropy' was ever present. Initially individuals and churches did what they could, but the tide engulfed them. In 1817 the Kingston Compassionate Society was formed to provide for 'the relief of the sick poor in their own homes and to forward destitute emigrants to their place of destination . . .'.[12] This society evolved into the Female Benevolent Society, which by 1829 found its work so extensive that it turned to government for help. It secured a small grant in that year and £3,000 a few years later to help build a new hospital.[13] These were the first of many grants to charitable organizations, preparing the way for state support of health and social welfare institutions.[14]

Today business interest groups are considered to be the most sophisticated pressure groups, but in the first half of the nineteenth century they were probably far less well developed than charitable organizations like the Kingston Female Benevolent Society or even the reading and discussion circles, such as the Canadian Institute, that were beginning to influence intellectual and political life in many centres.[15] The political impact of the latter groups was two-fold: they provided a forum for the discussion and dissemination of politically relevant ideas and promoted policies that would further the interests of at least some of their members. Between 1857 and 1860, for example, the Institut Canadien de Longueuil devoted more than a third of its meetings to issues in provincial administration, commerce, and the problem of emigration from Canada to the United States. Another third were taken up with local issues, particularly road improvement. Between 1856 and 1868 and between 1879 and 1898, the Drummond County Mechanics' Institute and Library Association devoted twenty-seven meetings to subjects such as the repeal of the union of Upper and Lower Canada, confederation, defence, the Intercolonial Railway, and so on — but approximately a dozen sessions were spent on local matters. Since these groups counted local political notables among their active members and since prominent politicians were sometimes invited to attend special meetings — the member of the assembly for Richmond County attended the discussion of defence and a visiting Duke of Wellington was treated to a debate on confederation — we can assume that these groups played a part in disseminating ideas about political issues and in the creation of local consensus. In other words, they were concerned with a combination of geographical and sectoral matters.

In major centres, such groups' chief political functions were the development of opinion and the encouragement of political institutions. In smaller communities they performed another function — one more clearly akin to modern pressure group activity, one that reflected the need for state institutions capable of providing services that could not be administered directly from London or even from the colonial capitals — the promotion of specific policies and programs. In Longueuil, for example, an interest in local affairs — especially local road works — clearly reflected the particular interests of members, some of whom were merchants. Nearly a fifth of the members held civic office. In Drummond County, the educational goals of the Mechanics' Institute were much to the fore in its early years. Soon after erecting a permanent home, the group rented part of the building to the local public school commission:

> The Institute having taken into consideration the difficult position in which the School Commissions are placed in [sic] for the want [sic] of a School House — and have no place to keep the school in operation — and the Institute being desirous of promoting the course of education that the following proposal be offered to the School Commissions by the president: that the Institute will finish the basement or understory of the Institute for the use of a School room to be left at the disposal of the School Commissions, paying to the Institute the sum of thirty pounds . . .[16]

As public education became widespread and as other forms of recreation overtook reading and conversation in popularity, these groups lost their vitality and died out. In their prime, however, they performed several functions still associated with interest group activity. By providing a forum for discussing public policy and a base for influencing policy — as in agitating for better roads and promoting education — they helped their members to understand the possibilities and responsibilities of citizenship.

These activities also helped develop local institutions of government, for their meetings enabled local representatives to test community opinion, which often helped to build consensus and thus gave moral support to civic leaders seeking concessions from distant officials. Moral support of this sort translated into enhanced legitimacy, not only for local government officials but for the municipal institutions they represented. Even at this early stage of pressure group politics we can see a tendency for interest groups to develop a supportive relationship with the institution — in this case, local government — with which they are most closely associated. We can also see the first indications that the political community was looking for ways to express sectoral interests, as in the Drummond County Mechanics' Institute's offer of a schoolroom to the public school authorities. For the most part, however, these expressions were latent or indistinct. These groups had not striven to develop a voice for themselves in any particular sphere of public policy. In general, they seem to have assumed that their range of concerns coincided with those of the community.

Other organizations had more clearly defined and lasting public policy objectives. Among them were the fraternal associations that came to social and political prominence during the industrialization and urbanization of the later Victorian period. The policy goals of some of these groups seem curiously mixed to modern eyes. While they promoted the ascendancy of either the Catholic or Protestant faiths, often violently, one of their important reasons for existing — and a source of their political strength — was mutual assistance. The most notorious of these, the Orange Lodge, which sometimes claimed 100,000 adherents in Ontario alone, attracted a good deal of middle-class, professional support, which saw in it a vehicle for meeting 'a need for the kind of welfarism which was, in other instances, provided by Catholic Hibernian societies and "sick and death benefit" societies organized by socialists in continental Europe. Orangemen had always been under the obligation to help one another. In some instances, this had meant joining in donnybrooks or helping guilty Orangemen evade justice, but it also meant finding work for a brother Orangeman, caring for indigent Orange families and, above all, providing decent burial for the deceased Orangemen.'[17]

The Orange Lodge, with other fraternal organizations and charitable associations, 'provided for social needs which could not be supplied easily by other agencies'.[18] As the state expanded its role in delivering social programs, theirs declined but was not abandoned. John Woodburn Langmuir, Inspector of Prisons and Asylums in Ontario from 1868 to 1882, shared the general belief that social programs could only succeed if they were assisted by private individuals and associations. Taking his cue from British and American experience, he encouraged the formation of prisoners' aid societies and secured for them financial support from the public treasury.[19] Similarly, the Ontario Royal Commission on the Prison and Reformatory System, which was concerned with the plight of destitute children, in 1890 recommended the formation of an association 'having local boards in every important centre of the Province who shall take upon themselves the important but delicate duty of looking after and caring for these children'.[20] Like Langmuir, the Commission recommended that the government should defray 'actual expenses incurred' by the association, which as the Ontario Children's Aid Society continues to carry out the function proposed for it a century ago.

Businessmen combined readily into groups to petition governments for measures that would promote trade, or protect it. As the nineteenth century progressed, informal groups and *ad hoc* committees gave way to more permanent organizations. Boards of Trade, as they generally called themselves, coalesced in every important town, advocating alternately expansionary and protective policies. The Toronto Board of Trade was probably typical. It received its charter in 1844, though it had been in existence for some years before that, and it represented the newer merchant class in the rapidly expanding town. Its concerns during the 1840s and 1850s were those of a frontier business community:

> First, it favoured 'development' of all sorts. Second, it sought 'freer trade', an end to various restrictions and burdens which were seen to exist. Third, it desired greater ordering and structuring of trade, in the interests of clarity and security. These objectives were not closely and precisely defined; they were not always logically reconcilable; they were often not even achievable. Above all, the board desired further development, and it supported all projects which it thought would add to Toronto's hinterland and tighten its control of it. It

welcomed government involvement in the achievement of these ends but preferred local control over such projects. During the [1850s] its horizons gradually broadened and shifted as the economy boomed and its ambitions grew.[21]

To achieve these ends, it established close ties with Toronto members of the legislature, several of whom were members of the Board. On occasion it would organize meetings to drum up wider support for its views and it would present resolutions to the Legislature, but 'it preferred to reinforce such pressure by sending representatives to call on members and ministers'.[22] This was a style of lobbying that Canadian business associations pursued for many years.

Although the promise of the frontier and the development of Canada's resources — usually described as 'boundless' — excited extravagant visions in which railways, immigration, and burgeoning industry figured largely and which could generally be brought about only through government action, business groups also wanted to protect their members from the rapacious behaviour that the ideology of free enterprise unleashed. Like the merchants of Halifax, who were anxious to perpetuate the protection offered by the navigation laws, countless merchants in Ontario's villages and towns sought to protect their businesses by establishing laws that would prevent some shopkeepers from undercutting their rivals by staying open late or on the sabbath.[23] The most adept protectionists, however, were professionals. Dentists, in particular, were very successful in securing legislative monopolies for their work and, according to one historian, by the 1870s had 'won a legitimacy in . . . Ontario [they] had not yet achieved anywhere else in the world'.[24]

The institutions active in pre-Confederation Canada were primarily local. Boards of Trade, which were being organized as vigorously and optimistically in tiny hamlets as in major centres, shared a name and had similar ambitions but were essentially oriented to specific communities. This is not to say that they were unaware of, or uninterested in, wider circles of like-minded people or sister organizations. A number, the Boards of Trade and the Mechanics' Institutes among them, were established in imitation of groups in Britain, the United States, and perhaps other parts of British North America. Their members corresponded with and visited their counterparts elsewhere, but beyond the local level organization was difficult and generally limited.

There were four reasons for this. First, travel and communications were extremely difficult in the sparsely populated colonies. As the British novelist Anthony Trollope put it in 1862, Canadians and Maritimers 'seldom see each other'.[25] Second, the groups were voluntary associations in the fullest sense. They employed no specialized staff to carry out organizational chores or to forge links with related groups. When these things were accomplished, it was because of individual members who devoted their own time and resources to the group's interest. Third, local loyalties often precluded co-operation between groups in rival centres. The Toronto Board of Trade claimed, at times, to speak for the interests of Upper Canada, but its members came exclusively from Toronto.[26] During the 1850s, co-operation between Boards of Trade was the exception rather than the rule. In 1852, a convention of Boards of Trade was brought to an untimely end by a squabble over tariff policy.[27] Fourth, the role of the state was limited. Pressure group politics could be decentralized and locally oriented because the greater part of public policy was concerned with local issues and was administered in a decentralized fashion. Today's great social programs were unheard of then and their predecessors were entrusted to local charitable and fraternal associations. Economic and development policy, which frequently did have imperial and colony-wide dimensions, could not be addressed readily by locally oriented business groups that lacked the cohesion needed to maintain a continuing lobby in London or the colonial capital. Even if that capacity had existed, it is doubtful whether it could have been effective in a legislative system where every member was a 'loose fish' uninfluenced by party discipline and bound to obtain for his constituency, and particularly his supporters, whatever patronage his vote would buy.*

As the nineteenth century passed the mid-point, these conditions changed, and pressure groups changed with them. Confederation brought new national and political configurations. As communications improved, local rivalries, though they burned brightly across the country, paled in the stronger light cast by the ambitions that Confederation aroused. The state started its inexorable extension into the daily lives of citizens and its agencies began to develop into complex bureaucratic structures. The trend to sectoral representation incipient in British North America quickened as latent interests became solidary interests and solidary interests perceived the advantages of organization.

The impact of improved communications is seen most dramatically in the national and international conventions that inspired interest in a variety of causes during the closing decades of the century. In 1887, according to Richard Splane, a conference in Toronto of Prisoner's Aid Associations,

---

*For example, New Brunswick legislatures during the 1840s and 1850s lacked disciplined political parties and Cabinet authority to initiate spending programs. 'Consequently, the dispersal of the Assembly's new found revenues was left to the local members. Each MLA used "his share" as a tool for patronage in his constituency....' Even after responsible government the support of MLAs was 'unpredictable. Until the twentieth century, it was a common practice for members who had previously supported the Cabinet to vote against a bill introduced by one of its ministers. Politicians solicited electoral support, based on their own positions on various issues. Their personal popularity was more important than their political party affiliations' (Arthur T. Doyle, *Front Benches and Back Rooms* [Toronto: Green Tree, 1976], 17).

presided over by Rutherford B. Hayes, former President of the United States, drew delegates from across the continent for a week of meetings that 'gave currency to a number of ideas relating to child welfare as well as to corrections, and stimulated thought and action in these fields. In particular, it prompted the members of the Prisoner's Aid Association [of Ontario] to make the advocacy of penal reform a more important part of its propaganda.'[28]

A succession of congresses provided similar inspiration to the forestry movement. In 1882, the American Forestry Congress met not once, but twice — in Cincinnati and Montreal — in the first 'parliament of forestry' in North America. The meetings 'served to focus all the hopes and criticisms that had been freely ventilated for so long on both sides of the border' and 'established a platform for leadership by outstanding forestry experts'.[29] They triggered institutional responses on the part of government and business whose effects were still felt decades later.[30]

These were not isolated events. Criss-crossing western Europe and North America, the new middle classes[31] were taking advantage of fast, luxurious railway and ocean travel, not only to see sights and sounds previously accessible only to the wealthy and intrepid, but to discover a world of ideas and a host of issues that cut across political boundaries. The dehumanizing consequences of urban industrialization, the reckless exploitation of natural resources, the limitations of democracy, and a host of other problems were to be found abroad as well as at home.

Furthermore, like-minded people were also to be found there. It became common for the leaders of movements in one country to visit and support their colleagues in another. The history of the temperance and women's suffrage movements, for example, is replete with instances in which Canadian, British, and American leaders visited one another and inspired and supported each other.* A meeting of the American Association for the Advancement of Women in 1877 encouraged Dr Emily Stowe to establish the Toronto Women's Literary Society, which in 1883 became Canada's first national suffrage association. The Chicago Women's Club served as a model for the Montreal Women's Club, established in 1891. The British National Union of Women's Suffrage Societies had some influence in Canada, and a prominent British woman, Lady Aberdeen, founded the National Council of Women to promote the interests of Canadian women.[32] Across the spectrum of interest group activity — from reform groups to business groups to labour

---

*Canadian women were less militant than their British and American counterparts, eschewing demonstrations and violent protest. They did, however, give their support to colleagues abroad, occasionally going so far as to join them in demonstrations and parades. Alice Chown led a group, each of whom carried a stem of Canadian wheat, in a London march; others participated in demonstrations prior to Woodrow Wilson's inauguration (Bacchi, *Liberation Deferred*, 34).

organizations — this pattern of interaction and co-operation recurs, inspired by the discovery of common interests and made possible by the revolution in transportation and communication.

Paradoxically, voluntarism and localism continued to be important characteristics of groups during the later 1800s. Visions of reform or of business development may have been international in scope, or even global, but they were still to be attained through local organizations influencing politicians at the community as well as at the national level. Most groups continued to be voluntary associations. Those with the resources to employ a permanent staff seem to have been rare. The majority persisted thanks to a dedicated core of volunteers, to the largesse of a patron, or because they formed ties with larger social institutions. The Women's Christian Temperance Union (WCTU) undoubtedly benefited in this way from its ties with the church. In Ontario during the 1890s, the work of the Sons of Temperance, the Independent Order of Good Templars, and the WCTU — which together claimed more than 40,000 members in the province — was vigorously supported by the Methodist, Presbyterian, Congregationalist, and Baptist churches.[33] Some evidence suggests that where church organizations did not encourage the formation of voluntary groups, reform efforts languished. Judith Fingard attributes 'the failure of the Quebec public to respond to . . . suggestions for sailors' homes' in part to 'the relative weakness of the Protestant middle class. It was the members of this group who were responsible for voluntary associations which promoted amelioration and social control in urban society.'[34]

The fruit growers' associations of Ontario initiated a new trend when they drew on government resources to support their organization. Most of these associations were fairly near each other in south-western Ontario. Their members were chiefly farmers keenly interested in the region's potential for fruit production. As local associations they could accomplish a good deal: they explored new methods of cultivation, developed new varieties, and exchanged information. But they lacked the capacity for concerted action on a wider scale, such as promoting the creation and expansion of the agricultural college at Guelph or disseminating scientific information from and to more distant communities.

This was a weakness of another solidary group that had interests in common with the fruit growers and that was simultaneously moving towards interest group status. Its members were drawn from the forest industries, particularly from the lumbering and forest products industries of the Ottawa valley and southern Ontario, where forest depletion had begun to have adverse economic effects. Led by several far-sighted businessmen, these interests had established contact with like-minded Americans. They had participated in and hosted lively, well-attended international and national conferences like the Cincinnati and Montreal congresses of 1882. They had even created a national organization, the Canadian Forestry Association. But they too lacked an organizational infrastructure above the local level.[35]

Both the fruit growers and the forestry interests solved their problem by persuading the Ontario government to establish the Ontario Bureau of Forestry. Because it was small — staffed by one person, grandly called the Commissioner of Forestry — the Bureau was ill-equipped to play an operational role. Instead the Commissioner devoted his energies to promoting the conservation cause: encouraging local volunteer groups, particularly those interested in farm forestry; helping to organize exhibitions, and publishing voluminous annual reports, which detailed the activities of local associations and catalogued progress in the field. He thus provided, at public expense, the institutional support needed by local interest groups in the conservation-agriculture field. It was a mutually beneficial relationship; while the Commissioner of Forestry served as a sort of corresponding secretary to a loosely organized provincial association, the local groups who called on his services provided the political support needed to maintain his office. Together they helped to keep alive a number of policy concerns — reforestation, forest fire protection, the maintenance of forest reserves — that became central to twentieth-century forest management policies.

We do not know how many such relationships existed before the First World War. Our knowledge of both administrative and pressure group history for that period is pitifully limited. Certainly the kinds of groups served by the Ontario Commissioner of Forestry existed in Nova Scotia and New Brunswick and similar offices could be found in several American states.[36] In Ontario, prison inspectors were ready to support the organization of prisoners' aid societies.[37] In Quebec a different pattern seems to have developed: a preference for a decentralized state led the provincial government to entrust some aspects of administration to societies organized by the interests most concerned. Instead of creating its own agency, the government encouraged the Conseil de l'agriculture, representing farmers and colonization interests, to organize agricultural circles or societies, and colonization societies. Similarly the government, instead of creating its own ministry of health, called on doctors to organize the Conseil d'hygiène publique. These and similar bodies flourished until the turn of the century; they then gave way to government-sponsored independent commissions structured to include representation from concerned interests.[38]

It appears that local voluntary groups represented the height of institutional sophistication for the period. They constituted the core of interest associations. National organizations with permanent headquarters and regular conventions were rare, though local groups seem to have corresponded regularly with one another on a provincial, national, and even international basis. National or provincial co-ordination — when it existed at all — was largely achieved by drawing on the good offices of a stronger social institution, such as religious denominations or, in some cases, the government.

All of this can be explained by the political economy Canada had developed during the nineteenth century. A limited degree of sectoral representation, much of it short-lived and issue-oriented, had been encouraged by the structure of colonial government. After Confederation, however, pressure group politics seems to have developed principally at the local level and seems to have been run almost exclusively on voluntary labour. Sectoral representation progressed slowly, still representing only a minor part of the political life of the late nineteenth century — even though some groups were extremely influential. Far more important were the political parties, which were the great engines of political communication. This was the heyday of grass-roots party organization. For a few decades, systems of political communication were sufficiently compatible with the structure of the economy for elected representatives to speak equally for the spatial and sectoral interests of their constituencies.[39]

Political communication in this period was based on the assumption that the private member of Parliament was the person best equipped to mediate between the demands of the constituency and the broad requirements of the national or provincial interest. This assumption had taken hold during the late eighteenth and early nineteenth centuries when our present institutions of representative government were germinating. They continued to be appropriate in the decades following Confederation because they meshed neatly with the economic fabric of the time. The economy was composed of innumerable relatively small enterprises — farms, mines, factories — which were owned by local interests and rooted in communities that in geographic terms corresponded more or less to the new political constituencies.

As party systems developed, the local élites who owned these firms found the formal and informal party organization in each constituency a viable tool for conveying their demands to policy-makers. Local owners might have boundless international visions, but their interests were still solidly parochial and could be safeguarded through participation in constituency organizations. Because industry, though part of an interdependent world economy, was still locally owned and because agriculture with its strong spatial orientation still employed a large part of the labour force, the heart of the party system was found in the single-member constituency. Both the local member and the riding association could be counted upon to exercise their influence on behalf of community business leaders in party conclaves. Party leaders had not yet imposed rigid discipline on their parliamentary followers; they therefore had a powerful incentive to accommodate local needs even as they grappled more and more with regional, provincial, and national issues.*[40]

In Nova Scotia, for example, the fate of provincial governments hinged for decades on purely local matters, such as the maintenance of roads and the introduction of municipal government.[41] The Lieutenant Governor of British Columbia, Thomas R. McInness, was dismissed because, as Prime Minister Laurier told the President of the Vancouver Board of Trade, 'so long as he was in office, business interests would be jeopardized and . . . the province would make no progress'.[42] Ontario's Sir Oliver Mowat, at the instigation of a supporter, secured the passage of a Rivers and Streams Act four times, only to have each version disallowed by the federal government, responding in its turn to the demands of an influential party member.[43] Sir J.D. Hazen, MP for Saint John, claimed that

> he had boldly risked his political career for the city. At that time, Portland, Maine, served, under subsidy, as Canada's winter port for overseas mail shipments. The Beaver Shipping line offered to operate the service from St John if it could get a federal subsidy of $25,000 annually. When the government procrastinated Hazen and his colleagues wired the government stating that they would resign their seats if the subsidy were not granted within twenty-four hours. It was granted immediately, and within a year it resulted in thirty-six steamers handling three million dollars in goods through the port.[44]

Such were the demands, and the power, of local interests in late nineteenth-century Canada. Though organized and persistent pressure groups were becoming relatively common and a few had national — and even international — presence, a decentralized economy and a decentralized party system made sophisticated pressure group politics unnecessary.

CENTRALIZING TRENDS

As the structure of the economy changed at the turn of the century, a need for organizational complexity and institutionalization emerged in interest representation. A revolution in transportation was making the world more interdependent. Less obvious but ultimately even more powerful were the

---

*This view differs somewhat from that of Norman Ward, who perceives, even in the early years of the House of Commons, 'a strong bias in favour of the executive'. However, Ward qualifies his view by stating that the private member was not only 'a loyal party man' but 'one inclined to be on the make for himself and his district as well as his party; his support of the party was always conditioned by his ambitions in other directions. The hope of patronage, both for himself and his supporters, may have made him dependent on his leaders, but the role he played as the real or potential distributor of favours in his district gave him a stature which few of his successors can enjoy today. . . . The member of Parliament was a strategic figure and a man of note. The House of Commons reflected the individuality of the members; yet the domination of the legislature by the executive was almost never threatened.'

changes in international finance — particularly the evolution of modern banking systems and the emergence of corporate concentration — that were radically altering patterns of industrial ownership. It was now possible for provincial, national, and international financiers to take the ownership and control of firms out of the hands of local élites.[45]

Political communication was profoundly affected by these changes, which dissolved the symmetrical relationship that had grown up at the local level between the party system and community business élites. The new corporations and their owners had little concern for local matters — unless they impeded efforts to integrate and rationalize production or otherwise affected business operations. Furthermore, because they sought economic integration between geographically distant enterprises, the new owners preferred to negotiate with government officials who had some authority to secure public policies that would encourage integration. Cabinet ministers and senior departmental officials could do this, but not individual constituency representatives. The new owners consequently preferred to approach government at its centre rather than at the community level. The individual MP or MLA became less influential, and so did the machinery of political communication that had been built around them — the constituency organization and, ultimately, the legislature. This decline forced local interests to appeal to the same key decision-makers who were increasingly being besieged by industrial moguls. Local delegations trekked more frequently, and with less effect, to Ottawa and the provincial capitals.*[46]

The experience of a northern Ontario community illustrates this. Nipigon had grown up at the turn of the century around the logging and sawmill industries. These industries were composed of a number of small concerns whose individual demands for timber holdings were relatively small and were generally processed in consultation with local riding officials from the party in power. The advent of the pulp-and-paper industry changed that procedure. Pulp mills required long-term leases of timberlands that were extensive enough to ensure a perpetual supply of wood on a sustained-yield basis. It became quite common for them to lease concessions of several thousand square miles — often exceeding the boundaries of an entire constituency. Consequently, the promoters of pulp-and-paper companies insisted

---

*The connection between corporate organization and government decision-making structures persists today. Christopher Leman suggests, for example, that 'one reason for the historic centralization of the provincial [natural resource] ministries was that the companies were themselves centralized, so that when a problem arose company executives would demand to speak to their ministry equivalent. Perhaps the pace of decentralization in the companies will continue to govern the extent to which the ministries will be able to truly decentralize [in the future]' (C. Leman, 'The Canadian Forest Ranger: Bureaucratic Centralism and Private Powers in Three Provincial Natural Resource Agencies'. Paper. Canadian Political Science Association, 1981, 28).

on dealing with the centres of power, arguing that because their affairs were associated with the province as a whole and not with any locality, they should bypass the local party machine. Furthermore, these corporations and their financiers were accustomed to dealing with governments rather than with intermediaries. As a result, though local political organizations occasionally played a significant role in the decision-making process, power came to reside almost exclusively in the hands of the leaders of the party in power. A February 1926 letter to an Ontario MLA from a riding official in Northern Ontario protesting the apparent allotment of three townships to a pulp and paper company illustrates the impact of this development:

> When in Nipigon you announced the deal that Hon. G. Howard Ferguson has promised to the people of Nipigon, that the townships of Booth, Purdon and Ledger would be open for settlement in the near future.
> Nipigon as you will remember gave the largest proportionate Conservative majority in the last elections in your constituency.
> Is that the reason why the interests of the people of Nipigon are *first to be sacrificed* by our Provincial Prime Minister? Do you expect me as President . . . to be forced by unprecedented nasty dealings apparently going on with the knowledge of the Prime Minister favoring the Nipigon Corporation to the exclusion of everyone else — do you expect me to be forced to announce that Hon. Howard Ferguson, whom I praised to my friends before the last election, is a man who does not honour his given word? If your Nipigon association can't trust in the word of our Prime Minister, can't have faith in the promise of the first citizen of the province, then who are they ever to trust in the future? I sincerely hope that such despicable action has not been confirmed, as yet, and that you will find some means to prevent it, so that I will not be made a liar among my political friends, in having advocated the interests of the Conservative party.[47]

The corruption of senior party officials, never entirely absent from Canadian politics, became particularly prevalent in this period as powerful interests, a few of them formally organized, discovered and enlarged the authority of the centre. The Taschereau regime in Quebec, the United Farmers of Alberta, and the Ferguson government in Ontario succumbed to corruption by major financial interests and were replaced, in Quebec and Ontario at least, by regimes that eventually followed the same path. The federal level, too, was touched by scandal, as Mackenzie King's difficulties with the Beauharnois affair demonstrated.[48]

The decline of local influence during the first three decades of this century was not confined to the forest and mining frontier. It also occurred in the larger centres, where for decades the business community had used social clubs to informally tell politicians about their concerns as individuals and as members of solidary groups. Two or three such clubs could be found in most major centres; they facilitated the informal élite interaction that was the essence of political communication in the late nineteenth and early twentieth centuries. The new political economy, however, reduced their influence. Most effective when they sat at the heart of an economic region dominated by their active members, the clubs lost their usefulness when outsiders took over large portions of their hinterland. The clubs could not help business élites sound out solidary-group feeling when important interests were not in any real sense 'part of the club'.[49]* Nor could élite members use traditional informal methods of influence when the increasing resort to bureaucratic methods required that propositions be put on paper and subjected to formal review. The informal and social orientations that had made these institutions such useful vehicles for interaction in an élite-dominated policy-making system became outmoded as the élites themselves moved to a few international centres, and as policy formation became more formal. Though business clubs still survive in regional centres, only the most important — Montreal's St James and Mount Royal Clubs, Toronto's York, Toronto, and National Clubs, and the Rideau Club in Ottawa — perform their original socio-economic function, and even their influence has been circumscribed by the introduction of bureaucratic processes into policy-making and by the shifting of economic power. Lesser clubs faded away, or concentrated on social activities. The importance of clubs as political entities declined immensely in the first half of this century.

The diminishing policy influence of local élites and party organizations was scarcely noticed by the average citizen. The razzmatazz and glitter of the party machine prolonged the illusion of power. Party leaders caught the eye. Strong personalities, they dominated the headlines and appeared to exercise almost despotic control over their Cabinets and officials. The legendary arrogance and arbitrary behaviour of men like R.B. Bennett, Howard Ferguson, Jimmy Gardiner, Maurice Duplessis, and Mitchell Hepburn symbolized the changes occurring within the parties.[50] Power was accruing to the leadership. The grass roots — losing policy influence and becoming instead simply 'a fighting machine'[51] — delivered votes and dispensed petty patronage, and lobbying focused on the Cabinet and a few influential advisers, where policy was now made.

New institutions emerged, better adapted to representing special interests. By the First World War these institutions had established their presence in the policy process; boards of trade and chambers of commerce were prominent at the national and regional levels, and sector groups were

---

*These comments are somewhat speculative, being based on the fragmentary evidence available in biographies, case studies, and general histories. To some extent they fly in the face of accepted wisdom amongst sociologists, which tends to see businessmen's clubs as bastions of privilege: exclusive preserves where members of the economic élite maintain contact with one another and arrange deals that seal the fate of thousands. However, the data actually presented by the leading students of Canadian élites reinforce the argument presented here.

making their presence felt.[52] The Canada Grain Act of 1912, for example, was the product of much debate and of representations by newly formed grain growers' associations,* whose appearance reflected a need for a higher degree of organization. Interests that previously had been able to resolve problems or promote policies satisfactorily through their local member found themselves building more formal organizations. As local influence declined, and as the costs of interest representation increased, community groups merged into provincial and national federations.

By pooling resources, groups could hire permanent staff to keep an eye on government policy-makers and to take care of the day-to-day representations that seemed essential as administrative structures developed around the executive.[53] Amalgamation eased the groups' cost of speaking to government, and enhanced their legitimacy — and their demands.

These more institutionalized pressure groups were making their presence felt by the turn of the century. The best known — and one of the few that have been properly studied — is the Canadian Manufacturers' Association (CMA). As early as 1900 the CMA actively and continuously lobbied federal and provincial policy-makers; by the end of the First World War it seems to have become an accepted part of the policy process. Although in its early years the CMA found it useful to have elected legislators as advocates, the growth of unions and other organizations with a strong popular base soon forced the association to try to exercise influence in other ways:

> The success of the Association, in the end, depended upon its ability to create opinions among the general public favourable to its policies, and to persuade members of Parliament and Cabinet ministers to translate those policies into governmental action. Thus its really significant influence was exerted through propaganda carried on in the country and lobbying directed by its representatives in the federal and provincial capitals.[54]

The CMA's attitudes and behaviour offer an insight into the emerging pattern of pressure group politics. Even before the First World War, the association concluded that its activities should be focused on the Cabinet, confirming the decline not only of local party influence, but of the significance of party politics itself. According to S.D. Clark, the CMA early found it desirable to avoid identification with any one party: 'The Association was interested in issues rather than in parties. "My politics today," said

---

*Roger Gibbins, *Prairie Politics and Society* (Toronto, 1980), 84; Hill, *Canada's Salesman to the World*. While the intervention of new groups was a sign of pressure-group development, the fact that the act was not passed until western farmers had protested on Parliament Hill underlines the decline of constituency influence in western politics. Similar pilgrimages to Ottawa characterized the Maritime Rights Movement; according to Forbes the failure of the traditional parties in the Maritimes to persuade Ottawa to accept Maritime claims reinforced a tendency to look to pressure groups to articulate the region's demands (*Maritime Rights*, ch. 7 'The Politics of Maritime Rights'; and 191-2).

one manufacturer, "are my business". By concentrating upon clearly defined objectives, pressure could be exerted upon the Government no matter which party was in power.'[55] As the century progressed and interest groups became more numerous, non-partisanship became an accepted feature of pressure group politics. Even in Nova Scotia, where party politics has retained a vigour almost unknown outside Atlantic Canada, a tradition of group non-partisanship developed. J.M. Beck, writing in 1972, reflected on a long tradition:

> The province's pressure groups normally do not work through the political parties, or their members as such; they present their requests to the cabinet, in some cases through annual briefs. Sometimes the opposition takes its cue from the government's failure to meet an interest group's demands, but since the membership of these groups usually cuts across party lines, they are often reluctant to have their interests adopted by any one party. . . . The exception to the general rule is trade unionism, which has been largely responsible for any success that the Independent Labour Party, the CCF, and the NDP may have had. However, the unionists, too, are pragmatic Nova Scotians, and they support the old parties when their interests seem to warrant it. Thus Nova Scotia pressure groups barely disturb the even tenor of the party system.[56]

Non-partisanship and the decision to focus on the Cabinet were the first stages of the access-oriented pressure group politics that characterized the Canadian system by the late 1960s. In Nova Scotia and some other provinces, this style of pressure group politics was associated with the long tenure in office of particular political parties.[57] It thus continued to reflect the general centralizing forces — economic and political — that were at work in early twentieth-century Canada. At the federal level, and eventually in the larger provinces, access-oriented pressure group politics came to be associated with the growing influence of the bureaucracy.

THE FIRST STAGES OF BUREAUCRATIC INFLUENCE: HANDMAIDEN TO THE HANDMAIDEN

Accompanying the centralizing trends of the first four decades of this century was the emergence of a new policy actor, the bureaucracy. Called into being by government's growing involvement in the technical aspects of economic development and by public demands for social services, administrative agencies expanded rapidly and were increasingly relied on for policy advice.[58] Their enlarged role, by the 1940s, had altered the entire process of policy-making. In the early stages of this evolution — the years of the First World War and the 1920s — the policy role of bureaucracy was limited, but gradually a few able senior officials — Adam Shortt, Graham Towers, Clifford Clark — won the confidence of the executive and came to exercise considerable influence.[59] Until the Second World War, however, political leaders seem to have doubted neither their own ability to 'work' the public service nor the soundness of their policy judgement. Bureaucracy was the handmaiden of the political executive. As political leaders absorbed the lessons of the Depression, and as the war forced governments more and more into managerial roles, policy-making became increasingly technical and a second generation of 'mandarins' — W.A. Mackintosh, John Deutsch, and Norman Robertson, among others — acquired a prominent part in the policy process. In subsequent decades that role was enlarged still further, to the point where the influence of senior officials came to be feared as a serious challenge to the legitimacy of the elected government.[60]

These developments are mainly responsible for the proliferation of pressure groups since the 1920s and for their expanded role. The administrative arm of government, in playing its own enlarged role, has found pressure groups a source of both information and legitimation. As power has leached through the administrative strata of government, the nature of the Canadian state has changed; and as the state has changed, so has pressure group politics. These changes have centred, first, on the failure of institutions of representative government to accommodate both territorial and sectoral concerns in the messages they send to government and, second, on the political system's consequent need to discover legitimate means of expressing sectoral needs. This presentation concentrates on the inter-war years and has two concerns: the effects on pressure group politics of the early stages of bureaucratic influence and the relations between pressure groups and the bureaucracy when the significance of widespread administrative intervention was first coming to be appreciated. In the next chapter we see how these developments contributed to the diffusion of power that bedevils policy-makers today.

The first effect of increased administrative involvement in the policy process was superficially innocuous, but presaged change: the processes of élite interaction became more bureaucratic, requiring the standardization of rules, the precise delineation of responsibility between offices, and the recording of official decisions. As bureaucratic methods invaded the corridors of power, politicians, élite members, and leaders of groups became entangled in a procedure that was inimical to their earlier *modus operandi*. A word in the right ear was no longer enough; officials had to be consulted, regulations checked, and the dangers of creating precedents thoroughly canvassed. Whimsy, personal inclination, friendship, chance — all became less regular ingredients in the alchemy of policy-making. The written record, justification on the basis of law and precedent, and formal procedures of review became more significant. The friendly support of a minister or a senior official might be helpful, and in borderline cases essential, but it could no longer serve as a means of bypassing paperwork and the need to 'go through channels'.*

The centralizing trends in the economy and in politics at the turn of the century also forced interest representation to become more formal. Local groups petitioning central authorities found that the very logistics of their pilgrimages to power required more advance planning, and more organization, than had ever been needed in the days of local consultation with the local member. As well, the increasingly centralized decision-making process was inherently less sensitive to local situations and the nuances of local power structures. Ministers and their advisers had difficulty evaluating delegations and the significance of their demands. More had to be explained; more had to be written down. Groups had to prove that they spoke for responsible opinion in the community. They had to establish their credibility, which had seldom been necessary when their demands had been addressed through politically sensitive local members. Formal organization made it easier to prepare delegations, to put together briefs, to orchestrate the adoption of weighty and impressive resolutions, and, above all, to demonstrate that the group was properly representative of the community; that its demands were legitimate.[61] The formal structure of the interest group was becoming a factor in its negotiations with government. As a result, local interests were gradually forced to change from solidary groups to interest groups.

Bureaucracy begat bureaucracy. To deal with the burgeoning agencies of government, pressure groups found themselves establishing offices and filling them with permanent officials. In some cases a spiral of institutionalization developed. As the permanent staff of pressure groups took up their positions they found that their work exposed new fields for policy development. For example, administering collective agreements led unions to monitor not only rates of pay, hours of work, and conditions surrounding hiring and firing, but also conditions of work, workers' compensation, the

---

*This transition may be observed in most aspects of public administration in this country, but nowhere is it demonstrated more clearly than in the long struggle to remove the civil service, at the federal and provincial levels, from the influence of patronage. For the spoils system, which gave the victorious political party immense freedom in the firing and appointment of public servants, successive reforms have substituted formal procedures governing appointments, including publication of openings, competitive examinations, precise descriptions of duties, establishment of classification systems, and a host of other regulations intended to ensure that merit, rather than the intervention of political friends, governs appointment and advancement in the public service. The long story of reform may be traced in a number of studies, of which the most complete is J.E. Hodgetts, William McCloskey, Reginald Whitaker and V. Seymour Wilson, *The Biography of an Institution: The Civil Service Commission of Canada, 1908-1967* (Montreal, 1972). Parallel experiences at the provincial level are analysed in J.E. Hodgetts and O.P. Dwivedi, *Provincial Governments as Employers* (Montreal, 1974).

employment of women and juveniles, and so on. Anomalies and abuses were brought to the attention of government, and as government responded it also expanded to take on the new workloads. As government expanded, so did the union organizations, for there was always more to monitor and always room for improvement in the conditions of work.[62] Similar spirals of institutionalization developed in many fields, though not, in most cases, until after the Second World War. The basic framework for the explosion of the policy-making system that followed 1945 was created in the inter-war years.

This spiral of institutionalization fed on a fundamental characteristic of bureaucracy: its capacity for dividing up work and assigning responsibility for specific tasks to different groups within the administrative organization. We call this 'differentiating function'. As each unit develops to meet its responsibilities, it also tends to divide up its work and create a more elaborate organizational structure. These tendencies are mirrored in the pressure group world, since each separate government agency strikes up a liaison with the parts of the public it serves. From the relationship, the government agency gets information, administrative assistance, and support in its dealings with other parts of the bureaucracy — and ultimately with the political environment. In other words, the handmaiden to government needed a handmaiden of her own and, in the policy system emerging in Canada between the wars, found that pressure groups admirably filled the role. It is from the inter-war period that we date an increased tendency for government officials to encourage special publics to develop their own organizational structures to benefit themselves and their bureaucratic partners. H.H. Hannam, president and managing director of the Canadian Federation of Agriculture, was encouraged in just this fashion by the Deputy Minister of Finance, during a discussion of the need for agricultural representation on the first board of directors of the Bank of Canada:

> In the course of our early remarks, Dr Clark said to me, 'We want to get one representative of agriculture. . . . We want to do that, the government wants to do that, and we are soliciting your help.' He went on to say, 'You have not a national organization representing agriculture, have you, which is a national interest group?' I said, 'No, we have not.' He said, 'It is too bad, isn't it?' That was a remark I will never forget. I used it quite often in the days when we were organizing the Federation . . . , that was the early part of 1935. We started and organized our Federation in the fall that same year.[63]

Thus was the development of formal interest groups encouraged.

Overtly political activity was not necessarily the first goal of this encouragement. Interest groups can perform para-administrative functions that cannot be as effectively achieved through the myriad, unorchestrated contacts that take place between agencies and the public at large. For example, the great flow of immigration to Canada in the first half of the twentieth century could not have been handled by government officials working alone. Local and national groups were needed to greet immigrants at the docks, to provide translation services, to help them through the first formalities, and to start them on their way across the country. Other groups were needed at major railway stops to guide the newcomers to their proper destinations, to provide medical help, and to explain what was happening. Still more were needed in the settlement areas as the immigrants selected and began to work their new lands.[64]

Some of the information-channelling activities of groups were also non-political and have been used by agencies to facilitate administrative work. Vincent Lemieux points out that the 'relayers' or popularizers of information, whether independent journalists or groups associated with particular agencies, play an important role in transmitting and translating data to the public. In André Holleaux's phrase 'l'association décode les messages administratifs et les recode dans le langage du public'.[65]

Interest groups also perform semi-political functions that make them valuable allies of government agencies. They help clarify the demands of the people they represent (we call this aggregating demand), they channel information, and they legitimize both the demands they make and the agencies that respond to them. Demand aggregation, for example, has been particularly important in industries where medium to small labour-intensive firms predominate — the textile and fishing industries, to name two. These industries could express their needs more effectively when they had developed formal organizational structures and procedures for discussing and reconciling their many divergent points of view. Without those structures, government received a flood of conflicting advice and was often at the mercy of the few interests who could command attention.* During the interwar years, Canadian bureaucrats and politicians discovered that those structures and procedures could be provided through interest groups.

The work of interest groups in aggregating demand also enhanced the legitimacy of the group's demands and the policy proposals agencies developed to satisfy them. An administrative proposal reflecting group-agency consultation and clearly having group support was more likely to win ministerial approval than one that could be described as merely a department project. Furthermore, an agency that clearly had the support of

---

*For example, when the government of Angus L. MacDonald came to power in Nova Scotia in 1933 one of its first acts was to appoint a Director of Marketing in the provincial Department of Agriculture. The successful appointee put forward a proposal that included putting 'order into the marketing of primary products. ... We planned to achieve this order both through co-operatives and marketing boards' (Quoted in A.A. MacDonald, *Policy Formation Process: Nova Scotia Dairy Marketing, 1933-1978* [Halifax, 1980], 35). During the 1930s marketing legislation was seen as an important vehicle for organizing a diffused industry.

the groups most affected by its work would also gain in stature. Finally, such support represented a counterpoise to the legitimacy of elected representatives. It permitted officials to claim that they too had a constituency, a functional one. It is no accident that officials often refer to their client groups as 'constituencies'.

Although these trends were developing throughout the inter-war years, they could be perceived only dimly. S.D. Clark in his study of the CMA gives an illustration:

> The development of lobby organizations by the Manufacturers' Association and other organized groups indicated the growth of a functional representative system outside the formally constituted machinery of government. Cutting across the boundaries of constituencies and provinces to give representation to groups organized upon the basis of common interests, the lobbyists expressed, more completely perhaps than members of Parliament, the diversified needs of the national community. They found it unnecessary to compromise principles or modify demands to meet the wishes of a great variety of groups.[66]

Not surprisingly, administrative agencies not only encouraged group participation in the policy process, they began actively promoting the creation of special interest groups. We noted an instance of this in 1873, when the Ontario Inspector of Prisons and Asylums recommended the establishment of prisoners' aid societies, but the practice seems to have become more common during the First World War. The official history of the Department of Trade and Commerce records, for example, that during the war years the department 'adopted a policy of encouraging the organization of industry-wide associations to seek out orders for their member companies'.[67] Similarly, N.J. Lawrie writes that at the end of the war the federal government, concerned with reconstruction, 'sought the close co-operation of industry. This, it believed, could best be fostered by dealing with associations representing industry's various components, and it was consequently desirous of having as many national organizations as possible.' He quotes A.K. MacLean, chairman of the Reconstruction Committee of the Privy Council, stating that if the founding meeting of the Canadian Construction Association had not already been planned ' "I had myself intended requesting such a gathering." As it was, various federal officials attended the meeting, urged collaboration and promised government co-operation.'[68]

Thus was entrenched a practice that has continued to the present day. In the 1930s it contributed to the founding of the Canadian Farmers' Association and in the Second World War to the development of the Consumers' Association of Canada. Early in the Trudeau administration there was a spate of pressure group formation as new co-ordinative agencies, such as the Ministry of State for Urban Affairs and the Department of Regional Economic Expansion, sought grass-roots reinforcement for policies of social and economic change.[69] From the beginning of his period as Minister of

Fisheries, Romeo LeBlanc devoted a great deal of time, effort, and regulatory encouragement to persuading the independent fishermen of the east coast to organize themselves. 'If I had to write the manual for dealing with government,' he told one group in 1978, 'I would put two main rules of the road: carry a flag — that is, have an organization — and sound your horn. Let people know you are there.'[70]

Though the sponsorship of pressure groups by government agencies was not entirely new, and though the practice was by no means as common in the inter-war years as it has since become,* its increased occurrence was symbolic. It indicated that though the role of pressure groups in policy-making was still modest and groups were very much under the tutelage of the state, they were acquiring a more significant role in the policy process. Since the beginning of the century many Canadian interest groups had become national and regional institutions. Responding to the centralizing influences of the concentration of economic and political power, they had grown beyond the local organizations that had given them their character during the nineteenth century. They had also acquired full-time professional staff, and so equipped themselves to deal on a continuing basis with the bureaucracies that were becoming increasingly influential in the Canadian state. Local organizations continued and volunteer labour was still the life-blood of most groups, but a growing number of interest associations now had the capacity and the stature to participate regularly in national and provincial policy debates and to work on a daily basis with officials as they implemented government programs.

The expansion of pressure group activity in the first third of the twentieth century sprang from two related but somewhat distinct causes. On the one hand, it was inspired by public realization that the most efficacious route to influencing public policy lay along the path of interest group organization. On the other, the state itself, finding its own tasks more numerous and complex, concluded that group participation sometimes facilitated policy formation and program implementation. Working generally through its administrative arm, but occasionally through its political arm, the state encouraged group formation. Both of these trends originated in the changing structure of the economy and its closer relationship with the state. The next chapter will examine these changes and look at how, during and after the

---

*By 1981 Kayyam Paltiel was commenting that since the 1960s growing numbers of citizens' groups had discovered that start-up and maintenance funds were increasingly available from 'benevolent sympathizers, private foundations in search of an agenda, and most importantly, public agencies, bureaucrats and politicians in search of an expanded constituency, votes and political support. Whereas private-sector groups depend largely on their membership for support, external funding in the past twenty years has apparently played an ever-increasing role in the funding of citizen, non-profit and even the mixed-sector groups' ('The Changing Environment and Role of Special Interest Groups': 206).

Second World War, they precipitated the realignments of policy-making institutions that we now associate with the diffusion of power and that have brought pressure groups close to the centre of our policy-making system.

CHAPTER 3

'To Have a Say, You Need a Voice'

Dramatic changes have taken place in Canadian pressure groups since the Second World War. They have become more numerous, more public, and more attentive to Parliament. Above all, they have come to occupy a more influential — and controversial — role in the policy process. This transition is rooted broadly in the changing relationship between government and the economy in the modern state, and more specifically in the expansion of bureaucratic influence and in the declining policy role of political parties. Hence, to understand how and why pressure groups have changed so much in recent decades, we must first review the transformations that have taken place in the role of the state and its policy-making institutions.

This chapter will show how business and political leaders came to depend on their professional advisers during the 1920s and 1930s and how that dependence caused a shift of policy-making capacity from the political executive to the middle ranks of the bureaucracy and its affiliated groups. Since pressure groups are adaptive instruments of political communication, I will not suggest that this change was the consequence of group action, but rather that groups have responded to the evolution of central institutions in the policy system. I will contend that the growth of government, with its inevitable elaboration of specialized bureaucracies, has precipitated a diffusion of power. That is, that the authority of the political and administrative executive has dissipated, leaching down into the middle ranks of the bureaucracy. The diffusion of power has transformed the methods used by government agencies to compete for resources and has forced them to look beyond the traditional relationships between Cabinet, bureaucracy, and Parliament in order to secure legitimacy for government policy. These two developments have helped to bring about the most recent changes in pressure group politics, especially a renewal of pressure group interest in Parliament — and possibly a revival of parliamentary influence in policy-making.

THE AGE OF THE TECHNOSTRUCTURE

By the late 1930s, governments had become equal partners with the private sector in the management of the economy. Governments had become involved in management because contemporary economies cannot function effectively without combining the human skills and physical resources needed to produce goods and bring them to market. Though this is achieved largely through the self-adjusting mechanisms of the market, the organizing ability of government is necessary to ensure that resources flow to industry as and where they are needed and that the economy can sustain demand for the goods produced. In other words, government plays an essential role in demand and supply management.*[1] A second reason for government's management function is that public-sector intervention is required if the world's depleting natural resources are to be prolonged effectively.

The evolution of this new role for government was related to the development of modern business organization, which radically changed the character of public policy-making in the late nineteenth century. As corporations in the twentieth century sought to integrate geographically distant resources, complex technologies, and sophisticated human skills, they increasingly depended on government to organize and manage the supply of resources to enterprises, and even to take a hand in the regulation of demand.

The forest industries provide a good illustration of these needs.[2] In Ontario, New Brunswick, and Quebec in particular, but to a lesser extent in other provinces, traditional lumbering gave way to pulp-and-paper operations. These enterprises could not be built around the principle of 'cut out and get out', which many lumber barons had been applying. They involved huge expenditures on plant and machinery and, to some extent, on the hiring of a skilled labour force. Capital expenditures had to be amortized over decades, not years. This meant that companies had to be supplied with forest reserves that could be made to last for a very long time indeed — preferably 'in perpetuity'. Even these vast tracts, however, would prove inadequate unless they were managed. Governments, which for the most part owned the forests and were in any case anxious to encourage their development, were drawn into co-operation with business to address the problems of forest management.

Each province handled the situation differently. Nova Scotia, and to some

---

*A. Pizzorno perceives a transformation in 'the formal aspects of the political system and the system of representation in particular, in capitalist societies just before and immediately after World War I.' Universal suffrage, mass parties, the institutionalization of interest groups, and new types of legislation represented 'a gradual shift away from the universalistic laws of the age of classical liberalism toward both more specificity in the content of laws and delegation of power to administrative agencies'. A common theme amongst writers who addressed these phenomena — Gierke, Maitland, Laski, Cole, Durkheim, Bentley, Michels, Weber — was the recognition 'that the idea of a direct relationship between the state and the individual was unrealistic' ('Interests and Parties in Pluralism' in S.D. Berger [ed.], *Organizing Interests in Western Europe* [Cambridge, 1981], 247-87, at 247-9).

extent Quebec, gave the companies virtually a free hand to develop and apply their own management plans. Other provinces, like Ontario, tried to monitor the companies' use of the forest. All took a growing part in the management process, first through forest protection work, then through reforestation programs, and ultimately in direct forest management. Nor was supply management confined to the resource itself. The companies needed large amounts of electricity, a need they sometimes met themselves but that was often provided through government-owned corporations such as Ontario Hydro, B.C. Power, and Hydro-Québec. The demand for human resources — for instance, competent people to carry out forest maintenance and protection work — was also met in part through government action. Forest ranger schools were established in several provinces, largely at public expense. At a more senior level, both private and public sectors also required professionals capable of supervising forest management and developing forest policy. By the 1920s, Quebec, Ontario, and New Brunswick had each established university-level professional training programs to meet this need.

The cycle of business-government interaction did not end there. Government also had to take a hand when transportation infrastructure was needed to get pulp and paper to market, when demand management became significant, and favourable tariffs had to be negotiated. Some provinces forbade the export of pulpwood and wood pulp in an attempt to protect the markets of companies manufacturing paper in Canada. At the height of the Depression, the Ontario and Quebec governments became deeply involved in rationing demand among surviving companies — it was the only way to keep most of them in business. Such examples of government intervention can be replicated, in differing forms, in the context of any modern industry. In aviation or fishing; atomic energy or automobile production; brewing, baking, and possibly even candle-making — government's role in supply or demand management has become essential and pervasive because government is generally the only actor possessing sufficient authority to orchestrate the flow of resources to business or to harmonize demand.[3]

In addition, there are times when government alone can help the community at large cope with many of the consequences — the externalities — of business activity. For example, the exploitation of any new resource or new technology involves social, environmental, and economic costs that can be met only through the careful management of other existing resources. Tapping the oil reserves of the Beaufort Sea involves enormous expenditures of public and private money, serious problems of environmental degradation, and the disruption of regional societies.[4] Likewise technological change alters many aspects of social and economic life. Though some of these changes will occur whatever the government does, most will generate some kind of public debate and government intervention. Communities that expand too rapidly will demand infusion of public money to maintain equilibrium; other communities, pushed into decline, will demand similar support to prevent, or at least to mitigate, the attendant human misery. In either pattern of development government will be deeply involved in the calculation and use of public resources, and in the channelling of private sector energies.[5]

These examples underline the high level of interdependence that was becoming increasingly central to state-business relations during the interwar years and that has a determining effect today on public policy-making. To cope with interdependence, government and industry need a much more sophisticated system of policy communication than had been created by business and political leaders in the early part of this century. The need was met through the creation of what J.K. Galbraith has called the 'technostructure' — a sophisticated communications network of technically proficient specialists that cuts across the lines dividing government and business and in which technical knowledge is the currency of power.[6] The technostructure, so far as the development and implementation of public policy is concerned, is the lace that ties the shoe. Through its network of professional relationships it pulls together the complementary capacities of government and business. It is strong because it works at virtually all levels of both systems; all participants speak a common specialized language, and its operations are largely informal. The technostructure enables the two sectors to make both large-scale policy and the day-to-day adjustments necessary to implement it, and in so doing has made possible the evolution of the modern economy.

At the same time, the technostructure has exacted a heavy price from democratic institutions because it fostered the dominance of technical competence in the policy process. It did this in three ways. First, in Gerard Timsit and Céline Wiener's words, it 'short-circuited' traditional institutions of political representation.[7] Second, it changed the language of policy-making in a fashion that excluded lay people, including politicians. Third, in promoting neutral competence it denigrated political participation in both administration and policy-making and substituted for it technical expertise.

Only to a very limited degree did these actions reflect conscious attempts on the part of technical experts to exclude the political element from policy and administration. For the most part, these patterns emerged informally and grew out of the situations in which specialists were working. Technical advisers and officials in government came to bypass elected policy-makers and speak directly with technicians in corporations and social institutions because they shared a common knowledge base, spoke a shared language, and often genuinely believed that the problems they discussed and resolved were 'technical' and not 'political'.* Only when they were looked at in their totality would it become clear that these informal, low-level exchanges between technicians created a framework of understandings and petty decisions that allowed the 'policy-maker' no freedom of action.

The effect of changes in the language of policy-making was equally unintentional but just as devastating.[8] The language of discussions between the public and private sectors became detailed and technical. In forest administration, for example, lumber barons increasingly found themselves negotiating with professional foresters whose concerns, and language, were entirely different from those of the party bosses. The bosses were concerned with jobs for the faithful and contributions to the party. The new forestry officials were steeped in the sciences of 'silviculture' and were conversant with the 'growth cycles' and 'succession' of trees. They allocated cutting rights according to 'forest management plans' that were based on 'forest inventories' and they insisted that lumbering 'operations' should be carried out in a fashion that promoted 'regeneration'. They even spoke of 'wood fibre' instead of trees.[9] Neither the traditional party system nor—except on rare occasions—political leaders could master the intricacies of the new language. Reviewing a seminar on the subject of government-citizen communications in Quebec, Jacques de Guise commented that the average Member of the National Assembly had been spoken of 'comme d'un fossile'. At the National Assembly, even in legislative committees, the MNA toes the party line, and while he or she is provided with a constituency office, it is not used as a place where local views on policy matters are discussed, but rather as a consulting room where constituents ask their representative to mediate between themselves and government. It is 'une sorte de confessional où chacun va demander à son "parrain" une réponse personnelle sinon privilegiée à un problème personnalisé'.[10] Even the MNAs present at the seminar concurred in this assessment, confessing that their offices were not places where citizens could develop and promote policy ideas. Like their counterparts in English Canada they saw themselves as ombudsmen.[11]

---

*A typical example of the technical nature of government regulation of industry was reported in the *Globe and Mail* on 11 December 1985 in a story on new controls governing the sale of table wines. The regulations limited permissible levels of ethyl carbamate—a chemical believed to be a carcinogen—to 30 parts per billion. A representative of the Canadian Wine Institute, which claims to represent 80 per cent of the country's wine producers, engaged in a vigorous debate with an official of the federal Department of Health and Welfare over highly technical issues, with the industry representative maintaining that testing apparatus was not accurate to 30 parts per billion. He demanded to know how the Department intended testing for that level and stated that the Institute would 'question the results of those tests very aggressively'. The Department representative, while admitting that testing apparatus would have to be improved, maintained that a yeast-enriching agent, urea, produces ethyl carbamate and that the dangerous chemical could be virtually eliminated if urea were no longer used.

Politicians are naturally alert to and understand a different language from that spoken in the technostructure. In the course of performing parliamentary and ministerial roles many politicians develop a good grasp of specialized fields, but their political survival depends on their being first and foremost 'community specialists', fluent in expressing the needs and aspirations of their constituents, but not in debating the merits of rival technical processes, the intricacies of corporate finance, or rarefied social and economic theory.

The promotion of neutral competence was more self-consciously directed at reducing the influence of politicians in policy and administration. The policy problem created by the gap between politicians' capacity to speak for the human needs of their constituency and their ability to engage meaningfully in debate with government's expert advisers served as the pretext for advancing the technostructure. Public dissatisfaction with the legislative branch's ineptitude in policy formation or its distaste for the corruption of machine politics — made apparent in the Beauharnois affair at the federal level and in numerous disputes over the distribution of mineral, forest, and other resources at the provincial[12] — grew during the inter-war years. The distributive politics of colonial and late nineteenth-century Canada that reached its peak in the 1920s had become less acceptable by the late 1930s. Its cost, particularly the wasteful management of resources and the corruption of the political machine, was too apparent.

By contrast, the competence and purity of technical administration appeared to hold great hope for the future. The implantation of neutral, professional competence in the public service was seen as part of a reform movement. In the United States, in fact, the divorce of politics and administration was an article of faith with many reformers. It struck a responsive chord in Canada as well, achieving its clearest manifestation in the federal Civil Service Acts of 1912 and 1918, which established the federal Civil Service Commission and provided that civil servants would be appointed on the basis of merit and not because of their affiliation with the party in power.[13] Provincial governments took longer to reach a similar stage, but there too the need for professional competence brought neutral expertise into the government service and eventually into positions of authority.[14]

Frequently the reformers' allies in their battles with party politicians were the associations that stood at the heart of each newly emergent profession. These bodies had many roles. They knit practitioners together as a group; they helped to determine what knowledge was required to practise each profession; they certified the competent; they worked to secure recognition of professional qualifications on the part of employers; and they monitored professional performance, particularly professional ethics. In several respects, these functions automatically aligned professional bodies with those who were fighting party patronage. The security of the profession depended on a security of tenure in the work-place that was unattainable in the traditional 'spoils system', in which civil service positions were taken away from the appointees of the 'losers' and handed out to a new group of government supporters each time the reins of power changed hands.

Patronage politics were not compatible with professional practices. A forester trained in university to strive for good forest management through crop rotation could only feel that his or her efforts had been wasted when local political leaders applied their own principles to the allocation of forest resources. During the 1920s and the 1930s, as the professions developed, these objections to party patronage became more widespread and generally known. They contributed to a growing public view that party-dominated policy-making and administration were inappropriate in the modern world, and they sometimes brought the administrative arm of government close to open warfare with party organizers. In the eyes of some administrators, the campaign assumed the proportions of a crusade against corruption as they sought to replace the influence of local party barons with administrative machinery run by technically competent professionals.[15] In so doing, they complicated still further the efforts of elected representatives to speak to both the spatial and sectoral concerns of their constituents, and they enhanced the representative functions of sectorally oriented institutions. That is, they promoted the political growth of the administrative arm of government and of its satellite groups at the expense of the legislative system and party government.

In short, the technostructure, necessary though it was, diminished the role of politicians in politics and administration and changed the relations between policy institutions. Just as the development of business concentration in the first part of the twentieth century drained power from the legislature to the executive, from the party organization to the party leaders, so the emergence after the Depression of technologically sophisticated professionals in business and government resulted in a further transfer of power from the political executive to the administrative branch of government. While the loss of power by the executive was certainly not complete, it was substantial, and it reduced appreciably the scope of the executive and its decision-making capacity.

As the accession of administrative power diminished the role of politicians, it enhanced that of pressure groups. Communication within the technostructure can, and frequently does, occur without the assistance of interest groups; but that assistance is often useful or even necessary. Because interest groups, like bureaucracies, are usually built around the principle of division of function, they easily link specific sections of administrative agencies and the parts of the public that are affected directly by those agencies' policies and programs. As well, while many aspects of the day-to-day administration of policy can be dealt with through one-to-one discussion between bureaucratic specialists and their opposite numbers in industry, the determination of industry-wide attitudes and needs can best be achieved through interest groups. They can draw together the various participants in each sector and can bring about some agreement over their conflicting demands. If necessary, interest groups can muster support within the specialized public for the policies that emerge from group-agency consultation.

This pattern of interaction and interdependence evolved gradually, beginning in the First World War as governments encouraged some solidary interests to organize themselves for the war effort. After the war, the new Crown corporations, boards, and commissions that were being set up proved as assiduous as traditional departments in fostering interest-group support. A number sought group representation on their directing or advisory bodies, much as Clifford Clark looked to H.H. Hannam to organize the farm community so that it could be represented on the Board of Directors of the Bank of Canada.[16] Interest groups were equally interested. According to S.D. Clark, 'the increasing importance of administrative orders of the Government' was one factor leading the Canadian Manufacturers' Association to change its focus. 'Emphasis tended to shift to influencing the policies and activities of government boards, commissioners, and department officials, and to the extent that parliamentary leaders became dependent upon such agencies, these influences were more effective than pressure exerted upon the party organization.'[17] Before the end of the Second World War, which on a country-wide basis accelerated the trend towards government participation in the organization of the economy, a pattern of technically oriented agency-industry-group interactions was in place in many industries.

GROUP POLITICS DURING THE REGIME OF THE MANDARINS

By the end of the Second World War pressure groups had become an essential part of the policy process, but they had not won a corresponding acceptance from the general public, or even from the officials who found them useful. This was because, first, group politics was antithetical to popular perceptions of democratic government, and, second, the mutual dependence of groups and agencies was not yet fully developed.

As recently as the 1960s the general public treated pressure-group participation in policy-making as illicit. Robert Presthus has called this 'a culturally determined orientation, semantical rather than substantive', attributable to the 'deferential style of Canadian politics'.[18] There were, however, more significant causes. There was a general tendency to equate pressure group activity with 'lobbying', which the public tended to associate with the corrupt and venal side of politics. This was probably a reaction to the publicity surrounding the exposure of American lobbying activity by the Muckrakers at the turn of the century and to the various scandals that plagued Canadian politics in the 1920s and 1930s and were often attributed to the demands of 'special interests'.[19]

However, 'guilt by association' only partially explains the animosity that frequently greeted pressure groups in the first two decades after the Second World War. A more important influence may have been the fact that pressure group intervention in policy-making offended public perceptions of democratic government. The institutions of representative government — the single-member constituency and the structure of political parties in particular — were sustained by myths that recognized no distinction between the representation of spatial interests and of sectoral concerns. Despite the growing incapacity of parties and legislatures, the belief persisted that they and they alone had the responsibility for articulating the needs of the people; that interventions on the part of other institutions were illegitimate. In Chapter 2 we cited J.M. Beck's observation that groups in Nova Scotia learned to avoid being identified explicitly with either of the main political parties. This approach stemmed partly from a fear of offending the leadership of one party or the other, but also from a public belief that interest groups had no business intervening in partisan politics. Beck quotes a 1911 editorial in the Halifax *Chronicle* reminding the Union of Nova Scotia Municipalities that its status was only that of 'a body of private individuals banded together for the furthering of what they conceived to be social progress. The Independent Order of Good Templars is another such.' Accordingly, the Union should 'leave politics severely alone if [it] wish[ed] to accomplish any good'. The demands of pressure groups, though not necessarily inimical to the public interest, were those of *special* interests and were therefore to be treated with great suspicion.[20]

Such attitudes were still prevalent in the years after the Second World War and provoked earnest debates when the public-spirited members of certain groups realized that their efforts to promote change in government policy bore an uncomfortable resemblance to pressure politics. Helen Jones Dawson, describing in 1963 the activities of the Consumers' Association of Canada, noted: 'through the years there has persisted a considerable body of opinion in the CAC that the Ottawa office, by being constantly in contact with the government, is turning the Association into a "pressure group"; there is very strong resistance to such a development.' One group within the organization 'felt quite strongly that CAC should not be submitting briefs to government as this turned it into a pressure group and did not contribute toward the education of the public on consumer matters'. Dawson came to the conclusion that 'there seems to be only one point on which virtually all members of the Executive during the past fifteen years could find agreement and that is that CAC must not become a "pressure group" or indulge in pressure group methods. It might be more difficult to get them to agree on what a pressure group is and does.'[21] Though these views seem naïve today, in the early 1960s the leadership of the CAC was probably reflecting fairly accurately a broad public distaste for pressure group politics.

These attitudes touched on fundamental philosophical issues. Though not always clearly articulated in public discussions, they were, and are, critical to any attempt to incorporate interest-group representation in public policy-making. (They will be discussed later in this study.) Probably their most significant effect on pressure groups in the 1950s and 1960s was to inhibit the development of pressure groups and thus to retard the resolution of the problems posed by the increasing incapacity of traditional representative institutions to express sectoral as well as spatial concerns. Inevitably too, public scepticism affected the impact that pressure groups could have in the policy process. In their dealings with group leaders, politicians and officials exploited the fact that pressure group legitimacy was constantly in doubt. It was never tactically sound to admit too enthusiastically that groups might be useful as sources of information, or as legitimizers of government policy.[22] The structure of the Canadian policy process reinforced the utility of this approach as far as government policy-makers were concerned, for the mutual dependence of groups and agencies was not yet well developed.

Unlike the American system — from which many Canadians, including many academics and policy-makers themselves, derived their ideas about pressure group politics — the policy process in the years after the Second World War operated through two relatively closed structures: the party system and the bureaucracy, both of which culminated in the Cabinet. The major political parties had, as shown in Chapter 2, turned their grass-roots organizations into 'fighting machines' for delivering votes and dispensing petty patronage. With the power to determine the distribution of party resources concentrated at the leadership level, the party hierarchy was able to impose on elected members a degree of discipline previously unknown in Canada. The same control extended, albeit less explicitly, through the party organization. Its framework was not likely to encourage vigorous internal party debate on policy issues. In fact, in the late 1960s, when the Liberal Party attempted to engage its constituency organizations in policy discussions, the grass roots had difficulty coping with their rediscovered role, and at the provincial level most Conservative regimes proved almost as hamstrung by power as the Liberals in Ottawa.[23] The structure and mores of the civil service contributed to this malaise. As far as the Ottawa civil service was concerned, by the 1960s it was 'generally accepted by students of Canadian Government that the senior public service has had a crucial position in the overall structure of power'.[24] It was the epoch of the mandarins, a period when the advice of some senior officials vastly outweighed that of most ministers; when more than one senior official could, like W.A. Mackintosh, confide to his colleagues that he virtually alone had written a major policy document (the *White Paper on Employment and Incomes* of 1945, which served as the base for Canada's post-war economic policy) and had inspired the original policy idea.* Mackintosh, R.B. Bryce, Norman Robertson, A.D.P. Heeney, and a handful of others derived their power from the trust confided in their considerable professional competence by the Prime Minister and his closest colleagues. Their position was strengthened by the factors we have already discussed: the unfavourable public repute of pressure group politics; the not yet fully appreciated decline in the policy capacity of the political parties; and the neutral competence of the public service. (The last had not yet been called into question, since it had not been widely recognized that the public service could be neutral in terms of partisan politics, but very much a supporter of specific policies.)[25]

Pressure group politics meant little to the mandarins. Some senior officials seem to have believed that they did not operate in this country. One confessed to a meeting of the Institute of Public Administration of Canada (IPAC), in 1953, that 'before I entered this meeting, I was under the impression that I had had no experience with pressure groups'.[26] At the same meeting, Wilfrid Eggleston quoted a remark by George McIlraith, then Parliamentary Assistant to C.D. Howe, to the effect that lobbying 'is most damaging but fortunately it is practically non-existent in Canada'.[27] Others were not so insensitive. K.W. Taylor, deputy minister of Finance, probably expressed a representative mandarin view when he remarked that

> the rapid expansion and growing complexity of modern government greatly increases the importance of administration. This means that policy is not so much a series of conscious decisions, but rather grows out of a stream of administrative decisions. For this reason there has been a growing tendency in recent years for lobbyists, the people who want to bring pressure to bear, to direct their attention as much to administrative officers as to political heads; for

---

*Mackintosh's comment is quoted by V.S. Wilson in 'Some Perspectives on Public Policy Analysis' in John H. Redekop, *Approaches to Canadian Politics* (Toronto, 1978), 247-79, at 251-3. Mackintosh, the archetypical 'mandarin', served for many years in senior positions and is considered by many economists to be the architect of Canada's post-war economic policy. Mitchell Sharp, who himself served as senior civil servant and as Cabinet minister, gives an excellent illustration of the changing roles of elected and permanent officials: 'I recall Dr Mackintosh's account of how he had been instructed to prepare a statement for [Prime Minister] King to use when announcing on the radio the overall price ceiling which came into effect towards the end of 1941. He showed his draft to the Prime Minister who, after reading the opening paragraphs, looked up and said: "This is important, isn't it, Mackintosh?" I couldn't imagine Mr Pearson or Mr Trudeau being so unaware of the momentous consequences of introducing overall price controls' ('Decision-making in the federal cabinet', *Canadian Public Administration* 19 [1976] 1, 1-8, 3). On the other hand, though Mackenzie King's successors may have had a better grasp of economic policy, they were much less masters of the policy process.

if you get a stream of administrative decisions started in a certain direction it tends to grow into established policy.[28]

The proceedings of the successive meetings of IPAC indicates that senior officials dealt regularly with interest groups and believed that they served a useful function in communicating with special publics and could sometimes be counted on to help with the delivery of programs.[29] Some departments — Veterans' Affairs, and to some extent Agriculture or Labour — might have very close ties with certain groups and might even be said to depend on them for support;[30] but for the most part senior administrators in the 1950s and 1960s were not prepared to admit that pressure groups had an essential role to play in policy-making. The idea of being in some way politically dependent on pressure groups would have been considered far-fetched, though instances of agency manipulation of groups were noted and condemned.[31] The consensus was that senior public servants had a special responsibility to guard the public interest and therefore should be concerned to test the legitimacy of the interest groups communicating with them and to maintain a polite but correct distance from them. According to Taylor, 'the public administrator has a very real interest in the techniques, in the tactics and in the varying degrees of subtlety with which administrators are approached. Among the things we have to develop in public administrators is a high order of sales resistance and a considerable skill in assessing the validity of representations that are made to us.'[32]

The mandarins presided over a disciplined bureaucracy. Today in Canada the media and the Opposition look to the public service for a constant flow of information concerning policy discussion within the executive and administrative branches. Competing agencies, interest groups, and even individual public servants committed to specific policy positions have discovered that public debate can be used to influence policy decisions. Consequently in Ottawa, as in Washington, the leak — authorized and unauthorized — has become an everyday occurrence. In the war years and the subsequent two decades such behaviour was considered unthinkable, and the discipline of the bureaucracy was strictly enforced to prevent it. This discipline extended not only to civil servants but to those whose dealings with government touched upon policy formation. Pressure groups in particular were affected by these constraints.

Attitudes and mores were reinforced by the mechanics of the policy process. Helen Jones Dawson pointed out that 'working in a Parliamentary system, it is inevitable that Canadian organizations find it essential to influence policy and legislation before the Parliamentary stage is reached.'[33] One senior civil servant put it more bluntly:

People who really want to guide and influence government policy are wasting their time dealing with members of Parliament, senators and, usually, even ministers. If you want results — rather than just the satisfaction of talking to the prominent — you deal with us, and at various levels. ... To produce results you need to see the key planners, who may be way down in the system, and you see them early enough to push for changes in policy before it is politically embarrassing to make them.

In effect this meant tackling senior politicians or the bureaucracy, or both. For the reasons we have already described, neither was easily susceptible to influence; this is reflected in the sequence of policy preparation summarized in Table 3-1. None of the stages reported in the table offered interests a very wide opening for exercising influence. In theory, as some members of the public service argued, groups opposed to new policies could make their views known at the legislative stage and, by capturing media attention, whip up public opposition to the proposed legislation. In practice this was seldom a viable strategy. Not only were governments reluctant to back away from legislation that they had formally presented as government policy, but the very attempt to discredit the proposals would incur the displeasure of senior officials who might capitulate on a single issue, but would punish the group on future occasions by withholding information or foreclosing opportunities for representation.[35]

It is therefore hardly surprising that Canadian pressure groups focused their attention on the mandarins and their departments, according the legislature only perfunctory attention.[36] This does not mean that the groups themselves necessarily favoured such one-sided relationships, but they were adaptive institutions that accepted the exigencies of the policy system.[37] As late as 1969-70, when the effects of a reformed committee system were beginning to be felt, Robert Presthus found, on interviewing 139 MPs concerning their relations with group representatives, that 58.2 per cent of them saw group representatives occasionally, seldom, or rarely. Admittedly, the largest proportion of them saw group representatives occasionally, rather than less frequently.[38] (See Table 3-2.) However, contact about twice a month (Presthus's definition of 'occasional') hardly constitutes a significant degree of interaction and contrasts sharply with Jean Pigott's comment, a little more than a decade later, that as an Opposition MP she was 'overwhelmed' by pressure group representations.[39] Presthus's data, however, is consistent with Dawson's impression that while groups in the late 1960s were paying more attention to Parliament, particularly to its committees, their contacts were not extensive and their tactics were by no means as sophisticated as those used at Westminster or Washington.[40] Even in dealing with committees, groups tended to confine their interaction to presenting briefs. There seems to have been little attempt to cultivate informal ties with committee members, to persuade them to pursue issues of concern to the groups, or to brief them in advance on technical aspects of their

Table 3-1: The Stages of Legislative Development in Canada during the 1950s and 1960s, with Points of Interest Intervention

1. CONCEPTUALIZATION

Traditionally the most elusive step in the policy process. Who conceives a new policy? It is usually argued that while specific individuals may initiate action leading to new policy positions they themselves have been inspired by a host of cumulative environmental and specific events. Obviously interest groups may have contributed directly or indirectly to these events.

2. DEPARTMENTAL PRELIMINARY EXAMINATION

Once initiated, the policy review or policy preparation process would call upon interdepartmental study groups to prepare background studies and policy alternatives, and draft policy documents. At this point, groups were generally invited to make their views known and were, in fact, most active in trying to influence the direction of policy, their rationale being that once a departmental position had been taken and advice tendered to Cabinet it was extremely difficult to change that advice, unless Cabinet itself called for change. Although one observer reports that groups were invited to participate in this process as a matter of course, there is at least one well-documented case in which key — and powerful — groups were not given an opportunity to influence discussion at this stage, and, in fact, remained ignorant of proposed policy until the parliamentary stage was reached.

3. MEMO TO CABINET

This memo, the product of the previous stage, was considered the most important document in the entire process. It laid out the general principles of the proposed policy and its financial implications. In its final form it was, and remains, a highly confidential paper and was not shown to group representatives or any others outside the decision circle. Cabinet might accept the proposal in its entirety or order changes. If changes were required, some of the steps already detailed were repeated. If not, the policy proposal would go to the formal drafting stage.

4. LEGISLATIVE DRAFTING

Drafting was carried out by the Department of Justice and seems to have been considered by some a purely technical process in which groups were not consulted. Anyone who has ever had any contact with the strictly legal aspects of policy-making will find this difficult to believe and will be more inclined to accept Dawson's statement that interests were consulted on matters of detail. It may have been true, though, that interests were not shown *final* drafts of legislation before submission to Parliament. Dawson quotes one minister explaining that interest groups were not provided with advance copies of a particular bill, 'because that insults Parliament. Parliament was the first to see the Bill. However, we did show many of these groups very carefully, specifically worded . . . draft instructions.' It is unclear how widespread such practices were.

5. PARLIAMENTARY STAGE

In the view of some civil servants of the day, the only really appropriate occasion for interest group intervention in the policy process came at the committee stage of the legislative process. This, naturally, was not a view that sat well with the representatives of established groups, and even the less experienced leaders of many issue-oriented groups realized that in the Cabinet-parliamentary system it is extremely difficult to modify proposed legislation once the government has formally committed itself to putting it before Parliament. During the 1970s this practice was modified somewhat and some legislation was considerably changed or even withdrawn at the Committee stage, but in the 1950s and 1960s only highly technical amendments stood any chance of success at the parliamentary stage.

Source: Helen Jones Dawson, 'National Pressure Groups and the Federal Government' in A.P. Pross (ed.) *Pressure Group Behaviour in Canadian Politics* (Toronto: McGraw-Hill, 1975), 27-59, and David Kwavnick, *Organized Labour and Pressure Politics* (Montreal: McGill-Queen's, 1972). Accounts of the procedures used to prepare legislation for Parliament in this period differ somewhat. We have assumed that these differences reflect inter-departmental variations in procedure, as the fixed points in the process were relatively few and procedure was apt to vary, not only between agencies but from time to time within agencies.

Table 3-2: Interest Group Interaction with Legislators

Conventional wisdom in the 1950s and 1960s asserted that interest groups had little to do with Members of Parliament. Robert Presthus's 1969-70 survey of approximately 1,000 interest-group directors generally confirmed that view. Asked which three elements of the policy system their groups targeted first, in general, Presthus's sample ranked the following first:

MAJOR GENERAL TARGETS OF INTEREST GROUPS

PROPORTION RANKING EACH TARGET FIRST

TARGET	PROPORTION	
	%	
Bureaucracy	40	(158)
Backbenchers	20	(80)
Cabinet	19	(74)
Legislative committees	7	(27)
Executive assistants	5	(19)
Judiciary	3	(11)
Other	6	(24)

A comparable US sample ranked the same targets as follows:

	%
Bureaucracy	21
Legislators	41
Cabinet	4
Legislative committees	19
Executive assistants	3
Judiciary	3
Other	9

Source: Robert Presthus, *Elites in the Policy Process*, Toronto, 1974, p. 255.

Presthus also investigated some 400 specific 'cases' in which he sought a similar identification of targets. As might be expected, in the particular circumstances surrounding each case the target of representations tended to shift according to the nature of the case and the needs of the group:

SUBSTANTIVE ISSUES PRESENTED TO GOVERNMENT ELITES BY INTEREST GROUPS, CASE STUDY

PROPORTION RANKING EACH TARGET FIRST

ISSUE	BACK-BENCHERS	CABINET	BUREAUCRACY	EXECUTIVE ASSISTANTS	OTHER	
	%	%	%	%	%	
Laws	11	51	19	4	15	(92)
Bills	30	33	19	4	13	(90)
Intraorganizational policy	15	26	16	4	22	(27)
Licensing	13	54	21	—	13	(26)
Administrative regulations	13	41	21	3	19	(79)
Fund-raising	7	13	60	3	17	(30)
Group jurisdiction	—	23	31	15	31	(16)
Other	6	36	24	1	22	(70)
	(60)	(154)	(107)	(15)	(50)	(406)

Presthus comments: These data provide an overview of both the substance and process of interest group-government interaction, in the case study context. Forty per cent of all groups contact the Cabinet; 26 per cent turn mainly to the bureaucracy; while only 15 per cent focus on the legislature as their primary target. Putatively administrative issues, such as licensing and regulations, exhibit a similar valence. Only regarding pending legislation do groups approach backbenchers with an intensity similar to that accorded the Cabinet. And only in fund-raising and problems of group jurisdiction is the Cabinet's dominance superseded by the bureaucracy. Even the final 'other' category, consisting of a *pot-pourri* of issues neither significant nor structured enough to warrant detailed categorization, remains primarily a Cabinet province. Here, in sum, we have the clearest evidence of Cabinet hegemony in the process of élite accommodation.

Source: Robert Presthus, *Elite Accommodation in Canadian Politics* (Cambridge, 1973), pp. 230-1.

presentations. Contacts with private members were even more limited, seldom rising to such heights of sophistication as lobbying them through constituency members of the organization; asking them to sponsor legislation; feeding them questions for Question Period; or even visiting them in their offices more than once or twice in the life of a Parliament. According to Dawson, some groups did not lobby private members 'as a matter of policy'. The Canadian Federation of Agriculture was cited in this category. These and similar findings led Dawson to conclude that 'traditionally Canadian pressure groups have not paid much attention to Parliament, its institutions, or its private members.'[41]

Thus in the two decades following the Second World War pressure groups developed in a contradictory climate. On the one hand the Depression, the war years, and the growth of the technostructure had all contributed to the extension of group participation in policy-making and the elaboration of pressure group organizations; on the other hand, negative public attitudes, the residue of power concentrated in the hands of the political executive, the disciplined structure of the policy process, and the dismissive attitude of the most senior public service advisers all militated against that expansion.

The groups that survived in this era did so because they came to terms with a central fact: the key to exercising influence in the relatively closed policy-making system that prevailed from the war years to the beginning of the Trudeau era was access. Oriented towards obtaining access to the policy-makers whose decisions had a vital impact on the concerns of their members, pressure group leaders concentrated on developing their capacity to communicate specialized, often highly technical information, and on their ability to engage officials at various levels of policy development and implementation. In order to maintain such an intimate association with the bureaucracy they also developed a high regard for discretion and a readiness to accept agency domination of the relationship.[42] This usually meant that the group would try to avoid public criticism of existing or proposed policy and would never indulge in media-attracting publicity that would arouse public opinion. Consultation, and the search for consensus, became the outstanding characteristics of government/pressure group relations.

These methods affected both group structure and organization. The need for expert knowledge dictated the hiring of specialists, or dependence on elaborate committee structures capable of tapping the expertise of group members. Equally important was the need to employ group representatives who had both intimate knowledge of the bureaucracies they had to deal with and an ability to work at the various levels at which policy was made. Publicists and animateurs, on the other hand, were not needed; nor, in general, was a large staff. As long as the information resources of the membership could be tapped fairly efficiently, and as long as group representatives knew their way around Ottawa, or the provincial capital, groups could function effectively from a modest base. More important than the scale of resources was the extent of their institutionalization. An effective collective memory, a relationship of trust with officials, and an intimate acquaintance with process and issues were vital, and these could only be acquired with time. Hence, few groups could be effective unless they established an institutional presence.

POWER DIFFUSED, POWER CONFUSED

A rough estimate of the number of associations listed in the *Canadian Almanac and Directory* suggests that between 1945 and 1982 their numbers rose from 1,700 to 5,500; another directory lists 8,000 in 1981. Coleman, in his study of national business groups, reports that in 1867 Canada possessed about 15 'nationally relevant associations', 70 in 1900, and more than 700 by 1980, with the most important period of association formation occurring during the two world wars and between 1960 and 1975. His figures make a key point: the rate of group formation clearly accelerated in the more recent period.[43] The 1991 edition of Land's *Directory of Associations in Canada* (iii) lists some 20,000 associations. Even more striking is the extent to which pressure groups, including institutionalized groups that formerly avoided publicity, now attract public attention. In the media they are ubiquitous; many advertise through newspapers, magazines, television, and radio to put their views before the public. They are assiduous in appearing before committees of enquiry, regulatory bodies, and reviews.[44] Nowhere is their presence more noticeable than in the parliamentary arena. In 1960, according to H.G. Thorburn, a particularly contentious public-policy issue — the regulation of resale price maintenance — saw twenty-nine groups attempting to influence government policy; of these only twelve appeared before the relevant parliamentary committee.[45] Twenty years later, by Hugh Faulkner's estimate, seven parliamentary task forces looking at issues ranging from federal-provincial fiscal relations to regulatory reform in general heard some 2,500 witnesses, many of whom represented 796 interest groups.[46] The activity of parliamentary committees shows the increased dynamism of public debate, of which pressure group activity is only a part. Committees working in the first session of the 32nd Parliament (1980-1) heard 3,326 witnesses. During the 1989-90 session of Parliament the Legislative Committee examining the government's proposed abortion bill met with 53 groups and individuals and heard from 2,198 groups and persons who contacted it by letter, fax, briefs, and telephone calls. By contrast, during the record-breaking length of the first session of the 27th Parliament (1966-7), 1,115 witnesses appeared before committees.[47] If the growth of pressure group activity in other parts of the policy system is any indication, a significant number of these witnesses probably represented organized groups. These signs of change reflect deep-seated alterations in the way policy is made and in the role of the institutions that make it. They are part of a long process of evolution that affects the legitimacy of our most important democratic institutions. Though much of this evolution is beyond the scope of this book, we must take account of its influence on pressure group development, and we must consider how it was itself affected by the proliferation and changing behaviour of groups. Broadly speaking we can divide our discussion into three parts:

  (i) The Growth of Government
  (ii) The Diffusion of Power
  (iii) The Search for Legitimating Institutions

The Growth of Government

The 1960s was a decade of frenetic activity in public-policy formation.[48] Vast new programs were undertaken in medical care and education. Major reforms were initiated in income-maintenance programs and regional economic policy. Other programs were proposed in the core policy field of taxation. Anachronistic policies relating to Canada's Native peoples began a long, and still incomplete, process of review and reform. Three major movements — the women's movement, the environmental movement, and the consumer movement — began to demand government attention. Shifting demographic patterns precipitated debate over appropriate urban development policies. At the same time, government confronted sweeping technological changes and major new demands in traditional fields of activity, such as resource development and communications, where capital-intensive methods of production rendered obsolete long-standing approaches to industry, labour, and trade. Above all, the country faced cultural and regional tensions of an order that it had not previously experienced.

All these factors precipitated growth in government activity. They also affected policy processes and the role of pressure groups. No longer could policy-making authority be contained in the hands of a small and intimate community of leading politicians and high officials. Policy-making had become so extensive and complex that it had to be divided up and parcelled out to the agencies and interests most concerned with what was happening in each particular field of government activity.

There followed an explosion of pressure group formation and participation, much of it stemming from the expansion of government.[49] That is, as government grew, interaction with its many agencies became increasingly difficult, both for smaller pressure groups and for individuals. Group formation, the elaboration of established groups, and the formation of 'peak' associations became necessary. (Peak associations are organizations that aggregate the demands of other organizations in order to express their collective demands to the state.) Similarly, group activity encouraged more group activity. Here a teaching role was played by television, which exposed the publicity-seeking activities of groups in one part of the country to appreciative eyes elsewhere. Because so many groups were now participating publicly in the policy process a more receptive climate for interest-group activity existed. 'Pressure-group tactics' were no longer considered politically unacceptable. Above all, the mounting clamour around the policy process made organization essential. 'To have a say, you need a voice,' advised a headline in the *Financial Post*.[50] 'Shout when not listened to,' admonished the *Bulletin* of the Canadian Association of University Teachers.[51]

Much of this increased activity was spontaneous. As David Truman and other pluralist writers have argued, when governments take steps to change policy or to create new programs, many affected interests coalesce to protect themselves or to take advantage of new opportunities.[52] Similarly, interests that have benefited from earlier policy become defensive and take a more active, often more public, part in policy debate.

Many of the reports on pressure groups that appeared in the press in the late 1960s and early 1970s can be seen in this light. A.E. Diamond, president of the Canadian Institute of Real Estate Companies, told his group in 1974 that they must 'make the public more aware of the difficulties faced by developers' in order to counteract 'the power that various interest groups have captured over the development process'.[53] Interest groups, according to the *Montreal Star*, were 'a new political force', and business reaction to much new legislation and regulation — such as the federal consumer-protection proposals of the late 1960s — suggests that the business community was taken by surprise by the influence of environmental, consumer, and women's groups.[54]

By 1976, according to the chair of the Canadian Association of Equipment Distributors, business executives were 'no longer surprised, though still dismayed, that government listens more to the consumer and environmentalist than the investor'.[55] His group was urged to learn the political process, and the role of its full-time president was redefined, making his chief concern that of achieving 'a closer liaison between the association and the federal government'. Other groups were taking similar steps. Small-business owners, led by John Bulloch and his Canadian Federation of Independent Business, were reported in 1972 to be 'building up their political muscle', and subsequent achievements — such as the appointment of a Minister of State for Small Business — were an object lesson to other interests.[56] Across the board business people sought 'more input in government decisions' and to that end were told by experienced lobbyists that they 'should do a better job of participation'.[57]

Nor were business and citizens' groups the only ones engaged, like the

Canadian Importers' Association, in 'widening the channel of communication' with government.[58] Long-established groups and newcomers alike found themselves building more and more elaborate organizations in order to keep up with policy discussions and to promote their own interests. The 1974 reports of the president and the executive secretary of the Canadian Association of University Teachers echoed many others when they dwelt on the growing lobbying role of the organization.[59] Not long after, CAUT appointed a full-time government liaison officer and — in an effort to halt the decline of research and university funding — was deeply involved, with other university-based groups, in organizing one of the most elaborate lobbying blitzes that Ottawa has ever seen.

Not all of this activity occurred spontaneously, however. As the critics of the pluralists have pointed out, many interests do not have a sufficient sense of solidarity or the necessary resources to participate fully in the policy process.[60] Governments, therefore, have considered it in the public interest to take a hand in group formation, identifying latent and solidary interests and encouraging them to organize themselves, often assisting them with financial support.[61]

Other methods of encouraging group formation and participation include the development of consultative bodies that solicit representation from weakly organized groups; the creation of regulatory regimes that force solidary groups into forming associations; and straightforward rhetorical encouragement. Group promotion of this sort is not entirely disinterested — a point I will return to shortly. Nevertheless it reflects in part the code of neutrality of the professional public servant: the public interest can be served best if all special interests are properly heard.

The Diffusion of Power

Interests and interest groups were not the only elements in the political and economic environment that had to adapt to the expansion of government activity in the 1960s. Government policy-making systems were themselves overwhelmed by the profusion and complexity of new undertakings. One response to the problems of overhead was to parcel out policy-making responsibility to those most competent and most interested in each field, preserving for the Cabinet and its immediate advisers the authority to create global policy and to monitor the work of individual agencies.

By the mid-1960s the flaws in this approach were becoming evident. Ministers, preoccupied with their own departmental affairs, were less and less capable of developing the broad conception of the public interest expected of them. The Prime Minister and his closest colleagues — usually the Ministers of Finance and Justice and the Secretary of State for External Affairs — because their responsibilities gave them a perspective on the work of all departments and often forced them to co-ordinate the work of agencies, were better able to develop a view of the national interest than the majority of Cabinet members. However, as the prime ministerial careers of both John Diefenbaker and Lester Pearson often revealed, even their ability to achieve an informed view of the sweep of public needs and government policy was hampered by their preoccupation with the major national and international issues facing the country.[62]

In their fields of jurisdiction, individual agencies had considerable freedom, which was often reinforced by the competence and stature of senior administrators who exercised great, though scrupulously non-partisan, authority over their departments. Unfortunately it was not sufficient for the departments to be well administered and to propose and implement intelligent and competent policies. Those policies had to avoid encroaching on the work of other governments and other departments and to respect the overall goals of the government in power. As the work of the Government of Canada expanded, the attainment of these objectives became more and more difficult — just as it did a few years later in the majority of the provincial governments. The response was to strive for centralization of policy-making by reorganizing the work of Cabinet and by creating for the Prime Minister and for Cabinet a series of central policy institutions that could co-ordinate the policy process and help the political executive develop global policies within which individual departments were expected to find their own mandates.[63] To reinforce the co-ordinative effects of these changes in structure and process, successive governments introduced a series of reforms in budgetary procedures and financial management that affected the distribution of power and, consequently, pressure group politics.[64]

Reform foundered on three obstacles that frequently impeded efforts to bring about better co-ordination through centralization. First, a power struggle developed among the co-ordinating agencies over their respective duties, and over the planning philosophy that was to guide policy-making. Thus, instead of achieving the structured development of policy envisaged by the reforms, the Privy Council Office, the Treasury Board, and the Department of Finance fostered confusion within and beyond government about which agency was actually co-ordinating policy-making and advising Cabinet.[65] Unsure of where sub-Cabinet decision-making was actually taking place, interests had to redouble their efforts to gain access to the process, expanding their physical presence and their lobbying activities.[66] Often finding their way to the centre barred — by the limited resources of the co-ordinating agencies, by the crush of rival groups, or by the policy-making procedures themselves — they changed their lobbying strategies, engaging more frequently in public discussion of issues in hopes of influencing the policy-makers through public opinion. Complaining that line agencies — such as Industry, Trade and Commerce; Transportation; Agriculture; the

Fisheries and Marine Service; and the Canadian Forestry Service — with which they had traditionally worked, had been stripped of their former substantive role in the policy process, they sought to restore to them some of their former power. In doing so they added their weight to the two other forces that were resisting the reforms: line agencies' unwillingness to give up power to the centre, and their concern that co-ordinating officials would pay too little respect to the more technical aspects of department advice.[67]

Thus motivated to resist the new co-ordinative regime, the line agencies employed various devices for avoiding, short-circuiting, or limiting central control — strategies that nearly always exacerbated the centre's penchant for extending its supervision. A vicious circle developed that gradually diffused power throughout the institutions of government. Though to some extent power still resided at the centre — particularly where the need to take critical decisions galvanized the executive — for the most part it simply trickled down through the bureaucracy, creating pockets of authority, even at fairly junior levels. The phenomenon led Andrew Roman to remark that 'the Government of Canada is secretly being run by persons earning no more than $20,000 a year',[68] but in general the influence of each policy actor was so restricted that power came to be expressed most frequently and most effectively in checking the activities of other actors. 'If power in our political system is diffused,' two students of British politics have observed, 'the power that is most widely diffused is the power of the veto.'[69] Canada's situation has been similar. 'Ottawa is full of "no" bodies,' one official commented after some months in the capital, 'all they do is press "no" buttons.'[70]

We can attribute much of the increased influence and growing public presence of pressure groups to this tug-of-war. Initially valued for their capacity to communicate with special publics, interest groups gradually came to be seen as allies of line agencies in their struggles with the centre. Within agencies, specific services would cultivate the support of groups particularly affected by their programs and policies. A 1968 report to the Canadian Citizenship Council complained that the Citizenship Branch had

> no non-governmental institution which is in a position of supporting or criticizing the overall organization, budget, policies or methods of the Branch ... [This] means that the Branch competes in the jungle warfare in this government for scarce resources all by itself. It gets no help from the public it serves. In fact, those publics who may depend on the Branch for support of critical experimental and innovative programs, may not even know that an internal struggle is taking place which will hamper their efforts.[71]

Other agencies drew the same conclusion and set about creating supportive institutions, or strengthening their connections to existing ones. The close affiliation between the federal Forestry Branch and its associates in the forestry profession, for example, succeeded in 1969 in securing the elevation of the Branch to departmental status. The March 1969 edition of *The Forestry Chronicle* applauded the success of a major campaign, and made it clear that professional foresters expected to be rewarded with 'adequate representation on the Forestry Development Board, and a substantial program of continuing research by graduate students and forest school staff members supported by the new Department'.[72] A few years later, the fledgling Department of the Environment considered a recommendation that it develop

> a coherent Departmental policy, including structures and procedures, which would encourage and regularize participation by public interest groups, private interest groups, professional associations and the public at large within a general framework that would allow for flexibility in its application by the various parts of the Department and would permit the continuance of on-going program-specific activities. By providing a consistent framework and ground rules, such a policy would contribute to the development of sustained relationships between interest groups and decision-makers which are an essential part of the mutual learning process required for effective public participation.[73]

In effect, agencies were building policy communities.[74] This was the self-serving aspect of the campaign to ensure that the weak and under-represented could participate in policy-making. A great many latent and solidary groups — like the independent fishermen of Canada's east coast — found themselves exhorted to organize themselves into interest associations.[75] For those who could not afford to organize themselves in this way, agencies provided financial incentives.

Core funding was an important factor in developing the modern Canadian aboriginal movement.[76] It has been made available to other minority groups and to organizations representing the economically disadvantaged.[77] Special grants have been made to groups preparing submissions to regulatory bodies and to established groups with limited means, such as learned societies, while contract research has been purchased from others.[78] Separately, or in conjunction with funding assistance, positional policies have been used to enhance the mandates of favoured groups or to co-opt unruly but influential ones.[79] Hence the proliferation of advisory boards commented on by some observers. Where moral support, funding, and positional inducements have failed, regulatory coercion has been applied. Thus fish quotas in the east coast fishery are divided up in consultation with sector committees representing the various elements in each fishery, an arrangement that may at last quell the individualism of the region's independent fishermen.[80] In these various ways federal agencies have sought to develop interest communities capable not only of creating a link with a specific clientele or sector constituency, but also of supporting each agency and its policies in the turbulent policy process that currently prevails.[81]

These relationships have not developed solely at the departmental level. Within agencies themselves, specific services have cultivated the support of groups particularly affected by their programs and policies. In fact, it is probable that the natural grouping for most policy communities occurs at the administrative level, where the functional responsibilities of agencies closely parallel the organizational structure created by interests. Thus a small department with very clear, relatively narrowly defined responsibilities, such as the Department of Labour, would relate as a department to its policy community.[82] The Department of the Environment, on the other hand, with responsibilities ranging from weather forecasting, to parks management, to environmental impact assessment, to name but a few, relates only with difficulty to its global constituency and so allows its individual branches, and often sub-branches, to discover and cultivate their own policy communities.[83]

During the 1970s, policy communities became prominent as line and central agencies struggled for influence in the policy process. At the centre the weight of the collective authority of Cabinet, and the capacity to influence budget allocations, weighed heavily on the side of the Privy Council Office, the Treasury Board, and the Department of Finance. On the departmental side the ability to generate public support through affiliated pressure groups transformed the latter from useful adjuncts into vitally important allies whose support enhanced the legitimacy of the departmental mission. However, in order to exploit the new group-agency relationship several changes had to be wrought in previous practice. It became less and less true to argue (as I argued in the mid-1970s)[84] that agency-group relations tended to be dominated by the government side. A dependency relationship became an exchange relationship.

The agencies today need their pressure group allies to a much greater extent than they did in the heyday of the mandarins. For example, as financial constraint bit deeply into agency budgets, officials turned to their policy communities for help, asking them to approach senior officials, members of the relevant Cabinet committees, and parliamentarians with a view to representing the urgent needs of each agency and service. Sometimes these efforts have been successful, as one official demonstrated in a 'thank you' letter he wrote to individuals and groups that had lobbied ministers and MPs on behalf of his agency:

> The numerous examples and suggestions were extremely useful. [The deputy minister] did obtain the strong support of the [other] departments and agencies belonging to the [budgetary] sector, and the two press releases indicate that his efforts were successful. I would also like to extend our thanks to those who have themselves approached politicians and high ranking officials to make them aware of the [agency's] difficult budgetary situation. It is obvious that taken as a

whole, the actions undertaken have had a considerable impact on the decision ultimately made.[85]

Agencies pay a price for generating this sort of public support. They have had to accept greater public involvement in policy and budgetary discussions. Similarly, as the policy process becomes more dynamic, and as more interests are stimulated to participate, agencies and their traditional policy communities lose their capacity to direct the course of policy debate.[86] Operating in a more uncertain environment, they must expect the policy process to take much longer than it did in the war years, and in the two decades following.

Obviously there are many ways in which the political system benefits from these changes in the policy process. The public agenda has been broadened and the policy-making system is more dynamic. Groups have been recognized as a viable part of the policy process and group intervention today is more generally accepted than it was in the 1960s. The new dynamism is extremely important because — as I will argue shortly — it has strengthened the role of Parliament in the policy process. And yet, despite the enhanced role of Parliament and increased public participation, this dynamism is flawed by its *raison d'être*. It grows out of a power struggle within the executive-administrative branch of government, rather than out of improved democratic institutions of government. Although those institutions have benefited from recent changes in the policy system, the principal effect of the changes has been to diffuse power and to elongate the policy process. In fact, it can be argued that these changes have introduced a new kind of pluralism into Canadian politics: bureaucratic pluralism. Agencies fight agencies intragovernmentally, thereby exciting the participation of pressure groups, which support their own respective positions. While this engenders more open discussion of policy issues from which the general public can benefit, experienced observers do not consider that democratic government has improved as a result; they see instead an excessive diffusion of power that emphasizes the political executive's lack of real control over the administrative branch. Even J. Hugh Faulkner — who argues from his own experience as a member of Cabinet that the system's legitimacy has not been compromised so far by these developments — expresses concern:

Short of an ideal definition of what is in the public interest, it becomes necessary to find a legitimate process for defining it in an on-going manner. That is clearly the role of Parliament and the executive. For them to fill this role effectively, they in turn have to enjoy widespread legitimacy as the final arbiters of the public interest. The process of accommodation and adjustment requires that the political act of initiation, leadership and arbitration must proceed from sources that command political legitimacy. The present Canadian context demonstrates the risks and dangers to the system when that is not present. The system of decision-making that I have referred to here is excessively dispersed. It leaves many Canadians confused and uncertain about how public policy is made; it increasingly puts a premium on group interaction — generally well-organized interaction — with the political and bureaucratic executive, and it leads many to conclude that the heart of the system, Parliament, has become weak and futile. All of these undermine the legitimacy of the policy-making process and they should command our concern.[87]

The next section of this chapter addresses the concerns raised by Faulkner.

The Search for Legitimating Institutions

'It makes me very, very nervous,' an interest group leader commented in 1981, 'that people out there look at our organization as being more legitimate at representing them than the government.'[88] The diffusion of power we have discussed above considerably strained the legitimacy of Canadian governments.[89] Expansion of government tends to erode public respect under the best of circumstances. A remote authority concerned with external relations, defence, and a few great national enterprises can, with a modicum of forethought and care, retain public confidence over a long period. An obtrusive, questing government, perpetually encroaching upon the private sector and diminishing the freedom of the individual, is bound to generate resentment, however necessary its expansion may be. When, as in Canada, the growth of government is particularly rapid and engenders intergovernmental conflict, mistakes are easily made, public respect is undermined, and the community's willingness to accept the authority of public officials diminishes. This is what we mean by a decline in the legitimacy of government.

Declining legitimacy has materially affected the roles and interrelationships of our three most important political institutions. Cabinets and bureaucracies at both levels of government, after a long accession of authority, have experienced a diminution of public regard. Parliament, and to a lesser extent the provincial legislatures, though often said to be institutions declining in influence, have in fact been more active in the policy process in recent years. This may be partly attributed to reforms in parliamentary procedure, and to a decline in executive legitimacy. Finally, the changing status of these institutions has been reflected in new forms of pressure group politics, including an enhancement of the role of pressure groups in the policy process. Before looking at these developments, however, we must explore what it means to say that the legitimacy of Cabinet and bureaucracy have declined.

Ultimately, the authority — the legitimacy — of the political executive depends on two intimately related factors: its capacity to control the legislature and its ability to direct the government. The development of the Cabinet has resulted from the need to select a group of members of Parliament to gather advice from civil servants on policy matters, choose from among policy alternatives, and oversee policy implementation. Thus, on the one hand, Cabinet, as the executive committee of Parliament, must secure its confidence. Equally, however, it must be able to show that it is in command of the public service. Inability to do so reduces the Cabinet's claim to public support, exposing it to a loss of legitimacy. It also casts doubt on the legitimacy of the service itself, for if the Cabinet is not seen to be in command of the public service, we cannot be sure that policy is being implemented in a fashion sanctioned by duly elected public authorities.

The conviction that the federal Cabinet has lost control of the machinery of government has gradually been taking hold of public consciousness since the late 1960s.[90] The need to reassert political control of the administrative arm was one theme of Pierre Elliott Trudeau's leadership campaign.[91] Yet, despite the vigorous pursuit and elaboration of central-agency reorganization, many observers soon came to feel that the bureaucracy was even less amenable to control and direction than it had been a decade earlier. As an assistant deputy-minister put it to a journalist in 1975, 'I always knew the politicians could never control the bureaucracy. But when you reach the point where the bureaucracy can't control the bureaucracy, you know it's time to look for another job.'[92] In other words, the alliance between the political leadership and the mandarins, which had ensured ultimate Cabinet control in the 1940s and 1950s, was effectively dead.

Such cocktail-circuit views were reinforced by a succession of reports issued by the Auditor General that drew attention to weaknesses in financial control and problems in policy implementation, going so far as to argue in 1976 that the government had 'lost control of the public purse'.[93] The stature of the Auditor General is such that his concerns ultimately led to the appointment of the Lambert Royal Commission on Financial Management and Accountability. The Commission *Report*, though more soothing in tone than the Auditor General's reports, nevertheless confirmed the existence of a serious problem. Released a few months before the 1979 election, the *Report* prompted major innovations in the budgetary process, financial management, and the institutions of accountability. Although the preliminary results of these improvements drew optimistic reviews, a decade of experience with them confirms the view of many politicians that the problems of control go far deeper than the reforms admitted.[94] Flora MacDonald, for example, after her stint in 1979 as Secretary of State for External Affairs, concluded that personal attitudes and long-established patterns of behaviour in the public service were as much at fault, and inherently much less susceptible to remedy, as weaknesses in financial and personnel management systems.[95]

Perhaps more important than the decline of Cabinet have been repercussions from the declining legitimacy of the public service.[96] The general public as well as informed observers perceived that diffusion of power had weakened the authority of the political executive. Traditionally Canadian government bureaucracies have acquired legitimacy first because they serve the political executive, which derives its own legitimacy from the support it receives in the legislature; and second because agencies apply neutral professional expertise to the development of policy and the delivery of programs.[97] Since the 1950s there has been a steady deterioration in the potency of these sources of legitimacy and thus in the status of the bureaucracy, particularly that of the federal public service. Flaws in the merit system were the first to cause concern. It was accepted that the public service was scrupulously non-partisan and highly competent, but in the eyes of many these advantages were offset by a system of management that undermined efficiency and effectiveness.[98]

Later it was realized that the merit system also tended to exclude certain parts of the population from the public service. French Canadians were poorly represented, as were Native peoples and, in the senior ranks, women.[99] Efforts to create a more representative and responsive service, particularly the attempt to build a bilingual public service, outraged many who had benefited from the system, but did not necessarily appease those who had not. These difficulties were lumped in the public mind with other problems of public administration: the seemingly endless growth of government; the extensions and sometimes arbitrary use of power; strikes in important services; the inflationary effect of some wage settlements and, above all, the growth of public-sector spending.

The public has grown increasingly sceptical of the authority of professional expertise and of the disinterestedness of bureaucratic advice. It became aware that political non-partisanship should not be confused with policy non-partisanship and that officials can be tempted into supporting policies because they enhance their own organizations or are administratively convenient. The public, therefore, began to question the legitimacy of the policies and programs developed by government departments. Respect for a neutral, highly professional service gave way to outspoken dissatisfaction. Public-service management became a political issue; critical journalism abounded, and the decline of public confidence was registered in the polls and the election of governments pledged to austerity.[100]

Bureaucracies sought to meet the decline of traditional sources of legitimacy in two ways: they surrounded themselves with their own form of representative institutions and cultivated the legitimating authority of Parliament. The first strategy is evident in the trend towards representative bureaucracy, observable particularly in agencies dealing with social policy or minority groups.[101] The most widely used strategy, however, has been the expansion and institutionalization of the policy communities operating in each field of government concerned. This approach seeks to enhance the legitimacy of agency proposals — and of the agencies themselves — by trying to give all who are most affected by specific policies an opportunity to influence them; agencies can then argue that such policies are a product of consensus within the affected sectoral constituency. The advantage of this strategy over others is that as long as agencies do not artificially limit participation, they can convincingly repudiate charges that they have manipulated consensus formation among their 'clients'. Thus we can see in the development of policy communities not only a response to the changing power relationship of central agencies and line departments but a groping towards more comprehensive representation of interests, which would enhance the legitimacy of agencies themselves.

Among the most important consequences of the search for legitimating institutions have been its effects on the role of Parliament. Although pressure groups have paid increasing attention to Parliament in recent years, this does not mean that interest-group leaders have revised their assessment of Parliament's capacity to change the policies proposed by the government. While it is true that the number of witnesses appearing before House committees increased significantly after 1968, and that a number of bills have been withdrawn, revised, or amended as a result of public intervention at the committee stage, experienced lobbyists seem to expect very little from their encounters with Parliament and parliamentarians.[102] John F. Bulloch, founder of the Canadian Federation of Independent Business, sees his early attempts to influence MPs and parliamentary committees as the misguided exertions of a 'very naïve' apprentice lobbyist. With more than ten years' experience behind him, he approaches parliamentarians only when 'it makes sense. . . . We do not have time to talk to people who have no influence.'[103] Other lobbyists agree and wonder why 'groups and companies persevere, given [the] limited pay-off'. They still believe that 'the important time to be having discussions with the government is before they actually draft legislation, or during the course of the drafting'.[104] The apparent futility of a time-consuming and expensive process is underlined by the fact that MPs themselves frequently bemoan their inability to effect real changes in legislation. One MP estimates that 'maybe' in 20 per cent of cases 'committees are useful in terms of decision-making, policy-making, or involvement of Parliament'.[105] A sense of inefficacy, not to mention the time constraints imposed on MPs by their other duties, often leads them to prepare inadequately for committee sessions, so that group representatives and other witnesses are often discouraged by Members' apparent ignorance of the issues under review.[106] Yet groups seem to appear more frequently and acknowledge that the days are gone when a major pressure group can conduct a national policy campaign with virtually no direct communication with Parliament, as the

Canadian Medical Association did during the medicare debate.[107] It is considered essential to invest time and effort in cultivating Parliament. As one labour representative has put it, 'we wouldn't lose any opportunity [to influence Parliament]. We'd always go and hope that somewhere, sometime, someone will take up some of the things we are saying. We would never back off from doing that.'[108] In the words of Ernest Steele, President of the Canadian Association of Broadcasters, it is 'a very necessary part of what we program for our association'.[109] Even John Bulloch maintains that 'if . . . you want . . . to put pressure on the system, there is nothing more effective than going to your Member of Parliament' and focusing public attention through caucus and question period.[110]

Two factors account for this anomalous behaviour. Simply by giving a hearing to challenging interests, Parliament first confers legitimacy on them and, second, publicizes their demands. Furthermore their participation galvanizes opposing and competitive groups who also want to mould public attitude and promote new policies. In the increasingly competitive environment of pressure group politics, the elders of established groups have to anticipate these interventions, or at least respond to them. In other words, the search for legitimating institutions resulting from the diffusion of power has alerted policy actors in the private and public sectors to the legitimating capacity of Parliament. As agencies sought to create in policy communities a source of external legitimation, they found in Parliament a vehicle through which those communities could publicize issues and secure their ultimate legitimation.

Many would disagree. A 1982 report of the Canadian Bar Association, for example, stated that 'Parliament is not only inefficient and ineffective, but . . . its reputation within the country is at an all-time low.'[111] Perhaps, but so is the reputation of the Cabinet and bureaucracy. The status of Parliament *has* improved. Kornberg, Clarke, and Goddard, for example, have analysed Canadian Institute of Public Opinion data to show that 'the *position* of members of Parliament is held in great esteem by the public. . . . The mean score for parliamentary office (82.3) was exceeded only by those for the Prime Minister (86.3) and the police (83.3).' Civil servants, the Governor-General, and the Queen scored much lower (68.4; 61.3; and 57.8 respectively).[112]

A diffused power system enhances the status of Parliament because it places a premium on what had previously been undervalued: the legitimating capacity of Parliament. Although this legitimating capacity is shared — Cabinet confers legitimacy on public policy by presenting it to Parliament; and the Crown, represented by the Governor-General, confers legitimacy on legislation by proclaiming it — no other institution possesses legitimacy of the same order as the duly constituted, properly representative Parliament, particularly the House of Commons. And of course the legitimating capacity of the Cabinet is derived from its ability to command a majority in the House.[113] The centrality of Parliament as a legitimating institution ensured that the collective groping for public support on the part of agencies and interests would in the long run bring public servants, pressure groups, and even the political executive to petition for the two benefits within its gift: publicity and legitimation. The government used Parliament to these ends during three important public debates in the early 1980s: constitutional reform, the National Energy Program, and the negotiation of federal-provincial fiscal agreements.[114] In each case the federal government, after long and unproductive discussions with the provincial governments, took its own case to the public, via Parliament. More recently the Mulroney government has used the Castonguay-Dobbie Committee to present its proposals for renewed federalism to Canadians. Similarly, public servants — in the past reluctant suitors for parliamentary attention — espoused reforms that would give them greater access on matters not involving the House's confidence.[115] Officials sometimes see in greater access a means of using parliamentarians and parliamentary committees to 'sell' favoured policy proposals to the public, even though, as Nord reports in a study of the Green Paper on Immigration Policy, such attempts sometimes fail in the face of determination on the part of committees to play a more independent, mediating role.[116]

In their relations with Parliament, public servants are constrained by the constitutional provisions of Cabinet-parliamentary government. In effect they may speak only when spoken to, and in all exchanges must be careful to respect the ultimate responsibility of the minister. For officials ambitious to foster policy development, or to secure the well-being of their institutions, this is a major impediment. The cultivation of policy communities offers an effective way around it. Interest group representatives are not bound by governmental agenda-setting. Intimately aware of the needs and objectives of agencies, they can express those needs when necessary in a manner that can be readily disowned by the sponsoring agency. Furthermore, in the sometimes competitive atmosphere of committee hearings friendly interest groups, rather than agencies themselves, are at times the most appropriate defenders of agency positions and proposals. Thus, in cultivating policy communities, agencies simultaneously achieve two types of legitimation. On the one hand they reinforce the support of their own functional constituencies, and on the other they use them to tap Parliament's capacity to publicize and legitimate agency goals and programs. In so doing they contribute to a revival of Parliament's role in the policy process.

This revival has not depended solely on a renewed interest in Parliament's capacity as legitimator and publicist. Parliamentary reform has facilitated, and perhaps encouraged, this trend. In particular the expanded use of committees to review legislation, scrutinize public expenditure, and investigate policy issues has made possible a greater interaction between Parliament, public servants, individuals, and interest groups. According to Rush, between 1945 and 1965 only 10 per cent to 15 per cent of public bills passed in each Parliament were referred to committee. After 1963, however, a growing number found their way there. In 1966-7, 23 per cent of bills were sent to standing committees. The number dropped drastically to 3 per cent in 1967-8, a period dominated by the Liberal leadership contest, but with the introduction of new procedures in the 1968-9 session, the proportion expanded to 75 per cent and in 1969-70 dropped only slightly to 70 per cent.[117] Impressionistic evidence suggests that, with the further integration of committee review in the legislative work of Parliament, this proportion has been maintained. The figures cited earlier leave little doubt that the public, including interest groups, has found committee hearings a useful forum for comment on proposed legislation. Case studies reinforce the point. Nord, in his study of the parliamentary review of the Green Paper on Immigration (referred to above), reports that the Joint Committee conducted well-publicized cross-country hearings that netted 1,400 letters and briefs and heard 400 individuals and groups.[118] The Commons Committee on Justice and Legal Affairs, which is credited with having pushed the 1968 reforms 'as far as possible',[119] has conducted several important inquiries into proposed legislation and into the penitentiary system, at times having to limit the number of briefs it would formally hear and on other occasions specifically inviting pressure groups — clearly members of the justice policy community — to comment on legislative proposals. Some of these hearings clearly influenced public opinion. The committee's hearings on gun control have twice aroused enough debate to persuade the government to revise proposed legislation.[120] These committees are but two of the many standing and special committees that have conducted similar reviews of legislation and investigations since 1968 and have attracted considerable public attention.

Although the search for legitimation, together with the effects of parliamentary reform, largely explain recent interest group attentiveness to Parliament, several other factors associated with the public aspect of policy formation also contribute to the changes we have observed. First, developments outside the governmental arena have placed a premium on publicity. Television in particular encourages demonstrative public participation. It also tends to encourage groups lacking established access to agencies to imitate the attention-catching behaviour of groups in other countries. Parliament, because it is able to focus attention to an extraordinary degree, becomes a target for Canadian groups. Challenged publicly by newcomers or the less privileged, established groups find they must respond publicly in order to safeguard their position and the policies they espouse. For them too,

Parliament is an important vehicle for gaining publicity and generating support.

Second, while it may appear to many MPs, and to those working to influence them, that the power of Parliament is extremely limited, so too, increasingly, is the power of other institutions, as our discussion of the diffusion of power has demonstrated. Relatively speaking, Parliament's authority in the policy process has expanded simply because that of other institutions has declined. While this does not mean that Parliament can actually formulate or determine policy, it does mean that interests must take into account Parliament's capacity to influence both policy and public opinion. Not all such revision is technical in nature. Finally the evidence suggests that Parliament today routinely changes legislation, particularly at the committee stage. Of the 100 government bills proposed to the 1990-1 session of Parliament, 40 were amended in committee.[121] Rush quotes Hockin to the effect that the Ministers of Agriculture and Justice 'spent many hours in the summer of 1969 consulting with committee members on proposed legislation, thus recognizing the political reality that both the Agriculture and Justice Committees were developing attitudes of their own — attitudes sometimes at variance with government policy'.[122]

Parliament, then, has become an important target for interests wishing to publicize their demands and/or receive the cachet of the legislature's support. This attentiveness to Parliament denotes a significant change in the behaviour pattern of groups. It enlarges the opportunity for nascent groups to enter policy discussions, and draws the more traditional institutionalized organizations into the public debate they once eschewed. It weakens the hold of government agencies on affiliated interest groups, diminishing their capacity to dominate the relationship and creating something closer to partnership in group-agency relations. It contributes, in short, to more dynamic public debate.

THE EVOLUTION OF A POLICY ACTOR

In these two chapters we have seen how pressure groups, never entirely absent from the policy process, have come to prominence in Canadian politics. Today national organizations lead public debate on many issues and are involved on a daily basis with the refinement and implementation of public policy.

Group politics, which played a limited role a century ago, has become an integral part of policy-making. Pressure groups now perform a vital communications function, linking special publics to government and often supplanting the élite interaction and party intervention that was the norm in 1900. They are often used to secure the legitimacy of government actions, something that would have been considered most unusual in the early part of the period we have studied.

Their form and behaviour has changed too. In the nineteenth century group activity occurred largely at the local level and depended on volunteer support. As the century reached its close, national associations were becoming prominent. Some of them employed a small professional staff, but they still owed their vigour and influence to the enthusiasm and dedication of volunteer supporters working in local chapters scattered across the country. We have seen how this decentralized group politics was superseded by the institutionalization of groups clustering around governments at the federal and provincial capitals. Local organizations did not disappear but their influence — and their spontaneity — declined as national associations developed, co-ordinating the views of individual branches, passing those views through the mill of committee review and convention ratification and, in general, 'aggregating' demand. Institutionalization turned pressure groups into complex organizations with elaborate federal, provincial, and local structures employing professional staff. Pressure groups also became more numerous.

Their behaviour became more complex. Early groups used petitions and personal lobbying with government leaders to obtain their ends. By the late nineteenth century the equivalent of today's mass media campaigns were not unknown — witness the public meetings organized by temperance groups and the extravagant parades of fraternal associations like the Orange Lodge — but Canadians seem to have exercised restraint in lobbying from the outset. As government expanded and the role of the bureaucracy in policy formation became more pronounced, restrained behind-the-scenes lobbying became the norm. Mass meetings, marches on Ottawa, demonstrations, and appeals to the media occurred but they came to be seen as the last resort of groups that had exhausted every other avenue of persuasion, or did not understand the policy process. The most influential groups eschewed publicity, accepting instead the norms of acceptable behaviour laid down by government. Ultimately, however, the scale and extent of government activity expanded beyond the control of senior administrators and leading politicians, fragmenting the policy process and unleashing an unprecedented level of group intervention — both public and behind-the-scenes — in policy-making. As a result, Canadians today possess a diffused policy-making system in which group politics is at the heart of policy communication and legitimation.

We have linked the transformation in the role of pressure groups to the evolution of Canada's economic and political life. The shift from a decentralized economy to one in which corporate concentration affects every aspect of life could not have been achieved without major changes in the role of the state and in the relations among political institutions. Governments became managers as corporations realized the need to plan. Supply-and-demand management became the common object of both the private and public sectors. Technostructures, often operating through the medium of interest groups, spun pervasive, binding threads of communication between the two.

The role of specific political institutions varied as the modern political economy evolved. Representative legislatures brought responsible government and paved the way for the political party and the Cabinet-parliamentary system of government. A decentralized, developing economy fostered Confederation and the emergence of the party system, giving only a minor role to interest groups. The latter, active at the local level, mitigated the harsher effects of industrialization and development and laid the basis for our modern system of social welfare. The party system and the provincial and federal governments were the preserve of business interests who saw the state as the guardian of law and order, the defender of the country, and, above all, as the mechanism through which economic development would be achieved. Thus, at the local level, benevolent societies established hospitals and shelters; fraternal organizations provided their members with insurance against the vicissitudes of life; and boards of trade brought pressure to bear on MPs and MLAs and party leaders to secure through the national and provincial governments the building of railroads, the settlement of new territory, the distribution of natural resources, and the erection of tariff barriers behind which an industrialized economy could emerge.

Industrialization, however, precipitated further changes in the relations among political and economic institutions. Initially corporate concentration fostered the dominance of the political executive and started the decline of party and legislature. Subsequently, as the complexity of economic management became apparent, the bureaucracy grew in influence, the technostructure emerged, the political executive became less competent at directing the public service, and Parliament reached such a low ebb of influence that many despaired of its revival. A revival of sorts has been achieved, however, growing out of the diffusion of power that complexity has spawned and based on Parliament's capacity to bestow legitimacy and publicity on those interests it chooses to hear. In this most recent evolution of our state and economic institutions, pressure groups have flourished, becoming more numerous and pervasive as they carry messages between interests and agencies; agencies and Parliament; Parliament and the media; and as they work to secure the legitimation of their demands. Their adaptability; their skills in communication; their capacity to represent interests; and, above all, their understanding of the policy process — all these give them an importance today that they never had before.

PART II

The Analysis of Pressure Groups: What They Do and How They Work

CHAPTER 4

Types of Groups*

Political science assumes that sound analysis has to be built on categorization. Without having defined what we are studying we cannot observe it, measure it, or describe it—and therefore we cannot make verifiable general statements about it. This chapter will look at the progress—or lack of progress—that political scientists have made in building a system of categories to investigate the relationship between a country's general political system and the pressure groups that work within it. We will also suggest a taxonomy of our own.

CATEGORIZING GROUPS

Pressure group studies boast remarkably few efforts to build systems for categorization (also known as typologies or taxonomies). Perhaps this is because it is quite easy to identify and to study formal interest groups that indisputably fit a broad definition, such as the one presented in the first chapter, once one has been agreed upon. Pressure groups are clearly not political parties (they seek influence, not power), not government agencies (they make their own decisions and appoint their own officers), and not even interests (they are defined as being formal associations). Scholars may quarrel over marginal cases, but the broad category, pressure groups, is generally recognized. Consequently the literature is full of case studies— many of them excellent—of particular groups and observations of groups engaged in various phases of pressure politics. There is even a growing number of empirical studies of groups that are clearly alike, such as business interest associations.

These studies tell us a lot about how groups have adapted to different political systems and have exercised influence. They are not, however, very helpful when we try to develop general theories of political life. They do not help us make verifiable generalizations about the political behaviour of organized groups, about their relationship to the state, or about their role in

---

*An earlier version of this chapter was read and commented upon by Sandra Burt, Henry Jacek, and Leslie Pal. I wish to thank them for their assistance and to absolve them of any blame for the shortcomings of the final product.

political systems, and it is very hard to set out a grand theory that does not include such generalizations. Of course, political scientists, myself included, have succumbed to the temptation to propose grand theories, but we all know that these theories are little more than informed speculation, flawed because the studies on which they are based are not comparable. While such studies generally share a common definition of the term 'interest/pressure group' — although even here, as we have seen, differences persist — there is only rudimentary agreement about the kinds of interest groups that are to be found. This prevents us from understanding why very different kinds of pressure groups emerge, why their behaviour varies, and why some groups appear to be more influential than others.*

Before exploring these issues more fully, it is useful to review the principles that guide categorization. We can apply those principles to some of the rudimentary typologies that have been used in studying pressure groups, and use them to build a system of categories of our own. The principles we shall draw upon, which have been widely used in the social sciences, can be expressed as five rules:

Rule 1: Pertinence.

The categories must be set up to address an explicitly defined research problem. For example, John E. Chubb, in *Interest Groups and the Bureaucracy*, divides the groups in his study of California energy politics into two categories: cost-bearers and beneficiaries. This approach is pertinent to a case study that tries to explain group behaviour in a single policy dispute, but it would not help us classify interest groups in general because groups are seldom consistently cost-bearers or beneficiaries.[1] In other words, the categories may vary a good deal according to our research interests, but it is important to ensure that they are appropriate to the research question being addressed.

Rule 2: Exhaustiveness.

The categories should take into account every type of group that exists in the system under study. If we want to study the pressure group system in a country, we cannot be content with a typology that captures only business, women's, or religious groups.

---

*Two factors may be forcing us to become more rigorous. First, the growth of empiricism in social science has fostered precision in definition and led to increasingly accurate observation of pressure groups. Second, the popularity of comparative studies has encouraged us to work out an analytical terminology that permits accurate comparision. The corporatists have contributed significantly to this effort.

Rule 3: Exclusiveness.

The categories should be mutually exclusive and independent. This is a most difficult requirement, but it is essential since it forces us to discriminate between groups and allows us to explore their differences. The distinction between 'public interest groups' and 'special interest groups' is popular because a public interest can be distinguished from a private, or special, interest.* On the other hand, even though a distinction between 'lobby' groups and 'protest' groups is equally popular because it evokes colourful images of the different beheaviour of the 'ins' and the 'outs', the distinction is not helpful analytically. This is because so-called 'protest' groups often lobby and occasionally even powerful lobby groups protest. The activities of protesting and lobbying, in other words, do not consistently differentiate groups.

Rule 4: One category/one principle.

We cannot build individual categories by combining characteristics that have been established on the basis of different principles. For example, when we refer to organizations as 'business', 'environmental', or 'civil rights' groups we are implicitly using a single principle to differentiate them. In this case, we are sorting them out according to their central objectives, which we have concluded are to promote business, or environmental concerns, or the protection of civil rights. Suppose that we tried to combine this principle with another one: the level of organizational complexity attained by each group. How would we do it? Would we say that all business groups are highly organized and all environmental groups not? If we were to do so, how would we categorize Greenpeace, which, with its extensive international network, is a highly complex environmental group — probably more complex than most business interest associations. Clearly, by combining two different methods of distinguishing groups we make the task of sorting them out much more difficult, if not impossible. We would be better off if we analysed one category in terms of another; we could look at protest groups, for example, to determine how many are highly organized, weakly organized, and so on.

Rule 5: Respect the level of analysis.

Each set of categories enables us to carry out analysis at a specific level. A set of categories designed to study the pressure groups operating in a particular policy field will not help us examine the efforts made by political parties, lobbying firms, corporations, officials, and individuals to influence

---

*Later we will show that this popular view can be misleading.

those policies. To do that, we would have to move to the next level of analysis, the policy system, and to employ a new set of analytical tools.[2]

How well do our categories for pressure groups adhere to these rules? When we set out to distinguish pressure groups from other political actors we seem to be on firm ground. The distinctions drawn between pressure groups, parties, government agencies, and so on in Chapter 1 have been generally accepted for a number of years and have helped keep us from violating the level of analysis precepts of Rule 5. Similarly, we have learned to distinguish between the three types of interests — latent, solidary, and organized or formal — and to maintain a clear distinction in analysis between organized groups and the other two types.[3]

When we attempt to distinguish *between* organized pressure groups we run into trouble, largely because we tend to ignore our first rule of categorization. We do not keep in mind the research questions that different methods of categorization are designed to address. Consequently we often fall into the trap of using a category designed to explore one question to address others. Equally, there is a danger of criticizing a typology developed for one purpose simply because it does not address another. To ensure that the following critique avoids this trap, we will briefly consider the research question that a general typology should address.

The questions at the heart of political science have to do with power, specifically, the power of the state — what it consists of, how it is used, who gets to use it, when and where. Pressure groups, by definition, do not seek to use state power directly, but rather to influence it. Consequently, the broadest and central questions that political scientists ask when they study pressure groups have to do with how groups exert influence and how their efforts are received by the state. In short, they are most concerned with the relationship between the state and pressure groups. There are, of course, many other questions political scientists ask about pressure groups — questions about how groups determine which issues they will pursue and about the effect membership characteristics and opinions have on group behaviour, for example — but the core questions have to do with state/group relations and all others are subsidiary. Any method of classification intended for general use in political analysis should be designed to address this central concern. Guided by this conclusion, the critique that follows is intended to assess the capacity of widely used typologies to assist our explorations of the core questions of political science. It should be remembered that typologies shown to be inadequate for this level of analysis may be extremely useful in addressing other questions.

Two methods of categorization are popular with academics, journalists, and interest group members themselves. The first divides organized groups according to their objectives — protest, environmental, civil rights, and public interest groups, to name a few. Collectively those groups that pursue public-regarding objectives are often referred to as 'public interest' groups, while those that attend to the exclusive and generally material benefits of their members are often labelled 'special interest' groups. The second classifies by the character of the members — business, ethnic, or women's groups for example.

Research that applies this two-fold division of groups shows that it fails to conform to two of our five rules of categorization, and therefore fails as a typology. It does not meet the requirement for exclusiveness or the requirement that a category should be based on a single principle. Some scholars assure us that despite the considerable overlap between groups that fall into the material benefit category and those designated as attitude groups, 'one is able to assign a group to one or the other category quite easily'.[4] This is not in fact the case. It is extremely difficult to show that there are characteristics unique to groups in each category.

A good illustration is found in Jeffrey Berry's survey of 83 public interest groups based in Washington in the early 1970s and his case studies of two of them. These studies show that when groups focus exclusively on public interest objectives, they tend to experience problems of organization, access, and resource mobilization, and that these circumstances generally lead them to use some pressure strategies — such as publicity, confrontation, and litigation — rather than others, like consultation and co-operation. However, if we compare Berry's findings with research into material benefit groups, we discover similar characteristics. Business interest associations are more likely to use consultation and co-operation rather than publicity and confrontation, but they may still use the latter techniques. Organizational characteristics are more likely to be distinct. Business interest groups tend to be better developed organizationally and to have more extensive membership participation in policy-making than public interest groups, while public interest groups are more likely to have been created by individuals whose charisma and entrepreneurial skills keep them alive and draw media attention to their causes. Even on this dimension, however, it is possible to find public interest groups that are more fully developed than many business groups and others that encourage membership participation.[5] It is also possible to find business interest associations, such as the Canadian Federation of Independent Business, that have been established by charismatic entrepreneurs.[6] We have to conclude, then, that we cannot create water-tight divisions between groups by associating material benefit objectives with one category of group and altruistic objectives with the other.

The second major approach to sorting out the different types of organized interests is to classify them according to their membership characteristics. Many scholars devote their lives to studying groups of this sort — women's, business, professional, ethnic, and labour groups in particular. Their approach does help us cope with the exclusiveness rule of categorization, which we found bedevilling attempts to classify groups according to their objectives. Groups can be unequivocally categorized according to selected characteristics of their members. This does enable us to investigate important questions, as the corporatists have shown. Unfortunately, the approach fails to satisfy the rule of exhaustiveness; not all groups are easily classified according to the characteristics of their members. It applies most successfully to occupational, business, and affinity groups, but is less satisfactory when applied to public interest groups. Conceivably commitment to a cause might be treated as a membership characteristic, for example, but it is much more variable than the physical, racial, and occupational characteristics that we associate with many member-oriented groups.

In summary, the typologies used most frequently in pressure group studies do not help us investigate the relationship between a country's general political system and its pressure group system; they violate either the rule of exhaustiveness or the rule of exclusiveness. Because this is the broadest and most important relationship to investigate in pressure group studies, it is reasonable to expect any widely used typology to be applicable to it.

But it is not the only significant relationship and there may be other contexts in which it is helpful to base research on the classification systems we have discussed, or on some other system.[7] This is in fact the case. When Berry and others asked whether public interest advocates encounter particular problems of access to and participation in policy debate, their studies of groups seeking altruistic objectives showed how sensitive public interest advocacy is to the rules for political discourse laid down by the state. They cited such examples as rules defining the tax status of charitable organizations and rules governing access to regulatory tribunals and the courts. As a result, steps have been taken, by regulatory bodies in particular, to facilitate their involvement in the policy process and, through financial assistance, to support their vitally important research work.[8] Some of these measures have been imitated in Canada — as in the early 1970s when the Berger inquiry into the proposed Mackenzie Valley Pipeline provided that assistance be given to Native and environmental groups wanting to intervene in the enquiry. However, the issues surrounding the participation of public interest groups have not been addressed as broadly or as systematically in this country as they have in the United States.[9]

Other benefits have accrued from research founded on objectives-based categorization. When scholars began looking into why European business and labour interests have been able to work with governments to create and implement effective industrial strategies, their findings had a world-wide impact and have influenced approaches to industrial strategy in Canada and the United States.[10] Objectives-based categorization tends to expose how the claims we make on society affect the behaviour of the group and the way in which the claim is assessed by policy-makers.

Membership-based categorization looks at the factors operating within groups to influence their behaviour. Groups drawing their membership from a particular culture, for example, can be expected to reflect that culture in their relations with the state. Alienation is a cultural characteristic of poor peoples' groups, many Native communities, and feminists. Their organizations tend to reflect that alienation in the way they organize themselves. It is common, for example, for groups representing these communities to reject conventional hierarchical organizational structures in favour of arrangments that promote full member participation and consensus-seeking in decision-making.[11]

There is no doubt, then, that traditional methods of categorizing groups can help us investigate significant questions. Yet they illuminate only a portion of the world of pressure group behaviour that we want to explore. They are concerned with pressure group sub-systems and, as we stated at the beginning of this discussion, we need a method of categorization that enables us to analyse full-fledged pressure group systems.

BUILDING A TYPOLOGY

The principles of categorization are not only useful in evaluating existing interest group typologies. Their greatest value lies in the guidance they offer for creating an alternative taxonomy.

Developing a new taxonomy starts by invoking the first rule of categorization and asking what research questions the typology will be designed to address. Our discussion so far will have made it quite clear what these are. We want to explore the relationship between groups and the state. We want to answer questions such as: Does the state's activities have anything to do with the formation of groups? Once formed, are groups influenced in their development by conditions created by the state — conditions of recognition; communication; regulation; and so on? Is the state's relationship with groups influenced by the group's functions, such as communication, legitimation, administration, and regulation? Are some types of groups more successful than others in persuading the state to follow the policies they promote? If some types of groups do tend to be more influential than others, what qualities do they possess that facilitate their success? Do they represent influential élites? Are they mass membership groups adept at marshalling public opinion? Are they especially good at understanding how to communicate with policy-makers and bringing pressure to bear on them?

Such questions — and these are only a few of those that are asked about group-state relations — demonstrate that even with the guidance of a central research question we must focus still further if we are to meet the demands of our second and third rules of categorization. Our second rule warns us that our typology must embrace all the groups meeting the criteria established by the definition set in Chapter 1. Our third rule says that we must establish clearly differentiated types. We can do this by noting that for the political scientist preoccupied with group-state relations, one set of questions seem more important than all others. These are the questions that have to do with groups' ability to influence public policy. This is because the political scientist, being principally concerned with how the state maintains and uses the coercive power of the polity, sees public policy as the formal expression of that power and considers the formation of public policy as being at the heart of state activity.[12] Therefore the processes through which influence is exerted are also of central concern.

This suggests that an explicit theory of differentiation might be built around the exercise of influence. Unfortunately influence itself is not a useful instrument for differentiating groups because it is extremely difficult to determine how influential specific groups are. Many claims to effectiveness have more to do with maintaining membership support and intimidating rival groups than with the actual outcome of lobbying campaigns. Even when lobbying input appears to be directly responsible for policy output, it takes a great deal of research to be certain that that is the case. A robust classification system has to be more accessible than that.

Nevertheless, the concept of influence might be useful. Perceptions of influence affect how individual groups are treated by the media, officials, politicians, the public, and other groups. The Canadian Labour Congress is seen to be influential because it has over two million members; the Business Council on National Issues because its small membership wields great economic power, and other groups because they have expert knowledge. Such perceptions about influence shape the strategies these groups and their rivals adopt; group strategists will try to exploit such perceptions or to attain similar advantages.[13] Strategic considerations often dictate the adoption of certain kinds of internal organizational arrangements. A group may decide to set up an office in Ottawa or to appoint a special officer to handle lobbying activities. In these ways perceptions of influence and perceptions about influence invest every aspect of a group's life with relevance for its relationship to the state. Clearly, then, we should be looking to influence-related characteristics for assistance in distinguishing one type of group from another.

What are these characteristics? The literature, especially the many case studies of interest groups and of their involvement in policy debates, strongly suggests that they are of two types. On the one hand, groups have inherent characteristics that give them weight in decision-making circles. The most commonly cited of these are membership size or the economic power of their members. In the following discussion I will refer to these as politically salient group characteristics, or *group characteristics* for short, and I will take care to ensure that the term embraces only those aspects of groups that give them policy significance but do not arise from self-conscious attempts to exert influence. The great majority of these groups exert political influence only as a by-product of their normal activities, so that they may develop politically salient strengths and weaknesses that exist apart from, and largely unaffected by, any explicit attempts to devise strategies and organizational competencies to influence policy. I also make this distinction in order to draw attention to those strategies and competencies that *are* intended to give groups influence. These constitute a second set of characteristics and I will refer to them as the *policy capacity* of groups.[14]

It is possible to describe each of these two sets of characteristics in some detail and to create a structure that allows empirical investigation and comparison of groups. Corporatist scholars have used a similar approach to distinguish between 'policy-capable' and 'policy-weak' organizations amongst business interest associations. However, this exercise has not given us the typology we are looking for. In particular, scholars working with groups that lack some of the characteristics of business interest associations have questioned the conclusions that have led the corporatists to define policy-capable organizations as highly differentiated and hierarchically structured. They maintain that large, complex organizations will sometimes appear to be less successful in attaining their objectives than others that are much smaller and less experienced in policy matters. Burt, for example, cites the relative success of some small women's groups in attaining their objectives while much larger and apparently more influential groups fail.[15] Such observations suggest that there is an additional ingredient in the mix of factors that secure access and confer influence. In the following discussion I will suggest that that ingredient is the complex phenomenon known as institutionalization.

The significance of institutionalization is one of the more persistent and pervasive ideas in pressure group studies. A link between organizational development and policy influence is commonly observed. Theodore Lowi, who sees 'institutionalization and formalization' as profoundly conservative forces in the policy process, argued in 1971 that in the United States' agricultural sector alone there were 'at least ten self-governing systems of policy-making, each of which is built on an institutionalized relationship between some bureau in the Department of Agriculture, some agricultural interest group, and some protective committee or subcommittee of Congress'.[16] European corporatists also appear to embrace institutional characteristics in the close association they have discovered between organizational sophistication and policy capacity, though, unlike Lowi, they emphasize the dynamic aspects of institutionalization rather than its conservative side.[17] Their research has shown that associations that are able to plan ahead and to accommodate themselves to changing circumstances are more likely to be invited to participate in policy formation and to be entrusted with administrative responsibilities than are associations that 'confine their activities to responding to short-term needs of their members, that find their structure changing as the economic environment of their members changes and that are unable to assume public responsibilities'.[18] The processes that the corporatists describe extend beyond organizational development into what we would call institutionalization.[19]

Although the term 'institutionalization' occurs frequently in the pressure group literature and is clearly used to indicate something more than organizational sophistication, it is seldom defined and little effort is made to distinguish between it and the mechanical aspects of organizational growth and elaboration. I will treat institutionalization as a process through which an organization — a 'technical instrument designed as a means to definite goals' — acquires a system of values and becomes an institution — 'a responsive, adaptive organism' that is 'peculiarly competent to do a particular kind of work'.[20] This is more than simply a mechanical process of organizational expansion. In the sociological language of Talcott Parsons and Neil Smelser, it is a process through which 'the value patterns of the common culture of a social system are integrated in the concrete action of its units in their interaction with each other through the definition of role expectations and the organization of motivation'.[21] In the case of pressure groups, institutionalization has the effect of linking a group's capacity to hear and respond to the demands of its members with its ability to carry those demands to the state. It creates an 'underlying normative orde'.[22] that sustains its internal social system and is understood, if not always accepted, by that part of the larger world with which it deals. Through institutionalization, group attitudes, norms, structures, and behaviour become internally coherent and attach the organization to its immediate environment. To quote Phillip Selznick:

> Beginning as a tool, the organization derives added meaning from the psychological and social functions it performs. In doing so it becomes valued for itself. To be sure, the personal and group bonds that make for institutionalization are not wholly separable. As the individual works out his special problems . . . he helps to tie the organization into the community's institutional network. Personal incentives may spark this absorption, and provide the needed energy; but its character and direction will be shaped by values already existent in the community at large. Similarly . . . the internal struggle for power becomes a channel through which external environmental forces make themselves felt. . . . Organizations do not so much create values as embody them. As this occurs, the organization becomes increasingly institutionalized.[23]

In our discussion of group characteristics and policy capacity we will touch on several aspects of group development that can be related to this description of institutionalization. In speaking of membership characteristics, we will note that groups whose members are drawn from the mainstream of society tend to find it easier to win general support than do groups whose members belong to minorities or espouse 'fringe' causes. This may reflect no more than the majority's calculation of what is in its best interest, but it may also signal the fact that the values institutionalized in the mainstream groups are more fully integrated with those of the broad community than are values of the other groups.

The nature of a group's interest is bound up with the normative order that it creates for itself and that helps to define its relationship with the state and the community. That is, the 'claims' groups make on society reflect their own prevailing values, while the response that the community makes to those claims indicate both the predominant values of the society and the extent to which the group has been able to capitalize on them and to affect how they are applied to itself. Claims may be expressed in material terms — benefits for the unemployed; tax relief for corporations; financial support for Native publications and for women's centres — but they reflect values that have been nurtured in the group and they appeal to values that the group hopes are prevalent in the community. The process through which the group identifies, enunciates, modifies, and builds such values into its ideology, culture, and manner of operating is a process of institutionalization. The clarity with which the group sets out its claims and the degree of member commitment to them indicate the extent to which it has institutionalized the values expressed in the claims.

Society's response to group claims also reflects institutional factors. If it is willing to respond to a group's demands through specialized agencies created specifically to deal with concerns like those expressed by the group, we can conclude that the group's values are considerably institutionalized in the society. We can also surmise that the agencies and their related groups will share many of the values and perspectives expressed in the groups' claims. This common outlook will be the product of institution-building on the part of both groups and agencies. Society's failure to address group claims is more ambiguous. It could mean that the values inherent in the claims are rejected by society, but it may also mean that they have not yet been institutionalized. That is, the claim appeals to existing values in a new way, a way that implies a reordering of the importance we attach to each of those values and hence a reordering of the power relationship associated with their authoritative allocation. I will look at such processes later when I discuss policy communities, but for the moment I illustrate them by recalling that governments were perplexed as to how to respond to early concerns about the degradation of the environment and about the status of women. As the environmental and women's movements developed and it became clear that they expressed values that were widely held, governments concluded that they would have to build structures that could assist governments and the two movements to communicate with one another. Since the late 1960s an immense variety of steps have been taken to achieve that end. First, attempts were made to establish a common language by mounting inquiries, sponsoring research and creating advisory groups. Second, agencies have been created to act as points of contact between the state and key groups in the movement. Such agencies frequently are comprised of existing units that have been responsible for programs that address some of the concerns of the movement.[24] The business of redesigning these programs reflects the lessons that have been taught in the building of a common language. More important, the creation of these agencies brings into the government people who are knowledgeable about the aims of the movement and conversant with its language. To a lesser extent the movement acquires people from government who are able to explain the language of government and its procedures. Third, language and people bring with them values and the perceptions that are shaped by values. Over time a sphere of influence is created within government where the culture and the ideology of the movement are understood, shared, and applied to the administration of programs of special concern to the movement. Equally, government establishes within the movement a similar understanding of its environment and approach. These processes of language learning and adaptation, of discourse, are processes of institutionalization.

We must be careful not to leap to the conclusion that the creation of shared understandings, the development of a common language, and the establishment of a mutually appreciated set of values guarantees that groups and agencies that work closely with one another will automatically agree on policy matters. After all, shared cultures and ideologies do not ensure unanimity elsewhere in political systems and the factors that make for disagreement elsewhere — such as differing perceptions of interest, loyalties to third parties, different organizational constraints and opportunities — can also operate in even close-knit and highly institutionalized policy communities.

Institutionalization can bring major benefits to established groups. Shared understandings and personal ties enhance the group's access to policy advisers, and the group's long-term involvement with a field deepens understanding of the field and an awareness of how the cause affects the larger community. The group may in fact have infused many of its own values into the language used in the debate and helped to establish the parameters of discussion. Even if the institutionalized group is at a disadvantage and is attempting to make its concerns known and to have them considered, accumulated knowledge and understanding enhances its credibility with policy-makers, the media, and the public. Understanding the context in which an issue arises also may help the group to articulate its concerns in terms that resonate with the public and so ensure a higher place on the public agenda than might otherwise be the case. That same understanding might even assist the group to convince the public that its objectives are banal and routine. Thus, a group's institutionalized knowledge of its focus of concern can help it to raise or lower the level of public conflict surrounding an issue. Institutionalization is most potent when it occurs with multiple politically salient group characteristics and considerable policy capacity. Groups so endowed have powerful claims to access to policy-making circles and to exert influence there.* They become the benchmark against which other groups measure themselves.

If such groups are widely regarded by both observers and participants in the policy process as those most likely to attain access and exert influence, why should not the analyst also treat them as a benchmark type? To do so would be consistent with our approach to the first principle of categorization because it would anchor the consequent typology in a central issue of group-state relations. After all, the evidence suggests that these groups have the greatest potential to secure access and exert influence,[25] and we have decided that we will learn the most about the role of groups in the state if we explore access and influence. With these thoughts in mind, along with a determination to observe the other four rules of categorization, we shall now attempt to set up the categories we need in our typology.

Our first step must be to label our benchmark type. We have suggested that it will score high on politically salient group characteristics and will have formidable policy capacity as well as possessing the attributes of institutionalization. We could call them 'policy-capable' organizations, as the corporatists do, but that would focus attention unduly on policy capability. For the same reason we have to avoid a label that emphasizes the politically salient characteristics of groups. Institutionalization, however, occurs as a group acquires politically salient characteristics and as it develops policy capacity and therefore should not distort investigation and analysis. Furthermore, institutionalization has a developmental quality that is useful in establishing the criteria for distinguishing between categories of groups. We shall, therefore, call our benchmark type the *fully institutionalized group*.

Some organizations may have the reverse characteristics of fully institutionalized groups. The example of protest groups springs to mind. At the first stage of formation they will have no previously established organizational framework to offer their members and no institutionalized values to provide them with roles and motivations, though they may well have political

---

*Access and influence do not always translate into attainment of group goals — other competitors may be more influential and some trends are simply too big to buck — but they enhance their prospects.

salience.* Theodore Lowi refers to these as 'groups in the process of formation', or *nascent groups*, and I will adopt his terminology.[26]

Most groups are neither fully institutionalized nor nascent. This, together with the developmental character of institutionalization, suggests that a continuum will be useful for the classification of pressure groups, nascent groups at one end and institutionalized groups at the other.** As long as we can effectively differentiate between them, the number of intermediary categories is a matter of convenience. For our purposes I will settle for two: *mature* and *fledgling* groups. Mature groups possess many of the attributes of the fully institutionalized group, but are less fully developed. Their political salience is more limited and their policy capacity reduced. Their behaviour may not reflect a complete grasp of the relations that prevail between institutionalized groups and governments. Forbes's characterization of the Canadian Cattlemen's Association and various poultry marketing groups suggests that they fall into this category, since they 'appear to be less broadly based, have fewer resources devoted to food policy, and have less depth and regularity of contact with government élites'.[27]

Fledgling groups are distinguished from nascent groups by differences in leadership roles and organizational orientation.[28] In the fledgling group charismatic leadership styles are less highly valued than they were when the group was first trying to attract members. Charismatic leaders either leave the group or adapt their behaviour. A new behaviour pattern is required because members of the group have learned to place a higher value on organizational attributes than they had previously. Instead of organizing solely to address issues, they also become concerned with the need to secure continuity within the executive and to achieve co-ordination of group policies and activities. These concerns reflect a growing interest in the institutional life of the group. Fledgling groups would differ from mature groups in the extent to which they have achieved organizational complexity; acquired the capacity to intervene in policy matters on a regular basis; supplemented the work of volunteers with professional staff; and so on.

---

*The members will, of course, bring to the group values that reflect commonly accepted patterns of behaviour and establish norms for the group. Speaking from my own experience, I have been struck by the ease with which nascent groups identify leaders and establish roles for them and for other members.

**Lowi, who employs a paradigm similar to this, is careful to dissociate himself from the evolution that 'seems to be an attribute of the ultimate theory' (*The Politics of Disorder*, 40). A similar disclaimer is probably necessary here. Groups may develop along the continuum, but it is quite possible that they could regress as group characteristics change, policy capacity diminishes, or even institutionalization dissipates. They might achieve a stable state at an early point on the continuum or, alternatively, as a result of changes such as an infusion of resources or new members or shifts in the environment, suddenly develop into highly institutionalized groups. I am grateful to Erika Simpson for drawing my attention to some of the problems inherent in the developmental cast of the institutionalization approach.

To sum up: I have argued that any effort to categorize groups should begin with the assumption that the taxonomy should primarily address questions that look at the relationship between groups and the state. Further, I have argued that all formal non-governmental associations active in a political community possess characteristics that give them policy significance, whether or not they are explicitly engaged in pressure politics. These characteristics have two aspects: those that have political significance but have emerged in the organization as a result of its internal life and without regard to policy considerations, and those that are explicitly developed as a result of the group's attempts to influence public policy. The first are labelled the group's politically significant characteristics ('group characteristics', for short) and the second, the group's 'policy capacity'. Institutionalization is a process that invests the group with a system of values that affect the application of these characteristics to the policy process. I use the term 'institutionalized group' to describe that category of group that has most fully developed its politically salient characteristics, its policy capacity, and an underlying normative order, and I have used the concept of the institutionalized group to anchor one end of a continuum that contains four different types of groups. Inherent in the concepts of institutionalization and of the continuum is the sense of a progression from one stage to another. While many groups do appear to go through such a progression, it is important not to assume that all groups will. We should assume that groups can become more institutionalized, that they can stand still, and that they can become less institutionalized. The following section will examine the components of political salience and policy capacity and consider the processes of institutionalization as they appear to reveal themselves in each of nascent, fledgling, mature, and institutionalized groups.

INSTITUTIONALIZATION: DEFINING THE CATEGORIES

How do we expect institutionalization to affect the components of politically salient group characteristics and of policy capacity? What are these components? In drawing on corporatist research I have adopted, with minor modifications, the general headings that they use to discuss the discrete features of groups.[29] These are: membership, resources, organizational structure, and outputs. Our understanding of each of these labels, which at times varies from that of the corporatists, is explained as I define each characteristic and show how it is manifested in Canadian pressure groups.* A summary of the categories is presented in Table 4-1.

---

*We cannot, of course, say with authority that these manifestations will be found in practice. Our typology is largely based on hypothesis, though it is informed by case studies and the comparative empirical research of the corporatists.

Table 4-1: The Policy Salience of Interest Groups

POLITICALLY SALIENT GROUP CHARACTERISTICS	POLICY CAPACITY
• *membership* –absolute size –proportion of domain held by business interest groups, professional associations, and co-ordinative/peak groups –socio-economic status of individual members –linkages • *resources* (tangible) –financial –extent –source diversity –staff –voluntary support (intangible) –leadership –internal cohesion –track record –public reputation • *organizational structure* –articulative capacity –aggregative capacity –strategic capacity –mobilization capacity –coalitional capacity • *outputs* –communication –revenue related services –mobilization related services	• *resources devoted to policy activity* (tangible) –financial –staff –volunteer –space (intangible) –experience –standing with related groups, e.g., leadership and collaboration –status with government (consultation; positional politics, organizational privileges) • *structures* –internal differentiation (at staff/member levels) –participation in inter-group differentiation • *outputs* –information and articulation –mobilization and lobbying –public responsibilities

Group characteristics represent the potential an association can exploit to bring pressure to bear on the policy process. The policy capacity of an organization determines how effectively that base can be exploited. Even if a group has great influence and immense wealth, if those resources are not exploited effectively its lobbying may be unsuccessful. As Bill Neville, one of Canada's most prominent lobbyists, has pointed out, the amount of money spent on a campaign is no guide to its effectiveness. Some of the most expensive campaigns are 'inept and ineffective' whilst some of the most successful have cost very little.[30] What makes the difference is luck and policy capacity. Luck, because no organization, however sophisticated or Machiavellian, can fully anticipate or manipulate the public agenda, and policy capacity because no amount of luck can help an organization that is not prepared to seize opportunity by the forelock. Policy capacity is thus an important independent ingredient in determining the influence of any organization.

A group's policy capacity has three components:

1.   A **strategic component**, which involves identifying, articulating, and agreeing upon the organization's public policy goals and the means it wishes to use to attain them.
2.   **Knowledge** of the substantive matters involved in the policy debate and of the processes through which the government will ultimately decide on its course of action, and a capacity to express that knowledge in language that is meaningful in policy debate.
3.   An **ability to mobilize** those group resources that confer political influence. That is, an ability to bring pressure to bear on policy-makers.

   Policy capacity tends to be associated with institutionalization. A group that is able to afford professional staff, for example, is likely to hire experts to promote public policies. Institutionalized groups that rely on their members and volunteers are more likely than uninstitutionalized groups to have the knowledge, experience, and links with other groups to mobilize their volunteers in a policy campaign. Outputs tend to diversify and expand as a group is institutionalized, and therefore such a group is better placed than one with fewer outputs to turn them to the attainment of a policy objective.

   A group's ability to carry out these activities will be registered in a variety of ways, most of them capable of being described in terms similar to those we have used to identify the other politically salient characteristics of interest associations. As we flesh out these characteristics, we will also assess the policy capacity of groups in terms of the resources they devote to researching and formulating their policy positions and to engaging in pressure politics; the structures they create to carry out these activities; and the products of these activities.

Membership

For our purposes the most notable dimensions of membership are size; the proportions of its domain actually occupied by the group; the socio-economic status of members and the knowledge they have of the substance of group concerns and of government in general.

Obviously the sheer size of an association has political significance, since very large organizations are inherently significant to vote-conscious politicians. The size and extent of major religious denominations, for example, give their leaders access to the media and policy-makers when they choose to speak out on public issues, as the Catholic bishops did in 1982 and 1991 when they criticized the increasingly laissez-faire bent of economic policy.[31]

However, another aspect of membership, 'domain', is more important. This is the proportion of the latent group represented by the organization. An association that is the sole mouthpiece of an interest and that is broadly representative of it has a legitimacy that enhances access and accords some influence. Conversely, organizations competing for the support of an interest have less credibility and may be played off against one another by officials and politicians. This is particularly so in the case of business interest associations, where, for example, Coleman and Grant have found that the lack of a single industry spokesman in the food-processing sector has fostered, and been fostered by, bureaucratic competition in the sector and inhibited the development of an industrial strategy.[32] It would also be so in the case of organizations that claim to be peak associations of the corporatist type and those — such as the Canadian Council of Churches, the Canadian Environmental Network, and the Coalition of National Voluntary Organizations — that claim to co-ordinate other organizations. On the other hand, public interest groups and religious groups could not be expected to claim a high proportion of domain because membership in such groups is generally a matter of choice based on conviction. These groups have few material benefits and no coercive inducements — such as are available to many professional groups — to persuade people to join. Affinity groups would occupy an intermediate position. Where their numbers are politically significant — as for many ethnic communities in major cities — their political influence would compel politicians and group leaders to pay special attention to the level of support each group could command in its community.

Members' socio-economic status — or in the case of businesses, the strategic importance of corporate members — affects the group's ability to gain access, the weight attached to its advice, and the extent to which it is integrated with the policy environment. Groups drawing their membership from the mainstream of society are more likely to be able to win sympathy and support from the broader community and to tap into widely held beliefs than are groups located on the fringe. Mainstream groups will have value systems in common with the community and thus shared understandings of reality. Members of the middle class and élites may have previous social and working contacts with policy actors, whereas the absence of social ties will work against groups that are already disadvantaged.

Socio-economic status also indicates the level of personal resources that members are able to commit to their organizations and particularly to the building of policy capacity. A wealthy membership might be prepared to pay for it; the less wealthy would be more constrained and would search for alternative approaches or for external funding. They might, for example, try to recruit members having access to business facilities that could be used to augment the group's own resources.

Members' levels of knowledge — both of the substance of group concerns and of policy processes — have special implications for policy capacity. Groups whose members possess advanced education are likely to have a broader understanding of the workings of government and the processes of group organization than other groups, an advantage that should enhance the groups' strategic planning ability and their knowledge of where and how to apply pressure. A membership familiar with bureaucratic norms could be expected to endorse the building up of policy expertise more readily than a group without that knowledge. Knowledge can, however, be offset by ideological factors. A membership ideologically opposed to differentiation, to executive dominance, or to the importation of experts would be inclined to resist the creation of special units for policy analysis and lobbying, or might experiment with unconventional alternatives.

A group's membership characteristics would affect its location on the institutionalization scale in the following ways. First, where domain is significant, we would attribute scores in proportion to the extent each group is able to dominate its domain, with monopolistic groups gaining the highest scores. Where only membership size is relevant, higher scores would be assigned to the most populous groups, bearing in mind that the absolute size of groups may vary considerably between policy fields and across territorial jurisdictions. Second, since we have associated institutionalization with value coherence and integration of values with those of the environment, our efforts to classify groups will be guided by indicators of coherence and integration. We would expect, for example, that a highly institutionalized group would have a stable membership and that for nascent groups membership would be extremely fluid. Behind this expectation is the assumption that membership stability reflects acceptance of the value system prevailing in the organization. A fluid membership suggests that the group has not yet agreed on its principle values or is subjecting them to fundamental re-examinaton. One would expect to find disagreement and tension over values in nascent groups, particularly when they begin to transform themselves into fledgling groups. At that point the charismatic figures and their zealous followers who give many nascent groups their initial impetus have to decide whether or not to accept a more managerial approach, with its attendant value system, to group organization. Many leave, to be replaced by members who will accept the new value system.[33]

Finally, members' socio-economic and educational characteristics would indicate levels of integration with the immediate and larger environment. We would associate higher levels of integration — and thus higher institutionalization — with those organizations whose members' status and knowledge levels are equal to or better than the society at large and comparable to the levels prevailing in the policy community.

Structure

Scholars disagree over the role organizational sophistication plays in enhancing a group's political salience and forwarding its policy capacity. The position taken here is that the structure and organization of a group is important insofar as it affects the group's ability to carry out the tasks set for it. From the policy-making perspective, what makes group structure significant is not the actual form of organization that is adopted, but the extent to which it can be used to give the group political influence.[34] Institutionalization is seen as a pervasive social process that imparts cohesion. In so doing, it may strengthen the salience and capacity of highly developed and relatively undeveloped organizations alike.

The group able to realize its potential for influence — that is, the fully institutionalized group — has become competent in five areas. First, it is effective in establishing internal agreement and in communicating members' wishes to others. That is, it has *aggregative* and *articulative capacity*. Closely related to these qualities is the ability to forecast and to plan ahead, the *strategic capacity* of the group. Third, an organization that regularly mobilizes its members in order to carry out its routine activities is likely to be able to mobilize them with a view to bringing pressure to bear on governments. We can call this the group's *mobilization capacity*. Fourth, organizations that are in regular contact with other organizations and cooperate with them frequently on joint projects have *coalitional capacity*.

Although these qualities will have been nurtured in activities that have little to do with exploiting the political salience of the group, it takes only a little political imagination to appreciate how they might be adapted to pressure politics. For example, an organization that is able to identify and articulate the views and demands of its members is more likely to be able to convey those views to government and to hold the attention of the public than one that is inconsistent and appears to be internally divided.

Again, we are often shown how important it is to be able to mobilize group members and sympathizers. The speed with which seniors from many organizations across the country responded collectively to the 1985 budget's attack on pension indexation is a case in point.[35] Individually the seniors' organizations were small and far from from wealthy. We would probably categorize most as fledgling groups, perhaps a few as mature groups. But they are used to moving people around—that is, they had a role structure that facilitated mobilization—and consequently had a mobilization capacity that would compare favourably with that of organizations that in most other respects would be considered much more institutionalized. As the case of seniors' mobilization makes clear, from the perspective of organizational analysis, what is important about the way in which a group exercises its structural capacities is not the elaborateness of its organizational form, but the effectiveness with which the capacity of the group is realized.

We must, therefore, expect groups to vary a great deal in the kind of organization they develop. Many highly institutionalized groups have built complex hierarchies in order to discover and articulate members' wishes; draw those wishes into some sort of collective will; forecast and plan ahead; and mobilize the membership to carry out the goals they have said they want to achieve. Similarly they have found that carrying out the many specialized functions involved in preparing briefs, organizing representations to officials, sitting on advisory boards, rallying membership support, and creating a positive public image demands a degree of organizational sophistication.

At another extreme are groups so uncomplicated that they try to avoid selecting executive officers. In between are small groups with very limited resources, yet still with the competence to do their task well. The John Howard Society, for example, is a highly regarded organization. Since 1929, it has been providing services for prisoners and ex-prisoners. It has the internal coherence and level of integration in its particular field to warrant our treating it as having many of the qualities of institutionalization. Yet it is not a complex organization. It has a small permanent staff and carries out its programs largely through volunteers.[36]

The debate over the importance of organizational sophistication focuses particularly on the properties groups need to acquire policy capacity. Coleman's studies of business associations suggest that the policy-capable association must be complex and hierarchical in structure. To meet the demands imposed by policy participation, groups are forced to create special units—task forces, committees, professional divisions, and so on—that are able to handle the different activities involved. The group with 'a flat organization, with all information being channelled to a central executive structure' that deals with problems *ad hoc* is 'policy weak'. 'Pressed for time, it will be unable to develop staff expertise or a comprehensive information base for participating in policy activity'.[37] In disagreeing, Sandra Burt argues that a number of Canadian women's groups have successfully created low-hierarchy organizations that respect the feminist movement's dedication to consensual decision making, yet have achieved important policy objectives. Clifford Gifford's study of seniors' organizations also suggests that a large number of quite small organizations can, by working together, achieve many of their policy goals. William Gamson found that, though bureaucracy was a feature of many of the American protest groups that he studied, hierarchy was often absent.[38]

The debate suggests several conclusions. An absence of differentiation and hierarchy does not necessarily indicate policy weakness. A proliferation of committees and task forces may in some groups compensate for an inability to assign professionals to policy development and lobbying tasks. Groups that work in close collaboration with a number of other organizations may share policy responsibilities with them. Some groups may develop expert knowledge in certain areas, while others may be especially effective in mobilizing supporters, communicating with the media, or gaining access to prominent officials.[39] If, therefore, we discover that a group lacking in the usual prerequisites of policy capacity often co-operates with other organizations on policy issues, we might be justified in assigning a high score to its coalitional capacity. In both types of cases, the social processes of institutionalization are important, particularly insofar as they promote organizational continuity and cohesion. The effect of continuity is to delineate responsibility and define channels of communication so that there is an orderly flow of information within the organization and individuals perform the tasks assigned to them. In groups having an elaborate organizational structure, these roles may be spelled out in formal, documented procedures that may reflect little institutional development, but where organizational development is more limited, informal processes of institutionalization will be essential. Cohesion is more clearly a social process than continuity, representing acceptance within the organization of a set of fundamental values pertaining both to the role of the organization and to its substantive objectives. This consensus is the foundation for the evolution of roles within the group and thus a motor for group action.*

The ability of bureaucracy to reduce these activities to routine gives an

---

*We should bear in mind, as well, the effect of two aspects of the policy-making environment on group structure and behaviour. Where the system demands a high degree of sophistication among policy actors, there is a considerable pressure on groups to develop commensurate structures. Where the demands of the system are less stringent, groups may be quite successful as policy actors despite having a limited policy capacity. This observation is consistent with the view, presented elsewhere in this book, that policy communities differ considerably in their methods of operation. It also suggests, however, that policy-weak groups that are effective in one sector may have great difficulty making an impression on policy communities that demand sophistication. Again it may be that the structure of an organization has to be commensurate with the complexity of its objectives and the type of claims it makes on society. An organization making extensive claims may have an elaborate organization, yet still fail to gain its objectives because it does not have a policy capacity that is able at one and the same time to mould public opinion, lobby officials and politicians, address a range of specific issues, develop wide-ranging information resources, and express itself effectively and persistently to government, other groups, and the public. Conversely a group with limited objectives may be more successful in achieving them simply because they demand less differentiated activity.

advantage to sophisticated organizations and leads us to hypothesize that they will, overall, rank higher on our index of institutionalization. At the very least, such groups should be able to substitute bureaucratic routine for social processes. Where bureaucratic routine has been melded with social cohesion — and the organization has become an institution — these groups are formidable indeed. Groups that lack organizational diversity may be able to substitute routines that depend on social forces, but they are likely to have difficulty maintaining and co-ordinating their various capacities and therefore we would expect them, in general, to rate lower on this aspect of institutionalization. Groups that have not established routines and have a low regard for organizational mechanisms will have difficulty developing and exploiting their capacities and therefore would be ranked at the bottom of the scale.[40]

In locating organizations on our institutional continuum we would generally give higher scores to groups that have highly developed organizations, especially where policy capacity is supported by professionally staffed information gathering, communications units, and lobbying ability. However, the score itself would depend on our assessment of each group's ability to exploit each of its separate capacities for aggregation, articulation, strategic planning, mobilization, and combining forces with other groups. A leading indicator of such potential would be the extent to which each group exercises its capacities as a matter of routine. Thus, as the 1985 mobilization of seniors demonstrates, groups that routinely mobilize their members and co-operate with other groups would tend to be rated highly on those dimensions.

Where capacities are not routinely exercised, groups tend to fail to exploit their political salience. For example, groups that do not have effective internal communications and do not regularly engage in policy discussions with government are likely to be inept in aggregating and articulating their members' views; unlikely to have developed policy capacity; and incapable of engaging in strategic thinking. Accordingly, we would not assume that formal structure alone indicates political salience and policy capacity; rather we would look for its conjunction with indicators that cohesion and continuity have provided the group with an additional or alternative means of exploiting its organizational and policy capacities.

Resources

Group resources are a characteristic with two very different aspects. Tangible resources are generally easily identified and quantifiable. Intangible resources are more difficult to identify but, because they are generally associated with institutionalization, are often more significant.

Tangible resources (such as financial strength, the presence of professional support staff, and the contributions of volunteers) can be quantified and the data used to assess the extent to which a group's resources confer autonomy on it, something that is extremely significant politically. A group that has diverse and largely institutionalized sources of funding is able to acquire facilities and other resources that are needed to respond readily to members' needs and to integrate the group's activities in the larger community. This makes it possible for the group to take an independent position in public policy debates. The group that depends on government support is, of course, susceptible to official pressure and less likely to act independently.

The accumulation of information resources is less easily identified, yet for many organizations knowledge is at the core of their existence. Information stored in a specialized library; access to databases; an ability to enter the many networks that provide, almost instantaneously, quantities of information that most people would consider arcane — these information resources are difficult to create instantaneously. They generally accumulate over time and with experience and hence we associate them with institutionalization.

The less tangible aspects of the group's resource base (such as the quality of an organization's leadership, its internal cohesion, its 'track record' in previous campaigns, and its public reputation) are as likely as its financial resources to be considered significant by other policy actors since they will in large part determine whether the organization will be able to put its views clearly and to sustain lobbying campaigns.

Both tangible and intangible resources are significant in developing policy capacity. Financial resources are needed to support research staff, lobby, mount policy committees and task forces, issue briefs, advertise, meet with officials, and co-ordinate activities with other groups. The intangible resources a group is able to commit are, as usual, harder to evaluate. Group experience, standing with other groups, and status in the policy community count for a great deal, but can be measured only in proximate terms. For example, an association that regularly collaborates with a number of other organizations and frequently takes a leading role in articulating and lobbying for policy can be said to score high on experience and standing. Its status in the policy community may be registered through the number of occasions on which it is invited by government to proffer advice and/or to take part in policy discussions, and is accorded 'organizational privileges' by the state.[41] These privileges will include not only invitations to participate in policy discussions but also financial support, assumption of responsibility for regulating members' behaviour, and delegated authority for managing programs.[42]

From these comments it will be seen that institutionalization is integral to the effective exploitation of resource strength. Track record, reputation, and cohesion are clearly associated with institutionalization, since they are the product of accumulated common knowledge, shared perceptions, and understandings acquired through experience in working as a group over time. Even organizations that cannot afford to pay staff generally find that institutionalization brings with it community recognition — which itself inspires material and volunteer support — and an accretion of knowledge and experience among its activists. Despite limited physical and financial resources, the organization is seen to have that 'peculiar competence' of which Selznick speaks. These same characteristics are normally extended further if the organization can afford to take on full-time staff, particularly professionals. These latter bring with them specialized knowledge of the substantive concerns of the organization — be it engineering, law, animal husbandry, social work, or whatever — and frequently a knowledge of the organizational environment in which the group is located. These two types of knowledge — substantive and process — contribute to the institutionalization of the organization in quite different ways. Substantive knowledge enhances the organization's ability to communicate in the special language of the field in which its concerns are focused. However, the expert only augments the group's institutionalization as he or she is is socialized into the organization and begins contributing to its internal coherence and its integration in the environment. The need to foster this process leads many organizations to appoint their permanent directors from the ranks of executives of member corporations or affiliated organizations. Such candidates should have access to the group's collective memory and so be in a position to foster internal coherence.* The person with process knowledge is more likely to come from government and will augment institutionalization linking the organization with the outside world.

How does an organization's resource base indicate its place on the institutionalization continuum? The institutionalized group we would expect to have considerable financial, staff, and information resources and institutional qualities — that is, the intangible resources — that permit the fullest realization of their potential. The quality of the group's collective leadership would be high. The group would be known for its internal cohesion. It would be widely accepted publicly — particularly in its policy community — largely on the basis of its track record. Through the leadership, the group's broad information resources would be augmented by extensive process and substantive knowledge.

An important part of its policy capacity would be its officers' knowledge

---

*Witness the qualifications sought in candidates for the position of executive vice-president of the Association of B.C. Professional Foresters: '15 or more years of practical experience as a professional forester, with at least five years in an executive position; good knowledge of the "players" in the forestry community; strong writing and oral communication skills; experience and ability in public speaking; a keen interest in furthering the aims of professionalism within the forestry field' (*Financial Post* 28 Jan. 1991).

of and ease of access to those sectors of government that affect their clients. We would expect fledgling and mature groups to have correspondingly fewer tangible resources and more limited staff support. However, as in our assessment of organizational structure, we would be prepared to find, particularly in the case of mature groups, that the effects of institutionalization might offset the lack of tangible resources, so that some experienced and long-established, but largely voluntary, organizations would be quite as salient and capable as more affluent, but less cohesive, groups. At the 'nascent' end of the continuum we would expect less developed organizations to draw their resources chiefly from their members only, to be dependent on contributions of cash and labour that would be sporadic and reflect attitudes toward the policies and personalities of the leadership. The institutionalization of the financial base would be indicated by the extent to which funding is derived from a variety of sources, the majority of them continuing in nature and possibly secured by contract.[43] Sources of funding would be narrowed at the nascent end of the continuum, with a dependence on government funding being seen as a source of instability.

Outputs

Finally, many groups are significant for the kind of services, or outputs, that they provide their members. Even though they have no apparent political significance, organizational services may provide unexpected benefits during a lobbying campaign. A newsletter is an obvious vehicle for debating policy concerns, aggregating opinion, and ultimately mobilizing action. Financially profitable services can be used to support the costs of preparing briefs, organizing demonstrations, sending delegations to see officials, and mounting legal challenges.

All those externally oriented activities that have explicit policy content can be defined as policy outputs and can be associated directly with policy capacity. They include not only policy positions that are formally adopted by groups and expressed in their letters, press releases, and reports, but also lobbying-related activities. A demonstration, for instance, should be treated as a policy output, since it embodies at least two policy messages: a statement for or against a particular government action or proposed action, and an indication that the group is able to mobilize support for that view. Demonstrations, like petitions, letter-writing campaigns, phone-ins, and so on, are messages to vote-conscious politicians about mobilization and support.

Quite different from these policy activities are the public responsibilities that many groups are assigned by government.[44] Although these involve routine program administration rather than policy matters and present little opportunity for the development of policy, they do engage the group in the program consequences of policies and alert it to the need for policy modification. They also make possible regular interaction with agency officials and so present opportunities for day-to-day communication about programs and their consequences. Out of these interactions may come more or less formal opportunities to influence policy changes to the programs in question. In certain circumstances — where group involvement is essential to the successful development and application of policy and where the groups themselves have acquired corporatist characteristics — such interactions may lead to corporatist style concertation (a continuous and highly institutionalized process of consultation between business, government, and labour) with its tendency to treat both groups and government as equal partners in the public enterprise.

Outputs are particularly likely to be associated with institutionalization, because those that are significant are likely to be developed over time, with experience. Consequently, we would expect institutionalized groups to have many diverse programs and to have maintained them for some time. A narrow range of outputs, delivered sporadically and variable in content, would indicate a nascent or fledgling group. Finally, the behaviour of each group is an output expressing its value system. Thus we usually interpret accommodative and co-operative behaviour on the part of a group and its policy community as a sign of the integration of the group's values with those of its environment — a sign of institutionalization, in other words. Discord and confrontation is associated with a lack of integration between the values of the group and those of the policy community and consequently suggest that the group is probably nascent or fledgling.

* * *

In operationalizing the concepts within our scheme of categorization, we have posited a system of scores that, in combination, can be used to locate groups on the institutional continuum. It is important to stress that in making a determination of institutional status, the evidence has to be sensitively combined. Data collected on each dimension must be balanced with that collected on all other dimensions of group character and policy capacity. For example, in assessing behavioural outputs we have to remember that the degree of manoeuvrability open to groups varies not only between political systems but over time and between policy communities within political systems. We might therefore find apparently institutionalized groups behaving in unexpectedly confrontational ways in regard to specific issues, particularly issues being processed in unfamiliar policy communities. Before concluding that these groups have changed their status — which is quite possible — we would want to relate the behavioural evidence to the data collected on the other dimensions of organizational character and policy capacity, and we would want to consider the general trend of their behaviour over time and over issues.

As in all such exercises, precision is more apparent than real. The relative importance of each dimension of membership, for example, will not be clear until the approach is used in empirical research. Other indicators might be more illuminating. Nevertheless, by analysing how the various dimensions of group characteristics and policy capacity may be associated with levels of institutionalization, we hope to have shown that it is possible to construct a typology that is methodologically correct* and that helps us to address central issues in group-state relations.

---

*It is contended here that the suggested typology meets the criteria of research pertinence, exhaustiveness, categoric principle, and level of analysis. Institutionalization is believed to offer a clear principle, of differentiation, but that cannot be asserted without empirical research.

CHAPTER 5

Context: Policy Communities and Group Functions

In the last chapter I argued that a robust scheme for classifying pressure groups must apply to many different contexts. Canada has experienced a series of transformations — or changing contexts — that render the political system existing today quite unlike the one that prevailed in Laurier's day or Macdonald's, or even John Diefenbaker's. In this chapter I will briefly examine the history of Canadian pressure groups to show how our scheme of categorization helps us to understand the way institutionalization has become integral to modern pressure group politics. I will then build on the review to develop a further analytical concept, the policy community. Finally, I will tie this knowledge of interest organizations to the policy community concept by exploring the functions that groups perform for their members and the political system.

EXPLAINING INSTITUTIONALIZATION

One of the striking features of early pressure groups is their lack of organizational complexity. Pressure groups as we define them did exist in the colonial and Confederation periods. We would classify a few of the early organizations as mature, possibly even fully institutionalized; the Orange Lodges, for example, constituted a complex organization. Some social movements boasted chapters across the country as well as international affiliations, though few hired professional staff.[1] Many of them were closely associated with religious organizations. Business associations were established in every community that considered itself enterprising.

However, the greater part of pressure group activity was carried out by groups that we would classify as nascent or fledgling. A group of businessmen would band together to persuade government to respond to an American trade restriction or to open a new frontier, or to fulfill its promise of building a railway to the West Coast. Its campaign completed, the group would disband. Groups promoting social causes would pass through a similar cycle. Very few groups, even among the more complex, seem to have considered it necessary to engage in strategic planning or to build an ongoing policy capacity. Instead they drew upon the cohesion of their own value system and its integration with broadly based social values — the temperance movements, for example — to promote a general climate of public opinion. In conjunction with élite interaction, public opinion could be used to influence political parties and their leaders.

We have seen that this pattern changed noticeably at the turn of the century. Political power was shifting from the legislatures to the political executives at both the federal and provincial levels. As a result, groups learned to focus their attention on the executive and to pay correspondingly less attention to parties and legislatures. In the early stages of this transformation, their behaviour suggests that groups working in an environment dominated by the executive were inclined to organize themselves to develop reasonably well-informed arguments on the broad features of policy and to study the political needs of ministers. They began to acquire policy capacity, particularly lobbying skills, but could still not be considered highly institutionalized. Few of them built complex organizational structures, since they depended on personal contacts with a few key actors and on a sophisticated understanding of the inner workings of élite politics.* However, it became increasingly common for geographically dispersed and very loosely associated groups to strengthen their ties with one another and to strengthen their national presence.[2]

During the heyday of the mandarins, established groups enhanced their ability to communicate with the bureaucracy and government leaders, becoming in the process more complex organizations with an orientation to technical expertise. We would classify a number of these associations — particularly those in agriculture and labour — as fully institutionalized.

In contemporary Canada, the diffusion of power through the governmental system compels effective pressure groups to add to these political and administrative capacities an ability to present themselves to the public. Only if they do so can they generate public support for the policies they favour. As well, particularly at the federal level, the tendency to delegate a great deal of responsibility to the administrative branch affects the structure and behaviour of groups. Organizational complexity is forced on a pressure group as it tries to cope not only with the political environment of senior policy-makers but with the voracious appetite of the administrative apparatus for technical adjustment of policies. The group becomes adept at

---

*George McCullagh, the influential publisher of the *Globe and Mail*, once said of former Ontario Premier Mitchell Hepburn's actions during a major strike that 'whatever Mr Hepburn did as a government leader was only as a result of information I placed before him in regard to government and trade unionism, a subject on which I have some knowledge.'(Quoted in Brian J. Young, 'C. George McCullagh and the Leadership League' in Ramsay Cook, *The Politics of Discontent* [Toronto, 1967], 76-102, 82.) Today it would be extremely hard for McCullagh to make the same boast.

research in order to master the required technical detail; it acquires legal and public relations skills to present its position effectively, and it builds a capacity to monitor the implementation and further development of policy.[3]

All of this is consistent with the argument of corporatist scholars that modern policy systems are so constructed that some degree of organization is a prerequisite to participation. To wield influence regularly in the formation and application of public policy, groups have to work with bureaucracies. As many protest groups have discovered, any group can influence a decision — but it takes a well-organized group to influence a policy. Without organization, even a strong strategic position is of limited value to an interest, though a strong organization considerably enhances a weak strategic position. Working in an environment of organizational complexity means that groups must be ready to contribute advice frequently on a number of issues, to serve on advisory boards, to represent their interests to the public, to co-ordinate their own activities with those of others, and to engage constantly in a host of undertakings that demand organization. The only way a group can do all of this is to develop its own organizational capability. It must have a formal structure, clearly defined roles, a system for generating and allocating resources, a collective memory, rules governing behaviour, and, most important, procedures for reaching and implementing decisions. Because the environment is bureaucratic, pressure groups have had to become increasingly institutionalized to work effectively in it.

To appreciate why the bureaucratic character of modern policy-making should so profoundly affect the character and behaviour of interest groups, we must briefly consider what bureaucracy is and why today's governments cannot live without it.[4] Bureaucracy divides complex undertakings into comprehensible and manageable units of work, and then, through hierarchy, provides a means for co-ordinating the separate activities that specialization has created. Specialization reduces all-encompassing projects to a scale that individuals can understand and, by working together, accomplish. Through specialization, tasks are identified and arranged in a sequence that will allow their successful performance to create a flow of work that ultimately produces a product, be it an automobile, a memo to Cabinet, a social assistance payment, or a transportation system. The responsibilities and attributes assigned to each position in the sequence of work are made explicit in job descriptions and regulations, recorded, and, finally, enforced by those who hold authority in the hierarchy.

Our survey of the evolution of Canadian pressure groups showed how the party politics of the late nineteenth century — with its random, personal style of policy-making — ceded ground to bureaucratic methods. Patronage was gradually reduced in the civil service because people working for government had to possess the skills needed to perform the job described for each position. Professional associations became prominent as a result, while the significance of local party organizations declined. The influence of experts on policy-makers grew apace in both business and government. As it did so, specialized organizations developed to facilitate communication between the pockets of expertise in the public and private sectors and to persuade lay policy-makers of the wisdom of expert advice. We ascribed the centralization of government administration to a need to keep pace with centralization in the economy.

Bureaucratic organization made centralization feasible; in turn, centralization made necessary the emergence of sectoral organizations concerned with the affairs of relatively narrow segments of the economy. By assigning responsibility for all but the most significant sectoral matters to what I will call policy communities, the political executive and the general public were able to conserve their energies for dealing with paramount issues.

But specialization does not end at the delineation of a policy field or sector.* In fact, it only begins there. Within each major policy field are many subfields — agriculture, for example, contains dairy farming, grain production, egg and poultry production, etc. There are frequently specializations within each subfield; dairy farming, for example, includes butter production, cheese manufacturing, the production of fresh dairy goods, and so on. Bureaucratic organization ensures that each field, subfield, and sub-subfield is attended by its own group of specialists, who deliver programs and contribute to policy development. Specialists in government and interests in the private sector find that they work most effectively together if they organize at the level of their specialization. The resulting structure of organized representation in agriculture is a common one: two national organizations, the Canadian Federation of Agriculture and the National Farmers' Union, represent agricultural interests on a variety of issues, but

---

*Nor are the effects of specialization confined to massive, complex structures such as the federal government . An editorial in *Plan Canada* notes that at the local level fragmentation of government, resulting from the practice of giving responsibility for a particular administrative or service function to some board, commission, or other authority separate from the elected council, means that 'apart perhaps from street cleaning, there is hardly a single function of local government which, somewhere or other in this land of ours, is not in the care of its own exclusive band of single-minded, loyal protectors' (*Plan Canada* 9 [1968] 2, 50). Peter Larkin, a prominent fisheries biologist, speaks similarly *vis-à-vis* fisheries policy and, in passing, makes a comment that illuminates our argument that those who do take part in policy discussions tend to opt for consensus rather than conflict: 'Characteristically, decision-making in fisheries management involves, either directly or indirectly, consultation with representatives of all the groups that may be affected — industry, fishermen, experts, ethnic groups, social groups, and in a vague sort of way, the people at large.... In these circumstances, the decisions are bound to have a certain character. "Why rock the boat?" is the usual theme of representatives. If disaster has not struck in the last three or four years, if things are more less the same, or only a little bit worse, why invite chaos or catastrophe?' (Peter A. Larkin, 'A Confidential Memorandum on Fisheries Science', in Brian J. Rothschild, *World Fisheries Policy* [Seattle: University of Washington, 1972], 189-98 at 193-4).

the detailed work of administering agricultural policy is carried out by subordinate, semi-autonomous, or independent government agencies, each of which has close ties to groups representing the interests of producers of the commodity it regulates. The Canadian Egg Marketing Agency, for example, may have dealings with the Canadian Federation of Agriculture and the National Farmers' Union, but its day-to-day relations with the industry are conducted through such organizations as the Canadian Egg Producers' Council, the Canadian Hatchery Association, the Canadian Egg and Poultry Council, and the Canadian Poultry and Egg Producers' Council.[5] Such structures attest to the importance of institutionalization in modern pressure group politics and account for the great increase in the number of institutionalized groups over the last thirty years.

At the same time, the bureaucratic organization of the modern state has not eliminated nascent and fledgling groups from the political scene. Their numbers, in fact, appear to have exploded — largely, it seems, because bureaucratic policy-making forces individuals to combine if they wish to have their voices heard. The nascent and fledgling organizations that they create serve important functions in the political system.[6] The chief advantage of these groups lies in their dynamism. Because they can develop quickly and are unencumbered by institutionalized structures, they can generate immediate public reaction to specific issues. Because their stake in the future is usually limited, they are able to indulge in forms of political communication that institutional groups are reluctant to use. These groups permit a responsiveness to emergent issues that could not be achieved if the community were to rely entirely on institutionalized groups.

This very brief attempt to apply our taxonomy to succeeding forms of the Canadian political system suggests that it does indeed help us to analyse the types of groups that are prevalent at different periods. In so doing, it also sheds some light on the central question of the relationship between the state and interest groups. It demonstrates very clearly that, because the state is the most prominent in the relationship, interests wanting to influence public policy have had to adapt themselves to its policy-making procedures. The bureaucratic structure of the modern state affects all those who must work with and through governments. To interact effectively with its complex machinery over a period of time, any interest must institutionalize its organizational capacity to a point where it is compatible with the policy system.

PRESSURE GROUPS IN THE POLICY PROCESS:
THE POLICY COMMUNITY CONCEPT

Society permits specialized publics to dominate decision-making in sectors of policy where they have competence, interfering only when larger concerns must take precedence, when systemic or technological change necessitates intervention, or when conflict within the special public spills over into the larger political arena.

Two terms are commonly used to describe these specialized publics: policy communities and networks.[7] A policy community is that part of a political system that has acquired a dominant voice in determining government decisions in a field of public activity. This is by virtue of its functional responsibilities, its vested interests, and its specialized knowledge. The policy community is generally permitted by society at large and the public authorities in particular to create public policy in that field. It is populated by government agencies, pressure groups, media people, and individuals, including academics, who have an interest in a particular policy field and attempt to influence it.[8] Networks are 'the relationships among the particular set of actors that forms around an issue of importance to the policy community'.[9]

Policy communities and networks are closely related but significantly different aspects of the policy process. A policy field draws together a community; policies and policy issues activate networks. Policies, because they are generally amalgams of decisions, tend to take shape over time and to have long-term implications. The communities that coalesce around policy fields reflect that continuity and, though not permanent, possess a longevity that gives significance to the evolution of idiosyncratic values, norms, language, and behavioural patterns. Issues arise in the context of policies. They precipitate network formation by policy actors who are drawn to make common cause with those whose interests are, or may be, similarly affected by efforts at issue-resolution.

The chief distinction between a network and a policy community lies in the fact that the community exists because a policy field exists, whereas a network exists because those in it share an approach to policy. What the members of a policy community have in common is an involvement — it may be a vested interest, an intellectual attachment, or a commitment to a view of the public interest — in the policy field. This does not mean that their approach to policy is the same. In fact, they may be in conflict over policy issues. (Free-traders and Canadian economic nationalists are deeply opposed on policy issues, but they must all be considered part of the policy community concerned with international trade.) Their relationships with one another are not unlike those of the residents of a small town or village. They may not always like each other and they may disagree on important points, but they know they have to live together and consequently they work out rules and relationships that enable the community to function.

Networks, in contrast, tend to be composed of similarly minded people. This is why issues are important in the formation of networks. Debate over issues helps to identify and bring together those who share values and perceptions about which policies should be adopted and which should not. Just as a village divides into camps over divisive issues, so policy communities divide into networks. Networks like camps may persist, sometimes creating relationships similar to those that are found in policy communities. This, of course, confounds observers and leads to academic debate in which the exclusive use of one term or the other is promoted.[10] As far as I am concerned here, both terms have value and describe essentially different activities. The value of the term 'network' lies in the image it conveys of actors who are consciously in touch with one another as the result of shared interests in the resolution of a specific issue.

A network's characteristic tendency to attract involvement from actors having an immediate stake in an issue also helps us to conceptualize what happens when an issue affects those who are not normally part of a policy community. Because networks tend to be open-ended, stakeholders may 'plug in' or leave as issues emerge and their concerns are aroused and resolved. Through networks, actors may cross the boundaries of policy communities. The value of the term 'policy community' is that it suggests communication that is both continuous and contained, and that it invokes the notion of a social pattern encompassing not only gradations between its members but shared, or at least commonly understood, belief systems, codes of conduct, and established patterns of behaviour.*

Most policy communities consist of two segments: the sub-government and the attentive public. In effect, the sub-government is the policy-making body of each community. It processes most routine policy issues and is seldom successfully challenged by dissident members of the policy community. It consists primarily of government agencies and institutionalized

---

*This aspect of the special public persuades this writer that the term 'community' is more apt than terms like 'special publics', 'sectors', and 'networks' which suggest communication patterns and shared concerns and perspectives, but which exclude a social dimension. Observation of several special publics indicates that the social dimension is a fundamental lubricant and a key in maintaining the community's dominance in a policy field. The fishing industry provides particularly strong evidence of this. Anyone attending industry conventions is immediately aware of social stratification within the industry and of the development of codes of conduct which are rigorously enforced. These are even more apparent in the advisory committees which help determine fish quotas and supervise harvesting arrangements. There the representatives of major companies, fishermen's organizations, and officials clearly work within a framework of understanding that defines permissible behaviour and punishes transgressors with chastisement and withdrawal of co-operation, and so on. Nor do these patterns exhibit themselves only in the work environment. Funerals and marriages in the families of individuals prominent in the industry serve as occasions for industry leaders from across the Atlantic region to meet, renew ties, come to informal understandings, and otherwise reinforce the bonds that hold them together in an often fractious but communal relationship. That similar patterns can be observed in other policy communities is demonstrated by J.D. House's superb *The Last of the Free Enterprisers: The Oilmen of Calgary* (Toronto, 1979).

interest groups. These alone have the resources and the incentive to meet the demands of sub-government work: day-to-day communication between agency officials and representatives of companies or groups; automatic group inclusion on advisory committees and panels of experts; invitations to comment on draft policy; participation on committees or commissions charged with long-range policy review; and continual formal and informal access to agency officials.

Because of the problem of limited resources, and because the policy process seldom allows time for full, meaningful consultation, sub-governments consist of very small groups of people: the minister in charge of the agency that is primarily responsible for formulating policy and carrying out programs in a field; the senior officials responsible for that field of policy, and perhaps their most important federal or provincial counterparts; and representatives of the few interest groups whose opinions and support are essential. Representatives of other agencies may also be included if those agencies are deeply involved in the policy field. For example, the federal Department of Health and Welfare is often a sub-government actor in the formulation of policy affecting Native peoples; the Departments of Energy, Mines and Resources and of Indian and Northern Affairs are usually involved jointly in decisions concerning the exploitation of northern resources. Other actors who may appear in the sub-government from time to time are parliamentarians whose constituency interests or committee responsibilities give them a special, if intermittent, authority in a specific field, and officers of central agencies responsible for Cabinet liaison and budget control.[11]

The attentive public, by contrast, is neither tightly knit nor clearly defined. It includes any government agencies, private institutions, pressure groups, specific interests, and individuals — including academics, consultants and journalists — who are affected by, or interested in, the policies of specific agencies and who follow, and attempt to influence, those policies, but do not participate in policy-making on a regular basis. Their interest may be keen but not compelling enough to warrant breaking into the inner circle. Often they may be excluded from it, particularly if they are opposed to prevailing policy trends.

The attentive public lacks the power of the sub-government but still plays a vital role in policy development. Conferences and study sessions organized by professional and interest associations offer opportunities for officials at various levels to converse with the grass roots of their constituencies, and with journalists and academics who have been studying public policy. They usually have views on government performance and are quick to put them forward. Though most are heard sceptically, sometimes patronizingly, they contribute to the gradual process through which policies and programs are amended, extended, and generally adapted to the changing needs of the community. Similarly, the newsletters, professional journals, and trade magazines that circulate through the policy community give both the sub-government and the attentive public plenty of opportunity to shore up, demolish, or transmogrify the existing policy edifice. In this turmoil of theories and interests, officialdom—which is almost never monolithic, nearly always pluralistic, and seldom at peace with itself—discerns the policy changes government must make if it is to keep nearly abreast of circumstance. The main function of the attentive public, then, is to maintain a perpetual policy review process. It introduces into the policy community an element of diversity inhibited at the sub-government level by the need to maintain consensus.[12]

Figure 5-1 represents the kind of policy community that might be active in a field in which the federal government is prominent. At the heart of the community are the key federal bodies involved: the lead agency (that is, the body primarily responsible for formulating policy and carrying out programs in the field); Cabinet, with its co-ordinating agencies; the Privy Council Office; Treasury Board; the Ministries of State; and the Departments of Finance and External Affairs. None of these are located at the very centre of the figure because no single agency is ever consistently dominant in the field. Because so much policy-making is routine, the lead agency tends to be most influential over time. Despite its prominence, the lead agency's activities are closely monitored by other federal agencies whose overlapping mandates bring them within the sub-government. Working through interdepartmental committees, they usually review and often greatly alter agency policy. For example, Canadian fisheries policy has often been influenced by External Affairs, which worries about Canada's relations with trading partners who fish off our coasts. Clustered around, keeping a sharp eye on 'the feds' and taking part in the sub-government, are the key pressure groups and provincial government agencies.

Hovering on the edge of the sub-government is Parliament—perennially interested, intermittently involved, sometimes influential. Provincial governments are variously involved: some might wish to be part of the sub-government but lack the resources to maintain a presence; others are simply not interested and are content to observe the activities of the sub-government, interfering when necessary. Provincial governments may be no more influential than the major pressure groups active in the community, some of which overlap one another, having common memberships, sitting together on advisory boards, and frequently combining their efforts to present a joint position to government and the public.

The composition of the attentive public ranges from institutionalized group members and government agencies to individuals and nascent groups. The degree to which a group is institutionalized need not dictate its status in the community, or its level of participation, which may be determined by the

Figure 5-1: The Policy Community

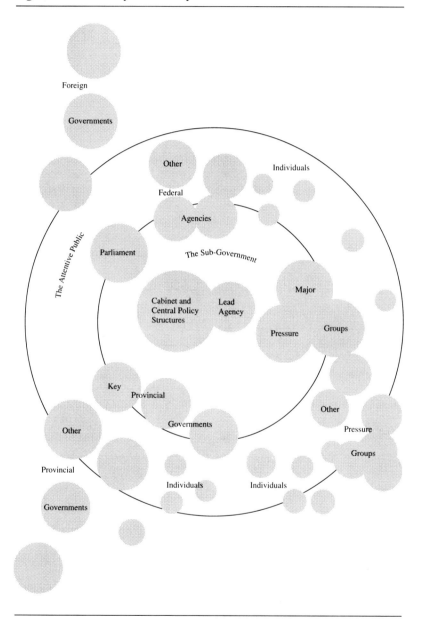

Foreign

Governments

Other

Individuals

Federal

Agencies

The Attentive Public

Parliament

The Sub-Government

Major

Cabinet and
Central Policy
Structures

Lead
Agency

Pressure

Groups

Key

Provincial

Other

Other

Governments

Pressure

Provincial

Groups

Governments

Individuals

Individuals

Source: A. Paul Pross, 'Pressure Groups: Talking Chameleons', in G. Williams and M.S. Whittington, *Canada in the 1980s* (Methuen Publications, Toronto, 1985).

strength of the interest of group members in the policy field and by their power in the economy and society. Prior to the 1970s, the chemical industries evinced very little interest in what we now call environmental policy; their participation in the formation of policies relating to water quality, for example, was minimal. With the growth of environmentalism, the industry mobilized itself to contribute to environmental policy. The Petroleum Association for the Conservation of the Environment (PACE), in particular, became a prominent actor—or member of the sub-government—in certain closely defined policy fields, such as that of oil pollution control.

Not all members of the attentive public need be as well organized as PACE, which has become an institutionalized actor.[13] The academic groups taking part in the foreign policy review of the early Trudeau years were linked to the Canadian Institute of International Affairs but could not otherwise be described as a highly institutionalized group.[14] To a considerable extent their meetings had to be arranged by the Department of External Affairs, whose readiness to do this indicated the value it attached to academic 'legitimation' of policy review, even though the department seems to have paid very little attention to the advice it received.

Even less organized, and generally less welcome, are the nascent groups whose spontaneous eruption into a policy field shatters the carefully contrived appearance of consensus and challenges both the routinization of policy and the conventional wisdom prevalent in the sub-government and, to a large extent, in the attentive public. They and other, less influential members of policy communities have good reason to excite public discussion of the issues that concern them: generally they have little standing in the policy community, and may have only limited knowledge of its methods, its language, and its philosophy—the essentials for participating in its discussions. Consequently an appeal to public opinion is the best way—sometimes the only way—to challenge a specific decision or to object to an undesirable policy and to embarrass governments into taking action.

Finally we should note that Canadian policy communities are not composed exclusively of Canadians, nor do they function only within our borders. Foreign governments follow closely our policies in fields of concern to them, as the American government demonstrated when Ottawa implemented the National Energy Policy. As Canadian nationalists frequently claim, foreign governments sometimes come close to participating in our sub-governments. So do multinational corporations. Coleman and his colleagues have demonstrated that the boards of directors of many business interest associations generally include senior executives of multinational firms, who strongly influence the views presented by those associations when they participate in sub-governmental deliberations.[15] Other external participants in Canadian policy communities include international organizations — such as the Organization for Economic Co-operation and Development, which regularly reviews Canadian economic policy, or the International Labour Organization, whose views on labour matters are often influential[16] — and international pressure groups, like Greenpeace and other groups that have used international public opinion to oppose the sealing industry. Conversely, Canadian policy communities try to influence the actions of foreign governments through, for example, international trade discussions or international aid activities.

Although Figure 5-1 suggests orbital movement around the lead agency and the federal executive, the other members of the policy community are actually in constant motion. Governments and key personnel change, provincial government participation varies, or changing economic factors compel provincial agencies to retreat or advance into the sub-government. In the energy field, for example, Alberta became prominent after the Leduc discovery, and Newfoundland after Hibernia. Similarly, pressure groups move back and forth from the centre.

Mobility is particularly evident in the attentive public, whose pressure groups and individual members are in constant motion, coalescing around or breaking away from more powerful actors, advancing towards and withdrawing from the core as their resources, their interests, and the public agenda change. In the early 1960s, for example, Douglas H. Pimlott, a University of Toronto biologist, was a prominent critic of Ontario forest policy. A decade later he had shifted his energies to national environmental policy and become a leading academic figure on matters touching northern development.[17] While individuals are more likely than organizations to shift focus in this way, groups do so as well. In the early 1970s, the Social Sciences Federation of Canada (SSFC) became involved in the environmental movement, establishing an interdisciplinary committee on the human environment that attempted, for approximately a decade, to monitor social science activity in environmental studies and to represent the social sciences in some of the policy communities concerned with environmental issues. Among its interests were codes of ethics applied by the federal government to social scientists working with Native communities, the development of environmental and social-impact assessment, and national parks policies. Eventually more appropriate institutions developed for representing the social sciences in these matters; the SSFC disbanded the committee and ceased being a part of the attentive public in the environmental field.[18] Such behaviour regularly occurs in any policy community. Organizations and individuals are constantly changing their interests, responding to new situations, developing new capacities, and shedding old ones.

The attentive public has two significant effects on the policy community. It is a dynamic influence. The most prominent members of the policy community are not primarily interested in making or reformulating policy.

For them the policy community is a protective device, limiting rather than expanding the opportunities for the public at large to achieve major policy changes. They use the sub-government to keep policy-making at the routine or technical level, thereby minimizing interference. Often, however, circumstances outside its control — economic changes, new technologies, changing public concerns — overwhelm the sub-government's system of formal communications and informal networks. At this point the attentive public becomes influential. Interventions from it draw attention to inadequacies in policy, force the pace of change, and introduce new blood and new ideas. They shake up the policy community. Policy debate broadens as levels of conflict rise, so that eventually central issues may be taken out of the hands of the sub-government and the policy community and resolved at the highest political levels.[19] When this occurs, both the policy community and policy are often vastly altered, perhaps even totally restructured — as in the early 1970s when several older communities were reorganized and combined to serve the newly defined field of environmental policy. Thus, the attentive public is a force for policy change.

The attentive public tends to exercise its greatest influence on long-range policy. Because it lacks ready access to the sub-government, its influence on day-to-day policy is minimal. Occasionally its members may need to intervene on specific issues or they may be called upon to defend existing policies from some outside threat, just as academics are currently being encouraged to participate in the effort to rescue Confederation. But the attentive public is more likely to be engaged in discussions of medium-term and long-term goals, chiefly because it cannot maintain the regular communication — virtually daily contact — with decision-makers that is necessary for involvement in day-to-day policy. The average member of the attentive public, who is seldom physically close to the decision centre and whose work does not make regular contact necessary, turns to more readily available links with the policy community. These may be local chapters of national organizations, national conferences, study seminars, or various types of print media, ranging from trade journals to academic periodicals. Such links keep members of the attentive public adequately informed, though not on short-term issues, many of which are resolved before information has filtered through these channels. Consequently the organizers of conferences and the publishers of journals concentrate on general trends and the larger picture.

The hypothesis that policy communities participate significantly in the policy process leads to a subsidiary hypothesis that the structures and functions of policy communities will vary from policy field to policy field.[20] Though most policy communities will contain common elements, the functions performed by specific components will vary significantly. In some fields, for example, citizens' groups, the media, and the academic community may play a larger role than they would in others. The structural relations between community members will differ accordingly. The determinants of variation will be extremely diverse and include such factors as the nature of the field, the longevity of government involvement in it, the extent of agency power and responsibility, the agency's significance in the power structure of its own government, and the resources and characteristics of the non-governmental members of the policy community.

While the policy field is an important variable in determining the nature of the policy community, so is the jurisdictional framework surrounding it. The structures and functions of policy communities will also vary according to the policy field's jurisdictional location. This is particularly important in the Canadian federal system, where vast differences can exist between policy communities operating exclusively within provincial jurisdictions and those operating on the national level. For example, in some of the Atlantic provinces government bureaucracies are much less aggressive and powerful than they appear to be at the federal level. The structure and organization of the policy communities are likely to vary accordingly. Similarly, a policy field restricted to the federal domain would be expected to possess a policy community significantly different from one that is continually engaged in the niceties of federal-provincial diplomacy.

Contrast, for instance, the policy community that seems to surround the Department of National Defence with the one formerly associated with the Ministry of State for Urban Affairs. The intense pressure brought to bear by provincial and local governments whenever the Department of National Defence talks of closing a military base indicates that while these governments and interests are not part of the defence sub-government — which appears to be a small, tightly knit group very much dominated by the military and including members of the international military organizations to which Canada belongs — they are very much a part of the attentive public. The short-lived Ministry of State for Urban Affairs, by contrast, had a very loosely structured sub-government that contained one extremely cohesive element, the sub-government surrounding the Central Mortgage and Housing Corporation, and a coterie of groups concerned about the co-ordinative and long-range policy roles of the Ministry. Several of these, like the Canadian Confederation of Mayors and Municipalities, had considerable influence inside and outside the Ministry's policy community, but the majority — nascent and institutionalized citizens' groups, research organizations, professional planners' associations, and so on — were unable to form an effective sub-government. They constituted a policy community so deeply divided that the Ministry and its supporters were ultimately unable to resist the attacks of those who wanted the federal government to abandon its venture into urban policy.[21]

A dispute over the Atlantic provinces' freight rates in 1982-83 displays both a policy community and a network in operation.[22] A small policy community has concerned itself with freight rates in the region since the 1920s. At that time, consolidation of railways in the Maritimes by central Canadian interests led to radical increases in rates. These were vigorously contested by the region's business community, which spearheaded a Maritime Rights Movement and ultimately, after a Royal Commission inquiry, secured a subsidy program.

Learning from experience that it was necessary to monitor the program continually, the Maritime Boards of Trade established the Atlantic Provinces Transportation Commission (APTC) in 1934 to provide manufacturers in the region with expert assistance in obtaining the 'best value for their transportation dollar' and to represent them in the discussion of transportation policy. Based in Moncton, the Commission employs a professional staff and is jointly governed by the business community and the provincial departments contributing financial support, usually the departments of Highways or Transportation. The Commission is closely affiliated with the Atlantic Provinces Chambers of Commerce (APCC), whose head office is also located in Moncton.

Since 1934, these two institutions have played a particularly important part in articulating and pressing for regional concerns in the transportation field. This has ensured that they exercise the collective memory of the region in the field and that they remain integral institutions — that is, sub-government members — in its transportation policy community. Other members of the sub-government are the federal Ministry of Transport (the lead agency in the community); the federal Treasury Board (which is particularly concerned about subsidies); provincial departments of highways and transportation; and, of course, the railways and the Canadian Trucking Association. Many other agencies and groups are active in the community but have to be treated as part of the attentive public. The Nova Scotia and Newfoundland Division of the Canadian Manufacturers' Association (CMA) and Nova Scotia's Voluntary Planning Board, for example, have transportation committees. The Atlantic Provinces Economic Council monitors transportation policy, as do many trade associations. Intermittent but significant participants in the community are federal parliamentarians and the Council of Maritime Premiers.

Though this policy community is small and concerned chiefly with routine, the significance of transportation to Atlantic Canada ensures that the APTC's role as business's watchdog is considered important by the attentive public and its communications are treated seriously. When, in the late 1970s, APTC signalled concern over Transport Canada's growing distaste for subsidies, members of the attentive public began to watch for signs that the federal agency would try to dismantle the program. These came in 1981, when the federal Minister of Transport and his regional counterparts agreed to revise the program by exchanging reduced subsidies for increased subventions for highway construction.

This radical change in policy precipitated two reactions within the policy community. First, extensive networks began to develop within the attentive public as more and more business people realized that transportation costs would rise dramatically as the subsidies were removed. Second, the level of conflict around the issue began to escalate. No significant sector was unaffected. Carriers and shippers, farmers, miners, forest workers and fishermen, processors and manufacturers, local Rotary clubs, Chambers of Commerce, the Maritime Lumber Bureau, the forest industry, sea-food producers, and a number of others joined in opposing subsidy removal. Very few business interest groups in the region failed to give at least token support. Agreement also cut across class barriers. Though labour organizations played no prominent role in the campaign, it was clear that they supported the pro-subsidy position. At the other end of the spectrum, the campaign was vigorously supported by significant regional élites. An *ad hoc* group representing major businesses and headed by McCain's vice-president Dr George McClure had considerable influence with political leaders at both levels of government. This was a formidable coalition. A few groups traditionally involved in the policy community — the CMA, the APTC, and the APCC — together with McClure's group, played central roles, but they were able to activate networks that extended into every corner of the regional economy. Group annual and special meetings made it clear that they were broadly supported. Information was shared readily, co-operation secured, and access to the media encouraged and facilitated. Above all, the regional business community accepted the guidance of the leading groups and spoke to the media, officials, and politicians with a united voice. Such a response could not help but convince the provincial and federal political leadership that the level of conflict surrounding the subsidy issue was too extensive to be ignored. In conjunction with a similar, and more highly publicized, dispute over proposed Crow Rate revisions in the West, it led to the replacement of the federal Minister of Transport and the abandonment, at least temporarily, of the subsidy reductions.

Without the policy community's special capabilities for studying alternative courses of action, for debating their merits, and for securing administrative arrangements for implementation, governments would have great difficulty discerning and choosing between policy options. Pressure groups are equally important within policy communities. It is in the policy community that they most frequently perform the functions we have attributed to them. They draw together the interests associated with the community and articulate their concerns. Their ability to secure the support of special publics for policies is often indispensable. They at times hold the collective memory for policy issues. With their annual meetings, newsletters, regional organizations, and, above all, informal networks, they have an ability to cross organizational lines denied to other more formal actors, such as government departments. They can therefore act as go-betweens, provide opportunities for quiet meetings between warring agencies, and keep the policy process in motion. They may also act as emissaries to other policy communities. These services, together with their ability to evaluate policy and develop opinion, make pressure groups integral members of the policy community. Pressure groups are vital to the life of policy communities and policy communities are essential to the development and implementation of public policy.

THE CONTEXT OF PRESSURE GROUP LIFE

Comparative studies of pressure group systems suggest that there are important variations in pressure group politics from country to country and that they are probably rooted in the different political systems of the countries involved.[23] Each system obliges the pressure groups working within it to adapt to its particular characteristics. The cumulative effects of individual group adaptations is the creation in each country of distinctive patterns of behaviour. In many ways, however, this diversity is misleading, as Robert Presthus suggests when he refers to pressure group politics as 'a process that seems functionally essential in any political system'.[24] If pressure groups perform one or more essential functions in each system, the functions are probably similar whenever they occur, and in carrying them out groups are likely to develop comparable techniques and structures. Comparing group activity suggests that pressure groups perform one func-tion — the promotion of members' interests — that is valued exclusively by their members, and four others that also meet the needs of the community in which they work. The most important of these are communication and legitimation. Less significant are the steps they take to regulate their members on behalf of the state and the assistance they give governments in administering programs. In the following paragraphs we examine each of these functions and identify their appearance in the pressure group politics of Canadian policy communities.

Interest Promotion

In Chapter 1 I said that pressure groups seek 'to influence public policy in order to promote their common interest'. They draw together people who see themselves as having common interests; they bring about agreement on which interests are indeed common and on how they can be best served, and enable these people to express their interests to government in a way they hope will influence public policy in their favour. In the jargon of political science, the first part of this activity is known as interest aggregation and the second as interest articulation. Taken together they constitute the function of promoting member interests. Not all members join groups out of a desire to promote their own narrowly defined interests. Furthermore, few pressure groups exist solely as pressure groups; many also act in the political realm as an inevitable extension of their other concerns. But whenever they engage in the policy process, such groups do so to promote what the members conceive as their common interest, whether it be a broadly stated public interest — such as will excite the Canadian Civil Liberties Association, for instance — or a narrowly conceived one, like the majority of issues pursued by trade associations. From the point of view of the members at large, promoting their interests is the chief reason why the groups they belong to should interact with government — should, in effect, act as pressure groups. Interest promotion, then, is a fundamental function of pressure groups.

The Systemic Functions

The desire to get some personal advantage from government policy is a common characteristic of interest group members. Can the self-interest of group supporters, however, explain why pressure groups are not only formed around the world but often welcomed and fostered — and are tolerated even in many states that, on ideological grounds, should be hostile? The promotion of self-interest is a subsystemic function: it helps those who are in the subsystem — that is, the group members — but at first glance it does not do very much for the rest of us in the larger system, the broader political community. Surely, to justify their prominence pressure groups must perform some functions that render them useful in the system at large. There must be what some scholars call a benefit-exchange relationship. To survive as effective political institutions they must offer services needed by their host political systems, receiving in return specific benefits for themselves and their members. The functions of communication, legitimation, regulation, and administration do this. These functions not only meet the needs of members, they facilitate the workings of the political system. I therefore call them 'systemic functions'.

Communications

When groups engage in the communications process they act as relay points, sending messages in four different directions. Best known is their role in transmitting demands from special publics to governments. When the federal government suspended commercial salmon fishing in New Brunswick and parts of Newfoundland, Denis Monroe, president of the Fisheries Council of Canada, complained that 'we simply weren't consulted. We learned about it third hand.' He urged the fishery interests to build up the resources of the Fisheries Council to enable it to make the fishermen's views heard when similar decisions had to be considered in future. 'You need a rifle, not a popgun to get through to the government,' he concluded.[25]

Besides transmitting messages to government, groups often convey the views, demands, and decisions of public officials from government to special publics. For example, the Union of Nova Scotia Municipalities began life as a ' "common" pressure group, trying to influence the government to follow the wishes of its members', but soon became a 'quasi-administrative' arm of the province, passing on to local governments the views and policy decisions of the government in Halifax.[26] Public officials encourage groups to act as the main conduit between themselves and group members, partly because this promotes dialogue, but also because they have found that interest organizations frequently offer the most effective means of reaching special publics.

One government agency working in the Lac St-Jean region of Quebec had a typical experience. Letters, use of the media, audio-visual displays, demonstrations, flyers, and press releases brought the agency's message to less than 18 per cent of its target audience. The officials concluded that members of the public create a wall of indifference to protect themselves from the barrage of information they receive daily from and about government. They might attend to those messages that seem to affect them personally — *'Ils ne sont touchés que par ce qui les poigne aux tripes. On les attrape avec leur bol de café, avec leurs oeufs, leur pain.'*[27] Even these, however, will not register unless they appear in a context and form that the individual is attuned to. Even though there are fields where the special public is numerous or has a recurrent contact with government (so that it is possible to convey information through officials), for the most part members of interest communities are too dispersed to be contacted in this way. The vital link between citizen and government has to be provided by interest group organizations. They understand how to catch the attention of their members, to show them how their vital interests may be affected by government messages, and perhaps even to translate the officialese of press releases, forms, and regulations into everyday language. They may be trusted where officials are not.

The two-way flow of messages between groups and governments is the most important communication process groups engage in, but not the only one. To a limited extent, groups can facilitate communication within government, carrying messages between agencies, cutting across the barriers that separate levels in the administrative hierarchy or divide the political and administrative worlds. They may simply be needed to interpret one part of government to another. They can render even more valuable service in intergovernmental communication.

In 1876, after repeated protests from the provincial government had failed to persuade Ottawa to begin work on the British Columbia end of the transcontinental railway, a group of Vancouver Island businessmen organized themselves into a club to lobby in support of the British Columbia government's demands. Ultimately the combined lobbying of government and business convinced the federal government that work should be started and that Vancouver — not New Westminster, whose own lobbying was in part responsible for the delay — should be the western terminus of the railway.[28]

On the east coast, the Atlantic Provinces Economic Council (APEC) took a leading role in promoting communication between governments, advocating intergovernmental meetings, supporting the work of the Deutsch inquiry into Maritime Union, and later championing establishment of the Council of Maritime Premiers. In itself, APEC serves as a mechanism through which governments can talk to one another on economic matters. Governments commission research that cuts across provincial jurisdictions; their representatives sit on APEC committees and study groups, and they participate in the Council's many conferences and seminars. These daily interactions provide the means through which governments can send messages to one another.[29]

Finally, groups spend a great deal of time communicating among themselves, as can be observed readily enough during any public debate. The discussion of 'freedom of information' legislation offers an illustration. To promote more open access to government information, the Canadian Bar Association, the Social Sciences Federation, the Canadian Association of University Teachers, and the Canadian Library Association, to name but a few organizations, co-operated extensively in presenting their views to government and bringing public pressure to bear. As the campaign developed, an umbrella group, ACCESS ('A Citizens Committee for the Right to Public Information') emerged and assumed most of the burden of co-ordinating the campaign.[30] Intergroup co-operation and communication has a long tradition in Canada; nearly a century earlier, the temperance movement promoted not only temperance but votes for women, the elimination of sweat shops, and the extension of educational opportunities for women.[31]

The direction of communications received and emitted by groups is important, but equally so is their content, which ranges from the routine to the urgent, from the banal to the extraordinary. Trade associations advise governments on appropriate standards for new products; fishermen's associations complain about inadequate weather forecasting and rescue services on the Pacific and Atlantic coasts; monarchists keep a watchful eye on governmental attitudes towards the Royal Family. Even the more unusual interest group communications are part of the flow of information government needs to exercise its vital functions.

Consider a series of messages delivered to the federal and Ontario governments by the Ontario Federation of Hunters and Anglers and the

Ontario Trappers' Association, among others, concerning the introduction into Canada of an Asian dog known as the coon dog. The dogs had been imported in 1980 by a Madoc, Ontario, fur rancher, who proposed to use their fur as a substitute for raccoon fur. The scheme had received the approval of the Ontario Department of Agriculture and it was only after the animals had arrived that wildlife groups learned that the importation 'had the potential for being the biggest environmental disaster since the introduction of the starling and the carp in the last century'. The coon dog, it appeared, is a voracious hunter of small game and a prolific breeder. Any dogs that escaped from the fur farm could, in a short time, extend their range throughout the eastern provinces and the northeastern United States. Urged on by the wildlife groups, federal authorities acted on two fronts. First, the Export and Import Act was amended to prohibit further importation. Second, after their owners were compensated, the dogs themselves were put down and a potential threat to Ontario wildlife was eliminated.[31]

Despite their variety and the diverse ways in which they are transmitted, interest group communications have two common features. First, they concern the vital interests of the groups engaged in transmitting and receiving them. Second, they are seen by public officials as essential to the business of government. The first makes them valuable to the groups originating them, and renders functional the formation of organizations capable of articulating them to government. The second renders those same groups valuable to government. Without that multi-directional flow of messages, modern government could not respond effectively to its environment, influence that environment, or attempt to create within it an element of order and stability.

Nowhere is this more clearly evident than in the experience of the east coast fishing industry. Here the role of government has steadily expanded, particularly in the period after January 1977 when Canada established the 200-mile limit and in effect undertook to manage the supply of fish to Canadian and foreign concerns. Not only is this resource highly unpredictable, the product of a complex environment we understand only inadequately, and prone to sudden and inexplicable fluctuations; the industry itself is excessively fragmented, technologically diverse, and rent by deep ideological differences. For years federal officials have sought to achieve order within it, to attain a degree of predictability for even minimal planning of stock management. This has been easy enough where the major fish companies have been concerned; they have experts who relate easily to the bureaucratic world of regulation and negotiation and who serve as the technostructure for the industry and government. The companies' trade association, the Fisheries Council of Canada, was for many years the main interest-group contact between the federal Department of Fisheries and the industry. Federal officials assumed that independent fishermen and small fish processors would communicate adequately with government through political parties and provincial governments. As the resource has been depleted, however, and market access has become more problematic, this assumption had to be abandoned. Federal officials sought ways of persuading the 'unorganized' fishermen to build organizations through which they could hear and speak to government.

Romeo LeBlanc, Minister of Fisheries and Oceans in the Trudeau government, pointed out that 'most groups and professions have some means to influence events. But in my first speech as Minister I had to urge fishermen to organize, not just to deal with processors but so we in government could begin to hear their views'.[33] Time and again since the early 1970s, incentives were offered to independent fishermen to organize themselves. When incentives failed, regulatory regimes were established to coerce them into collective decision-making and communication. Using its ability to control access to the resource, the government succeeded in establishing more than 100 stock management committees composed of officials, representatives of major companies, and fishermen chosen through local or association elections. These efforts have helped to improve the day-to-day management of the fishery but have not led to general acceptance of stock management regimes by the industry nor to appropriate and coherent federal policies. The east coast fishery needs a stable environment—consistent regulation, sufficient and predictable catches, orderly exploitation, and secure markets—but without effective communication within the industry, neither industry members nor governments can determine what policies will best secure these objectives, nor can they ensure that members of the industry will respect fisheries policy and make them work. Organization of the diverse interests within the fishery would go far to securing stability; it would facilitate the flow of communication government needs to fully play its role in demand and supply management.[34]

Legitimation

Both interests and government treat groups' ability to proclaim or undermine the legitimacy of the government's measures as important weapons in the policy battle. Interest groups confer legitimacy when they acknowledge and support the work of a particular individual, institution or policy and use their influence with the community at large to extend that support. Government thus finds in the pressure group system a device for testing policy proposals, neutralizing group objections to proposed legislation and engaging support for it. A typical instance occurred in 1983 when the Minister of Consumer and Corporate Affairs attempted to end nearly fifteen years of debate over reform of competition policy by drawing leading business groups into a privileged advisory position. Officials and some two dozen representatives of the Chamber of Commerce, the Business Council on National Issues, and the Canadian Manufacturers' Association met behind closed doors to work out the latest proposals. Consumer groups were pointedly ignored. Their support was not essential to passage of the bill; that of the business groups was. As one newspaper report put it, 'Ottawa has tried six times in the past dozen years to update its competition laws but has failed each time after colliding head-on with business'.[35] This process ultimately gave birth to a policy that appeared to have business endorsement.

Legitimation not only benefits government agencies — which sometimes go so far as to stimulate pressure group activity in order to generate support within the community — but can be used by groups to secure benefits from government, since government recognition enhances their own stature and guarantees a measure of influence over policy decisions that are of concern to them. This symbiotic relationship can help to keep government abreast of changes within the social system as a whole, thereby promoting general political stability.

However, it may also be a source of rigidity. Much depends on the sensitivity of governmental and pressure group sub-systems to changes in their environments and on their willingness to change with them. Through a failure to absorb external demands, closed and captive agencies and groups may compound rigidities existing elsewhere in the system. Quasi-judicial tribunals, such as motor carrier boards or natural product marketing boards, are prone to do this. Because they deal with complex, highly technical matters, they often depend on the information resources of the groups they are meant to control and even — by defining very narrowly the public's right to intervene in regulatory hearings — lose the capacity to assess the broader public interest.[36] Eventually such atrophication can lead to policies that are so clearly self-serving that an offended public repudiates their legitimacy and imposes new rules, new terms of reference, and new decision-making processes on the policy community.

In the field of tax policy, for example, it came to be widely accepted in the early 1980s that the 'closed and secretive' character of tax policy-making had undermined the legitimacy of many measures. When he was appointed Minister of Finance, Michael Wilson heeded the advice of reformers to 'mobilize new support to offset the opposition of aggrieved interests' and established a regular program of consultation with interest groups inside and beyond the traditional circle of advisers on tax policy.[37]

Regulation and administration

Finally, pressure groups frequently act as the agents of government to regulate their members and to administer programs. Their role in the regulation of professional activity is perhaps the best known example of this function. The governing bodies of the professions decide what lawyers, doctors, chartered accountants, engineers and other professionals need to know before they can be allowed to practise.[38] In many cases, they test recruits to the profession and establish periods of probation. They determine some of the conditions that govern the conduct of professionals — lawyers must not solicit business, for example; accountants must observe strict rules when they report the financial affairs of clients — and they discipline those who break the rules, sometimes by dismissing them from the profession. The state permits the professions to exercise this 'private interest government' partly because neither politicians nor administrators feel competent to regulate matters that are often highly technical and complex and partly because our political culture tries to limit the intervention of government in the conduct of economic activity.[39] For these reasons, the community is prepared to entrust a great deal of power to the self-regulating professions, hoping that a sense of public trust will encourage their governing bodies not to abuse authority.*

On many other occasions, the work of interest groups supplements that of government agencies. I have discussed the role charitable associations played in establishing and supporting hospitals and shelters for the poor. As the state assumed the burden of responsibility for these institutions, the role of voluntary organizations declined but did not disappear.[40] Increased state responsibility brought some groups new duties, and even fostered new ones as officials suggested that volunteers might assist them in carrying out their duties. Thus Ontario prison officials encouraged the development of prisoners' aid societies. Again, 'over the whole post-war period . . . voluntary agencies have given considerable (and largely unpaid) service to the government in the reception, welfare, settlement, and adjustment of immigrants'.[41] Many social welfare agencies (such as Children's Aid Societies) provide similar administrative assistance to government.[42] An indication of how extensive this form of 'privatization' of government activities has become appeared in 1982 when the Ontario government, in imposing spending cuts on the public service, insisted that the restraint measures extend to the salaries of individuals working for charitable institutions under contract to the government.[43] In other fields, government and group co-management of programs, though less extensive, has been seen as a means of holding down

---

*Other groups may exercise self-regulation in order to maintain cordial relations with the public and perhaps to forestall government intervention. For example, the Canadian Direct Marketing Association responded to 'constant complaints' by consumers by announcing that its 450 members would be required to remove names from mailing lists on request (*Globe and Mail*, 14 Feb. 1991). Simultaneously the NDP government was telling Ontario farmers that it would impose stringent environmental regulations on the use of herbicides and pesticides if farmers did not regulate their own use of these chemicals (*Globe and Mail*, 6 Feb. 1991).

costs and limiting the extension of bureaucracy. The idea of interest group participation in co-management of the fishery has tantalized policy-makers in the Department of Fisheries and Oceans for some years.[44] The success of the British National Trust has led Parks Canada to assign some aspects of parks management to 'co-operating associations'.[45] The Canadian International Development Agency contracts with non-profit organizations, as well as with private companies, to administer graduate fellowship programs for students from less developed countries and to provide expert support for projects in those countries.[46]

Research and data collection is frequently assigned to interest groups by governments and the interests themselves. The Alberta government's Environmental Trust enables non-government bodies to carry out environmental research. In Ontario, the Canadian Environmental Law Association has been assisted to carry out research into environmental impact assessment, toxic waste disposal, sand and gravel extraction, and other procedures and practices that are in dispute. Such research helps regulatory tribunals and informs legislation.[47] Throughout Canadian industry, associations carry on research activities that aid the public, governments, and industry. The Canadian Home Builders' Association conducts research into energy efficiency. The Canadian Masonry Contractors Association and the Machinery and Equipment Manufacturers' Association of Canada fund research on behalf of government and industry.[48] In the health field, the National Cancer Institute is known to all Canadians for its work in channelling government and private funding to medical research. Less public is the work of the Institute of Public Administration of Canada in supporting research and publication concerned with the management, operations, and conduct of government. The list could go on and on.

The administrative and regulatory functions of pressure groups are less significant than their legitimating and communication functions because they have less impact on the operation of the political system. They are, nevertheless, important in the delivery of government programs — many government functions could not be performed without them — and in the maintenance of economic relations, particularly the relations between professional groups and the community at large. In the climate of government restraint that currently prevails, it is quite possible that these functions will become more important as governments attempt to turn over to the private sector responsibilities and activities that they can no longer afford. If this should prove to be the case, it is also probable that increased responsibilities will bring interest groups increased influence in policy-making.

CONCLUSION

To understand the role and behaviour of pressure groups in our political system, I have assumed that pressure groups behave differently under different political systems even while they perform functions that are similar. This strategy is useful because it helps to avoid the risks of adopting too freely the conclusions about group behaviour reached by students of other systems, while at the same time it helps order information about groups in general and Canadian groups in particular. It suggests the examination of two types of characteristics in pressure group systems: those that are universal and those that seem to vary from country to country, which can be called system-specific. Applying this strategy leads to identifying the critical functions groups perform for their members and for the system at large: interest promotion, communication, legitimation, regulation, and administration.

The first of these is subsystemic in orientation. It is far more immediately important to group members than to the political community as a whole. Nonetheless, interest promotion is the *sine qua non* of pressure group politics, since very few pressure groups would exist at all if group members did not feel a need to combine in order to forward their own interests. While the remaining four functions are of varying significance to group members, they play a vital part in the life of most modern political communities. To the extent that each of these functions is indispensable to a given polity, pressure groups will develop and take the shape peculiar to that specific system. In the Canadian political system, groups perform all four systemic functions, but they generally perform them within the confines of the policy community. Of these, by far the most important for both politics in general and policy communities in particular are the communication and legitimation functions.

CHAPTER 6

Groups In Action: Influencing the Policy Community

Discussion, coercion, and corruption are the means groups use to obtain their goals. How they use these methods depends on their concerns, the resources they have at hand, and the environment surrounding the policy process.

Most pressure group persuasion is carried out through political debate. Briefs are presented to royal commissions, parliamentary committees, tribunals, and officials. Legal arguments dispute the validity of government policy. Placards shout distress, anger, hope, despair. Theatre, film, pantomime, music, and every conceivable kind of tactile art express opinions about government and are aimed, however indirectly, at government.* Books are written; advertisements concocted; speeches rouse multitudes — or leave them indifferent — all in the name of rational discourse.

Threats and promises are implicit in much political debate. Few demonstrators thrusting placards at politicians or shouting into microphones are simply expressing their right to petition. They are also threatening to use the political process to work — and vote — against the party in power unless it accommodates their demands. Even more ominous are the messages contained in the murmur of voices around a boardroom table, the unemotional recitation of a brief or press statement, as the holders of economic power indicate whether or not they will challenge public policy by withholding investment, cutting back production, or eliminating services. The fury that leads protesting fishermen to ransack government offices is less devastating.[1] More commonly, a hint of publicity acts as a powerful solvent for reducing the intransigence of groups and officials who prefer the status quo.

---

*Examples leap to mind. The films of Saul Alinsky. Songs such as 'We shall overcome'. The satiric theatre of Newfoundland's 'CODCO'. Nor are they new inventions. At the end of the eighteenth century the Committee for the Abolition of the Slave Trade persuaded William Cowper to write 'The Negro's Complaint' and Josiah Wedgwood to issue a black and white medallion bearing a kneeling slave in chains and proclaiming 'Am I Not a Man and a Brother'.

When driven, every interest will use whatever tools it can muster to protect its own. Illegal means may not be excluded. It is increasingly common in Canada for groups that feel excluded from political life to explode their frustration through 'monkey wrenching', blockades, and violent demonstrations.[2] Bribery and other forms of corruption may not be common, but they occur more often than Canadians like to believe. There are enough cases on record of the bribery and corruption of public officials for us to assume that on occasion lobbyists do buy policy decisions.[3] This suggests not that everyone who represents interest associations in our capitals is venal or that corruption is a common tool for pressure groups, but that venality and corruption do exist in Canada and can be used to influence public policy.

How group representatives use lobbying tools to sway policy decisions depends on the objectives of the group, the resources at its disposal, and the prevailing conditions at each gateway to the process. For some groups with extensive resources, sure that their views carry weight in policy circles, the polished tactics of traditional lobbying are ideal. They can afford to give 'the best power parties in Ottawa' where 'Cabinet ministers and deputy ministers mingle with captains of industry'. They can afford professional preparation of briefs and other documentation demanded by our increasingly bureaucratized policy process, as well as the costs of litigation or appearances before regulatory bodies. If necessary, they can pay for campaigns of mass persuasion. For other groups access to the policy process — even at the local level — is hard to obtain because they do not understand the bureaucratic ways of policy-makers, because the trappings of democracy are beyond their means, or because their plight is too banal to stir a flicker of interest among crusading journalists.

Within the range of these extremes, groups seize on the policy system where and how they can, struggling to insert their claims in hopes of satisfying their demands and interests. I will look at this struggle from the vantage point of the policy community concept, first exploring the relationship most significant to the group — that between it and the lead agency. I will then consider how the amorphous and elusive ties that hold together the sub-government influence the way groups in the sub-government behave towards one another. Next I will look at a lively, though not powerful, part of the policy community, the attentive public, and try to assess how it relates to the core members. In the next chapter I will begin by asking how, when, and why groups bring their messages to the general public. I will also look briefly at the role of other governments in pressure group politics and will glance at the increasing use groups are making of the judicial system.

INFLUENCING THE POLICY COMMUNITY

The ascendancy of the policy community is a relatively new phenomenon, growing out of the decline of bureaucratic influence and the subsequent search for legitimation. To achieve their goals, public officials must now build support in the policy community and win the approval of those other government agencies, pressure groups, corporations, institutions, and individuals with an explicit concern in the policy field. Departments foster constant contact with their 'clientele'—sounding public opinion and obtaining new ideas. Usually this is done by building on relations with organized groups or specific interests concerned with the work of the agency. If interest groups do not exist, departments encourage their formation.

With this reciprocal relationship comes a growth in the complexity and number of ties that bind the various players in the community. Forty years ago, lobbying and government were much less complicated. David Kirk, an official of the Canadian Federation of Agriculture, recalls that it was possible 'to work with just one minister and department. Policy recommendations would come up through the department; the minister would decide what he wanted to do; then he would take his proposals to Cabinet'.[4] Action would be authorized with a minimum of fuss. Interdepartmental committees would not haver forever over the pros and cons of alternative options. If the minister was obstructive, there would be little mystery about the reasons why, and it would be fairly clear whether ministerial lobbying would overcome the problem. Today lobbyists know that persuading key officials, or even ministers, will not suffice, since these apparently powerful personages will seldom act without receiving clear signals from other interested parties that they too support the proposed changes in policy. This does not mean that politicians avoid involvement in the selection of policy options; but it does reflect the fact that 'Cabinet ministers are in general enormously over-extended and do not have adequate time to devote to any single special interest, unless it happens to be central to the management of the portfolio'.[5] They are forced to rely on their officials.

In most cases, the only alternative opinions available to the minister come from affected interest groups:

These are primary constituencies. Their backing is often essential to maintaining ministerial clout within Cabinet, even of surviving on the job. Their support in the implementation of programs and policies is usually important. A minister who loses the confidence of his primary constituency is in trouble. You can quickly read in the political columns the impending political mortality of a minister who has lost that support. The primary constituency is also a minister's principal alternative source of information for his department. Any minister who decides he can run a department on the basis of the advice he gets from his bureaucrats is bound to be in trouble. Not because the advice from bureaucrats is mischievous or malevolent or badly thought out, but because it represents a particular point of view; and in a world where the public agenda is increasingly broad, a single source of information, a single point of view, can no longer be relied upon.... The primary constituency ... provides a minister with grass-roots feed-back on issues and the concerns of its membership. So political heads of agencies need very good communications with that primary constituency to provide intelligence on what programs are working and on how they are working. They need their views on what policies should be changed. In short, they depend on the primary constituency as a source of policy countervail to departmental advice.[6]

Officials, aware that the ministers see key interest groups as a countervailing force, also consult them and attempt to win their support in campaigns for the policies and programs favoured by departments and agencies.

The competition for support on policy issues exacerbates tendencies towards bureaucratic forms of communication. Senior agency officials, however well informed, will want supporting documents from the subordinates who will be responsible for implementing decisions. They know that decisions taken without that support will be carried out half-heartedly at best. Junior officials who are deeply opposed may sabotage the policy or initiate a bitter public debate led by their affiliates in the policy community. Consequently, subordinates have to be brought 'on side' by being given a lead role in developing an appropriate policy analysis and in generating support within the policy community. To generate that support, other units, agencies, individuals, and groups must be consulted, committees established, and both the unit and the group advocating the change of policy must spend a great deal of time and effort explaining their proposal and then reshaping it into a form that is acceptable to the key actors in the community. What was once a straightforward process involving only a handful of individuals has become a highly bureaucratic one, demanding the time and talents of many.

Because the policy community works in this bureaucratic fashion, a group wishing to be influential in it (i.e., to be part of the sub-government) must share some of the attributes of bureaucracy. Power — the ability to control the flow of human, material, or financial resources to the sector — may enable the group to have a say in policy development, but the impact of that contribution will depend on how well the group understands and exploits its strategic position in the policy community. Access to decision centres, a strategic place in the information flow, and the possession of technical expertise are also essential. Expert knowledge of the policy field is valuable, particularly if the group holds a monopoly or near-monopoly on vital information. Such information can be exchanged for access to decision-makers and for a continuing place in the information flow, such as group representation on advisory committees or automatic inclusion in technical conferences and consultative exercises. Access to key decision-makers denotes more than recognition. It is an acknowledgement of power in the community, of the possession of vital information, and/or the ability to persuade others to support or abandon a cause. Above all, it is an acknowledgement of the group's familiarity with the policy process and its ability to deal with a bureaucratic structure and to share bureaucratic values, such as a high regard for accurate information and rational decision-making.

To influence its policy community, a group must be prepared to deploy its lobbying activities in four different directions. The most important target will be the sub-government. For the group's purposes, this is made up of three targets that function separately and must be approached differently: the political executive and its supporting agencies; the lead agency itself; and the other groups and agencies that are regularly consulted in the formation of government policy. Finally, from time to time the group will have to address the entire policy community, including the attentive public.

The executive

Most established groups prefer not to take action-oriented messages to the Cabinet and the central agencies. To do so would be to admit that they had failed to reach agreement within the policy community and, in effect, are breaking ranks with the other members of the community. Invoking the superior authority of the political executive disturbs the balance of power within the policy community. Even if it achieves its purpose, it does so at the cost of good will and smooth working relations with their immediate associates.

There are two even more important reasons for many groups not to appeal to the centre. First, they want to avoid Cabinet interference. Cabinet — particularly the inner Cabinet — occupies the overview position in the government. It is responsible for overriding the self-regarding tendencies of departments and their allies, for finding ways of co-ordinating the policies and programs of individual agencies, and for ensuring that issues that have been organized out of politics are pushed back in. These responsibilities are often pushed aside by Cabinet workloads and the natural tendency of ministers to defend their own departments by not encroaching on others'. However, since major reforms were made to the central policy structures during the Trudeau years, officials in the Privy Council Office, the Treasury Board, the Prime Minister's Office, and Finance have frequently assumed the task of representing Cabinet's co-ordinative and monitoring roles. Their many interventions during the 1970s earned them the dislike and bitter opposition of line agencies and their allies, who became determined to contain issues within the policy community and to reduce the central agencies' influence.[7]

This determination is given a further edge by the second reason for avoiding the involvement of the political executive: groups have discovered that an appeal to the centre may force them to engage in public debate. The agenda of Cabinet and its committees is so constrained that only a few issues inherently and obviously of national importance find their way automatically to Cabinet consideration. The majority have to fight for a place on the agenda, usually by attracting the kind of media attention that persuades Cabinet ministers that the public is concerned and wants policy decisions. This kind of publicity attracts the interest of opponents as well as the support of friends.

Nevertheless, circumstances often force issues into Cabinet's purview — as in 1985 when the failure of two regional banks precipitated a major review of bank regulation and inspection. On such occasions, groups must contend with the mysteries of central decision-making. This is when the maintenance of offices in the federal and provincial capitals pays off. Since access to Cabinet is virtually impossible to obtain, groups must focus their attention on the officials of the central policy structures and aides of influential ministers. Groups whose staff are familiar with the workings of the central agencies and know their officials have a considerable advantage. Familiarity with the policy review process gives them a sense of when to inject supporting information and whether, when, and where to apply pressure, as well as the ability to monitor discussions at the centre and to use personal connections to communicate group concerns to officials. Some may be able to brief key ministers. Groups that do not have staff members who are able to achieve this level of access — and they are probably the great majority, even among members of the various sub-governments — must use the services of the many legal and consulting firms who specialize in this type of lobbying. Described as 'door openers for the lobbying trade', firms like Executive Consultants Limited will, for a sizeable monthly retainer, advise clients about which people to see and what to say.[8] Groups that are not affluent enough to pay for professional lobbying must depend on the pressure tactics we described earlier: communicating with MPs; asking friends and members with influence to intercede on their behalf with Cabinet members; and party officials; writing to Cabinet members; and generally trying to create the impression that the public at large supports their cause.

Influential members of policy communities are chary of taking action-oriented messages to the centre, but they treat the delivery of legitimating messages — messages that convey acceptance and support — as a mark of recognition, a telling point in the game of positional politics. Groups with particular influence — either because they represent a broad cross-section of the community or because they can command extensive economic resources — frequently have access to Cabinets and from time to time make formal presentations to them. For many years it was a tradition that the Canadian Federation of Agriculture, the Canadian Labour Congress, and business groups such as the Canadian Manufacturers' Association annually presented the federal Cabinet with briefs on the current state of government policy in fields concerning them and urged the executive to further measures that each group favoured. Some of the positions put forward in these briefs were 'ritual demands' — demands that the leadership and the politicians knew could not be met and followed up — that were presented as tokens of the group's long-term commitment to certain goals. Others, however, signalled to the executive the group's current policy agenda. These 'serious demands' were related to the group's mandate, its privileges and prerogatives, and other matters affecting the organizational integrity of the group, as well as to major current issues.[9]

As the proliferation of pressure groups has made it more and more difficult for the federal government to appear to favour even very broadly based specific groups, the tradition of the Cabinet briefing has been discouraged and major groups have had to be content with influencing those they hope will influence the Cabinet.[10] By 1980 a representative of the Canadian Farmers' Association reported that 'in recent years' his organization had made presentations to the several federal caucuses rather than to Cabinet.[11] In the provinces, where such meetings still continue and may be more numerous, group briefs may be concerned with immediate issues and problems.

Groups reluctant to take specific concerns to the Cabinet level make an exception in the case of 'their' minister. The minister responsible for the community's lead agency is generally expected to be sympathetic to the community's concerns and to speak for them in Cabinet. Self-interest accounts for this. The community's successes tend to cast the minister in a favourable light; its failures nearly always find political expression, and unless handled adroitly, they can undermine a promising ministerial career.

The policy process itself also enables interests to develop friendly relations with their minister. He or she is in constant contact with the lead agency and its clients and depends on it for an introduction into the details of the community's concerns. Inevitably an element of indoctrination creeps into what is already a mutually dependent relationship, but the process has the advantage of making the minister a member of the community — a person with whom it is possible to discuss issues that many members would not discuss with anyone outside the community. This relationship should enhance the minister's understanding and capacity to lead and to represent.

Finally, the policy process puts the minister in a position to arbitrate between officials and private sector members of the community.[12] The working relationship that makes possible the arbitrator's role, and gives the community the link it needs with the political executive, is developed and maintained in a variety of ways. Community members generally have freer access to the minister than do non-members. Consultations may take place fairly frequently. Some ministers like to meet regularly with a small group of trusted advisers, some of whom will be members of the community. Symbolic appearances — official openings, presentations, key-note, and after-dinner speeches — are important and numerous, not because of what is said in public, but because they sustain acquaintanceships, permit brief confabulations, and remind the minister of the group's work, influence, and interests. They also have positional importance. The Canadian Club of Toronto takes pride in the fact that, since Donald Fleming addressed its members in 1958, it has played host to every Minister of Finance. The event reinforces the group's image as a gathering of the business élite and, not incidentally, permits a few of those who attend to exchange some words with the minister. In a succession of days crowded with events of this sort, ministers establish their affinity with the community, take its pulse, and connect it to the Cabinet and the larger political scene.

The lead agency

The bureaucratic nature of the policy community is reinforced by the fact that government agencies sit at their centre. Even though agencies may not dominate their relations with groups as easily as they once did, they are still very powerful. Their capacity to dictate terms has diminished, but not evaporated. To work with agencies, interest groups must organize themselves in similar fashion and, to some extent, must abide by the norms of consultation preferred by them. This is particularly true of the relations with the lead agency and, where their authority is significant, the regulatory boards and commissions in the policy community.

The group begins to adapt to the structure of the target agency as soon as it decides to attempt to influence the bureaucracy. To wield influence, the group must become familiar with the agency's institutional framework. It must know who in the organization deals with what issues and how much weight their advice carries, who their rivals are and how likely they are to attack. The group must also have an intimate knowledge of the programs administered by the agency, a thorough understanding of how they work, how they affect the public, their shortcomings and benefits, and whether or not they come close to meeting the objectives set out for them. To accomplish this, the group must have professional staff or volunteers who are familiar with both the institutional framework for policy development and delivery and the pattern of thought the agency applies to the policy field. Often groups will organize themselves to mirror the structure of the agency and its chief affiliates. They will hire professionals to maintain a continuing liaison with those parts of the agency whose work is vital to them; they will organize members' committees to evaluate the information derived from monitoring, and to respond to initiatives from the agency and related groups.

A budget prepared by the Social Sciences Federation of Canada gives an idea of what is involved:

> A sizeable portion of the Federation's staff, elected officers' and members' time is devoted to liaising with government departments and agencies. The work accomplished in this area by members and elected officers is considerable, but obviously very difficult to quantify. It is possible, however, to give an indication of the nature and scope of the Federation's staff involvement. During the course of the past year, the Executive Director and/or the professional staff have had ten meetings with MPs and ministers, more than twenty with senior civil servants, thirty with SSHRC's committees or members of staff and a dozen with representatives of other Councils or agencies (Science Council, National Science and Engineering Research Council, Economic Council, etc.). In addition, a substantial amount of correspondence is carried out with various departments on topics which concern the academic community.[13]

In support of this work and as part of it, the Federation prepared and distributed a number of discussion papers, briefs, and reports; conducted several task forces; reviewed the work of a consultative exercise on the strategic concerns of its member organizations; and attempted to monitor and react to the policy initiatives and legislative program of the Mulroney government. The Federation also maintained up-to-date databases on current and projected legislation and departmental programs of concern to social scientists, and similarly current lists of elected officials, public servants, university officials, and members. It also developed departmental profiles for the five federal departments with which it was most regularly involved: Secretary of State, Health and Welfare, Solicitor General, Environment, and Communications. Its 'public awareness' program and special programs for members were additions to these activities. It is hardly surprising that even a modest interest group like the SSFC becomes a complex organization.

These developments occur over organizational space. Staff is added and new units are created as the group's work evolves to keep pace with government initiatives. Frequently the interest group's development takes place over physical space as well. Groups first established at the provincial level, often in only one or two provinces, have frequently moved their headquarters to Ottawa or set up a major office there, and have had to establish a physical presence in each of the provinces. This reflects the tendency for groups across the country to recognize their common concerns and to merge provincial organizations into federated ones able to speak with a national voice.* It also reflects the expanded role of government. Organizations that at the end of the Second World War existed only at the provincial

---

*The Canadian Chamber of Commerce was one of the first and most prominent of these. Originating in numerous boards of trade created by local business communities during the nineteenth century, it has grown into a national organization representing 165,000

level found that in the next quarter-century the expansion and interpenetration of federal and provincial responsibilities necessitated their presence at the federal level as well. Without it, they were unable to maintain a continuous liaison with the federal officials whose decisions were crucial to group members.

This was the experience of the Canadian Trucking Association, which in the 1950s was a loose confederation of provincial associations. A series of court decisions recognizing Ottawa's constitutional role in interprovincial highway regulation, together with the federal government's Trans-Canada Highway program — which made a national trucking network feasible — drew the federal government into a more prominent and authoritative position in the policy community concerned with motor vehicle transportation. Ultimately the Canadian Trucking Association strengthened its national organization and built up a major office in Ottawa.[14]

At least one Canadian academic society, the Canadian Political Science Association, followed a similar route. Until the late 1960s the CPSA's 'head office' was located at whichever university employed the organization's part-time secretary-treasurer. By the mid-1970s, the association's involvement with federal programs in support of national academic associations and the publication of learned journals had forced a change in policy: head office had to be located at one of the two Ottawa universities. There the association, which still has a part-time secretary-treasurer but employs several administrators, can participate readily in the numerous committees and consultative activities organized by the Social Sciences Federation of Canada to lobby federal agencies, particularly the Social Sciences and Humanities Research Council of Canada and the Secretary of State.

The experience of these, among many, national organizations suggests that the growth of government activity has fostered a concurrent physical centralization of interest groups, drawing them into an increasingly bureaucratized policy community. Perhaps physical centralization has also reinforced bureaucratization of the policy community, facilitating as it does committee interaction between groups and agencies and fostering the extensive consultation that is a hallmark of politics in modern policy communities.

The bureaucratic influence of the key agency does not end there. Most agencies will want affiliate groups to accept their own bureaucratic mores, including a high regard for bureaucratic modes of communication. A good deal of emphasis will be placed on formal research and analysis of policy options, and on written presentation of group positions. Above all, they will want to ensure that the groups will have little resort to publicity — unless, of

businesses in 500 centres and operating offices in Ottawa and most of the provincial capitals. *Financial Post*, 2 Feb. 1985.

course, it promotes the legitimacy of the community and its dominant policies — and even less resort to confrontation. As Tom d'Aquino, president of the Business Council on National Issues, puts it: 'Most businessmen avoid confrontation and are uncomfortable promoting causes on public platforms . . . and there is the further underlying concern that high visibility can attract reprisals from either government or labour'.[15]

In the 1970s, Canadians became aware of how influential the bureaucracy had become. The widespread realization that in agency-group relations the agency tends to dominate[16] fostered a small mythology of bureaucratic behaviour. An article in the September 1980 issue of *Canadian Business* describes some of the perceptions many interest group representatives developed of the lead agencies in their policy field, and indicates some of the strategies deployed to deal with them. Entitled 'Getting Your Way With a Bureaucrat', its subtitle suggests a power relationship in which the official calls the shots: 'Show respect. Be patient. Take him seriously. Sounds easy, but a lot of businessmen don't know how to get to first base'.[17] According to author Larry Smith, a consulting economist with experience as a federal civil servant,

> The need for business to be able to defend its interests before the civil service has never been greater. But many business representatives not only fail to advance their causes, but actually antagonize the very persons they wish to influence. The ineptness that many lobbyists bring to their relationships with the civil service arises from a single source — their failure to understand the bureaucracy's aims and the way it works. The bureaucracy is not, as too many business people tend to regard it, some inscrutable mandarinate out to thwart the legitimate ends of the free enterprise system. It is a collection of for the most part reasonably principled and reasonably intelligent civil servants who can be swayed by reasonable discourse.[18]

To get their way, lobbyists were urged to adopt a set of procedures that reflected a shrewd understanding of how human foibles and motivations affect the operations of bureaucracy. The bureaucratic machine lives on information. It demands raw data from those it serves and sophisticated analyses from those who want to influence it. It is also complex and slow-moving. Decisions, rather than being made quickly by an individual, are generally the product of internal consultation and often reflect the public service's mandate to defend the public interest.

These rationalistic aspects of bureaucracy intimidate many, who come to resent and fear the quest for information. They see the need for formal analysis and the complexity and slow pace of decision-making as an encumbrance. However, the mingling of these classic attributes of bureaucracy with people's everyday need to advance and take satisfaction in their work offers the experienced lobbyist an opportunity to exercise influence. Smith's message is that civil servants are human, 'reasonably competent and conscientious'. They are even 'susceptible to the most basic bargaining techniques'. The artfully prepared brief has greater impact if it is presented 'by someone the civil servant knows and may already have co-operated with. That circumstance alone guarantees a reading, which is the first, most critical step in advancing your case'.[19] The request for information may be an opportunity to establish a contact and to do a favour. Respect for the civil servant's expertise and concern for the public interest builds trust that may be important in future bargaining sessions. Smith also argues that 'when you are dealing with a complex organization, it is futile to try to impose simplicity where none exists. But handled knowledgeably, the very complexity of the bureaucracy can work to your advantage.' People who complain that 'I cannot find the right person to talk to; everyone refers me to someone else' are turning an opportunity into a problem:

> it is a mistake to take the absence of a single channel of responsibility as a vice; it is an outright virtue. If you are lobbying for a cause down a single pathway, a turn-down becomes a rejection without recourse or appeal. In the more tightly structured private sector, one imbecile often has the power to bring an entire line of activity to a complete halt. But in the civil service, where responsibility is diffused, any particular refusal need be only a roadblock around which it is possible to manoeuvre. The likelihood of ultimate success grows in direct proportion to the number of avenues of pursuit.

Aware that no single, knowledgeable official can navigate 'the dark labyrinths of the mandarinate', the effective lobbyist obtains referrals from one civil servant to another in an effort 'to get each of them involved in your problem'. Furthermore, the canny lobbyist does not simply generate lists of names:

> in your initial conversations with any civil servant, find out exactly what he does. Then try to find something about your problem that fits his bailiwick. Consider, for example, a company seeking support to make an investment in a new plant. Each of the following aspects of the question involves *different* civil servants: job creation in general; job creation for a specific region; job creation for a minority; export stimulation; import substitution; improvement in the competitiveness of the market; enhancement of research and development; environmental improvement; and national unity. And that is a short list, any aspect of which may make the critical difference for obtaining a favourable hearing. Broader lobbying causes, of course, involve an even wider range of possibilities.

Like much sophisticated advice, these suggestions over-simplify the world of policy formation and present too optimistic an account of the benefits to be derived from Machiavellian manipulation. Nevertheless they give us a glimpse of how lobbyists work with the public service and a sense of the rules they often apply. We can condense those rules into four basic strategies.

First, even though the lobbyist may want to exploit the complexity of the bureaucracy, it is essential to have a very clear idea of what the lobby group wants. Bureaucracy has its own rationality. It divides the world into innumerable activities, which it approaches separately. The group that does not know its own mind may find itself queuing at the wrong wicket, wasting resources in attempts to influence officials who themselves are unable to affect the policies that are of greatest concern to the group.

The group that does know its own mind is able to exploit the complexity of the bureaucracy and to apply the second rule in the lobbyist's operational guidebook, which is to know and understand its target. This enables it to look ahead, identify the agencies it is most likely to deal with, and become familiar with their policies, their programs, and, above all, their problems. This is necessary because working with government is a process of collective bargaining. A group may be able to negotiate modifications in the policy it is concerned about in exchange for support — in the policy community, with other agencies, or with the public — for the agency's pet policy. Alternatively, it may be able to barter information or administrative facilities for policy concessions, financial assistance, or a position in the sub-government.

Professional lobbyists also get to know the agency's organizational structure and the people who work in it. Some call this 'creative loitering'. With a knowledge of structure, lobbyists can identify who decides what. By working on the assumption that the best way to stop an adverse decision is never to let it be born, they can familiarize officials with the group's point of view and assess their attitudes towards it. If a cordial relationship has been created, the lobbyist may also obtain advance warning of policy reviews and the guarantee of an opportunity for input at the right time. Obviously a sense of timing is important.[20] Lobbyists know that addressing an issue too soon may be as dangerous as reacting to it too late. Being over-eager may waste group resources and irritate policy-makers, and may even precipitate the very discussion that the lobbyist hoped to avoid. Lobbyists also learn how to use the budget cycle to put forward proposals and develop a sixth sense about the issues they should leave alone, those they should monitor, and those that demand immediate and decisive action.

Such strategies virtually compel the lobbyist to become professional, working full-time towards understanding the bureaucracy and attempting to influence it. Being professional is, in fact, the third rule of lobbying, one of the mores that the bureaucracy imposes on its relations with groups. Officials and senior politicians deal with groups continuously and are not impressed by tantrums. As one community activist puts it, 'don't wing it — and don't whine. Don't make outrageous demands, or back government people into corners. Do your homework'.[21] Nor do they tolerate poor organization and amateurish presentations. They expect groups to make the best use of their time. They prefer to read briefs that are crisp, well documented, and effectively organized, culminating in recommendations that are clearly set out and take account of the changes in programs that would be caused by changes in policy. They like group representatives to be well organized in their oral presentations with their facts at their fingertips. They do not like the group's supporters to become abusive and 'physical' — to get out of hand.

The sanctions against confrontation present many groups with a fundamental question: should we try to embarrass policy-makers and expand our public support by criticism in the media, or is it better to work quietly behind the scenes and forsake a public image? Many groups formulate a fourth, and final, guide to action: avoid confrontation, but remember that sometimes it is necessary to embarrass politicians and officials. In all situations, it is important to avoid strident exposure that alienates them permanently and may antagonize the public as well. In the words of one activist:

> Avoid confrontation, but don't ignore its potential. Better to be seen as a lion than as a pussy cat! Confrontation — like the theatre that it strongly resembles — can generate emotions, rousing passions, touching people at their deepest levels, stimulating a catharsis. If the media are present they magnify and transmit the images to thousands of people. But confrontation is a two-edged sword: it can ruin an organization's credibility as well as enhancing it. Use it at specific times, to achieve specific goals (media coverage, mobilization of interest, to reach politicians who have ceased to listen). Plan confrontation so that it is effective in achieving these goals, and keep it under control.[22]

It is equally important to avoid boxing in policy-makers. They must have an 'out', a compromise that will allow them to save face and permit them to maintain an equable relationship with the group in the future.

This list of lobbyists' informal rules underlines the significant role of the bureaucracy in policy formation, and the extent to which its characteristics colour the policy community. It also emphasizes the inequalities groups face in the policy process. In 1985-6, the Social Sciences Federation of Canada budgeted over $300,000 for representing the concerns of its members and for fostering 'a greater and more positive awareness of the social sciences'.[23] The SSFC is not a wealthy organization. The Consumers' Association of Canada was reported in 1980 to have revenues of $1.7 million, derived from federal grants and from its 145,000 members. It too is considered a 'brown bagger in the lobbying crowd'.[24] In contrast, the Canadian Nuclear Association budgeted $2,644,000 for its 1987 public information program and $4,260,000 in 1988.[25] Such comparisons underline the handicaps that encumber groups with small resources — particularly groups attempting to represent the poor and disadvantaged — that cannot work easily in a bureaucratic environment. Their capacity to help make policy is limited.

Some observers argue that these disparities are not as debilitating to such groups as they might seem, and that citizen commitment and energy can overcome the gap between their resources and those of major interests.[26] These observers fail to take into account the bureaucratic nature of the policy process and its tendency to require repeated infusions of energy and other resources. A major lobbying campaign by the academic scientific community is a case in point. The culmination of months of planning by a number of associations,[27] the campaign involved identifying the attitudes of politicians and the agencies many science academics were associated with. The politicians and agencies were assigned selected volunteers representating the scientific community. Buttressed with carefully researched fact sheets and position papers, group and individual meetings in 1978 achieved some success, but by 1981 much of the work had to be done again. A second visit in December 1980 revealed that:

> The average MP is much better informed on [research and development] than in 1978, but the absence of large scale lobbying by us during the two years of musical chairs in Ottawa has taken its toll. Even some of our old allies in the House now need updating and re-educating to a considerable extent. . . .
>
> As of December 11th, the short term picture for research seems bleak. . . . The only factors which might influence [it] are the lobby just held, the next lobby in March, and resistance from presidents . . . of the granting councils.[28]

It was clear that continued effort was necessary to keep the scientific community's needs before decision-makers. The lobbying coalition developed a long-term strategy that involved supplying MPs with questions for question period; being prepared to respond immediately to budget decisions; and extending the canvass of MPs and ministers to senior civil servants and media leaders. All this was in addition to the normal round of lobbying conducted by most of the organizations participating in the coalition. The campaign continues today. If a lobby engaging the kind of effort just described could achieve such tenuous results, how much greater are the odds facing groups whose resources are even more limited?

The sub-government

Apart from its concern for promoting its influence with the lead agency, two factors are paramount in a group's relations with other members of the sub-government. The first is position. The second is co-operation.

Status, recognition, and position are essential to being consulted. Securing a recognized position in the sub-government is a first priority for any group intending to exert continuing influence on policy.[29] For many, this involves continual struggle and competition. The National Farmers' Union, which has a reputation for radical farm politics, has never been able to join the Canadian Federation of Agriculture in its privileged position in the agricultural policy community.[30] Other groups, however, gain recognition from their work, or else their status was earned so long ago that it is no longer questioned. The Canadian Bankers' Association and the Canadian Tax Foundation, for example, are confirmed members of the policy community that regularly discusses fiscal policy with the Department of Finance. The Canadian Federation of Independent Business (CFIB) and the Business Council on National Issues (BCNI) were created only in the 1970s and have had to earn a consultative position in the community concerned with the economy. The CFIB mounted a flamboyant, belligerent publicity campaign that asserted the right of small business to be heard. The BCNI was equally flamboyant, but deliberately conveyed the impression that an organization speaking for the wealthiest corporations in the country would automatically have a seat in the councils of the mighty.[31]

Once they have survived the first round in the game of positional politics, groups tend to become less vocal, less inclined to invoke public opinion. Problems of legitimacy give way to problems of communication. Instead of clamouring to be consulted, they are hounded for advice. When governments and their agencies decide that specific groups speak for a significant part of the population and that their views are legitimate, they turn to them frequently, inviting them to sit on advisory committees and consulting them on issues far afield from the immediate concerns of the groups themselves. Responding to these overtures takes considerable effort. Membership opinion may have to be elicited, or specialized knowledge tapped. More frequently, the organization may have to dedicate the time of its research staff to the government's question, diverting it from tasks more important to the group and its members. Even participation on advisory boards can siphon off valuable executive time.[32]

Despite these problems, groups hesitate to turn down invitations to advise and participate. Participation helps maintain the organization's position as an integral part of the policy community; taps it into the information flow; guarantees consultation on issues of real concern to the group; and provides opportunities for group representatives to form personal links with civil servants, leaders of other groups, and sometimes senior politicians. The cost of participation is the price the group pays for acceptance as a full-fledged member of the policy community.

Monitoring is an important aspect of any established group's relationship with its policy community, and particularly with the key agencies. Being a part of the information flow and establishing friendly ties with the representatives of other groups help the group keep abreast of opinion in influential circles, enabling it to anticipate proposals for policy change, and thus to react and adapt to them. Informal ties, and even a prominent place in the community, do not in themselves guarantee adequate monitoring of trends in public opinion and government thinking. It is often necessary to introduce more systematic monitoring devices, such as clipping and analysing the general and specialized press; scrutinizing government policy, proposed legislation, and policy reviews in related fields; following academic discussions that have a bearing on the policy field; and even commissioning research into emergent issues. Often groups will themselves organize seminars, workshops, and conferences whose major function is to engage in forecasting activities — summing up the results of current monitoring activities and extrapolating from them.

Position confers the privilege of consultation and of access to strategic information, both of which facilitate the process of bringing influence to bear. These privileges reconcile group members of the sub-government to the bureaucracy's norms. Indeed, these norms are not necessarily distasteful to groups that have worked their way to the sub-government. While competition and conflict are a part of group efforts to secure the support of public opinion and to influence the political and administrative executive, a search for consensus is an even more important part of the life of the sub-governments. Those with a vested interest in established policy prefer to maintain its stability by 'organizing issues out of politics' and restricting discussion to their own narrowly defined special public. Maintaining consensus within the sub-government helps to achieve that end.[33] But consensus, as much as the predilections of officials, imposes norms and sanctions on group behaviour — particularly norms and sanctions of discretion and confidentiality.

This preoccupation with keeping issues out of politics is related to the tendency to co-operate — the second feature of sub-government relations that concerns most of its members. For as long as organized groups have existed to influence government, they have allied themselves with other groups. There are several reasons for this. First, they promote stable relations between groups. As Kwavnick puts it: 'To leave a group outside the circle of accepted groups is to invite its leaders to adopt unorthodox tactics, to make exaggerated demands, and, generally, to be a disruptive and uncertain element'.[34] Second, alliances strengthen group credibility. Third, they broaden the base of support and increase the resources available to specific groups. Fourth, they reflect the communal nature of policy-making. Most members of the sub-government are aware that they will have to live with one another in the future. Tomorrow they may have to ally themselves with the groups they are tempted to revile today. There is therefore an incentive not only to reach compromises and to exercise restraint and civility, but to act together.

At the turn of the century, for example, those who supported 'votes for women' often found themselves working with temperance groups. In 1916, the president of the Saskatchewan Grain Growers' Association, which like many western farmers' groups was strongly prohibitionist, wrote to the Acting Premier, J.A. Calder: 'I am instructed by the executive...to memorialize you stating that the body sincerely hopes that provision may be made fully enfranchising the women of Saskatchewan so that they may vote in December next on the referendum on the liquor question.' Though the biographer of the Canadian women's suffrage movement wryly comments that 'the evidence reinforces the hypothesis that women received the vote primarily because they represented puritanical, moralistic values and not because of the growth of genuine sentiment in favor of sexual equality', the fact remains that it was through a succession of alliances of this sort that women in all the provinces influenced public opinion — and ultimately governments — to the point where they won the right to vote.[35]

Such alliances are often entered into with misgivings. In the early years of the suffrage movement many prohibitionists felt that their association with the suffragists offended many who might otherwise have supported the temperance cause. Later, as the narrow focus of the rural-based temperance movement became a liability in an increasingly urban country, the suffragists came to doubt the wisdom of aligning their cause with one that was considered less and less relevant to modern needs.[36] Nevertheless, for a crucial period at the turn of the century the alliance was a great help to the suffragists:

> The connection between prohibition and woman suffrage, like the connection with the social gospel, contributed to the esteem of the woman's movement and to the eventual suffrage victory. The temperance reformers remained a powerful group in early-twentieth century Canada and their endorsement undoubtedly aided the women politically. The close alliance between the WCTU and the suffragists and the actual overlap in the two memberships also convinced the men in power that the suffragists were really quite an inoffensive group. Woman suffrage ceased to alarm.[37]

While the struggle for women's suffrage is uncharacteristic of sub-government behaviour, in that the issue was taken to the general public, it nevertheless illustrates the advantages of co-operation. For the suffrage movement, the alliance with the temperance movement, at least in the early days, brought access to leaders of religious groups and others who regularly influenced government policy concerned with moral issues. Elite sub-government support of that kind made an impression on politicians. In the more public aspects of the struggle, the mass support for the temperance movement was to some extent transferable to the initially less popular suffrage cause. More commonly, co-operation between members of the sub-government will present opportunities for making joint approaches to policy-makers, reinforcing each other's influence, forestalling challenges to the authority of the sub-government, and trading off benefits between groups. Co-operation, in short, is an essential tool for maintaining the hegemony of the sub-government.

A group's relations with other members of the sub-government is seldom defined explicitly. Admission to the circle of sub-government members is a recognition of a group's policy capacity. It can use the same levers to obtain concessions from officials, politicians, and other members that other key groups and agencies can use. It can regulate the flow of information to government and the public, secure the success or failure of government programs, and confer legitimacy on public policies. Consciously and unconsciously the group exploits these attributes to form alliances, win support, oppose rivals, and try to crush the pretensions of groups that would like to supplant it. As in most élite groups, however, real influence is maintained in a more subtle manner. The sub-government is a spontaneous social phenomenon formed because its members share a power relationship with a government agency. Over time, recognition of mutual interests and the habit of working together lead to the evolution of a more or less cohesive social organization that is maintained through an informal web of mores, norms, and sanctions. Admission to the sub-government sets up a reciprocal relationship in which the privileges of membership are conferred and the leaders of the newly accepted group 'become susceptible to socialization into the mores and modes of behaviour appropriate to interest group leaders'.[38] The most important aspects of this socialization have to do with positional politics and with maintaining stability.

> By recognizing the mandate of a group, the leaders of other groups provide themselves with someone with whom they can bargain. At the same time they reduce the possibility of another group developing to represent the same interest. Such a group might attempt to consolidate its position among the membership by means of a radical or uncompromising stance or by use of rash tactics, either of which could only hurt all interest-group leaders.
>
> The recognition of the mandate of the group and its leaders by those outside the group, by government and by the leaders of other interest groups is advantageous for both sides since they are both interested in assuring that the equilibrium is not unduly disturbed. So great is the desire for stability that although 'an organized alternative leadership is almost always absent, when it appears, the Government usually refuses to deal with it anyway'.[39]

In the processes of intergroup bargaining, however, these norms are a powerful instrument, not only for those within the sub-government anxious to maintain stability, but also for those who are bargaining with them. Because these norms exist, the threat of publicity becomes the ultimate weapon and a powerful incentive for securing accommodation within the sub-government. Like confrontation, with which it is closely associated, publicity is a bargaining technique that must be used with care. It is also an important element in the uneasy relationship between the sub-government and the policy community's attentive public.

The attentive public

The attentive public is the lively part of the policy community. It does not share the privileges of access and does not necessarily have a vested interest in keeping issues out of politics. In fact, many of its members are excluded from power and influence and see public debate as one way of obtaining them. They are therefore prepared to challenge the status quo and are less inclined to accept the norms with which sub-government members are comfortable. As a result, relations within the attentive public are more volatile than those within the sub-government and the relations between the two parts of the policy community are often uneasy and at times frankly hostile.

Relations between environmental groups and other members of policy communities concerned with economic policy are often particularly hostile, perhaps because environmentalism attacks the ideological underpinnings of much economic activity. It is common to hear that the leadership of environmental groups 'is exclusively in the hands of extreme dogmatists'.[40] Ron Arnold of Bellevue, Washington, has presented workshops to Canadian forestry and agricultural agencies and groups in which he warns that 'a small but vociferous minority . . . is effectively stopping the use of vital agrichemicals . . . to forward the lifestyle, world view and political goals of antipesticide activists.' He tells workshop participants that 'your goal must be to destroy the antipesticide movement once and for all, because there is no other way to avoid your own defeat'.[41]

Some agencies share these views, at least to the extent of maintaining 'databases' on certain groups. In the mid-1970s, according to the *Globe and Mail*, Ontario Hydro gathered information on anti-nuclear groups in the province, including, it was alleged, personal information on members' social and economic backgrounds.[42] In 1988, Atomic Energy of Canada Limited developed a database on some 100 anti-nuclear groups. Most of the information in the database was publicly available from corporate and association registries. In some cases, however, the professions of group executives and the salaries of staff were included. Most important, the database identified strategic information, such as the financial resources of groups, their strengths and weaknesses, and their current research activities.[43] Environmentalists have responded by doing their own studies of their opposition and working to counteract industry strategies, such as the creation of pro-industry groups, public education campaigns, and expensive litigation.[44]

The attentive public cannot be ignored. For the majority of issues it is the sub-government's public, and for those few issues that attract general public attention it occupies strategic territory between the sub-government and the public at large. Its capacity to generate informed support or opposition to policy makes it an ally worth courting and an opponent to be feared. From a system perspective, the attentive public has value as a source of renewal, even though challenges to conventional wisdom, however apt, are seldom welcomed by those who hold power. It is a forum for exploring and testing new ideas and new approaches without disrupting the stability that is so important to charter members of the sub-government.

The components of the attentive public are disparate. Allies and affiliates of sub-governments have a significant presence. Groups, agencies, and corporations whose policy capacity and power base are inadequate to sustain membership in the inner circle will nevertheless share many of the values of the more powerful. In return for access to information and consultation on issues that concern them, they can be counted upon to give public support.[45] Many groups, agencies, and corporations with only a secondary interest in the policy field maintain membership in the community primarily to monitor events that might affect that interest. They are likely to share the attitudes and policy goals of the centre, as are the many individuals and consulting firms that depend on the larger players for their livelihoods. Divergent ideas are more likely to come from groups, corporations, individuals, and even some agencies that are avowedly challenging the status quo. Their opposition stems from a conviction that the conventional wisdom is in error and that a new policy paradigm must be put in place. They consequently attract both public attention and the interest of the more venturesome participants in the policy establishment, some of whom hope that supporting important new approaches or concerns will put them in the fast lane to success.

Because of its greater extent and more varied composition, the attentive public lacks the communal qualities that facilitate interaction within the sub-government, though the members often meet face-to-face. Leaders may be known personally to a large number of people and a great many more know a surprising amount about them; but barriers of time, space, and divergence of interest prevent regular discourse. Intimate understanding of conflicting views is rare and stereotyping is common. The interest group living in this policy climate must work hard to secure the support and understanding of other members. It must monitor their activities, attempt to build alliances with affinity groups, and strive to maintain a position in the community that enables it to hear what is being said and to contribute to debate. It may feel compelled to 'educate' the public at large and the policy community — particularly government decision-makers — about certain problems and about the value of the alternatives available.

For these reasons, the attentive public tends to use some of the techniques that link it to the public at large for internal communications. Teleconferencing, electronic mail, networks, special databases, and the circulation of videos on specific topics are increasingly common, but for the moment the print media dominate. Many groups publish their own journals and newsletters. Some fields are affluent enough to support an independent specialized trade press that provides a forum for debating policy issues. When community issues erupt into public debate, such publications become a source of background material for the general media, and their specialized journalists often act as communications intermediaries between the community and the press at large. Other means of communication favoured by the attentive public are books and pamphlets.[46] Anti-establishment groups favour critical reviews of policy, but other groups also support writers and publishers who can produce commemorative volumes. It is not entirely clear who reads these—reviewers abhor them—but they can be valuable in positional politics. They have symbolic value, and are a method of sending legitimating messages, being quoted frequently at testimonial dinners and generally expressing the permanence and importance of the sponsoring group.

Although there are some similarities between communications in the attentive public and communications with the public at large, the business of influencing the policy community calls for different strategies and skills. The communicating group does not have to start by persuading the community that it ought to be interested, but assumes that it has a definite interest in the policy field. The community is also relatively small, making competition for attention less fierce, so that face-to-face communication is often possible, and language barriers are lower. In most policy communities, professions and trades have defined the terms that are used in the policy field. Even though a variety of professions and trades may be found, long association with one another has created a basic vocabulary that helps discussion about matters of common interest. To the outsider the language is obscure, even arcane. To the community member, it is a useful tool that defines differences precisely and smooths negotiations between groups, corporations, individuals, and agencies. Also implicit in a common language are assumptions about the way in which the community works, about its relationship with the broader environment, and the nature of the processes, materials, and relationships it deals with. Though not all of these assumptions are fully shared, they provide a framework for policy discourse within the community, and they underlie the norms and sanctions that guide behaviour within it.

Conferences are vital for developing opinion within the special public. The most frequently used means of bringing sub-government members into contact with the attentive public, conferences create opportunities for all sides to try to persuade others, to exchange information, and to attempt to assert community solidarity.

A typical conference was held in October, 1983, when the Automotive Parts Manufacturers' Association of Canada and the Japan Automobile

Manufacturers' Assocation (JAMA)—with the Institute for Research on Public Policy, the Canadian Institute of International Affairs, and the Canadian Studies Program of Columbia University—held a one-day symposium in Ottawa on 'The North American Automobile Industry and the Canadian Interest'. The conference tackled the question of 'What to do with the automobile industry?' Should the federal government support restructuring of the industry, or resist its decline? The conference organizers, aware that the federal government was considering a task force report on the future of the industry, built their agenda around discussions of world trends and 'current Canadian concerns'. Prominent analysts, senior representatives from the automobile industry, and influential public servants attended the conference, read papers to one another, briefed the media, and engaged in a debate over how government policy should address the problems created for the Canadian industry by the influx of imports from Japan and Korea.[47]

No major decisions were made. It would have been unusual if they had. But, like most meetings of its sort, the conference brought the community together in a debate that helped to build community understanding of what policy options were available to government and which of them were feasible. It would be impossible to say whether the conference influenced the government's decision to continue to work within a system in which Japanese manufacturers voluntarily limited exports to Canada, but it undoubtedly played a part in creating a receptive climate of opinion in the community for such a policy.[48] An active participant in any policy community must devote a considerable portion of its resources to such exchanges, in order to hear contending points of view and to put forward analyses and statements that will advance its interests.

Though members of the attentive public do not enjoy the nearly daily contact with the lead agency, or the almost automatic consultation that is the privilege of sub-government members, they are not excluded from consultation. Some are represented on advisory committees and are regulars at conferences and closed-door seminars. Individual members—academics in particular—are likely to be chosen to sit on task forces and royal commissions. The assumptions behind these appointments are two-fold: the appointees are expected not only to represent a point of view, but to be fair-minded about the opinions of others, and they are understood to have considerable knowledge of the field. In general, these assumptions are probably correct, but such appointments also offer opportunities for promoting preferred positions and interests.

Alliances and co-operation are valued even more by members of the attentive public than they are by the sub-government. Smaller groups co-operate to the point of sharing office space and resources. In every major urban centre, there is an office building (a little past its prime but at a respectable address) where a cluster of smaller groups share equipment and low-rent office space — sometimes even staff. Similar clusters are found on many university campuses. Usually such groups will belong to the same, or to a closely related, policy community, and their interdependence may extend to sponsoring joint activities and sharing mailing lists and information. Even when it is not necessary, co-operation can be a regular part of a group's relations with organizations close to it in orientation and interests. Co-operation enhances each group's ability to project an impression of legitimacy.

Co-operation is also extremely valuable in winning public attention inside and outside the policy community. An alliance had a considerable impact on the decision to revise freedom of information legislation. The extent of administrative secrecy (an inheritance from Britain) had long disturbed lawyers, journalists, academics, and many others concerned with the study and discussion of public affairs. For years individuals — Professors T. Murray Rankin and Donald Rowat and Progressive Conservative MP Ged Baldwin, among others — had written and spoken in favour of more open access to government documents. In 1969, Baldwin proposed a motion to the House of Commons to this effect, but it was not until the mid-1970s that the House and Senate agreed to have the issue investigated by the joint Committee on Regulations and other Statutory Instruments. The hearings, at which a large number of groups and individuals testified, resulted in a strong report urging implementing freedom of information. Although the report was endorsed by the House, the government responded with a green paper whose 'meagreness . . . provoked many organizations . . . to protest and to suggest more wide-ranging legislation'.[49] The Clark government did introduce legislation that, while not entirely satisfactory to the interested groups, went a lot further than that projected by the green paper. But that legislation succumbed with the defeat of the government. The Liberals, while reintroducing the legislation, seemed far less anxious to implement it, and 'seemed gradually to retreat, using the opposition of some of the provincial attorneys-general as an excuse'.[50] At this point the interest groups that had been active in the debate — the Canadian Bar Association, the Canadian Library Association, and the Canadian Association of University Teachers, among others — extended the informal alliance that had gradually emerged under the umbrella group ACCESS and joined forces to conduct a series of press conferences that precipitated strong public pressure on the government, which reluctantly honoured the promise to implement legislation like that introduced by the Conservatives.

For the majority of groups in the attentive public, the game of interest politics is played within the policy community using the communication tools that we have described. Consultation, the giving and receiving of advice, and participating through conferences and the printed word in the formation of the ideas that underlie policy are, even for the majority of those who have little standing in the community, the chief instruments for influencing policy-makers. But the attentive public contains the policy community's more outspoken critics — those who feel that they will not be listened to unless they can excite support from the public at large. As I will show in the following chapter, their activities tell us a great deal about the relationship of the policy community with the greater world of government and public opinion.

CHAPTER 7

Beyond the Policy Community: Strategies for Dealing With Contentious Issues

Not all issues are resolved within policy communities. Some are considered too important to the country at large to be left in the hands of a small number of government agencies and their associated interests. They have to be resolved by the political leadership after full-dress debate in the media, in Parliament, and often at intergovernmental meetings. Policies that affect relations between the English and French communities often require such debate. At other times, issues may be discussed by the Cabinet and public at large because they have generated conflict between two or more policy communities. Disputes that pit environmentalists against proponents of economic development may be the most common of these. Finally, when serious disagreements occur within policy communities it is sometimes necessary to resolve them through the larger political system.

Groups concerned with issues that have escaped the policy community have to deal with processes and institutions quite different from those they are accustomed to working with. They may have to convince members of the general public, who know virtually nothing of the circumstances that have led to a particular dispute but who have strong opinions concerning the dispute itself. They may be forced to meet the intense, hectic agenda of the media and Parliament. Alternatively, dispute may take groups to the courts or to intergovernmental meetings. Often a variety of institutions will participate in policy discussions that are highly contentious.

Wherever the path of conflict resolution leads, the affected interests must be prepared to follow. They must adapt themselves to the conditions established by each new policy environment, whether it be the judicial environment, the arena of high policy, the court of public opinion, or any other forum in which major policy debates take place. This chapter examines how groups approach three of these: the public at large, the courts, and intergovernmental bodies.

INFLUENCING PUBLIC OPINION

Groups have one of two ends in view when they seek to influence mass opinion: they hope to use an aroused public to dictate a specific decision, or, through public education, they hope to create an environment of ideas and attitudes that will encourage policy-makers to take certain kinds of actions rather than others. We are usually more aware of the first kind of action-oriented campaign; but the transmission of legitimating messages is probably more widely practised, and perhaps more effective.

Each of these endeavours is precipitated by entirely different circumstances and makes diverse demands on groups and on the policy system. Attempts to influence specific decisions are often reactions to a proposed or adopted course of action. They may entail appeals to the general public through the media, the use of demonstrations, perhaps even attempts to force candidates and parties to address certain issues during an election campaign. In contrast, the creation of a broadly supportive environment is a long-term process involving the regular and steady seepage of ideas into the public consciousness.

Groups influence public opinion through advertising, via direct lobbying, by capturing media attention, and by exploiting Parliament.

Advertising

Although advertising is not a standard pressure technique in Canada, as it is in the United States, it is becoming more common. The shift probably reflects the adaptation of groups in this country to the diffusion of power that has occurred in the last two decades. Since in other respects Canadian groups have begun to adapt to a redefinition of the power system by exploiting a more open policy style, it is quite possible that advertising will become more prominent in the future.

Isaiah Litvak has traced a trend to advertising beginning as early as the late 1960s, when 'the trauma of tax reform made the [mining] industry public-relations conscious'. As part of its battle against changes in mineral industry taxation, the industry launched its first major radio and television campaign.[1] This was an action-oriented campaign, but most of those that Litvak cites in the 1970s stressed legitimation.

The Canadian Petroleum Association tried to persuade Canadians to abandon their negative perception of the oil companies and to accept the legitimacy of the industry's attack on the National Energy Program.[2] During the debate over the building of the Mackenzie Valley pipeline, the oil industry used television extensively to present a series of advertisements intended to persuade the public of its respectability, its regard for the environment, its respect for the culture and way of life of the Native peoples, and its concern for energy conservation. More recently, Goldfarb Consultants advised the Canadian Nuclear Association that in order to counteract the negative public image of the nuclear industry, it should conduct a three-year public information campaign to foster 'a greater sense of trust' in the industry; 'move people from opposition to neutrality' and 'demonstrate and justify the need for the nuclear energy option'. The campaign would be multi-faceted, incorporating mobile information displays, films, high school education kits, and symposia and speaking tours to 'almost overwhelm people with the number of credible scientific experts coming out in support of the nuclear energy option'.[3] The association budgeted $1,671,000 for advertising in 1987 and $3,039,000 in 1988.[4]

Action-oriented messages also appear on Canadian television, but their use has been constrained by their cost—only groups with substantial resources can afford them—and by media policy. The CBC, for example, since the early 1960s has refused to allow advertisers to broadcast 'controversial material'. It defines controversy as 'a matter of public interest about which there is a significant difference of opinion and which is . . . the subject of public debate'.[5] The Media Foundation, a coalition of environmental advocacy and media-studies groups operating in Canada and the United States, has challenged these policies. It argues that they are not genuinely intended to protect the public from manipulation by wealthy groups, but rather to protect the sort of advertisers who sponsor legitimating messages. The Foundation has not yet altered media policy—it expects that will occur only as a result of litigation—but it did persuade the CBC to refuse a $7-million-dollar ad campaign promoting the environmental image of British Columbia forest companies.

Environmental issues have generated the most heated debate over advertising in general. The campaign against sealing made dramatic use of television and newspaper advertisements in Europe, urging consumers not only to boycott seal products but to express their abhorrence of the hunt to their legislators. A traditional industry was destroyed.[6] Today strongly worded animal rights advertisements are similarly affecting the fur industry,[7] and forest industry executives fear that attacks on forest management practices will inspire a comparable and even more devastating European boycott of Canadian wood products. The film *A Paradise Despoiled*, which is critical of logging practices, has been credited with inspiring European concern and precipitated intense industry reaction. The Canadian Imperial Bank of Commerce withdrew its sponsorship of a CBC program that had shown it, and Frank Oberle, the federal Minister of Forestry, announced a campaign to offset this 'obvious effort by the environmental movement in Canada to discredit our industry'.[8]

Direct lobbying

Legitimating and action-oriented messages can also be conveyed directly to members of the public. A traditional direct approach is often used at the local level. Door-to-door canvassing, meetings organized to attract concerned citizens, and campaigns to obtain signatures on petitions are all believed to affect the thinking of municipal politicians and public officials. Provincial, national, and international groups 'go direct' in a more sophisticated fashion. Mailing lists obtained from magazine publishers and sympathetic interest groups can be used to identify people likely to respond positively to flyers, appeals, and 'personal' letters from prominent figures urging 'Mr and Mrs Citizen' to express support for the group's position.* Often, too, the literature will solicit funds to support the group's work.

Capturing media attention

The most widely used technique for influencing public opinion is to capture media attention, largely because it brings a triple benefit. It is less expensive than advertising, it lends legitimacy to a campaign, and it can be used to whip up public support for a cause.[9] These benefits are not easily obtained, however. Competition for attention is fierce and once the novelty of a situation has evaporated a high degree of organizational competence is required. Because of their fundamentally different characteristics, the electronic media and the print media demand different strategies and techniques from those who seek to exploit them. I will look first at the relationships between groups and the electronic media.

The electronic media search out and focus on dramatic action that vividly expresses a group's feelings. Demonstrations, riots, bizarre happenings, and harrowing personal events grip media attention, serving as a backdrop to a group's message and driving home its point. Radio and television time is precious. Only events high on the national agenda can be assured exposure. Competition for air time is intense, and is not confined to each group's own backyard. A local group attempting to capture the attention of its immediate community must vie for air time with the latest atrocities in the world's trouble spots. Like its competitors working on the larger stage, the local

*In the Spring of 1984 the Canadian Coalition on Acid Rain made a typical direct mailing to individuals aware of environmental issues. The mailing consisted of (1) A letter from Farley Mowat, which began 'How long will your garden bloom if you water it with vinegar?' and requested financial support for lobbying the federal and American governments on the acid rain issue; (2) A postcard to be sent to the Prime Minister, which read 'The recent Gallop Poll indicates that 75% of Canadians would be willing to donate one day's salary per year to beat acid rain. I'm one of them, and to show I'm serious I just sent a donation to the Canadian Coalition on Acid Rain. I'm sending this card to you to show my concern about our acid rain problem. Will you act too!' The card's reverse showed a highway 'stop' sign with the words 'Stop Acid Rain'. (3) A flyer itemizing the dangers of acid rain. (4) Two forms, one for donations to the Canadian Acid Precipitation Foundation, which would be eligible for the tax deductible receipts issued by charities, and one for donations to the Coalition, which would not. The latter began, 'Yes, Farley, I want to stop acid rain. I'm sending...'

group must strive to exploit the dramatic, to force complex issues into snappy slogans, to seek the essence of issues, and, inevitably, to caricature them.

Groups attempting to attract media attention must become skilled in staging media events. Those with action-oriented messages have the greatest choice, ranging from demonstrations to carefully staged conferences that provide a podium from which to expound a group position. At the furthest extreme are the violent techniques used by revolutionary and profoundly disaffected groups.

Legitimating messages are less amenable to dramatization, though their proponents can still take advantage of the same techniques. Drama is diminished, but symbolism is more readily available. Conferences can be used to reaffirm a group's support of a widely accepted public position. Historic events can be commemorated, citizens honoured, and worthy causes espoused. All of these techniques serve to associate the group and its message with sentiments ingrained in the public consciousness.

The policy process offers opportunities for legitimating communications that are not as readily seized by proponents of action-oriented messages. Public hearings are important opportunities for doing this. Ironically, though public hearings are often seen as occasions for groups to influence policy recommendations, they are probably more important for providing groups with an opportunity to familiarize the public with their concerns and points of view. Many groups appear at public hearings principally for this reason. Hearings generally assure them media coverage, and thus free advertising for their cause. Such considerations may explain the pattern of representation before the Royal Commission on the Economic Union and Canada's Development Prospects. The *Financial Post*, reviewing representations to the commission during 1983, noted that the major steel companies had presented no formal briefs, none had been received from the influential financial firms based in Winnipeg, and only a few from the major oil companies. By contrast, an unprecedentedly high number of interest groups appeared, an indication that though individual firms saw little advantage in appearing before the Commission, they felt that the interest groups that represented them should treat the occasion as symbolic and as an opportunity for public education.[10]

When they take advantage of public hearings, groups are aware that they are stepping from one level of interaction with the media to another. The electronic media may draw attention to public hearings and outline for the public the issues and rival policies under debate, but the format used at hearings does not lend itself to television and radio reporting. The presentation of briefs, the testimony of expert witnesses, interventions from lawyers, and questioning by commissioners make for pallid television, forcing a group anxious for a spot on the evening news to mount a side show — a demonstration, perhaps, or a dramatic, visible example of its concerns — to capture camera attention. For the print media, however, public hearings are a source of good copy. The sequential elucidation of issues and concerns, the analysis of underlying causes and the presentation and explanation of data are the basis of the in-depth background reporting and analysis that newspapers, magazines, and public affairs books do best. Group leaders consequently strive to use the electronic media to draw public attention to an issue and to create a mood of concern, and the print media to convey reasoned proposals that will have some bearing on policy formulation. They know that policy-makers will be as influenced as much by the groups' briefs, the mass of clippings flowing from public hearings, their internal analyses, and immediate political concerns as they will be by the conflict transmitted by radio and television.

The preferred technique of groups wishing to influence public opinion is to try to persuade the media to focus public attention on them. This gives broad, relatively cheap exposure, and also implies legitimacy. It is achieved both through attention-catching activities and through exploitation of the policy process and the political system. In attempting to influence the public at large, groups assume either that strongly expressed public opinion will in turn influence the decisions of key policy-makers, or that they can foster a climate of opinion that encourages some kinds of decisions rather than others. The first assumption applies when groups send action-oriented messages to the public, the second when legitimating messages are sent.

To transmit either type of message to the general public, groups must fight hard for attention. This nearly always means they must catch the eye of the camera and the ear of the microphone, and must be skilled at exploiting the fleeting opportunities presented in the brief exposures the media allows. They must understand the needs of the media as well as the rhythm of the policy process. This takes imagination, expertise, organization, and individual commitment. The long-term demands of influencing public opinion place a premium on these attributes. Though many smaller, less-experienced organizations get public support and sympathy, they cannot assume that their policy preferences will be implemented. To translate public acceptance into policy action, the group must secure the co-operation and support of the policy community, particularly the bureaucracy.

Exploiting Parliament

Parliament is a vehicle not only for transmitting demands and proposals to policy-makers, but for engaging public concern. Here, too, the different media fasten on and exploit separate features of the policy process. Question period is the focal point for all journalists, but it fosters a short, pungent, and pointed style that is more effectively exploited by the electronic media and by groups with an action-oriented message. The routine business of Parliament, particularly the major debates on the budget, the throne speech and the second reading of the government bills — together with the hearings of parliamentary committees and task forces — are, like public hearings, more effectively reported by the print media and are likely to attract the attention of groups with long-term policy concerns.

In recent years, lobbyists have paid increasing attention to Members of Parliament, and even to provincial legislators. The more open policy process that has evolved has encouraged more groups to channel issues to question period and has swept away the reticence that used to bar institutionalized groups from parliamentary discussion. While the diffusion of power has freed groups, it has also imposed new burdens on them. It is now necessary for them to cultivate Parliament. MPs report that they receive a constant flow of background material from groups — much of it related to issues being debated, but a good part of it intended to educate the MP to a broader understanding of the group's concerns.[11] Some campaigns are intensive and though individual MPs are not lobbied as persistently and continuously as are American Congressmen, there may be a growing tendency for groups to seek to speak to caucus. Backbenchers are considered capable of influencing policy while it is still in caucus, particularly where regional issues are concerned.[12] The independent views of members can be truly influential only during 'free votes', when the member is permitted to vote according to his or her conscience. On those occasions, the average backbencher is submitted to a degree of persuasion comparable to that normally endured by Cabinet ministers. Votes on capital punishment produce the most notable examples of such pressure, both in Canada and elsewhere.[13]

In some countries prominent groups secure the election of legislative advocates.[14] This ensures not only that the group has a sponsor and speaker in the legislature, but that it is tapped into the flow of policy information as it circulates through the country's busiest talk-shop and rumour mill. The small size and the spatial orientation of the House of Commons inhibits this tactic in Canada, though special interest representation has long been a feature of the Senate, where a number of Senators identified particularly with business interests articulate group concerns on Senate committees.[15] Nevertheless, prominent interest communities often believe that a good way to influence public policy is to win the election of individuals who can broadly represent them. This has been true of the women's movement, which, despite continued male domination of politics, has had some success both in persuading women to run for political office and in electing them. Similarly business executives often urge one another to enter politics in order to secure a more sympathetic hearing for the business point of view in Ottawa and the provincial capitals.

Electing representatives to Parliament, however, will not ensure their adherence to a point of view endorsed by the interests that sponsored them. Legislators, as representatives of a geographically located community, must strive to speak for its broad needs rather than for the needs of a sectoral interest.[16] They must also consider the general needs of the country or province and usually they must accept their party's view of how best to address those needs. When elected, business people are not seen as delegates for groups such as the Canadian Manufacturers' Association or the Canadian Federation of Independent Business, even though they may be expected to sympathize with the views of the business community and to have ties to specific organizations. In the words of Robert Stanbury, general counsel and secretary to Firestone Canada and a member of the first Trudeau Cabinet, MPs from business must accept that 'in government, whether it is the bureaucrat or politician, there is a different point of view that has to be adopted', and that they do not speak only for business. 'You're forced to think in national terms.'[17]

Some groups have tried to influence public opinion by intervening in the electoral process. Though it is not easy to influence party platforms — and many doubt the utility of engineering inclusion of a favourable plank in the platforms of the major parties — groups often expend great effort trying to win promises from the parties and their leaders. Prior to the 1984 federal election campaign, the business community worked to persuade party strategists 'that the best contribution Ottawa could make to future growth and stability would be to regain control over federal finances'. By the end of the campaign, when each of the three major parties announced that the cost of their election promises would amount to about $5 billion, the Investment Dealers' Association, the Business Council on National Issues, and the Canadian Chambers of Commerce, among others, admitted despairingly that the politicians had been more prone to promising new programs than to championing the need for deficit reduction and financial housecleaning.[18] Nevertheless, the groups' efforts forced the public to debate the deficit issue and though the election campaign itself generated little of the 'responsible leadership' that business people hoped for, the Mulroney government, once elected, maintained that it had a mandate to cut the federal deficit. The struggle with the deficit has influenced its economic policies since. In other words, by successfully injecting business issues into the electoral debate, the business community laid the ground for the government to claim that deficit reduction was part of its electoral mandate.

Several recent elections have witnessed more focused interventions, some of them directed at specific candidates and parties. In 1977, *Maclean's* reported that gun associations had effectively intimidated some MPs by threatening to encourage association members to vote against them if they supported gun control.[19] The NDP's Svend Robinson was vigorously attacked during the 1980 campaign by groups opposed to his and the NDP's

position on the abortion issue. Though the attack failed, the then Chief
Electoral Officer, Jean-Marc Hamel, was sufficiently disturbed by it and
other incidents to recommend changes in the Elections Act.[20] Parliament
took his advice and on 25 October 1983, with remarkable unanimity, the
House of Commons adopted an amendment to the Canada Elections Act that
declared that Canadians might not 'incur election expenses' in support of or
in opposition to a party or candidate during an election campaign, unless the
benefiting party or candidate consented. Parties or candidates accepting
such support would have to include the cost of the advertising in their
allowable election expenses. Anyone convicted of advertising in violation of
the act could be liable to a fine of $5,000 or five years in jail.

The amendment opened a new chapter in a debate over the role of parties
and pressure groups in election campaigns. The issue is rooted in the 1974
revisions of the Canada Elections Act, which regulates public donations to
political parties and limits election expenses. According to Toronto lawyer
Aubrey Golden, 'restricting candidates' spending was a cornerstone of the
act', but 'if candidates and their parties were to be restricted, the obvious
loophole that others could spend in their support had to be closed.'[21] The
1974 act did this in part by providing that only registered candidates and
parties could spend money campaigning to oppose or support some other
registered candidate. However, since Parliament at that time was not
anxious to restrict the right of individuals and groups to debate issues of
public policy, the act also provided that a citizen who was not a candidate
could spend money for 'the purpose of gaining support for views held by
him on an issue of public policy'.[22] The citizen could even support a non-
political organization engaged in the same quest, as long as the debate
involved an issue in public policy and was entered into 'in good faith'. This
'good faith' clause, when tested in the courts, acquired an interpretation so
liberal that it permitted campaigns like the attack on Robinson. In Parliament's eyes it was clearly too liberal.

The new provisions were soon challenged by the National Citizens'
Coalition.[23] The Coalition, which frequently places advertisements in major
newspapers exhorting the public to persuade politicians to adopt the conservative posture it favours, was supported by a variety of other organizations, including the Canadian Daily Newspaper Publishers' Association and
the Canadian, Ontario, and Atlantic Provinces Chambers of Commerce.[24]
The Coalition's argument that the amendments represented an undue limitation on freedom of expression was accepted by Mr Justice Donald Medhurst
of the Alberta Court of Queen's Bench. Medhurst ruled that because the
sections limited freedom of expression they would have to pass the test
established in the Charter of Rights, which requires that 'the limitations
must be considered for the protection of a real value to society and not
simply to reduce or restrain criticism, no matter how unfair such criticism

may be'. As far as Justice Medhurst was concerned, 'fears or concerns of mischief that may occur are not adequate reasons for imposing a limitation'. He ruled that the amendments were an unreasonable and unjustified limitation of the freedom of expression guaranteed in the Charter and therefore were unconstitutional.[25]

When the federal government — faced with hostile editorial opinion[26] and on the eve of an election — decided not to appeal the decision, it closed a chapter in the debate over freedom of speech during election campaigns, but it did not close the debate itself. The issue remains: if candidates themselves must observe limits to the amount of money they may spend on election campaigns, how can they be protected from the irresponsible use of advertising by groups and citizens who face no similar constraints? Mr Hamel has called a system that limits election spending by parties and candidates, but not other interested groups, an 'exercise in futility'.[27] He argued that the restrictions, rather than unduly limiting freedom of speech, simply prevented wealthy interests from overwhelming their opponents with expensive media campaigns. He was clearly anxious to avoid a Canadian version of recent American experience. There 'Political Action Committees' (PACs) have spent many millions supporting their preferred candidates. The level of support has often been grossly lopsided, generally favouring incumbents.[28] Such support has caused Fred Wertheimer, president of the public interest group Common Cause, to label the PACs 'a corrupt system. It is a visible national scandal totally undermining the integrity of Congress.'[29] The Chief Electoral Officer, Jean-Marc Hamel, called repeatedly for a complete overhaul of federal election spending laws and on 15 November 1989 the government responded by appointing a commission, chaired by Quebec business executive Pierre Lortie, to inquire into electoral reform and party finances.

The commission has to consider a difficult question. It is not clear that the abuses that have occurred are as threatening as Jean-Marc Hamel believes or that they must be constrained in the way set out in the 1983 amendments. The 1984 election campaign witnessed few instances of advertising excesses by groups, but the 1988 campaign, with its intense debate over free trade and abortion, rekindled fears that Canada is contracting the PAC disease. Janet Hiebert reports that the Commissioner of Canada Elections has said that if the legislation were enforced he would have prosecuted those advertising on the free trade issue, regardless of whether or not they actually named the Conservatives. In the Commissioner's view, party positions were so clearly identified that support or opposition to free trade was tantamount to support or opposition to the Conservatives.[30]

These fears are probably excessive. They ignore the differences between the Canadian and American party systems. In the United States 'individual candidates remain the relevant units of campaign politics'. They reach Congress 'as individuals, and ... they govern as individuals'.[31] Canadians generally vote for national or provincial parties, either on traditional grounds or because they support the party leadership. While interest group advertising might influence the outcome in a few ridings, it would be unlikely to have a significant effect on policy. To influence the vote significantly on a national or even local basis, interests would have to spend a great deal more than is available to most of them. Spending of this order would itself become an election issue, as in fact advertisements in favour of free trade became in the 1988 election. If third-party election advertising should become a serious problem, it could be addressed in a less draconian fashion. Specific abuses could be prohibited. For example, advertisements might be banned in the closing days of a campaign. Defamatory and highly misleading advertisements could be heavily penalized and might serve as grounds for nullifying results in individual constituencies. Such refinements of the election law, rather than an outright ban on third-party advertising, would be a suitable response to abuses of freedom of speech.

VARIATIONS ON A THEME: ADAPTATIONS IN PRESSURE GROUP TACTICS

Pressure groups have been quick to take advantage of changes in the Canadian policy system. We have already seen how, in responding to the diffusion of power, they have expanded their legitimating role and have paid increasing attention to Parliament. Their quest for influence has led them to other points of access. Though sometimes baffled in their attempts to exploit intergovernmental relations in Canada, they have been assiduous in their efforts to influence the first ministers and their colleagues. Some have been quick to seize opportunities to influence international public opinion and, most recently, to take advantage of the growing policy role of the courts.

Influencing intergovernmental negotiations

Between the Depression and the collapse of the Meech Lake initiative, intergovernmental meetings assumed a more and more significant role in public policy formation. Prior to Quebec's post-Meech insistence on bilateralism, many of the most important public policy issues were resolved at the intergovernmental level, either at meetings of the first ministers or at conferences of ministers responsible for particular policy fields. Not surprisingly, interest groups tried to influence these negotiations.

The success of their attempts has been much debated, with some scholars arguing that the Canadian federal system represses group demands and others that it encourages them by providing a multiplicity of opportunities to influence policy-making.[32] Thorburn expresses the consensus eventually reached on this point: though interest groups are generally frozen out of the intense intergovernmental negotiations that ultimately reconcile conflicting regional demands, the governments participating in the debate have strong ties to important interests in their jurisdictions and try to promote and protect them.[33] Group influence on intergovernmental relations can be considerable, albeit indirect. The actions of groups themselves suggest that they believe that is the case.

Group behaviour is profoundly affected by the conditions that prevail in the forum in which intergovernmental negotiations take place, which is reflected in both the organizational forms and the strategies that groups adopt to cope with them. Groups with strong national and provincial interests structure themselves to work with both levels of government. This reflects the fact that not all intergovernmental negotiations have been as tense and conflict-ridden as the televised meetings of the first ministers. The majority of intergovernmental conferences have been at least as concerned with maintaining intergovernmental agreement as with coping with disagreement. Most issues on the agenda of these meetings have related to the joint programs essential to Canada's social and economic life. To accommodate this co-operative federalism, many groups have adopted 'either a federal structure or a confederal one in which the major power rests in the provincial or regional offices'.[34] As well, many groups have found it useful to belong to regional or provincial intersectoral associations.[35]

For strategic reasons, groups have preferred to play a bipartisan role. Thorburn argues that even groups whose fortunes depend primarily on one level of government, and which consequently are often compelled to support it, have been careful to avoid total commitment. 'It is in the interest of a group to have friends in all governments and on all sides.'[36] Bipartisan strategies were most evident in those meetings where outside groups were permitted to attend and even to participate in forging compromises between jurisdictions and interests. Federal officials and mining representatives attended the annual conference of provincial ministers of mines, for example.[37] In a sense, many of these meetings were simply the conclave of the national policy community in their specific fields. They were important opportunities for consultation and joint decision-making, rather than occasions for resolving burning issues. They testified to the fact that interest groups have been significant and active participants in intergovernmental affairs.

The constitutional crisis — a trauma that has beset Canada since the 1960s — has gradually undermined this consensual and bipartisan pattern. Its principal effects have been four-fold.

First, the crisis has strained national organizations. Regional tensions within groups have mirrored and interacted with those being played out at the political level. This is illustrated by the steps a number of groups have taken to change their names and structure in order to accommodate the increasingly separatist orientation of Quebec. The Quebec division of the Canadian Manufacturers' Association became the Quebec Manufacturers' Association; the Canadian Peace Alliance created a 'binational' structure; even the Pro-Canada Network changed its name to the Action Canada Network in order to distance itself from its predecessor in the 1980 Quebec referendum.[38] Regional and provincial branches of organizations often find themselves at odds with their national associations and act independently, especially in matters affecting the regional application of national policies. Like intergovernmental tensions, these reflect differences of interest from region to region. What is good for the southern Quebec milk industry is not necessarily good for milk producers in Ontario and the Maritimes.[39] Provincial branches of organizations can have as much difficulty working out differences between one another as the first ministers. That is one reason why some issues escape the policy community. In Coleman's view, this centrifugal bias of Canadian regionalism offsets the tendency for business interests to adopt unitary forms of organization in their associations and fragments business's ability to achieve collective action nationally.[40]

Second, as intergovernmental tensions have risen, groups have found it increasingly difficult to resolve interjurisdictional issues at the bureaucratic and ministerial levels. Matters that were once considered housekeeping chores for federal ministers and their provincial counterparts have become contentious and have found their way to the first ministers' agenda. This means that groups are not able to rely solely on the tactics of consultation that used to be effective. They experience problems of access. Meetings with premiers are not easily obtained and the Prime Minister is nearly inaccessible. Even if access is obtained, meetings have to be so short as to be almost symbolic. This compels the groups to act through intermediaries, senior politicians, the ministers active in the policy field, caucus, other group leaders, and above all the officials around the leader. Since few of these will be fully aware of the nuances of the group's position, it is quite likely that the group will achieve less than it would like. Probably the most difficult intermediaries will be the officials of the leaders' support staffs. Used to the overview position and sometimes predisposed to suspect the importunings of groups whose normal allies are the line agencies, such officials are often elusive and difficult to persuade.[41] Groups are consequently forced to resort to publicity to generate support for their positions; public participation is thus encouraged.

The third effect of the constitutional crisis is that groups find themselves participating in intergovernmental rivalries. The intensification of competition between governments has seen the growth of a tendency for groups to ally themselves with one level of government or the other. There has been a long-standing tendency for groups to support those governments whose policies and jurisdictions have the greatest impact on their interests.* Governments — particularly provincial governments — have reciprocated by championing allied interests in intergovernmental negotiations.[42] This reciprocity, in Cairns's view, has led some interests to become virtual hostages of the governments to which they are beholden:

> Each government transmits cues and pressures to the environment, tending to group the interests manipulated by its policies into webs of interdependence springing from the particular version of socioeconomic integration it is pursuing.[43]

Such strategies not only constrain groups' freedom to manoeuvre, they diminish their role as intermediaries between levels of government. In turn, the differences between federal and provincial governments become ever more sharply defined as interests line up behind their champions and the spiral of confrontation extends, drawing more and more groups into the mêlée.

The fourth effect of the constitutional crisis has been to draw groups into the constitutional debate itself. There are several reasons for this. For some groups, like Quebec's St Jean Baptiste Society, constitutional change has always been a major objective, and the growth of tension between the governments and peoples of Canada has presented opportunities for achieving it. Equally, groups committed to the preservation of Confederation have marshalled their forces. For the great majority of groups, the constitution was not a concern. It established the political framework within which they had to work and, except when they sought judicial interpretations of the division of powers, they accepted it as a 'given'.

The crisis over the constitution has made these groups aware of the extent to which this fundamental document shapes their environment. For some, the debate portends important and unwelcome changes and they have acted

---

*Kwavnick, 'Interest Group Demands', 70-86. In such circumstances the interest's chief concern is the extent of its champion's own influence. This can have interesting consequences. For example, the smaller provinces can do very little for local interests if their concerns run counter to those of Ontario and/or Quebec. The problems posed by inter-regional rivalries led Maritime business interests to encourage the formation of the Council of Maritime Premiers, and experience has shown that when the Maritime premiers can be persuaded to speak collectively, they are more likely to obtain the concessions the interests want. To achieve this, however, groups must themselves achieve a high degree of agreement and they must become sophisticated diplomats, juggling the concerns and shibboleths of provincial administrations as they search for the compromises and convincing arguments that will hold the premiers together at the bargaining table.

to support the status quo — as the major fish processors did in the late 1970s when they opposed provincialization of fisheries management[44] — or to secure an orderly evolution of the constitution, as the Business Council on National Issues has done in the most recent phase of the crisis.[45] Other groups have seen the constitutional debate as an opportunity to achieve political objectives. Thus Native people, the handicapped, the elderly, and women worked to secure special recognition in the Charter of Rights and opposed the Meech Lake accord because it appeared to limit that recognition. Their use of the constitutional debate has meant that the constitution itself has become a part of pressure group politics, a development that makes the task of national reconciliation more complex and more difficult.* Furthermore, organizations claiming to represent Charter groups have successfully challenged the legitimacy of the processes through which we have traditionally negotiated constitutional changes. In doing so, they have raised fears that an alternative process will be dominated by interest groups.[46]

Domestic/external influences

Many Canadian groups are involved with intergovernmental relations on a quite different level: that of international relations. Nor is Canadian public policy free of external influence from foreign interest groups. Although I do not have space here to explore the many ways Canadians use groups to influence events outside the country, or are in turn affected by international pressure groups, I will catalogue the several manifestations of international pressure group activities that are significant to Canadians.[47]

The first has to do with economic issues. Given this country's dependence on international trade, we should expect Canadian interest groups to keep a watchful eye on the domestic influences affecting the policies of our most important trading partners, and to try to counteract unfriendly influences. The latter will involve efforts to persuade the Canadian government to take counter measures, but it may also prompt groups to take their campaign into

---

*This point is illustrated by the role of aboriginal groups in the most recent constitutional round. A number of claims put forward by them clearly have constitutional significance, the demand for self-determination, for example. Others — like the need for expeditious settlement of land claims — could be resolved politically, but are being raised in the constitutional arena because that is where they are most likely to be addressed and resolved.(See *Globe and Mail*, 10 Nov. 1990 [John Dafoe], 6 and 9 Feb., 12 April 1991.) That this is effective strategy is attested by the decision of the Mulroney government to revive its 1990 promise to conduct a Royal Commission inquiry into aboriginal issues and by aboriginal leaders' insistence on a role in constitutional renewal.

their rivals' camp.* It is not unusual for Canadian industries to lobby extensively in other capitals, particularly Washington, for tariff concessions and purchasing opportunities. Sometimes this kind of lobbying is also engaged in by Canadian governments in conjunction with diplomatic representations by officials.[48] In Washington, where Ambassador Allan Gotlieb and his successor Derek Burney have urged Canadian business people to adopt the techniques of American lobbyists, the embassy provides lists of lawyers and lobbyists and gives briefings on US government agencies and their policies.[49] This approach represents a change of style for Canadian diplomats, who for many years were accused by the business community of preferring to represent Canada abroad but not Canadian business interests.[50]

Interest group involvement in trade issues has long been a fixture of Canadian politics. Earlier, for example, I noted Norman Robertson's unsympathetic comments on the Canadian Manufacturers' Association's efforts to influence R. B. Bennett's trade negotiations in the 1930s. Ethnic groups, too, have lobbied Canadian governments to use diplomatic pressure to influence policies in their lands of origin. Many of their concerns have to do with the rights and interests of minorities in other countries, but not all. Trading relationships, air links, economic development, defence, and sovereignty also bring ethnic group briefs, delegations, letters, and demonstrations to Ottawa.[51]

The international activities of humanitarian, environmental, and peace groups are generally a more recent phenomenon. In the past, many of these groups and their predecessors had contacts in other countries and were influenced by them. The temperance movement in Canada was influenced by its American counterpart. The women's suffrage movement was encouraged by women in the United States and Britain. The forestry movement in the late nineteenth century was inspired in part by American example. The labour movement had international connections. Today, many international groups go beyond sympathizing with and encouraging their colleagues in other countries. They take direct action in foreign capitals. Perhaps the best-known recent example of Canadians taking this step is the alliance between the federal and several provincial governments and a number of environmental groups to lobby the United States on acid rain. Of the interest groups involved, the most prominent was the Canadian Coalition on Acid Rain, which, with an annual budget of between $200,000 and $400,000, lobbied

---

*Not all efforts to persuade the federal government to counteract the lobbying abroad of foreign pressure groups are successful. Provincial ministers of fisheries, for example, have complained that while the federal Department of Fisheries and Oceans prepared material countering the anti-sealing campaign, the Department of External Affairs refused to distribute it (Interview with the Hon. John Leefe, Minister of Fisheries, Nova Scotia, 20 March 1984).

American governments in ways not available to Canadian officials. They asked Americans owning cottages in Canada to lobby for a new acid rain policy, they drew prominent politicians into the debate, and they persuaded provincial governments to advertise the issue on non-resident fishing licences. A new policy, together with a supporting treaty, was finally achieved in early 1991 as a result of close collaboration between this alliance and a similar one in the United States.[52]

Conversely, foreign groups often take direct action — both in Canada and through international pressure — to influence Canadian governments. The International Fund for Animal Welfare, in its attack on Canada's seal hunt, seems to have had relatively little support in this country and was bitterly opposed in Newfoundland. By inflaming European opinion and embarrassing the Canadian government, it first secured changes in the regulations governing the hunt and ultimately destroyed the market for pelts.[53]

International public opinion has also been used by Canadian groups to exert pressure at home. Native peoples in particular have done this effectively. The highly publicized lobbying of the British Parliament by Native groups secured concessions from the Trudeau government as it negotiated repatriation of the constitution. The northern Quebec Cree were the first Canadian aboriginal group to win non-government status at the United Nations, a status they have used to lobby against the James Bay projects.[54] Similarly, Native women, angry that the Indian Act deprived women married to non-Natives of their Indian status, achieved a change in policy by appealing to the United Nations Human Rights Committee.[55] International human rights groups were appealed to again following the 1990 Oka confrontation.[56]

For many groups, the international environment is an extension of domestic politics. They use that environment — represented by international public opinion and accessible through international organizations, governmental and non-governmental — to influence policy at home, or to create conditions abroad that further their own interests. For other groups, the world is truly a global village. They exist primarily at the international level to influence events in whatever country they choose. Oxfam, the Red Cross, Greenpeace, Amnesty International, and many others, though they work through governmental agencies to achieve their objectives, often find that international public opinion is their most effective weapon. Through spectacular stunts as well as through appeals to the consciences of wealthier citizens of the world, they not only acquire resources to carry out their own programs, but goad governments and international agencies into modifying their policies.

Using the courts

The number of groups prepared to resort to the courts to challenge the actions of others, including the actions of government, appears to be on the increase. I have already referred to one such case, the successful attack launched by the National Citizens' Coalition to the 1983 amendments to the Canada Elections Act. The aboriginal community has conducted numerous actions intended to secure its rights. Environmental groups have invoked environmental assessment regulations to constrain development. Women's groups, human rights groups, and organizations representing the handicapped, the disadvantaged, and minorities have taken a variety of rights issues through the courts, many of them to the Supreme Court itself. At the level of local government, it is common for citizens' groups to engage in long battles before administrative tribunals and the courts in attempts to preserve or improve civic amenities.[57]

One of the factors inhibiting a resort to law has been the fact that the legal system was not, and in large part still is not, friendly to citizens' groups. Swaigen explains:

> The challenges facing public interest groups and their lawyers are difficult ones. In many instances, the full weight of big business or big government can shatter the financial and organizational capabilities of citizen groups before such groups have had the opportunity to effectively present their cases.... [G]etting a case into the courts is only the beginning of what can prove to be a lengthy, frustrating and very expensive lesson in how the law works.... Because of the costs involved if a case is lost, few citizens are willing to use the courts to seek redress. A wealthy corporation that stands to lose millions of dollars because of a consumer protection policy will challenge the policy in the courts. But thousands of consumers who individually lose a few hundred dollars because they have had to repair a defective product will never sue the manufacturer as long as each of them is liable for what may amount to several thousands of dollars in costs.[58]

A group of Cape Breton landowners discovered the truth of Swaigen's assessment when they challenged the right of Stora Koppaburg, a forest products firm, to spray herbicides on lands sharing their own watershed. The landowners lost the case, and found themselves responsible for paying court costs that far exceeded their resources. Several faced bankruptcy. Ultimately public opinion, including public opinion in Sweden where its head office is located, persuaded the firm to accept a much smaller sum and a commitment that the group would not appeal the case or pursue the issue farther. Quite apart from this commitment, such experiences cannot help but intimidate other activists.[59] As far as one legal scholar is concerned, it also encourages government indifference to group pleas for intervention:

> The first response of government is often to tell a group ... with a rights concern: 'We'll let the courts decide.' Most governments are well aware of the limited resources of groups seeking to challenge laws or administrative action and are well aware of the high costs of litigation. The assumption made by

government, and I fear it is fairly accurate, is that many of these claims will never be pursued.[60]

Groups also face legal barriers to court action, notably the courts' reluctance to grant them 'standing'. Standing relates to the court's view as to whether a would-be litigant has 'an interest in the subject matter of the legal proceedings that is greater than and different from that of the general public'.[61] In other words, the courts, and many regulatory bodies, insist that before they will listen to requests to interfere with the actions of others, the parties making the requests should prove that they are directly and substantially affected by those actions. Until recently Canadian courts have defined standing narrowly, and have not been very willing to permit interventions by individuals and groups concerned to show how the public interest might be affected by the outcome of a case.[62] These narrow definitions have limited pressure group use of the courts. They have made it difficult for public interest groups to intervene, and have discouraged efforts to draw larger issues from the particular differences that concern the original disputants. As a consequence, many individuals and small groups have to fight public battles on their own, without the financial support, experience, and expertise of larger and more established public interest groups.

The trend towards increased litigation flows from disparate sources. On a superficial level, it might seem to be another example of Canadian emulation of American strategies, but changes in the constitution and in legal procedure are probably stronger influences. It may be that the diffusion of power I discussed earlier is having some effect. A community that finds it difficult to locate responsibility and to fix authority, and whose policy process is highly discursive, is almost forced to turn to law. The constitution, the statutes, and the body of legal interpretation are perceived as being among its more stable and reliable institutions.

Changes in the constitution and in legal procedure are closely related. The introduction of the Charter of Rights has opened a new branch of constitutional law concerned with the impact of legislation on the public in general. In order to address these concerns, the courts have shown an increased willingness to hear interventions from groups holding views on how the public interest might be affected by the outcome of specific cases. The Charter has also forced a policy role on the courts. When the courts are asked to decide whether a legislative constraint on individual rights is reasonable, it is being asked to make a judgement rather than to interpret a law. In the words of Supreme Court Justice John Sopinka, the courts are now making 'the kinds of decisions that were previously made by elected representatives who got their information from a variety of sources'. This has encouraged the Supreme Court in particular to 'broaden the sources of our information to make sure we hear all sides of the question'.[63]

The legal profession and some governments have also shown interest in developing procedures that would help individual citizens and smaller groups. Groups such as the Public Interest Advocacy Centre and the Women's Legal Education and Action Fund frequently provide legal assistance for smaller groups, as well as individuals. Finally, some legislative reform has been attempted to ensure that public interest issues can be brought to the courts through class actions. These are cases brought by individuals on behalf of others who may not have given their consent to the action. This practice has been widely used in the United States by public interest groups. It is intended to overcome the barriers created by court requirements that cases be brought by aggrieved parties, each of whom must plead individually. To date, only Quebec has introduced a class action law. Though the Quebec law provides financial assistance to litigants, it is so encumbered by restrictions that it has had very little effect and has led one legal authority, H. Patrick Glenn, to conclude that class actions have an 'inherently problematic character' that makes them inappropriate for use by interest groups and that undermines legal institutions.

> Class actions procedures, where they exist, now appear to be failing, both as significant measures of social reform and as procedures viable even on a limited scale in the court system. There are profound and systemic reasons for this, which no amount of legislative design or fine-tuning can overcome. Parties and counsel are rejecting class actions because they are too onerous and problematical (aside from questions of costs) in a judicial system which responds to radically different priorities. Judges reject class actions because they see them as incompatible with both their procedural and adjudicative functions, and in this they are probably correct. Class action implementation therefore accomplishes little, and anything which is accomplished is at the critical expense of judicial authority and the principles of fundamental justice.[64]

The Quebec experience could be a first step towards more effective class action legislation and provision of financial assistance for appellants — part of a larger effort at law reform that, in Swaigen's words, is 'necessary just to ensure that people have the right to speak out about injustice without fear of harassment and to use the courts without paying crushing costs'.[65]

CONCLUSIONS

The last two chapters have discussed the way in which groups relate to and attempt to influence their environment. I have treated that environment as consisting of two distinct entities: the policy community and the larger world of institutions and mass publics beyond the policy community. The general public — which has superordinate authority over the policy community — has its say from time to time, but to influence policy consistently, groups must influence the policy community. The policy community, as long as it is not disbanded or reshaped, possesses the collective memory for policy and organizes the application of knowledge to the resolution of policy problems. Over time, it exercises a continuing sway over the evolution of policy and its implementation.

The strategies that win support in the policy community reflect its bureaucratic orientation. To participate, groups must organize themselves along bureaucratic lines — preferably along lines that parallel the structure of the lead agency itself. They must accept many of the bureaucratic mores of the governmental actors in the community. They come to think in bureaucratic terms, finding that elaborate analyses of groups' positions help them push their ideas through the information machine that we call the policy process. Even when groups appeal to the general public they cannot escape the bureaucratic imperative. The media can only be 'used' over time by groups aware of media strengths, weaknesses, and prejudices and able to maintain contact with its many levels of operation. Even the staging of a 'spontaneous' demonstration involves more preparation than most observers will realize. Legislators are often sympathetic to small groups of constituents, but to influence them to the point of securing policy change citizens must bring continual pressure to bear, which also demands organization. Even groups that have won a victory at the public level cannot be certain of translating their gains into programs, unless they achieve organized participation in the policy community.

Bureaucratic strategies are expensive. They demand elaborate organizations, often located in several centres. They call for expertise in the preparation of analyses and in the conduct of lobbying campaigns. Professional help is seldom cheap. The maintenance of position in the community, even if it does not depend on the operation of well-staffed offices, will generally involve member or representative participation in advisory committees, co-operative actions and the mounting of conferences. The travel and communication costs incurred by these activities are particularly high in a bilingual, sometimes multilingual, country whose major centres are far apart. The commitments of participation do not always end at the boundaries of the immediate policy community. International connections are frequent and sometimes essential supports for domestic campaigns. They too are expensive to maintain. Finally, the resort to law can be the most expensive of all pressure activities.

In sum, the cost and level of organization demanded of group actors in the Canadian policy system places an immense burden on most committed groups, but it places the greatest burden on groups that lack a strong resource base, a category that includes most public-interest groups. Even the diffusion of power which has developed in Canada since the late 1960s does not necessarily assist these groups. Today they have a wider choice of avenues to policy discussion than they had two decades ago, and it is easier to generate policy discussion. But it is not easier to participate in that discussion over the length of time required to put a policy in place. Public interest groups are therefore not able to make the contribution to the evolution of policy that their origins and composition warrant. Their limited role may be a comfort to interests that dominate policy fields, but it restricts the benefits the polity at large can derive from group politics.

CHAPTER 8

The Interior Life of Groups

No group will achieve political success unless it can sustain the support of its members, employees, and friends. This can never be forgotten by those who organize interest representation in the policy process. It is a condition of survival. For that reason, the manner in which group support is created and maintained — the interior life of groups — deserves careful attention.

I will examine the internal operations of groups from three perspectives. First, I will consider the motivations individuals, corporations, and other groups bring to membership in an interest association, arguing that the aims and concerns of members affect not only the success of the group, but the way it works to achieve its goals. This argument will build on the discussion of group types presented in Chapter 4. Extending that discussion further, in the next section I will review the types of resources used by pressure groups and explore how their availability differs among various kinds of groups. Finally, I will consider the complex problem of group management, an aspect of group life that affects not only the pursuit of a group's political goals, but its capacity to survive.

THE BASES OF SUPPORT

I have argued that pressure groups have a role in the political system because they perform some or all of four functions: communication, legitimation, administration, and regulation. To carry out any of these functions, a group must attract enough members from its potential clientele to sustain its work and, where legitimation is important, to ensure that it can be considered adequately representative of the interest community. This fundamental requirement raises the extremely important question of member motivation. Why do people join pressure groups?

It is sometimes suggested that awareness of the need to promote a common interest accounts for the decision of individuals to join specific groups. Often quoted, for example, is David Truman's argument that formal interest associations are most likely to take shape when the interest community they represent is in some way threatened:[1] a common peril forces solidary group members to recognize their mutual interest and to band together. It is generally argued that recognition of a shared interest is a necessary condition for joining a formal interest association, but is not in itself a motivator to lead a person to make this sort of commitment. This view, implicit in many early case studies, was put forward as a generalization in the 1950s by V.O. Key, who pointed out that many people did not join pressure groups *per se*: they joined labour unions, voluntary associations, clubs, and many other organizations for the services, personal opportunities, and social life they offered.[2] Pressure group activity was very frequently an unanticipated, and often unwelcome, aspect of membership. In 1965, Mancur Olson fostered a major, still-flourishing, controversy by making this point the centre of a new theory of pressure group behaviour. In *The Logic of Collective Action,* he argues that most people rationally, if imperfectly, calculate the benefits and costs associated with taking part in interest organizations, and will not join them unless membership brings with it some benefit they would not otherwise obtain. In the absence of such inducements the only other motive would be that membership is a condition of employment, of practising a profession, or even of enjoying some benefit provided by government.[3] Olson's theory rests on the view that human beings are motivated by fear or greed, or both.

For the moment, I will not quarrel with this depressing perspective, but will consider instead Olson's explanation of how this view of human nature affects pressure groups. He argues that, in the eyes of members and potential members, interest organizations produce two kinds of benefits: 'collective benefits' and 'selective benefits'. Collective benefits are available to everyone in the community, regardless of how much or how little each has contributed to its creation and upkeep. Many people will share a common interest in obtaining a collective benefit, but if they can obtain it without exertion they will do so, in effect taking a 'free ride' at the expense of those who joined groups dedicated to providing it or to urging the government to provide it.[4] Evidence for this argument can be obtained on any summer day in any federal or provincial park. Millions of people enjoy these facilities every year, but very few support the Canadian Wildlife Federation and the other organizations that have lobbied for these parks and for the amenities they provide. While many who enjoy the parks may be aware that they share that enjoyment with others and that they all have a common interest, that awareness is unlikely to encourage them to join the Wildlife Federation, or any other parks-oriented pressure group.

Faced with the free-rider problem, Olson argues, groups develop selective benefits. These are:

> private benefits which, precisely because they are private rather than collective in nature, can operate selectively on the membership as a whole: they can be conferred upon those who contribute. . . . If a person wishes to obtain selective incentives he cannot do so by waiting for others to shoulder the costs. He will

have to 'qualify' to receive them, which in practice, ordinarily means paying dues and becoming a formal member.[5]

Members of the Wildlife Federation receive special literature about Canadian wildlife. They take part in conservation projects or are offered excursion rates to travel to conservation areas. According to Olson, these selective benefits — material, social, and psychic — are unavailable to non-members of the Wildlife Federation and are an inducement to join that body.

Similarly, the majority of Canadians cannot subscribe to the group life insurance plan available through the Canadian Association of University Teachers. Furthermore, Canadian university teachers who are not members of this association are ineligible to obtain the legal and other advisory services the CAUT makes available to affiliate groups engaged in collective bargaining; nor, if they are driven to strike action, can they draw on the association's strike fund. Even business associations, which are particularly oriented towards political intervention, develop selective inducements. As intermediaries between competing firms and government, they are often privy to information that is otherwise available only to individual firms and government regulators. Without breaking confidences, they are thus frequently in a position to offer mediating services to rivals within their membership.[6]

In Olson's estimation, selective inducements are in most cases the *raison d'être* of interest associations. Lobbying is, in effect, a by-product of group life:

> The lobbies of the large economic groups are the by-products of organizations that have the capacity to 'mobilize' a latent group with 'selective incentives'. The only organizations that have 'selective incentives' available are those that (1) have authority and capacity to be coercive, or (2) have a source of positive inducements that they can offer the individuals in a latent group.[7]

Other organizations are formed primarily to participate directly in policy-making. In Olson's view, they are groups with limited capacity: small bands of idealists caught up in a wave of public passion, and small solidary groups content to promote very narrow interests for limited returns. In effect, these groups are also using selective inducements to attract and sometimes to hold their members. The inducements are the promise of group social life or the psychological rewards of direct participation. Such inducements cannot easily survive organizational growth. When they are found in larger organizations, they are accompanied by other, more tangible incentives.[8]

Olson's theory explains a good deal about pressure group politics. It forcibly reminds us that for the majority of members, participation in the association is related to the specific benefits the group can provide, rather than to the promotion of the public interest. Though we have very little comparable Canadian data, one cannot help wondering whether Olson's thesis explains in part the low level of popular support for the Consumers' Association of Canada reported by Helen Jones Dawson:

> Membership has been a grave disappointment to the CAC since its earliest days when it was assumed that every woman in Canada would be happy to pay a fifty cent fee to belong to an organization which would inform her about consumer goods, represent her before the government, and protect her from unscrupulous manufacturers, producers and advertisers.[9]

Olson would diagnose the free-rider problem. He would note that two of the three benefits listed are collective benefits and would ask how the third — provision of information — had been made available. On learning that the organization's capacity to deal with individual concerns was extremely limited, he would conclude that the CAC really offered virtually no inducements to encourage Canadian women to become members. Considering these deficiencies in combination with the other problems identified by Dawson in her 1963 article — lack of money, poor communications, weak organization, and regional jealousies; executive procrastination and lack of agreement on organizational role, and pursuit of too many objectives — Olson would probably wonder how the CAC managed to survive at all.

The CAC did survive these difficult years and survives today, often appearing prominently in the news.[10] Yet its range of selective inducements is no more extensive than it was thirty years ago. Many other well-known organizations have also done as well or better — without offering selective inducements any more appealing than those offered by the CAC. Transport 2000 is an active lobby for public transportation systems that offers its members little more inducement to join than a mimeographed news-sheet and the exhilaration of lobbying in a cause that appears to be doomed. Yet Transport 2000 regularly prepares elaborate briefs for the Canadian Transport Commission and for ministers and parliamentary committees, and has become a force to be reckoned with. Though some of Transport 2000's members have been put out of work by rail closures or may fear for their jobs, many have joined because they feel government policy is misguided and they want a different kind of public transportation system for Canada.[11] For that collective benefit, they are prepared to put far more into Transport 2000 than the organization can ever give them in return.

The experience of such organizations forces us to question the Olsonian calculus of participation. If human beings are self-interested, rational, and calculating, why do so many devote much of their leisure time to the CAC, Transport 2000, Greenpeace, Planned Parenthood, and the thousands of other groups whose chief concern is to work for collective benefits? Olson and his supporters offer two explanations. First, non-material rewards, such as social rewards, enter into a personal calculation of marginal utility. Lifelong friendships can be made camping around a nuclear power station or sharing a paddy wagon. There can also be psychic rewards. Working for the CAC simply makes some people feel good. People may derive a great deal of moral satisfaction from helping to protect the consumer or from promoting world peace. The second explanation offered by Olsonian theorists is that while human beings are rational, calculating, and self-interested, they must also work with imperfect information.[12] They may underestimate the extent of the resources they will have to dedicate to a cause, they may overestimate the personal satisfactions they will derive from it, or they may simply not realize that they could derive as much satisfaction from doing something else. It is hard to believe that such miscalculations explain the dedication many men and women bring to the often disheartening work of the John Howard and Elizabeth Fry Societies, and the efforts to breathe life and vigour into many parent-teacher associations, and organizations such as the Canadian Cancer Society!

A third explanation, put forward by Terry M. Moe, introduces another dimension. He argues that people's assumptions about marginal increments are shaped by perceptions: 'behavioural expectations are contingent in specific ways upon perceptions.'[13] For example, a person with a well-developed sense of personal efficacy will consider that his or her participation in a cause 'makes a difference' in the struggle to persuade public authorities to pursue a particular, desired policy. In other words, both selective inducements and group goals can attract members.

All of these explanations are more or less plausible, but they push Olsonian theory beyond its limits. It may be true that a volunteer in the Elizabeth Fry Society derives great personal satisfaction from the exacting tasks that organization undertakes even in its policy-oriented aspects, but that satisfaction cannot be quantified in order to make Olson's concept operational. More important is the question of why members of the public should wish to devote themselves to group life when the rewards it brings seldom seem commensurate with the effort they must put into it. Nevertheless, Moe's observation is helpful because it suggests that the desire to participate may be rooted in the individual's experience of the processes of socialization. That is, the kind of people who join these groups have been taught a sense of civic responsibility from an early age. This supports the argument put forward by students of comparative politics that variations in political culture have a great deal to do with association-joining and political participation in general. A high degree of political efficacy and cognitive orientation in a community increases its chances of producing a lively group life.

I can accept Olson's notion that some groups find it useful to attract or hold members by offering secondary inducements, but I cannot agree that the concept of a calculus of participation explains all association-joining. It is true that virtually any satisfaction obtained from group participation can be labelled a secondary inducement; but since the great majority of these satisfactions cannot be quantified in the manner suggested by Olson, it will be more useful to consider them on their own merits rather than to rely on a spurious calculus.

What are these satisfactions and how do they lead people to join interest associations? Social or psychic satisfactions have little to do with the political aspects of interest group activity. Others, however, are related to political life. Moe's argument is that some people have a sufficiently high sense of personal efficacy to feel that their participation does make a difference. This is also experienced by the provincial or regional leaders of CAC and by many local members. They will point out that politicians believe that for each person participating directly in the CAC, many others in the general community hold similar views on issues. They thus feel they play a representative role. Such people provide the core of group life.

Many of these people also feel that they have a responsibility to participate, that a democratic society remains democratic only so long as the public at large monitors the work of government and lets public officials know when they are performing poorly, unjustly, or corruptly. Such sentiments explain the speed with which a protest movement can arise, and account for the longevity of organizations concerned with improving public policy, whether it relates to the prison system, public transportation, or the state of the environment. There is quantitative justification of this view in Moe's survey of five associations. Although over 50 per cent of respondents cited secondary inducements as the reason for joining, in three organizations 20 per cent or more were attracted by the association's work in promoting collective benefits. Obviously these three organizations would be much smaller if they did not offer secondary inducements, but a core of supporters seems willing to work chiefly for collective benefits. Had Moe surveyed public interest groups, he might have shed light on this willingness to work for collective benefits. As it is, he gives us some reason to believe that civic responsibility does play a part in motivating people to join interest groups.[14]

It may be that people who engage in group life because they feel their participation makes a difference or because they feel a responsibility to work for collective benefits derive their motivations from cultural factors. From childhood, in the family, in school, and in the organizational life that surrounds school and university, they have absorbed ideas — about human relationships, about the role of the individual in the community, and about the government's responsibility to promote the general welfare — that foster a tendency to take part in collective action. Since individual socialization experience differs — as does the response to it — some members of a political community will be strongly motivated to participate fully in it, while others will not feel that their involvement makes a difference or that they have a responsibility to take part.[15]

Not every active pressure group member wants to take part in group life, not even in exchange for selective benefits. Though potent social and psychological rewards often accompany membership, for many loyal members of interest associations the social contacts and duties of group life are painful rather than pleasant, tedious rather than gratifying. The parent who caps an exhausting, stressful week at work with a weekend of living out of a suitcase in order to take part in drafting a policy statement for a regional home-and-school association must — if we exclude sheer masochism — be motivated by a very strong sense of collective responsibility as well as a desire to benefit his or her own offspring. The parent would be inclined to agree with J.A. Corry: 'not many of us derive our satisfactions out of moulding complex collective decisions and carrying a heavy and ill-defined responsibility. We would much sooner leave the burden to someone else.'[16] Given a choice, that parent would likely prefer to communicate directly with educational policy-makers; to sit down with curriculum planners and argue the value of various teaching methods. He or she knows, however, that such opportunities are rare and that even when they do occur they are unlikely to lead to any direct change in public policy, because so many other opinions must be considered. As Leon Dion observes, 'Canadian institutions have evolved in a shape more or less consciously designed to discourage direct personal involvement in the political process.'[17] This is not solely a Canadian problem. André Holleaux, discussing group politics in France, notes that senior officials now see fewer and fewer individuals in the course of their working day, meeting instead with delegations representing groups.[18] Meynaud argues that this is a natural outgrowth of the increasing collectivization of modern life: individuals can interact less and less with the state when so many corporate interests — each representing many interests — are anxious to speak to various authorities. Such groups take precedence. To gain access the individual must combine with others.[19]

In an earlier period, the policy-conscious citizen might have chosen to exert influence on decision-makers through the political party, but that option, for the reasons outlined in earlier chapters, is no longer viable. The development of bureaucratic power, the diffuse nature of party concerns, and the increasing recognition given to sectoral groups all suggest to the questioning citizen that the only effective way to participate in the policy process is to work through pressure groups active in the relevant field. In short, there is a strong institutional incentive to join interest associations. This incentive borders on coercion, since the majority of citizens cannot exercise the rights of citizenship apart from group affiliation. Faced with a choice between remaining mute or engaging in group life, most citizens opt for silence. The minority who elect to join associations provide the semi-captive labour force that keeps those organizations going.

I have identified five factors that I believe motivate individuals to become members of interest groups: selective inducements, the promise of collective benefits, socialization to a sense of civic responsibility, a strong sense of political efficacy, and institutional coercion. Before discussing the different ways these factors influence the interior life of groups, I should note that they are not mutually exclusive. A person may join a group for one, several, or all of the reasons embodied in the five factors. For example, a lawyer is coerced into joining the bar association, but may also feel the attraction of deriving both direct and selective benefits from it, while feeling a civic duty to influence the development of the law in the belief that the bar association is a useful vehicle for attaining that end. Because such motivations very often combine in a given membership, both observers and leaders of groups have difficulty in assessing precisely what group members hope to achieve by joining specific organizations — and how those organizations should be made to serve them. I will discuss this point in the next two sections of this chapter.

One other point should be made first. I have tended to speak in terms of, and to cite examples of, the motives that lead to participation in established groups. How does our argument relate to individuals who join — or form — new groups? While coercion is unlikely to prompt people to join such groups, all the other motivations can come into play, though cultural incentives and the promise of direct benefits are probably the most important. An environmentalist, for example, on first learning about the destructive effects of clear-cutting, could — if sufficiently endowed with a sense of efficacy and of social responsibility — decide to join with others to create an organization to combat the problem. The decision to select group action rather than elite action or individual intercession might well reflect awareness of institutional imperatives, even though that awareness might be accompanied by the knowledge that nascent groups do not easily obtain access to the policy system. Even selective inducements may play a part in the decision to join or create a new group: the yearning for a sense of solidarity, the gratifications of participation, the sense of leadership — all these can be significant non-material inducements to take part.

GROUP TYPES AND THE AVAILABILITY OF RESOURCES

Interest group resources fall into three categories: knowledge, mandate, and wealth. The capacity of a group to muster these resources depends largely, but not entirely, on the capacities and inclinations of the membership. There is consequently a direct relation between the type of group that members are disposed to create and the resources available to it. I will first examine what is meant by knowledge, mandate, and wealth, and then will discuss how various kinds of groups use them differently.

Knowledge

Interest group knowledge is of two kinds: knowledge about the substance of policy, and knowledge about the policy process. Extensive acquisition of the one does not necessarily entail a grasp of the other, as both specialists and generalists have sometimes learned to their cost. Substantive knowledge derives from the experience an organization acquires in meeting the needs of its members. Most of this work may have little to do with policy-making, but in doing it the organization develops an intimate understanding of its special field and ultimately that understanding may become highly relevant to some policy debate. Substantive knowledge is generally expert knowledge,[20] which permits one to say to public decision-makers, 'If you do this, that will happen,' and to know that the statement will be accepted. For many groups this is a precious resource. It is their key to access and influence, for in many instances government has no expertise of its own and no other source of information. Thus critics of the National Energy Board complain that the Board and the Department of Energy, Mines and Resources is totally dependent on the oil companies and the Oil Producers' Association of Canada for their knowledge of the country's resources of hydrocarbons.[21] Coleman and Jacek note that intra-industry surveys carried out by chemical industry associations sometimes offer the only data available to regulators, either because Statistics Canada has cut back on data collection in recent years or has never generated data of the type required. According to them, 'the Canadian Fertilizer Institute suggests that its Canadian Fertilizer Information System is now the only authoritative source on the production and consumption of fertilizers in Canada.'[22] Information monopolies of this sort are doubly valuable in group relations with government: not only do they assure the group of a place in the policy process, but discreet manipulation of data can be used to shape the thinking of policy-makers. Critics of energy policy have argued that Canadian reserves of hydrocarbons have at times been grossly overestimated in order to persuade public authorities to allow producers to export large quantities of oil and natural gas deemed 'excess' to Canadian needs. Even when it is not of strategic importance, information can be valuable currency in winning the regard of public decision-makers, as the following cautionary tale suggests:

One civil servant conducting a background study on a certain industry needed information that, although in the public domain, required laborious collection. Realizing that these data would have been collected by the industry's trade association, he called, explained his purpose and requested the information. He was refused, abruptly. And what did this refusal accomplish? Because the information in question was still obtainable for the report, the only result was one very irritated civil servant. And since this civil servant was a specialist in the industry he was studying, the next time the trade association might have occasion to lobby Ottawa, this same civil servant would become involved and he would remember.[23]

John Bulloch, of the Canadian Federation of Independent Business, maintains that '75 per cent of our time is spent responding to requests by government institutions for advice and assistance on every facet of public policy—federal as well as provincial.'[24] Even allowing for exaggeration, this suggests that the Federation has at its disposal a resource that can, if adroitly used, win it important concessions from government. While the diversity of the CFIB's interests and the size of its membership probably makes it unusual in the information business, it is conceivable that a significant number of other interest groups occupy strategically useful positions thanks to their command of information resources.

Besides being useful in government-group relations, information is of value in the relations between the interest association and its members. An organization that stands in a relation of trust between its members and government not only obtains a perspective on the membership that is not available to individuals, but acquires an authority over and above the willingness of members to support it. This is one of the factors that makes the organization necessary to its supporters and it contributes to the independence sometimes shown towards members by the organization staff and leadership. The tendency of government agencies to use the interest organization as a vehicle for communicating with its members also enhances the stature and independence of the leadership and staff, and gives them core assets—advance intimations of policy change, for example—that can be used in bargaining with members. Government, simply by using the organization as an information conduit, enhances its status with its supporters.

Policy-process information is not the hard currency that substantive knowledge can often be, but it is nonetheless valuable, as the success in Ottawa of many lobbying firms attests. Without a considerable knowledge of how the policy process works, it is easy to waste valuable substantive information. According to John Bulloch:

> The crucial thing is to know to whom to talk. It follows that you get better at lobbying over time, because it takes so long to infiltrate the system and find out who really makes the decisions. Organization charts are useless. You have to find out who sits on the interdepartmental committees. Every department has its own power structure, and it takes a lot of digging and a lot of contacts to find who makes the decisions. In some cases the ministers are very powerful, but in others they have very little power and major decisions are made for them by their senior advisers.[25]

Knowing who does what, and where, helps the lobbyist place information. A minister does not want to see a complex brief on a technical point; a deputy minister objects to being troubled with minor questions; a junior official may give useful advice on a major proposal, but is probably not the appropriate person to receive a formal proposal on the agency's behalf. The lobbyist wise in the ways of the policy process selects each contact with care, attempting to gauge the impact of each nugget of information on different policy actors, and its subsequent effect as it works its way through the policy system. Implicit in each decision on the placement of information is a further decision about the overall objective of the policy exercise. If hoping to achieve only a minor modification of policy — or wishing to present as routine a more significant change — the lobbyist will probably initiate the process at the lowest level in the bureaucracy competent to deal with the matter. First contacts may be made with technical specialists. A more complex proposal might involve multiple contacts — lobbyists handling complex proposals are sometimes advised to engage as many officials as possible in the undertaking since each, if properly approached, will develop an interest in promoting the scheme.[26] Major change may take years and engage an entire policy community (a process I discussed in Chapter 6) or may be approached more vigorously via a frontal lobbying of parliamentary institutions and ministers. To quote John Bulloch again:

> if what you want is to put pressure on the system, there is nothing more effective than going to your Member of Parliament who can be influential in caucus — and in the question period. In earlier days, when we were involved in a less sophisticated form of lobbying, the question period was one of our most powerful instruments because Members can obtain information that the government would not give us. It became a great game of providing the Opposition with material for the question period. We go about our business differently now because we have access to government. But smaller groups which lack clout and access do find the question period a valuable lobbying tool and an important instrument of influence.[27]

Bulloch suggests that the parliamentary route is used primarily by nascent groups that lack a sophisticated knowledge of the policy process. However, as we saw in Chapter 3, institutionalized groups have in recent years tended to approach Parliament partly because the changing nature of the policy process demands it, but also because there is a new leverage to be obtained from contesting departmental decisions before Parliament. Labour groups, for example, because they frequently challenge the prevailing economic structure, are often to be seen demonstrating on Parliament Hill and bringing pressure to bear on the government through question period and other parliamentary devices.

The kind of information available to a group is determined by the composition of its members, its organizational structure, its ideological orientation, and the policy field it chooses to participate in. These factors are often interrelated, and tend to govern the way information is used.

Group type has a profound influence. A group located at the nascent end of the policy continuum I presented in Chapter 5 is less likely than a highly institutionalized group to have at hand process information or to know how to use it. Donald Chant, in his account of the early days of Pollution Probe, noted the naivety of his younger associates when faced with determined attempts by industry to suppress information about the fluoride pollution emanating from the Electric Reduction Company plant at Port Maitland, Ontario.[28] Though many of them were science students at the University of Toronto and were knowledgeable about chemical processes and pollution, they were baffled by the policy process. As the environmental movement gained ground and their own organization became influential, they acquired even greater respect for sound substantive knowledge — their capacity to prepare a thorough and accurate brief helped win recognition — and they became more sophisticated in the ways of policy-making. Yet they did not abandon a lobbying style that many interest representatives consider dysfunctional. A penchant for publicity and a conviction that 'when seeking decisive action . . . one should approach the real centres of power: Cabinet members . . . and other political leaders', are not recommended long-term strategies.[29] Nevertheless, this approach was effective for Pollution Probe — for reasons that illustrate our earlier point: the availability and use of information reflects group type, membership, ideology, and the policy field it works in. When Pollution Probe was launched, no distinct field of environmental policy existed; there was merely a series of discrete policy fields, many of them belonging to quite different sectors. Water-quality issues tended to be associated with the Department of Mines and Technical Surveys, because water was used in the production of energy, or was necessary to the majority of mineral extraction or manufacturing processes. Water purity was seldom considered, except in regard to its potability. Further issues raised by the environmental movement were treated by other agencies and from different perspectives. Consequently, Pollution Probe and other environmental groups could not affiliate themselves with a ready-made policy community. Instead they had to create one, which entailed shaking up the policy system as a whole. Therefore it made sense to tackle the centres of power, as Chant recommended, since only premiers and Cabinet ministers could bring about the major structural changes needed to create agencies to which environmental groups could attach themselves. Once those agencies were created, environmental groups changed their communication tactics, becoming much less visible and developing the more traditional characteristics of institutionalized pressure groups.

It was not the nature of the policy field alone that dictated a particular communications style. Although Pollution Probe at first knew more about the nature of the policy problem than about bureaucratic processes, it did not experience the setbacks endured by other nascent groups when it insisted on going to the top as well as appealing to the public at large because it was part of a widespread movement. Nevertheless, its strong issue orientation became an organizational problem for the group as it developed. David Hoffman, observing it several years after its formation, commented:

> The experience of Pollution Probe illustrates an aspect of the question of the most effective strategy for groups who wish to make major changes in the system. It seems that there has been considerable controversy within the organization about what the strategy should be and the discussion has focussed on whether efforts 'within the system' are worthwhile at all. Some of the Pollution Probe staff feel that attempting to influence environmental policy through accepted channels will only bring about short-term benefits, and that longer-term results require 'confrontation' strategies — that is, challenges to the entire system of decision-making. Partly in response to this difference of opinion the staff has now been divided into four distinct 'teams', each of which tends to have its own approach to influencing public policy. The energy team, for example, participates actively on various government boards and hearings, but an educational team that operates in Ward 3 of the City of Toronto, on the other hand, is deeply committed to the promotion of citizen participation.[30]

This shows the intimate connection between group type, ideology, and membership characteristics. Formed around a specific issue (a particular problem of air pollution) and building on a strategy of starting with limited, 'clearly identified, highly visible local issues with which the public can readily identify before moving on to large issues of more far-reaching importance', Pollution Probe took the first step towards institutionalization: it broadened its mandate. Its membership — mainly young people inclined to take strong ideological positions — was oriented more to issues than to process. As the resolution of specific issues proceeded differently, ideological positions developed differently. In the energy sector, where some goals were achieved, members softened their ideological view of the tactics of change. This made them feel more effective; they understood, or felt they understood, how to make the system work for them. Where more resistance was encountered, their ideological orientation to confrontation became a commitment and they used their information more abrasively. These divergent approaches produced cathartic tensions within the organization. Pollution Probe experienced 'horizontally' an information problem that the majority of groups experience 'vertically': the vertical information problem arises as leaders of nascent groups become knowledgeable about the policy process, come to feel more effective in it, and consequently tend to move away from their followers — who begin to worry that the leadership has been co-opted. As one group leader put it, 'we're dealing with incredible anger . . . you have to play a game of taking swings at people just to keep the troops in line.'[31] It is not enough for leaders of pressure groups to have process knowledge; their followers should have it as well.

Pollution Probe shows the interdependence of information and organizational characteristics in a group in the early stages of institutionalization. The committee system used in the interest associations representing the chemical industry illustrates the way highly institutionalized groups structure themselves to convey technical information. According to Jacek and Coleman, the 26 interest associations active in the field involve representatives of their member firms in over 100 specialized committees dealing with matters that range from product development to the transportation of dangerous goods, consumer relations, taxation, planning, and tariff matters.[32] The industry considers many of these committees crucial to the successful representation of its interests; companies are willing to underwrite the travelling expenses and time of their employees selected to serve on them. In certain cases, company delegates come from the executive ranks. The Canadian Pharmaceutical Manufacturers' Association requires constitutionally that senior executives serve on its major committees. Coleman and Jacek found that for two associations 32.6 per cent of committee representatives were company presidents; 27.4 per cent were general managers; 24.2 per cent were vice-presidents, and only 15.8 per cent were divisional managers or held lower positions in the hierarchy. To support their activities, twenty of the industry associations employed in 1979 an average of 4.85 permanent staff members, though the ten major associations employed an average of 7.25 permanent staff.[33] On the surface, these figures seem modest, compared with the 30 permanent staff employed by the one union in the chemical field, the Energy and Chemical Workers' Union. It must be remembered that senior executives serving an industry association in this way can, and do, draw on company expertise to accommodate their committee assignments. Unions do not have these supplementary resources. Business-interest associations are expected to devote a considerable proportion of their energies to conveying information between members and government, as well as between members themselves. The scale and complexity of the effort they devote to information-processing alone is impressive. There can be no surer indication of its importance as an interest-group resource.

Mandate

Mandate is the other face of legitimacy. Legitimacy ensures that a group will be heard in policy conclaves, and mandate is the express assignment of representative capacity to a group's leadership by its membership.[34] As long as group representatives retain that mandate, what they say is the legitimate expression of the group will. If that mandate is withdrawn or overreached, their legitimacy is diminished—and to some extent, so is that of the organization.

Mandate does not depend entirely on membership support, any more than legitimacy is a function exclusively of that support. The other organizations the group deals with can, by conferring legitimacy, also assign a mandate to the group. According to Kwavnick:

> The demands for organizational recognition made upon government by interest group leaders may overshadow the demands which they make in pursuit of the interests of their group's membership and are among the most important demands that they make.[35]

A labour union that wins the support of a collective-bargaining unit has a mandate from the members of that unit; in the eyes of the unit's members the union has legitimacy. In the eyes of the public — and possibly in those of the management of the firm involved — true legitimacy is not achieved until the appropriate labour relations board certifies the union and recognizes that it, and it alone, has the right to represent the employees in that bargaining unit.

So it is with most pressure groups. Any entrepreneur can, by establishing an organization, claim to speak for a particular interest. Government must be assured that the organization adequately represents the interest it purports to speak for, and that the leadership of the organization is itself duly constituted. Failure to provide these assurances exposes government to the difficulties I enumerated in Chapter 5, where I discussed communication and legitimation as functions of pressure groups. Once its mandate is secured and its legitimacy established, an organization can obtain from government supplementary mandates that reinforce its legitimacy with members, with government, and with other groups.

The quest for mandate, then, may be important enough to group leaders to lead them to take decisions that affect the structure and policies of the organization. I noted how Pollution Probe had diversified its organization in order to reduce tensions emanating from the different perceptions of strategy and tactics held by members. In part, diversification was an exercise in reasserting mandate. Elements that had difficulty working together on middle- and short-range goals might continue to adhere to the organization if they could work separately on those goals. Thus the overall mandate of the group would be maintained. Not all groups find decentralization an entirely satisfactory solution to the mandate problem. For many organizations in the Canadian political system decentralization is essential, but not necessarily conducive to reaching agreement on global objectives. The leadership of the National Indian Brotherhood (NIB), for example, in working with a specially established federal Cabinet subcommittee to consider major Native issues, found that its powerful provincial affiliates frequently challenged the mandate of national representatives and thus undermined the legitimacy of the NIB in the eyes of federal politicians and officials.[36] Faced with a similar problem, the Canadian Labour Congress responded by seeking to reinforce and extend the portion of its mandate derived from government:

> The weakness of the central organization, the limited role or *raison d'être* of the Congress and the fact that even this is subject to challenge by the larger affiliates and the AFL-CIO have resulted in an attempt by the Congress leadership to institutionalize the Congress as a recognized component of the Canadian political and social system. The ultimate aim . . . is to create a position for the Congress in the minds of the trade unionists, government and the public at large in addition to the position which the Congress occupies within the trade union movement.[37]

As these illustrations suggest, mandate as a resource is subject to constraints very similar to those that affect information as a resource: constraints that stem from the composition of the membership. Organization type and group ideology will affect the leadership's capacity to secure a firm mandate and thus to win recognition from government. At the same time, the leadership can secure or reinforce membership support if it obtains some token of recognition from government. For example, the Union of Nova Scotia Municipalities (UNSM) was established as a mechanism for transmitting the demands of member municipalities to the provincial government. Even though it was hampered by the reluctant support of some members, the UNSM found that an equivalent factor in securing legitimacy was the provincial government's decision to use the organization as a mechanism for the downward transmittal of government views to members. Government recognition and legitimation consequently encouraged member support.[38]

Our illustrations have also suggested some of the strategies used by groups to secure mandate. Clearly these can be too numerous to outline in detail here. Among the most important are:

1. Pursuing issues that members can identify with and that, while associated with larger goals, are limited enough to be resolvable through group action. This strategy is especially appropriate to small nascent groups.
2. Development of selective inducements that may persuade members to remain loyal to the group, even if they are not strong supporters of primary group objectives.
3. Diversification of goals in order to tap a larger membership pool.
4. Securing external recognition and material support. The former, whether obtained from government or from other groups, heightens legitimacy in the eyes of members; the latter gives group leadership some independence from the membership.
5. Decentralizing group organization along territorial and/or sectoral lines. As we have seen, this strategy creates difficulties of its own, but it broadens participation and helps to resolve conflicts within specialized committees and branch associations.

This list by no means exhausts the strategies available to groups in their efforts to create and bolster their mandates, but it suggests what can be done.

Wealth

Lobbying is popularly associated with illicit distribution of wealth by 'monied interests' anxious to buy political favours. History has shown that this is often precisely what lobbying is all about, but it has also shown that the reality is more complex and that the monied interests are not the only ones that must be prepared to spend considerable sums to achieve their aims. In fact, the nefarious, cigar-smoking lobbyist who bribes public officials very likely spends far less than does the average public interest group that, with the purest of motives, seeks to persuade the community to follow what it conceives to be the community's own best interest. The lobbyist buys decisions, but the public interest group buys policies, which are far rarer and far harder to obtain in the political market-place.

The object of any lobbying exercise cannot be obtained without the expenditure of money, or a money substitute. The modest group defending trees in an urban neighbourhood finds it needs financial resources, just as does the sophisticated, established, institutionalized group fighting its way with batteries of lawyers and consultants through law courts, regulatory bodies, agencies, and legislatures. The pertinent questions to ask relate not to the expenditure of money — though it is important to know how much money must be spent — but to where it can be obtained. Broadly speaking, there are four principal sources:

1. Members
2. Friends
3. Governments
4. The sale of goods and services

I will look briefly at each of these sources and at what their assistance might mean for different kinds of interest organizations.

But first, what are the costs of lobbying? Much depends on the type of lobbying. Between 1979 and 1984 Gulf Canada spent $21.6 million on its public affairs budget, a major part of which was used to finance an advertising campaign intended to enhance Gulf's public image and to win support for the company's energy policy position.[39] Ongoing lobbying of one or two agencies can be much less expensive. Coleman and Jacek report that in 1979 the Canadian Soap and Detergent Association cost its backers only $8,000. Of the twenty business associations surveyed by Jacek and Coleman, the average expenditure in 1979 was $303,740, with the most costly, the Pharmaceutical Manufacturers' Association, spending $900,000. In addition, like most business interest groups they received free services from their members. The Petroleum Association for the Conservation of the Environment (PACE) drew from its members some 216 executive person-days of work for each of its committees. At executive rates of pay, such activities represent a substantial supplement to formal membership dues. Labour organizations do not as a rule have available money substitutes of this kind, but because their costs are spread across many thousands of members they can generate financial resources equal to, and often greater than, those of the larger business groups. Thus the poor relations in the interest-group family tend to be the smaller professional groups and many public-interest groups. Of nineteen environmental groups surveyed in 1987 for Atomic Energy of Canada Limited, only one, Greenpeace Canada, had a budget of $1.5 million. The combined budgets of the rest came to only $2.4 million.[40] Variable though they are, these figures give us an idea of the sums involved in run-of-the-mill interest representation.

Where does the money come from? Foremost on the list of financial supporters are the group members themselves. This is so for two reasons. First, because membership implies a commitment, however modest, to sustain the group's organization in its endeavours, the organization can reasonably expect each member to contribute something — money, labour, or material — to its work. Second, membership support is a symbol to the members of their own commitment, while to government and other groups it is one of the few indications of the extent to which the group represents the interest it claims to speak for. That is why politicians and officials often question group representatives closely about the number of dues-paying members and other supporters involved with their organizations. Such inquisitions are intended to establish the organization's credentials.

Actual membership dues are often modest, particularly those of voluntary organizations. Labour and professional organizations that can employ an element of coercion to obtain members are generally more pressing in their demands, as are business interest associations that provide a vital service to their supporters. Dues reflect what the market will bear. In the case of many public-interest groups, they also reflect a trade-off between the need for funds and the desire for representativeness: it is better to impress government with 30,000 members, each paying $15, than to fix dues at $50 and attract only 8,000 members. Other financial considerations may also dictate lower fees. Some selective inducements may be more feasible if offered to a larger market: for example, if a group publishes a trade journal, a membership and subscription fee of $50 may not cover the costs of running both organization and journal; but securing a wider readership may guarantee that the organization can sell more advertising space — and at a higher price — to firms wanting to reach its membership.

Most organizations include members who are prepared to donate their own time, the resources of their firms, or their own personal resources; some organizations can attract supplementary financial supports in the form of donations, 'sustaining members' fees, and so on. Charitable foundations and public-interest groups can sometimes count as well on receiving bequests.

For many groups, friends as well as members are a source of support. This is particularly true of public-interest groups, the more affluent of which solicit donations from people anxious to support their cause or from corporations that wish to be seen as 'good corporate citizens'. Sometimes such donations are given for specific projects, sometimes for the work of the organization in general. Friends may also include allied groups that are interested in promoting a particular cause but do not wish to undertake all, or even part, of the campaign themselves. Church organizations, for example, gave support to the issue-oriented groups promoting the Canadian recognition of Biafra during the Nigerian civil war, but they were reluctant to jeopardize their own ties with the Department of External Affairs by vigorously and publicly promoting the same cause.[41]

When the contributions of friends and members are insufficient to sustain the work of a group, the most likely alternative source of funds is government, particularly the federal government. Such support comes in a variety of forms. Perhaps the most bizarre was the catch of squid used to underwrite the Eastern Fishermen's Federation (EFF) in its first years of operation. Until the late 1970s, squid was not a species strongly exploited by Canadian fisheries. At the end of the decade, however, the Japanese sought permission to take squid off the east coast. Permission was granted, but rights to the fish were given to the EFF, which then earned a commission on its sale to the Japanese.[42] Less unusual forms of government support include direct and indirect financial assistance; training; recognition; secondment of personnel to specific groups — a practice more common in Europe than in Canada[43] — and access to government resources such as office space, databanks, telecommunications equipment, and libraries.[44] William T. Stanbury has analysed the 1986-7 *Public Accounts of Canada* in an attempt to determine how much the federal government paid interest groups to support their advocacy activities; that is, activities such as making representations on policy issues, organizing conferences, policy research, and negotiating with government. Even after excluding payments to groups for services that had nothing to do with policy advocacy — such as providing shelters for battered women — Stanbury calculated that in 1986-7 17 federal departments had paid $184,995,000 to over 500 groups.[45]

Direct financial support comes in the forms of sustaining funding and project grants. Sustaining grants — or core funding as it is often called — is intended to assist groups to meet general expenses. For example, Consumer and Corporate Affairs Canada, in providing core grants to national voluntary consumers organizations, requires that the grants must be used to meet operating costs arising from the organizations' 'on-going work, including permanent staff salaries, rent and overhead expenses'.[46] Project funding supports groups' discrete activities. These can include organizing conferences, carrying out research, administering programs, developing and distributing publications, and offering training programs, to name a few. Many projects could as easily be carried out by private sector firms, and they are subject to the type of controls that apply to government contracts with businesses, including strict financial reporting requirements and little freedom to change the terms of agreements. A special category of project support is intervenor funding, which helps organizations to prepare submissions for public inquiries and administrative tribunals, such as environment assessment panels.[47]

Indirect government financial support is obtained through the tax system: businesses can treat association dues and employee involvement in business-interest groups as a legitimate business expense for tax purposes; individuals can deduct union and professional dues from gross income when calculating their taxable incomes; and contributions to a large number of public-interest groups are tax deductible. Designation as a charitable organization also often entitles groups to be excused from paying income, sales, and property taxes. In addition to federal government support, groups receive similar assistance from provincial governments and, to a much more limited extent, from municipal authorities. In theory, indirect support through the tax system allows the public — rather than government officials — to decide which public interest groups deserve the most support, but, as we shall see, official discretion has a role to play here as well as in determining which groups should benefit from core and project funding.

Many different types of groups receive government support. Public-interest groups are prominent among them. According to Stanbury, 160 groups interested in public interest matters received $23,367,000 from the federal government in 1986-87.[48] Core funding is often provided to organizations representing disadvantaged sections of the community, particularly the groups recognized in the Charter of Rights as deserving special protection and support. These include the groups representing and promoting equality for aboriginal peoples, women, senior citizens, and the handicapped.

A glance through the federal and provincial public accounts quickly reveals that many other groups receive substantial governmental support. The majority of cultural, professional, and academic groups as well as a number of ethnic groups derive a significant part of their revenues from government.[49] In many cases they could not exist otherwise. Even some business-oriented groups receive government assistance. We have already cited the support given to the Eastern Fishermen's Federation. In another field, the federal and Alberta governments have provided the Sulphur Development Institute of Canada with a substantial portion of its income since it was first established in 1973; in that year, 78 per cent of the association's income came from government, and six years later, in 1979, it still amounted to 50 per cent.[50]

Government financial support of interest groups raises important questions not only for government and groups, but for the public at large.

From a strictly financial perspective, governments are concerned about the rising costs of supporting interest groups, about the problem of deciding which should receive support, and about ensuring that funds are used for the purposes for which they were allocated and are properly accounted for. The accountability of groups has been a concern for some years. It has prompted studies by the Auditor General, inquiries by parliamentary committees, and, in some cases, alleged misallocation of funds has figured in criminal prosecutions.[51] These concerns in part account for an agency tendency to move away from core funding in favour of project support, because the latter can be more closely monitored. The federal government took steps to address the problem of rising costs by imposing cutbacks on grants and contributions to interest groups in the 1990 and 1991 budgets.[52] The outcry from groups affected by the cuts drew attention to the great variation in the criteria agencies use to allocate funds to groups.[53] This had been a concern to groups since the 1970s and had been the object of internal reviews within some agencies.[54] It is unlikely that a standard set of criteria will be adopted easily. Agencies have a great variety of reasons for wishing to support groups and are themselves apt to be influenced by the special pleading of those groups that are closely affiliated with them and dependent on them.

As far as groups are concerned, public funding, however necessary it may be, brings with it problems of uncertainty, dependence, and a tendency to distort the goals of their organization. Distortion occurs because governments frequently see groups as instruments for achieving their own goals, so that groups 'must fight to retain their integrity in an environment where there is often a conflict between the ultimate objectives of the donor and those of the association'.[55] Consequently, a group, anxious to obtain the funds needed to keep valued staff members employed, 'may gradually and almost unconsciously accommodate itself to the funder over time'.[56] Uncertainty is a product of inconsistent procedures for handling applications, a lack of standard criteria for determining which groups should be funded, the short term of most grants — often six months, sometimes a year, with renewals far from automatic — and, of course, the limited resources available for governments to distribute. Uncertainty means that organizations with limited resources must spend disproportionate amounts of energy making applications, meeting with officials, and generally lobbying for support. It also means that organizations deriving a large part of their income from government become dependent on the agencies with which they are affiliated.

It is on the issue of dependency that the concerns of groups, governments, and the public at large come together. Although public-interest groups are funded by government because society values their capacity to contribute to public debate, the very fact that they are supported by government is a problem. As Don Smiley puts it:

> Can anyone seriously believe that effective challenges to the social, economic, and political order can be made by groups relying on federal organizational and financial support? ... Even under benign circumstances, private associations dependent on the state are corrupted as their tests of their own performance and that of their leadership comes largely to be success in deriving financial support from government.[57]

The public naturally suspects that a dependent relationship cannot be disinterested.

The experience of the Nova Scotia Fishermen's Association is a case in point. The NSFA set out to organize inshore fishermen by espousing a philosophy of independence quite different from the collective bargaining approach adopted by its chief rival, the Maritime Fishermen's Union. A start-up grant of $50,000 from the government of Nova Scotia became an embarrassment. It earned the association the stigma of being 'government controlled', while government recognition entailed an obligation to participate extensively in fisheries policy discussions. The association's resources could not sustain such a level of participation; members came to feel that the leadership was losing touch with the rank and file. Despite their criticism of government support, members resisted a reorganization and revised fee structure designed to ensure independence from government so that ultimately the association was forced to abandon its attempt to speak for all Nova Scotia's inshore fishermen.[58] In a similar vein, Dominique Clift argues that Montreal's English-language community was unable to evolve a credible independent response to the Parti Québécois's 1980 referendum position because its interest associations were heavily subsidized by the federal Privy Council Office and Secretary of State.[59]

The fact that agencies exchange material and positional support for group endorsement of their policies and organizational demands reinforces public doubt. The director of policy studies at the Canadian Arctic Resources Committee, Don Gamble, commented: 'Interest groups should probably not rely on government for funding. It is unhealthy. Not only does it leave them vulnerable to a sudden policy change, but they might well find that the more effective they become, the faster their funding dries up.'[60] It is implicit in the conclusion reached in a study of federal funding trends that 'funding is relatively secure for groups — official language minority associations and multicultural groups — which support the symbolic order of the Canadian identity, but has declined considerably for groups which promote rights of other collectivities, notably women and Aboriginal peoples.'[61] The criticism by constitutional experts, who fear that Charter groups are distorting constitutional renewal processes by demanding participation and special protection, is an immediate and practical expression of these same concerns.[62]

Nor are groups and agencies insensitive to them. The criticism of one group representative, Don Gamble, has been cited. Groups appearing before a 1977 task force on voluntary organizations made the same points, repeatedly.[63] Fear of reprisal influences group behaviour, especially when organizations that have criticized government policy are seen to suffer cutbacks.[64] Although officials do not readily admit to manipulating groups, they too voice related concerns about the tendency of groups that have received core funding to develop a conviction that they are entitled to it on a continuing basis and that they are in a sense the 'chosen instrument' of the agency in the policy community.[65] This concern is closely related to a second one having to do with the representativeness of the groups that agencies support. How truly do these groups reflect the concerns of their supporters and of similar members of the public?[66] In providing support for some groups, are agencies inadvertently embroiling themselves in the factionalism that is found in many interest communities? The role of Agriculture Canada *vis-à-vis* the Canadian Federation of Agriculture and the National Farmers Union and of the Secretary of State *vis-à-vis* the National Action Committee on the Status of Women and REAL Women are two well-known examples. Are they fostering one point of view at the expense of others that deserve a hearing?

Such concerns invite the fundamental question of whether or not governments should assist groups at all. Although in the long run groups do not benefit from being subsidized by government and dynamic public debate is constrained, the answer to this question — in Canada, at least — is that government has little choice but to support them. There are two reasons for this. First, even if government were to abstain from providing direct financial and material support to any group, it would still influence group development and group behaviour. Even the most rudimentary processes of consultation favour some groups over others. Again, the decision not to fund any groups would favour those groups that do not need funding. If public funding were not available to some portions of the community, they would very likely not be heard from at all, which would weaken not only those sectors but the quality of public debate.

Consequently the public, groups, and governments have to accept the inevitability of public funding for groups, and the real issue becomes one of finding a means of ensuring that all elements of the community have a reasonable opportunity to be heard in public debate. In other words, because an independent pressure group system is as important to competent and democratic government as are a dynamic party system and a free press, every effort should be made to structure the processes of group-state relations so that the dangers of intimidation, favouritism, and manipulation are minimized.

Given the realities of politics, such a goal would always be an ideal, but some remedies are possible. Tax provisions for affecting interest groups could be revised to eliminate the advantages accruing to business interest associations and to make more realistic provision for groups speaking to the public interest.* An explicit policy of neutrality on the part of governments would go a long way to ensuring a vibrant and beneficial interest group politics. Governments could ensure that criteria for awarding support are standardized and applied in an even-handed way. 'Sunset rules' might be applied to groups looking for seed money. That is, a group might be granted

---

*Those who would argue that many public interest groups have an alternative source of funding in charitable donation should note that even that area is not immune to manipulation. Although public interest groups claim charitable status as trusts for 'purposes beneficial to the community', they are constrained by the view of the courts that trusts established for political objectives are not valid charities (John Swaigen, *How to Fight for What's Right* [Toronto: James Lorimer, 1981], 126). Since the term 'political' has not been authoritatively defined in this context, it puts great discretion in the hands of the officials responsible for determining whether or not an organization is entitled to charitable status. A 1977 circular issued by Revenue Canada defined the appropriate activity of charitable groups so narrowly that many groups complained of harassment. (See House of Commons, *Debates*, 1 May 1978.) In 1984, group leaders noted that Revenue Canada began a vigorous review of the political activities of groups with charitable organization status shortly after Prime Minister Trudeau harshly criticized groups opposing cruise-missile testing (a point made by a public interest group director during an off-the-record interview. Mr Trudeau's comments were reported in *Maclean's*, 23 May 1983). By April 1984, the media were reporting complaints that Revenue Canada was threatening 'a growing number' of charitable organizations with removal of status if they took stands on public policy issues. George Rohn, Director General of the Canadian Mental Health Association, was reported to know of sixteen groups receiving warnings. Ian Morrison, chairman of the National Coalition of Voluntary Organizations, claimed that many of the 126 organizations in his group would not admit to being threatened because they 'don't want to draw attention to themselves'. He cited the experience of the Quebec Social Rehabilitation Association, a prisoner rehabilitation organization that was denied charitable status because it had publicly argued against the building of more prisons (Halifax, *Chronicle-Herald*, 4 April 1984; Andrew Cohen, 'Who makes the rules?', *Canadian Associations*, June 1984, 10-12). In response, the 1985 federal budget provided that organizations would be entitled to participate in political activities if the activities were 'ancillary and incidental to their charitable purposes' (Hon. Michael Wilson. Minister of Finance. *Technical notes to a bill amending the Income Tax Act and related statutes* [Ottawa, Nov. 1985] Revenue Canada. Taxation. 'Registered charities — ancillary and incidental political activities', *Information Circular No. 87-1* [Ottawa, 25 Feb. 1987]; Arthur M. Timms, 'The complementary interplay of charitable organizations and governments', *Canadian Associations*, March 1986, 32-33). Although this clarifies the position of many groups providing services directly to the community (e.g., social welfare groups, prisoners' aid societies, and so on) the status of those formed to promote public debate was left in doubt. Doubt was not dispelled by a recent discussion paper from Revenue Canada (*A Better Tax Administration in Support of Charities* [Ottawa, 1990]). Its bias was clearly against those groups that devote themselves primarily to promoting debate over public policy; its promise of a clear exposition of the rules relating to political debate is ominous; and its suggestion that groups will be required to report their policy interventions more fully renews fears of policing of public debate.

sufficient funds to finance its initial operations for several years, but the funds allotted would be distributed on a declining scale, so that as the grant ran out the group's organizers would have to find alternative funding or give up. If alternative funding is completely unavailable, and the public interest clearly dictates that an interest be heard, as in the case of poor people's groups, it might be possible to arrange grants through systems of peer review, or perhaps to abandon a group approach altogether, in favour of an advisory board approach.

The final means of raising funds essentially turns the group away from its primary thrust of serving its members and its secondary thrust of communicating with government. This is the practice of using the organization's strategic position to develop some sort of saleable commodity. A group with a large membership can at times derive secondary revenue from the sale of selective benefits: life insurance for members, for example, or trade journals. Some groups take advantage of their position in the policy community to act as purveyors of information, either by organizing specialist seminars or by publishing specialized journals.[67] While not abundant, such opportunities present an alternative to the pitfalls of government funding and the risk of leaning too heavily on members and friends, but there is the danger that the group's entrepreneurial activities will supplant its other, more fundamental, functions.

ORGANIZATION AND MANAGEMENT

By outlining some of the factors that make each interest organization a unique part of the political community, I have suggested the complexities surrounding the business of organizing, running, and leading groups. These complexities make the management of groups a fascinating but formidable task for those who undertake to lead them.

Membership characteristics, wealth or (more likely) lack of it, ideology, mandate, the nature of the policy field in which the group is situated — all establish boundaries to action and dictate the conditions under which the leader must work. None, not even the task of carrying the group's goals into the political arena, will likely influence its leader, first, foremost, and continuously; they will be summed up in a presence that is palpable: the organization of the group itself. For the organization of the group is its membership. The organization expresses the strengths and weaknesses of the membership. It reflects the resources the membership can bring to bear, and its structure is the product both of their goals and of the environment in which those goals must be expressed. Supple or rigid; well-endowed or poor; newly created or well-established; nascent or institutionalized — whatever its characteristics and qualities, the organization is the instrument through which the leadership must give expression to the concerns of its supporters and achieve their goals.

Two features in particular of the many aspects of group organization will illustrate the challenges that face any group leader: the question of sectoral and territorial centralization versus decentralization, and the task of reconciling staff needs and goals with those of the members.

The first feature is endemic in Canadian group life. Even organizations that concern themselves only with the work of a single provincial government must contend with the divisive influence of territorial or sectoral particularism. Helen Jones Dawson's early study of the Consumers' Association of Canada demonstrates the extent to which the CAC reflects the problems of working in a political system with a strong central core and weak peripheral hinterlands.[68] She found intense feelings of isolation among eastern and western members of the association, and considerable resentment of the concentration of members from the central provinces on the board of directors. Other groups have similar problems, which are not lost on public officials: they frequently question the extent to which a group's leadership truly represents its national membership. Many, like the Canadian Construction Association, add sectoral differences to territorial cleavages:

> [Since the Second World War] the Canadian Construction Association's organizational network [has extended] to encompass an impressive array of industrial and regional components. This has not satisfactorily reduced the association's remoteness from the industry; instead, it now finds itself in competition with a multitude of organizations for the attention and support of contractors. In its attempts to rationalize its relations with those competitors, the CCA has threatened to become a confederation of associations, characterized by a decreasing contact with individual firms. This may be a necessary price to pay for having a sizeable organization; in an industry so varied as construction and in a country so large as Canada, it is difficult to see how any national association could remain at once highly centralized and broadly representative.[69]

Such tensions impinge heavily on the work of group leaders, and particularly on key staff members. Not only must they spend a good deal of time visiting branch groups and accommodating their sensitivities, they must accept certain organizational inefficiencies in order to ensure the continued loyalty of important constituencies. For example, functions that could be managed more efficiently in a single place are sometimes dispersed across several provinces. Nor is inefficiency manifested solely in higher telephone bills and higher transportation costs between headquarters and branch offices; unless the travel funds of the branch office match those of the head office, the branch may find itself less in touch with the general membership than the centre. In effect, it will be working only for a small local part of the organization. Because it symbolizes the importance of the regional group, the branch office may resist direction from the central leadership and become a focal point for regionally based internal opposition to the leadership.[70]

Sectoral cleavages also produce tensions that sometimes can be resolved only by allowing organizations to splinter into independent or loosely affiliated units. The Canadian Library Association has become an organizational maze of regional bodies and large specialized sub-groups, such as those representing school librarians and public librarians, and lesser groups—committees, co-ordinated groups, and interest groups—whose presence is intermittent and whose organizational status is vague.[71] Many academic associations have split into independent groups. The Canadian Political Science Association was once considered capable of representing not only political scientists but economists, sociologists, and anthropologists. Today three organizations represent those disciplines. Business interests in mining and forestry are represented by a large number of sectorally differentiated groups.[72] Such divisions are the natural product of growth, but they inevitably interrupt the work of the group and create severe problems of resource dispersion, which group leaders must manage with minimal fuss.

Managing staff requires talents that are in many ways different from the diplomatic and political skills needed to keep a disparate organization functioning harmoniously. The most striking difference is that the job of managing the staff belongs not to the group leadership as a whole but to the professional and permanent head of the organization. It is an internally oriented activity, and if it is managed successfully it is almost unnoticed by the membership. Nevertheless, it is crucially important because for many members the attitude of the staff makes or breaks their affinity with the organization. The group manager who considers the members a necessary but tedious part of the organization will soon transmit that attitude to staff, among whom it may be magnified, prompting lack of courtesy in the treatment of members, disregard for their concerns, delay in handling inquiries, and the subordination of members' goals to those of staff. The manager who exploits staff, or leaves personnel matters to an unsympathetic subordinate, is likely to create tensions in the office that can have very similar effects, leading gradually to a falling off of membership participation and eventually of membership support.

Relations between staff and the group manager are crucial in many other ways. Few groups have staff resources commensurate either with their ambitions or with the projects they have in hand. Staff are called upon to do far more than would be expected of them in government or in the majority of large businesses. This applies as much to the secretary who must give up a weekend to type an important brief as to the specialist who has spent hours of overtime researching it and melding into it the members' divergent views.

The group manager, as the one member of the leadership who is in daily contact with the staff and who is their representative before the board, can elicit willing, efficient staff support. Effective staff management includes the things one would expect of any competent manager: recognition of merit, constructive and sympathetic criticism of failures, support before the board, a flexible approach to the widely varying circumstances in which a group finds itself, and so on. A good manager has the ability to imprint on staff a loyalty to the organization, a sense of sharing in its identity, and a commitment to its goals — in short, an ability to so motivate staff that the organization makes the difficult metamorphosis from organization to institution that was discussed in Chapter 4.

This is particularly important where professional staff is concerned. Since most group organizations cannot afford the high salaries that experienced, top-flight professionals command, they must depend on bright, energetic but inevitably inexperienced younger people. This is not necessarily a bad thing. Such people bring with them a vigour and a fresh outlook that are very important in the dynamic, often changing world of pressure group politics. However, to produce results that will impress senior officials, politicians, group members, and representatives of rival groups, these specialists must stretch their talents to the utmost — often beyond what they themselves thought possible. It is a form of apprenticeship that demands of the 'master-lobbyist' considerable talents of leadership and instruction.[73]

A final aspect of the group's relationship with its staff must be handled with care by the manager and the leadership as a whole. This is the natural and understandable tendency of staff to superimpose their own goals on those created by the membership. Staff, after all, are far more involved with the organization than are the majority of members. They work for it daily. They have, as a consequence of their strategic location in the information flow, a perspective far broader than that of most members. Many are personally ambitious and tend to tie their own mobility to particular policy initiatives. They are often influenced far more by the views of colleagues in the public service and other groups, whom they see daily, than by the members, whom they see sporadically at best. Their tendencies may be shared by the group manager, who is subject to many of the same influences. They are frequently the source of considerable tension within institutionalized organizations, capable of setting staff and membership at odds with one another unless handled with restraint by the group manager and the elected leadership.[74]

The complexities of group management indicate that the successful group manager must be a paragon of professional virtue, if such an individual exists. Even so, I have touched on only *two* aspects of the management task. I have not discussed the talents required to make limited financial resources go far beyond what might be reasonably expected; to superintend the development and provision of selective benefits; to organize the more commercial aspects of group work; or even to juggle personnel and staff resources in order to meet the constantly changing set of issues and problems that the group must deal with. Nor have I mentioned the outstanding diplomatic and political skills required by anyone who must lead the group in the public arena, negotiate with officials, and bargain with friendly and competing groups. Finally, I have not mentioned the need for substantial, expert knowledge of the policy field in which the group is located and of the policy process in which it must work.

It is highly unlikely that many group managers possess all these talents. Nevertheless the proliferation of pressure groups in the last twenty years shows that enough individuals with some of these talents have been available to build groups, to serve them, and to enhance their role in the policy process. There are even enough professional managers to warrant creation of their own interest organization, the Institute of Association Executives, which publishes a professional journal and concerns itself with professional development, conditions of work, and ethical issues. Between 1977 and 1991, its membership grew from 1200 to 2000 — surely a sign that the recent expansion of the profession of group manager is likely to continue.[75]

PART III

Group Politics
and
Democratic Government

CHAPTER 9

Models of Interest Representation: Corporatism, Pluralism, and Post-Pluralism

Our experience with pressure groups demonstrates their value to Canadian political life. In many ways they are indispensable. It is hard to imagine how we could organize policy debate if pressure groups, with their specialized knowledge, did not focus discussion in policy communities. Even our political parties, suspicious as they are of pressure group influence, are indebted to them. Broad-based, middle-of-the-road parties such as Canada's cannot easily reconcile the conflicting demands of their members, particularly when sectoral aspirations in one region clash with those of another.

The existence of pressure groups permits party leaders to relegate potentially divisive issues to 'technical levels' where they can be defused piecemeal by officials and interest group representatives.[1] As well, pressure groups are far more sensitive than political parties or government bureaucracies to subtle shifts in public opinion. For individual citizens they are a more flexible vehicle for articulating policy demands. From the authorities' perspective, they offer quick access to public opinion. That same flexibility and sensitivity allows them to render service to the political system generally, helping it recognize and adjust to the changing needs of the community.

Inevitably, there are drawbacks. There are great disparities in pressure group influence. Some pressure groups represent individuals and organizations that already have immense economic power. At the outset these groups have status beyond that of other groups. Access to senior policy-makers is, for them, a right, not a privilege. Participation in key decisions is a matter of course.

To the problem of inequality between groups, we must add the problem of group legitimacy and mandate. Is a particular group genuinely supported by the people it says it represents? Have they given it the mandate it claims? Public officials are often at a loss to evaluate these crucial aspects of group intervention in policy-making. On another front, the public at large must be concerned about the affinity between groups and the bureaucracies they work with. Does working together lead to scheming together? Do group leaders and bureaucrats manage the public and its elected representatives? The dynamic of the sub-government makes this a possibility. How can the public monitor the relationship?

Finally, there is the difficulty of assigning roles to pressure groups and political parties. As seen at the beginning of this study, the vitality of the party system has caused concern for years. The hoopla of traditional party politics cannot conceal the fact that the party rank and file long ago ceased to have an effective role in policy formation. Bureaucrats proffer the advice once given by constituency organizations. Some Canadians have responded by joining new political parties — the Reform Party, the Bloc Québécois, the Confederation of Regions — but the majority of civic-minded individuals appear to have decided to devote their time, money, and energy to interest groups. These seem not only to be more interested in and better prepared to achieve their public policy goals, they also appear to have some influence with officials. The net effect is to make pressure groups competitors with political parties and to lead thoughtful Canadians to worry about the dangers of Canada becoming a special interest state.

Their concerns can be expressed in many ways. I have cited only a few. Fundamentally, they revolve around a single question: which is to be paramount in the Canadian state, representation by sector or representation based on place? Superficially there can be but one answer: the constitution provides for a system of representation based on the election of legislators from geographically defined constituencies. No other system of representation has legitimacy. Sectoral representation is a more potent force than this suggests, however. Bureaucratic influence in the Canadian policy process is extensive, as it is in most industrialized countries. The natural constituency for bureaucracy is the sectorally oriented policy community. Together specialized bureaucracies and their surrounding policy communities are a powerful force — conceivably powerful enough to be, *de facto*, the paramount system of representation. The problem of representation is therefore a fundamental one for the Canadian state.

Does this justify putting the problem of representation at the centre of a discussion of the role of pressure groups in the Canadian political system? It does, because in democracies the legitimacy of the state rests on public understanding that the government serves with the formal consent of the governed and is chosen through a process of election in which all citizens have an equal vote in electing representatives who are responsible for determining fundamental policy and for monitoring the government as it carries them out. Even though we recognize that the complexity of modern public policy prohibits the legislature from actually formulating policy, or supervising its implementation on a daily basis, it is able to hold the government accountable for its actions. As long as the general public believes that these conditions prevail, it will consider that the government to be is legitimate and will accept and abide by its decisions.

Interest group politics threatens the legitimacy of the state when it undermines these broad understandings. Bureaucratic expertise coupled with that of private interests makes the policy community a significant counterweight to the authority of the legislature, even though the legislature derives its legitimacy from the constitution and from its quality as an elected representative body. When the representativeness of its interest group members is thrown into the equation, the policy community acquires an authority that may challenge that of the elected legislature. Ministers and officials often characterize the policy community as 'the functional constituency',[2] a term that implies comparability with the constituencies of legislators. It implies a similar legitimacy. Even though the policy community is not truly representative of the sector for which it speaks, its ability to be seen as the 'functional constituency' diminishes the legitimacy of the legislature.

Policy communities do not usually directly challenge the authority of elected legislatures. Frontal attacks would fail in the face of constitutional rights and the legitimacy of election. Nevertheless, policy communities steadily undermine the authority of the legislature. By seeking to obtain delegated authority to implement the details of broadly expressed legislation, the policy community acquires an extensive, virtually unsupervised territory for policy-making. This practice has troubled thoughtful democrats for decades.[3] There has been a tendency for ministers and senior officials — who today seek the support of Parliament to a degree that they never did in the past — to come to legislatures armed with the support of the functional constituency. Their claims that 'the affected have been consulted and have agreed to the policies proposed' are difficult to refute — especially for legislative committees whose members may have little knowledge of a field. Legislative committees have little opportunity to escape the confines of specialization and to consider proposals from the perspective of the broad public interest, while policy communities, through their specialization and through the claims they can make because of consultation, effect a steady attrition of real legislative authority. As the public learns the extent of attrition, it loses confidence in the legislature's ability to monitor government and to review policy. The public also realizes that the policy community is by no means fairly representative of all the interests its decisions affect — and that the people are being governed through an unequal distribution of power.[4] As a consequence, the public's confidence in the legitimacy of the system as a whole dwindles.

This study of pressure group politics began with expressions of the fears aroused by these developments. I then traced the developments themselves and looked at some of their root causes. Now I will examine how practitioners and theorists have tackled these issues.

All theorists and practitioners do not diagnose the problem in exactly the way that it has been done here. For several whom I quoted at the beginning of the book, the issue is one of the rivalry between parties and pressure groups. Others are concerned about illicit influence. Many theorists, focusing on the state's desire to organize functional constituencies and to look for corporatist structures that are truly representative of the sectors for which they speak, pay little attention to traditional representative institutions. Others, writing out of the pluralist tradition, conceive of a less structured, more dynamic group politics than do the corporatists.

WHAT IS CORPORATISM?

A striking feature of modern politics is the extent to which government institutions seek to organize the political world. In democracies as well as in totalitarian states, in countries espousing 'free enterprise' as well as in socialist systems, governments arrange the way in which various interest communities communicate with public authorities. Elaborate formal structures — often called corporatist structures — have at times been created to regulate communication and economic decision-making, as is the case in Austria, Germany, and the Scandinavian countries. In other countries, the structure of 'concertation', as the French call it, is not as rigidly defined, but there is an intimate and continuous liaison between government agencies and the groups they consider have an interest in the development of specific aspects of policy.

In Britain, Canada, and the United States, pluralist approaches are still prominent. That is, governments expect interests to organize themselves as the need arises and to compete with one another for government attention and for influence. Even so, many agencies in these countries have encouraged some groups to organize themselves and others to expand, and there has been talk of creating more structured relationships, similar to those found in northern Europe.

The development of highly structured relationships — even the more modest instances of government encouragement of groups such as we see in Canada — has set off several important debates. Many observers ask whether these changes are symptomatic of fundamental changes in the nature of the state. Some ask whether the state is being forced to share power more as the activities of government increase and the state itself becomes more obtrusive — is the state itself less authoritative?[5] Others, particularly in countries like Canada, where the state itself has never been very obtrusive, ask whether the state is becoming *dirigiste*, as it is in Europe.[6] That is, are government bodies gradually becoming more and more capable of directing every aspect of our daily lives? Still others look at more immediate and less fundamental aspects of these developments, asking the kind of questions that were raised in the first chapter: are we witnessing the development of new systems of representation — systems for more effectively bringing sectoral concerns to public attention? If we are, what are the implications for party politics and, above all, for Parliament?

There are many different interpretations of these developments. It has become customary to divide the proponents of specific interpretations into two classes: the corporatists and the pluralists. Corporatists emphasize the role of the state in determining group participation in policy formation and execution, while pluralists focus on the voluntary, competitive, and unorchestrated quality of group involvement in the policy process.

The first and most difficult problem confronting anyone who investigates the applicability of corporatist ideas to Canada is that of definition. What is corporatism? A great deal of time is spent on this question, which suggests that the concept is less generally applicable than was at first supposed. Furthermore, scholars in various parts of the world have concluded that though the concept says something about their own political systems, it does not say as much as they had hoped.[7] Although I agree essentially with that position, I intend to explore the concept briefly because, despite its deficiencies, it contributes to our understanding of government's growing tendency to orchestrate the relations between groups and the state. Hence, I too must dwell a little on the problem of definition.

The most widely accepted definition has been developed by Philippe Schmitter, who sees corporatism as

> a system of interest representation in which the constituent units are organized into a limited number of single, compulsory, non-competitive, hierarchically ordered and functionally differentiated categories, recognized or licensed (if not created) by the state and granted a deliberate representational monopoly within their respective categories in exchange for observing certain controls on their selection of leaders and articulation of demands and support.[8]

This complex definition consists of the following elements:

1. The relationships between the state and the many interests in the community are organized into a system of representation. A structure is consciously imposed on them, which allows some groups to have a recognized role in policy communication and to count on being heard, while other groups are not recognized in the same way and cannot count on being heard. In terms of the continuum framework I developed in Chapter 4, institutionalized groups would probably fit into the first category, but nascent groups generally would not.

2. In this system, each group is recognized as having certain kinds of

expertise and acquires a role consistent with that expertise. Most, for example, represent quite specialized interests — the United Auto Workers of Canada might be deemed to represent auto workers, the Canadian Brotherhood of Railway Trainmen might represent railway workers, and so on — and are expected to speak for those interests. Each of these functionally differentiated groups monopolizes its field, but is expected to co-operate with other groups in such a way that agreement can be reached on their collective views and demands and can be represented to government and to other peak associations by a few superordinate associations — such as the Canadian Labour Congress.

This hierarchical system filters policy ideas and proposals in order to reduce them to manageable proportions at the bargaining table. In the process, many groups find that demands important to them have been ignored or grossly altered. They generally tolerate such abuses, partly because this is a bargaining process, which — like any other — involves compromises and even the loss of valued position, but also because the system accords each group a definite status and a monopoly position as representative of a particular interest community. To object too frequently and too strenuously about the way the system works not only antagonizes other actors, but may lead them to redefine the status of the group and even to remove its monopoly.

3. This complex of rewards and punishments holds the system together. The state recognizes the monopoly of functional groups, but assumes in return that they will respect the hierarchical authority of peak associations. For the latter, participation in the policy process entails the advantages of being recognized as the sole peak association in its field, and responsibility for ensuring that its membership accepts the decisions reached by the state and the peak associations. Participation also involves maintaining a degree of representativeness consistent with popular ideas of legitimacy. This is extremely important because in the long run the acceptability of the policies devised through corporatist processes depends on the extent to which the public at large feels they have been properly arrived at. If the general public believes that the developers of public policy do not properly represent those they speak for, the policies themselves will be considered illegitimate. For this reason, the state insists that groups participating in corporatist exercises must accept externally devised standards of representativeness and due process.

Schmitter identifies two kinds of corporatism — state corporatism and societal corporatism. State corporatism comes from 'above', from authorities at the centre of power who consciously try to create a system of group-state relations through which they can control and dominate the various interests in the community.[9] At its most extreme, state corporatism resembles the highly structured relationships created by the Fascist regimes in

Italy and, to a lesser extent, in Germany. In Italy, Mussolini subdued a strong labour movement by transforming various unions and professional groups into corporations that, along with similar groupings of business interests, were substituted for traditional political parties, becoming in effect instruments of the state. They did not survive the restoration of parliamentary government after the Second World War.[10] Schmitter points out that since this type of corporatism entails almost complete loss of autonomy for hitherto independent associations and may, as in the Fascist states, involve their suppression, state corporatism is usually resisted and is unlikely to be effective in the long run. In his view, societal corporatism is a more feasible system for harmonizing relations between the state and interest communities. This type of corporatism develops from 'below', from the gradual evolution of 'interassociational demands and intraorganizational processes'.[11] It is the product of the will of associations to achieve consensus between themselves and, in conjunction with government authorities, to agree on public policy and on their own interrelations. This view of corporatism is the one most commonly adopted by present-day scholars. It has the advantage of presenting the development of structures for state-group relations as the product of the state's desire to create order in its communications with its many publics, and of an equally vigorous desire by the business and labour communities to build institutions of communication that not only strengthen their hand in their relations with the state, but help to protect them from its full coercive authority.

Corporatism, as defined by Schmitter, captures aspects of state-group relations that are reflected in no other term currently used to describe the totality of relations between the state and interest communities. The term expresses the will of both government officials and interest representatives in all fields to avoid conflict in the development and implementation of policy, and to do so through the creation of monopolistic representative groups working through formal structures for collaboration. Because of this, I will use Schmitter's term to refer to all forms of corporatism, regardless of where they occur; however, I will use the term 'tripartism' to designate those forms of corporatism that are concerned exclusively with the development of economic policy.

CORPORATIST TRENDS IN CANADA

At first glance corporatism seems to have very little to say about Canadian politics. We tend to think of ourselves as adhering generally — though a little less tenaciously than our neighbours — to the liberal, pluralist ideology that dominates the United States. We recognize that our governments play a larger part in the economy than does American government, but we tend to agree with Whitaker when he describes this form of intervention as little more than 'private ownership at public expense'.[12] The idea that public policy should be concocted through a system of interest representation such as that defined by Schmitter offends our notions of legitimacy, which hold that public policy should be developed by Cabinet and approved by Parliament. Our reactions when confronted with corporatist, particularly tripartite, proposals have been distinctly negative.

Nevertheless, there is a strain of corporatism in Canada, both at the level of ideas and in actual practice. Furthermore, given the fact that corporatism seems to be associated with advanced industrial economies, such as Canada's, it is possible that corporatist trends will strengthen in the years ahead. Consequently we must look closely at what corporatism means in and for Canada.

From an historical perspective, Leo Panitch argues that this country's ideological orientation has always been antagonistic to corporatism and that attempts in the late 1970s to institute corporatist practices have fallen on stony ground. Even though this country has experienced a great deal of 'private ownership coupled with state control', its form has been generally pluralist.[13] He is willing to acknowledge that some such ideological background for corporatism exists in Quebec Catholicism, agrarian populism, and Mackenzie King's Liberalism, and identifies two periods when corporatist ideas have reached the public agenda: in the years between the First World War and the Depression, and in the 1970s.[14]

During the first period, corporatist ideas were espoused by the Catholic Church, which in Quebec, as in several European countries, applied them to trade-union organization.[15] Later these ideas were taken up by Duplessis, who spoke in terms of abolishing Quebec's Upper House and replacing it with 'an advisory council in which all "corporations" would be grouped to formulate policy for the economy as a whole'. These corporations would be associations of employers and employees in each industry, and would have 'considerable authority to make decisions regarding prices, wages, and general policy for the industry'.[16] On the Prairies, corporatism appealed to the farm community, which saw in it a means to eliminate the corruption of traditional parties and the influence of the eastern interests. The United Farmers of Alberta, like Duplessis some years later, advocated government through groups. In Ottawa, no less a figure than Mackenzie King came to the leadership of the Liberal Party with corporatist ideas in mind. Industry, he argued, in *Industry and Humanity* (1918), should be controlled by a 'partnership' of labour, capital, management, and the community. As Panitch has demonstrated, none of these proposals were ever put into effect or even seriously discussed, despite their having been suggested by leaders who could have taken steps to implement them.[17]

In the 1970s, Canadian interest in corporatism was rekindled — partly as a result of concern over the direction of economic development, and partly as a reflection of institutional imperatives. For Panitch, the revival was rooted in the class struggle, notably capital's growing need to channel and contain the demands of workers. The years following the Second World War had created conditions — 'a stronger organized working class, conditions that the government considered to be full employment, inflationary pressures, a squeeze on private capital accumulation, the failure of "stop-go"' — similar to those that had fostered corporatist developments in Western Europe.[18] Nevertheless corporatism, in Panitch's view, did not develop. Beginning in 1968, Prime Minister Trudeau initiated discussions with business and labour leaders that eventually led to the creation of the Prices and Incomes Commission. This body, though not tripartite, 'set about a series of meetings with the organizations of business and labour to secure agreement and co-operation in a price and wage restraint program'.[19] Despite some minor successes, the project was constrained by labour's refusal to support it and was abandoned at the end of 1970.

As inflationary difficulties increased during the early 1970s, the government again sought tripartite arrangements, but despite generous participatory inducements labour again resisted, 'finding little substantive response to their demands for cheaper housing, higher pensions, full-employment policies . . . and close controls over corporate investment to create jobs'.[20] The Anti-Inflation Program that followed not only earned bitter criticism from labour, and a total denial of support, but led labour to withdraw from the few tripartite bodies that had been established, notably the Economic Council of Canada. Even so, the dispute served to familiarize Canadians with corporatist, and particularly tripartite, concepts.

Both labour and government sought a mechanism for achieving tripartite consultation, though neither side was willing to go as far as the other wanted. The Canadian Labour Congress edged towards large-scale social and economic planning under tripartite auspices, while the government, protesting that constitutionally it could not share power and that the CLC proposals would undermine Parliament's role in policy-making, sought safety in number and proposed a multipartite 'consultative forum'. Based on a combination of regional and sectoral representation, the forum would consist of thirty to fifty members and would discuss economic policy. In 1977, the Department of Industry, Trade and Commerce followed up the consultative forum proposal by initiating 'Enterprise 77', a series of interviews with leading business executives. In response to the very critical view of government that emerged from this exercise, Ottawa embarked on a more elaborate consultative process — known as the Tier I and Tier II discussions — built around the work of twenty-three task forces, each of which examined the government/business partnership in a particular sector of the economy. According to Coleman and Jacek, business at least was impressed with the 'seriousness with which the government took this exercise'. They concluded that some federal officials had been encouraged to consider creating 'a permanent structure for consultation that can only be described as "corporatist"'.[21] At the very least these initiatives are, in Panitch's words, 'indicative of the tendencies toward corporatism in Canada'.[22]

Brown, Eastman, and Robinson are more cautious. The exercises provided governments with a 'wealth of information' about the private sector's view of the problems and challenges facing Canadian industry, but the sector reports did not 'present government with a basis for making decisions about which sectors should be encouraged to lead economic recovery'.[23] Furthermore, the consultative process used in Tier I 'encouraged each sector task force to make a special case for itself, and worked against the formulation of recommendations which would permit government to choose between sectors and between firms'.[24] The second round of consultations (Tier II), led to 'uneasy compromises' that testified to 'the difficulties involved in formulating proposals for the manufacturing industry as a whole'.[25] Brown, Eastman, and Robinson concluded that the 1978 exercise barely went beyond elementary consultation. Certainly, 'a broad joint consensus on objectives for industrial policy' was not achieved.[26] The Tier II consultations were, however, 'a step toward more effective collaboration on economic and industrial issues'.[27] They did involve much closer collaboration than had occurred previously — at least within a framework of discussion cutting across sector policy fields — but they were a long way from corporatism itself.

Full-fledged corporatism entails far more extensive rationalization of interest intermediation than that described above. Despite periodic calls for a march towards corporatism, it is unlikely that we would easily or quickly overcome the barriers standing in the way, even if we wished to. In 1982, when Prime Minister Trudeau urged Canadians to apply the corporatist models of Japan and Germany in order to pull out of the recession, Montreal's *Le Devoir* replied:

Au sujet de l'Allemagne et du Japon le chef du gouvernement avait raison d'invoquer l'habitude de la discipline et de la concertation. Cette habitude est ancienne dans les deux cas, et de plus en plus fragile dans la République fédérale. Des générations de leaders patroneaux, syndicaux et politiques l'ont patiemment construite et mise à jour. L'expérience canadienne, les attitudes des partenaires économiques et celles des politiciens ont plutôt maintenu le cap vers une autre direction. Nous en payons le prix aujourd'hui. Nos improvisations restent hésitantes. Peut-il en être autrement?[28]

Brown, Eastman, and Robinson, in their assessment of the Tier I/Tier II experience, reach similar conclusions. Attitudinal and ideological barriers inhibit the translation of the consultative exercise into a corporative arrangement. As well, the representative capacity of most groups is limited:

[N]o single business organization exists to legitimately represent the private sector. The Canadian Manufacturers' Association, the Business Council on National Issues and the Canadian Federation of Independent Business each represents a significant proportion of business, but none are as all-encompassing as, for example, the BC Employers' Council or the Conseil du Patronat in Quebec are for their regions. Nor do they speak with the authority that business, labour and agricultural groups in many European countries do. Foreign ownership is one significant obstacle to this; the cleavage between large and small business and the regional dispersion of business are others. The . . . exercise did bring together firms in the manufacturing sectors (many for the first time) but, as a whole, small business was neglected. . . . The Canadian Labour Congress does not have the same degree of structural weakness for consultation, but it, too, has limitations. Only a minority of the Canadian work force is organized, and a significant minority of unions are not affiliated with the CLC.[29]

Finally, Coleman, after extensive study of business interest associations in Canada, concludes that in combination with divisive economic factors — such as differences in market orientation, sectoral organization, and territorial dispersion — federalism and the Cabinet-parliamentary system contribute to the fragmentation of business interests in this country.[30]

In terms of practice and of ideology, Canada has followed a path that is far removed from corporatism. The hesitant moves of the late 1970s and early 1980s towards a more integrated system did not replace two centuries of individualism. Powerful ideological convictions militate against corporatist discipline, and these convictions are reinforced by the institutionalized tendencies towards decentralization found in groups and government. Our political structures are in many ways incompatible with corporatism. Divided jurisdiction means that key elements of the economy must be managed by different sets of institutions owing no obedience to one another. It may be possible for the federal government to arrange corporatist structures to deal with matters within its competence, but there are few such matters today that can be handled without in some way affecting, or being affected by, provincial policies. As long as that is the case, the integrated hierarchical system of policy development and implementation, which is the essence of corporatism, will not take hold in Canada. The recent accelerated institutionalization of interest groups encourages participation in corporatist forums, but as long as power in groups remains decentralized, these forums will lack authority. The exercises in consultation that have taken place do not go beyond consultation. Views are exchanged, understanding is extended, and co-operation is achieved, but authoritative agreements are not reached.

These realities were evident in the 1985 economic summit organized by the Mulroney government. First suggested in 1979 by Robert de Cotret, then Minister of State for Economic Development in the Clark government,[31] the National Economic Conference brought to Ottawa representatives of most sectors of Canadian society. Primed with a series of background papers prepared by government and many of the participating groups, the delegates were expected to address, on national television and radio, an agenda that extended across the economic spectrum. This they did, but with disappointing results. The media and many delegates themselves concluded that most speakers had time only to present established groups' positions. Dialogue did not take place, much less a movement towards consensus.

From the perspective of the early 1990s, the 1985 economic summit appears to have been the end of a cycle of government interest in corporatism and not a step towards harmonizing the work of business, labour, and government in economic management. As Atkinson and Coleman have pointed out, in the early 1980s the Canadian government had a choice of shaping Canada's economy through a trade policy geared to international market forces or through an industrial strategy arrived at in concert with labour and business.[32] In embracing continental free trade, the Mulroney government chose the trade route and apparently abandoned the corporatist initiatives. The Mulroney government was not ideologically sympathetic to corporatism's interventionist assumptions. Those same assumptions, together with corporatism's structural emphasis on a hierarchy of monopolistic institutions, were also an embarrassment for a government that was initially determined to renounce the penchant for centralism of the Trudeau years. Institutionally, the government's choice was reflected in the changes that have been made since 1984 in the central policy structures. The ministries of state for economic and social development have been dismantled. The small Operations Committee has become the Cabinet's decision centre. The Privy Council Office, where a concern for planning had been an important factor in promoting tripartism, has seen its central role shifted from co-ordination for planning to co-ordination for 'communications'. A planning-oriented budgetary system has been abandoned. The Department of Finance has re-emerged as the key agency for co-ordination of economic policy.[33] Collectively, these institutional changes spell a return to the agency-centred policy process that had prevailed during the Diefenbaker and Pearson years.

Despite the decline in political and bureaucratic interest in corporatism in recent years, both the concept and the approach will probably continue to have a role in the theory of group-state relations in Canada and in the practice of those relations. Corporatist-inspired studies have produced considerable empirical information about the organization of business interests and have stimulated research in Canadian pressure group studies in general. In common with corporatists elsewhere, scholars in the field have turned to sector level studies, where they have found some evidence of corporatist ('meso-corporatist') institutions.[34] More important, their analyses of the problems confronting the development of an industrial strategy for Canada provide the groundwork for a renewed debate over the role of the state in the future Canadian economy. Such a debate may seem unlikely at a time when the country is grappling with the threat of political fragmentation and is coming to terms with free trade. Nevertheless, Canada's exposure to international economic forces means that ultimately, regardless of changes in constitutional structure, this country will have to develop institutions comparable to those used by her trading competitors. Since many of those competitors rely heavily on state intervention through corporatist institutions, similar arrangements will be considered for Canadian needs and adapted to them.

PLURALISM AND POST-PLURALISM

Corporatist ideas are relatively new in Canadian approaches to state-group relations, but perceptions of pressure groups in this country have been permeated for many years by the pluralist philosophy espoused by American scholars. The pluralists saw the political system as a dynamic mass of activity in which new groups constantly evolve and old ones are killed off as society adjusts to change. Any change will advance some interests, but will have an adverse effect on others, which will exercise group influence, including political influence, to solve their common problem. In the process of maintaining equilibrium, the pluralists argued, society will naturally produce groups to champion an interest disadvantaged by a recent change in social and economic conditions. The same dynamic forces will ensure that there will always be challengers to groups that seek to dominate policy-making. An atomistic, bustling, vibrant, self-organizing interest-group politics is, they believed, healthy, natural, and optimal.[35]

Pluralism has been under attack for several decades, largely because of its implications for democratic theory. In 1947 R.M. MacIver took exception to the assumption of Arthur Bentley, whose 1908 treatise *The Process of Government* set out the initial tenets of the approach, that 'a legislative act is always the calculable resultant of a struggle between pressure groups, never a decision between opposing conceptions of the national welfare.'

> [T]he whole logic of democracy is based on the conception that there is still a national unity and a common welfare. The fact that the interest in the common welfare cannot be organized after the fashion of specific interests should not conceal from us either its existence or the need to sustain it. Democracy itself is the final organization of the common interest.... Democracy affirms the community.
>
> This affirmation is constantly being threatened by the imperialism of powerful groups. It is the eternal problem of democracy to keep them in their place, subject to the democratic code.[36]

A sustained attack began in the 1960s when American political science was riven by an intense argument over the validity of the pluralist understanding of politics. This critique argued persuasively that the natural dynamism of the American system could not ensure the equal representation of all interests or even their partial representation. As Mancur Olson pointed out, the argument 'that "suffering", "dislocation", and "disturbance" will almost inevitably result in organized political pressure' is not sustained by the facts.[37] The evidence brought to light by the civil rights movement and the ghetto uprisings indicated that the distribution of power, and consequently of the benefits of American civilization, was very unequal indeed. It was no longer possible to accept Robert Dahl's argument that the 'independence, penetrability, and heterogeneity of the political stratum' virtually guarantee that the concerns of disaffected groups would be expressed in political debate. Such pluralist arguments ignored the fact that 'political penetrability' is compromised by the capacity of many office-holders to ignore policy options known to be disliked by political and economic élites and to keep some political issues from reaching the public agenda.[38] Powerful special interests with a fierce grip on the levers of power had put the resources of the American state to their own use, creating, as Theodore Lowi put it, 'Socialism for the organized; *laissez-faire* for the unorganized.'[39]

Lowi has been one of the most strident critics of the pluralists. His book, *The End of Liberalism*, proclaims the fall of the system of democratic government upon which the United States grew to greatness, and its replacement by a 'second republic' — the tool of powerful interests who manipulate the system. For Lowi, the crux of the problem has been a growing incapacity on the part of American representative institutions to reconcile spatially oriented and functionally oriented demands. He associates the growth of the special interest state with the rise of specialization and thus with the increasing power of the bureaucracy in American government. The American party system, with its strong bias towards geographically defined community interests, has been no match for the combined power of the functionally oriented administrative units and their affiliates, the interest groups. It has been reduced to packaging and selling presidential candidates, and to providing a nominal affiliation for the sectoral chieftains who dispense congressional patronage.

Not all American theorists follow Lowi to this point. One of the foremost American students of pressure groups, Robert H. Salisbury, while critical of the pluralist approach, takes a more clinical, less despondent view of pressure group influence.[40] Similarly Mancur Olson, who is himself critical of the pluralists for their failure to consider properly the impact of individual and national interest on group politics, espouses a rational-choice interpretation of group life and behaviour that is not inconsistent with the pluralist approach.[41]

Nevertheless, even these scholars present data that sustain Lowi's interpretations. Salisbury's view of the origin of groups offers a case in point:

> As a consequence of various processes of social differentiation ... there is within a given population more and more specialization of function ... and from this comes greater and greater diversity of interests or values as each newly differentiated set of people desires a somewhat different set of social goals.[42]

Lowi would argue that it is this very process that precipitates the special interest state.

Emerging from the criticisms of the anti-pluralists was a new perception of the structure of relations between the American state and interest groups. Post-pluralism takes account of the dynamism of traditional American interest group politics, on which the pluralists focused. In addition, by identifying a more active role for agencies of the state, it pinpoints an important shift in the structure of American politics — a shift that creates a similarity between the American system and the corporatist regimes of Europe.[43] As well, the post-pluralists were not convinced that the political system is self-regulating and capable of maintaining an equilibrium in which all members of society have confidence because they share a common right to participate. On the contrary, though there may be a common right to participate, there is no common *opportunity* to participate. There are great inequalities in political life that reflect enormous social and economic disparities between individuals and that will provoke disequilibrium in the system. Where the pluralists had envisaged a dynamic, atomistic environment in which individual groups engaged in one-on-one relations with the offices and legislators whose decisions affected their interests, the post-pluralists described tight-knit alliances between key legislators, influential groups, and the leaders of agencies. Some post-pluralists envisaged group politics as a monstrous engine of inequity capable ultimately of destroying the society that created it.

At the heart of this revised view is the argument that 'some issues are organized into politics while others are organized out of it'.[44] Contrary to pluralist theory, politics is not a competitive market-place for policy options. Instead, the majority of participants consider politics a vehicle for limiting competition and for securing a tranquil environment for themselves and their enterprises. Just as in business many entrepreneurs attempt to control their environment by forming cartels or in other ways limiting competition, so in politics various actors try to achieve consensus and to avoid conflict. The most effective way to do this is to control the instruments that define which issues will appear on the public agenda, and — just as important — which alternatives will be chosen to resolve them. For E.E. Schattschneider:

> [T]he definition of alternatives is the supreme instrument of power, the

antagonists can rarely agree on what the issues are because power is involved in the definition. He who determines what politics is about runs the country, because the definition of the alternatives is the choice of conflicts, and the choice of conflicts allocates power.[45]

Of the various institutions engaged in defining issues and alternatives, organized interests are among the most important because they have specialized knowledge — unlike political parties and most of the media — and because they derive a degree of legitimacy from their claim to represent an interest community.

Four factors contribute to organized interests' bias toward articulating some issues rather than others. First, not all interests are represented. In particular, the poor or disadvantaged have no voice. Second, not all elements of specific interest communities are represented by the groups who speak for them. Third, Schattschneider finds that people involved in interest organizations, particularly those who take leadership positions, tend to belong to the more affluent classes of society. Thus, by dominating both the organizations at large and their executive positions, the upper classes steer interest group concerns toward issues that affect themselves and toward alternatives that favour them. Fourth, in this system of unequal representation, Schattschneider finds that certain kinds of associations have a great deal more influence than others.[46] Business associations in particular tend to be more effective than most unions or professional groups in attaining their ends and infinitely more successful than voluntary groups. They have resources and commitments that normally far outweigh those of voluntary groups and the majority of unions.

Schattschneider, like other post-pluralist theorists, reminds us that the management of conflict is only a small part of what politics is about and that the use of consensus underlies the greater part of political decision-making.[47] When he maintains that some issues are organized into politics, while others are organized out, he is suggesting that conflict can be contained through the management of consensus.[48] When Bachrach, Baratz, and Crenson argue that non-decision-making is the other face of pluralist democracy, they are also suggesting that consensus is being managed to prevent issues from being articulated.[49]

The vehicle for achieving consensus management is the sub-government. Because complex societies depend on specialization of function to accomplish the majority of economic, social, and political goals, a tendency towards sub-government is endemic in all modern political systems, but particularly in the United States. There sub-governments are built around three mutually dependent elements: administrative units, congressional committees, and pressure groups. The diffusion of power within the American system of government spawned a triangular symbiosis between these three political elements. Congressional committees, and particularly their chairpersons, with their power to create, halt, or mutilate legislation, and their control over appropriations, are courted not only by officials of the administrative units whose budgets and legislation they influence, but by the interest groups most closely associated with the same sphere of activity. Congressmen also have needs. Pet pieces of legislation or budget allocations designed to benefit their constituencies often need the kind of public support that can be generated by interest groups. Groups, too, can often dispense patronage. The decisions of members of business associations, for example, can be vitally important for Congressmen worried about unemployment back home or anxious to build on their constituency's economic base. Again, the associations can be important intermediaries between public decision-makers and specific interests, and between agencies and the public at large. For all this, the organized interests expect benefits in return: recognition of their own status, policy benefits for their interest at large, and, where appropriate, patronage for individual members. Finally, the implementation of policies desired by legislators and groups depends to a considerable extent on the goodwill of the administrative agency.

According to Ripley and Franklin:

> Most of the policy-making in which sub-governments engage consists of routine matters. By 'routine' we simply mean policy that is not currently involved in a high degree of controversy, policy that is not likely to change very much and policy with which the participants in it are thoroughly familiar and quietly efficient in its implementation and minor alteration.[50]

They reinforce Schattschneider's argument that routine is the nub of consensus management. By not drawing attention to what is being decided, sub-governments can arrange public policy to their own satisfaction. 'Since most policy-making is routine most of the time, sub-governments can often function for long periods of time without much interference.'[51] The key to being left alone is to maintain the fiction that what is done is 'routine'; it involves maintaining agreement within the sub-government and ensuring that potential rival interests, in both the public and private sectors, can be co-opted, suppressed, or safely ignored. 'If the members of a sub-government can reach compromises among themselves on any disagreements about a policy, they can reduce the chance of calling a broader audience together that might become involved in their activities and their output.'[52] Consensus management, then, becomes the main task of those employed at the heart of the sub-government: the key political decision-makers, interest representatives, and agency leaders. By striving to maintain an alliance among themselves, members of the sub-government ensure that (as far as the public is concerned) new policies are 'routine' and 'incremental', even though they may have engaged in heated debate. Sub-governments have thus been successful in keeping out of politics many issues that, according to the pluralists, should naturally find their way into public debate. The process of mutual accommodation creates an extremely powerful relationship that, as Schattschneider pointed out, for the unorganized, the under-represented, the poverty-stricken — the weaker elements of American society — is very difficult to challenge, much less break down.

Post-pluralist theory does not exclude the role of conflict in policy-making. There will always be times when it becomes impossible to contain debate within the sub-government. The issues involved may be so important that leading members will be driven to public disagreement. Proposed policy may trench too aggressively into the domain of another sub-government. The leaders of the sub-government, complacent in their long exercise of power, may have failed to recognize the importance of challenging groups, or of fundamental shifts in public opinion. A probing journalist may have exposed a major scandal in the policy field. Such factors can turn a quiet policy backwater into a maelstrom of public debate. Raising the 'level of conflict', to use Schattschneider's phrase, will nearly always lead to revision of policy and disruption of the sub-government itself, ultimately changing to some degree the conditions operating in the particular policy field. In most cases, the traditional dominance of the sub-government in that field, its capacity to dispense patronage and co-opt critics, and the sheer weight of the expertise it can muster ensure that controversy will eventually subside, whereupon the sub-government, somewhat mauled and slightly changed, will be able to retire again to a comfortable obscurity. Nevertheless, the penalties for failing to maintain consensus or for incompetently adapting to the changing environment will cause the leaders of the sub-government to redouble their efforts to 'routinize' public policy and to organize out of politics discussion of the issues that most concern them. The elemental force of conflict, always present in sub-government relations, is kept at bay through the management of consensus.

APPLYING POST-PLURALISM TO CANADA

How useful are post-pluralist concepts to an understanding of Canadian pressure group politics? Are issues organized in and out of Canadian politics? Is consensus management a key goal of state-group decision-makers? Is policy specialization within sub-governments the mechanism through which consensus is managed? If post-pluralist analysis is an aid to understanding Canadian pressure group politics, are the normative concerns of the post-pluralists also relevant in this country?

Consensus management clearly exists outside the United States. Observation of consensus management in Britain, in corporatist European regimes, and in Asia confirms the transferability of post-pluralist concepts.[53] Important differences do exist. For example, though British scholars adopt the concept of the sub-government, there are significant variations between their allusions to sub-governments and the post-pluralist's conceptualization. Where American post-pluralists speak of a tight-knit group of officials, politicians, and interest group leaders managing the sub-government, British scholars envisage mechanisms that are more loosely structured, more divided, and less authoritative.[54]

These variations suggest that observers of non-American systems apply post-pluralist concepts with the same reservations shown by their predecessors in using the original pluralist notions. The analytical concepts of one culture and one system cannot be transplanted without modification to others. In the case of the post-pluralists, it is clear that, though many vital elements of the concept—the tendency towards policy specialization and the management of consensus for example—can be found in most modern systems, institutional, cultural, and ideological variations modify the way in which groups, agencies, and legislators interact. The most notable distinction between the American and other systems is expressed in the concept of the 'iron triangle'. Few systems accord individual legislators the power possessed by members of Congress. Outside the United States the image of the triangle does not apply, though the concept of the sub-government remains useful.[55] Similarly, ideology and culture decree a different role for the American state than prevails in many other countries.

We, too, must use caution in applying post-pluralist concepts to Canada. In some respects, these concepts offer a plausible framework for interpreting the Canadian experience of group politics. It is not hard to find consensus-seeking behaviour, despite the tendency towards confrontation in recent Canadian political history. Indeed, institutionalized pressure groups found for many years that they had to conform to a certain kind of consensus-seeking behaviour if they wished to maintain access to, and exert influence on, governmental decision-makers. Recent studies of Canadian business interest associations have identified many instances of consensus-seeking behaviour. One approach uses joint committees composed of officials and business representatives to formulate policy, 'with senior level committees discussing its general shape and junior committees deliberating over technical details'.[56] Alternatively, agency officials will write to interested groups advising them of proposed changes and inviting comment. In other instances—for example, in the case of marketing boards—agencies will delegate responsibility for policy formulation to bodies representing various interests.[57] Despite such evidence of consensus-building within specific industries and policy fields, and despite the interest in tripartite consultation that we noted earlier, scholars have been forced to conclude that regional differences, jurisdictional rivalries, and the tendency of widespread foreign ownership of Canadian businesses to encourage fragmentation of interest associations inhibits the building and maintenance of consensus on the broader policy level.[58] In short, the post-pluralist concept of consensus-building identifies a characteristic of interest group involvement in the Canadian policy process, but we must be careful not to assume that consensus-building occurs in the same way or has the same effect it does in other countries.

I have used the post-pluralist concept of the sub-government extensively in interpreting Canadian group politics. However, in applying the concept, I have modified it considerably, abandoning the image of the triangle and treating the sub-government as the central core of a greater policy community, which organizes the special public concerned with a particular policy field, providing mechanisms for policy communication, legitimation, and, to an extent, renewal.[59] I have introduced these modifications because, as the earlier discussions have suggested, sub-governments in Canada lack the cohesion and authority of the American. I can attribute their lack of authority to the fact that, despite the diffusion of power that has occurred in recent years, the Cabinet-parliamentary system still creates a focal point for power in the Cabinet. The co-ordinative role of Cabinet renders the independence of sub-governments in Canada less certain and more variable than it is in the United States. When Cabinet chooses to exert its power, as for example when it chooses to reverse the orders of regulatory boards and commissions, then no sub-government can resist it in the short run, however successful it may be in routinizing policy-making over the long term. Ultimately, the administrative structures bargaining with interest representatives do not need to share power with them to the same extent as do their American counterparts. This was very clear in the days of the mandarins, but is less so today.

Again, the Cabinet-parliamentary system imposes an important structural variation on Canadian and British sub-governments. There is no place for the powerful legislative committees that form the third partner in the American triad. In Canada and Britain, sub-governments consist of two sets of partners — the lead agency and the major interests — each of which still needs what the other has to offer, but one of which — the agency — is more authoritative, less dependent, than the other. We must not conclude from this, however, that we can substitute the British model of sub-governments for the American one. The extensive diffusion of power found in our federal bureaucracy is reinforced in Canada by the structure of federal-provincial decision-making and the decentralization that comes with federalism. Thus, while Canadian sub-governments are less powerful than those in the United States, they have more authority than their British counterparts, simply because they have more opportunity to manipulate decision centres.

Throughout the discussion, I have emphasized the consensus-seeking activities of policy communities because I accept the post-pluralist argument that the majority of participants in sub-governments are anxious to create and maintain a stable environment. Officials seek the 'quiet life' — not simply because general agreement makes life 'easier', but because consensus equates with legitimation. As long as the policy community, even including its less important members, appears to the public at large to agree on policy fundamentals, the general public is likely to feel that the policies being followed are legitimate, and thus acceptable. Such legitimation permits the modification of policy to be treated as routine, or incremental.

The co-optation of interests into policy-making allows issues to be organized out of politics. If this fundamental aspect of consensus management is neglected, dissident groups will circumvent the policy community and almost invariably will appeal to the public at large. Their efforts may be relatively inconsequential, but they can awaken public unease about the conduct of the policy community. If the dissidents include individuals and groups whose views can be respected, the public may challenge the conventional wisdom prevailing in the policy community and raise questions about issues that in the past had been treated as routine and kept out of politics.[60] In short, the level of conflict will rise to a point where issues escape the control of the policy community — and of the sub-government in particular — so that the environment for decision-making becomes extremely unsettled.

To avoid these major disruptions, the policy community has to engage in a constant process of assimilation. New issues are raised, new individuals brought into the community, changes in the environment accommodated and so on. This may create more turmoil in a policy community than meets the eye of the uninitiated, but it is a necessary part of building and maintaining consensus. Most community members, even the competitively inclined, prefer a stable environment, but to secure stability they must accept a degree of change.

Issues do escape the policy community frequently enough. They reflect either serious internal disagreements within the community or major changes in the external policy environment. For the leaders of the sub-government, the former are easier to stomach. Internal conflicts may entail unwanted publicity, the assimilation of unwelcome policy ideas (and often their proponents), and momentary destabilization. But normally the community will remain intact. As I have suggested, these minor eruptions can be a source of renewal for the community. Not so the major exogenous changes. They can lead to a dismantling of the policy community or, at the very least, fundamental changes in policy.

The evidence reviewed in earlier chapters suggested that since the mid-1960s, Canadian policy communities have experienced the second kind of challenge to an unusual degree. They are being forced to adjust to fundamental changes in the country's social, economic, and political systems: the spread of new technologies; urbanization; regionalism; the growth of the multinational; the accelerating interdependence of economies; the decline of traditional communities; general changes in life-style; concern for environmental quality; and so on. Individually such changes introduce, often very rapidly, dramatic alterations in the specific environment of policy communities.[61] Collectively, the effect of these changes on policy communities is even more profound because it transforms long-standing relations between social, economic, and political systems. Governments, as I noted in Chapter 3, have become inextricably involved in demand and supply management, an involvement that has forced a total redefinition of the relations between the public and private sectors in every aspect of public policy. Instead of being the distributor of public wealth, government has become the redistributor. Instead of maintaining an appropriate environment for social and economic life, government has found itself trying to create that environment. Instead of playing a basically passive role in relation to society, government has had to participate very actively indeed. The impact of these trends has been registered particularly at two levels of the political system. It has precipitated the diffusion of power that I described in Chapter 3 and has led to confrontation at the intergovernmental level. Both of these effects have made a considerable difference to the way policy communities function.

In essence, the diffusion of power represents a loss of control over the machinery of government on the part of the political executive and the senior public service. A consequence of the rapid evolution of new policies and programs, and thus of the even more rapid growth of agencies, diffusion not only precipitates loss of control, but sets in motion the crisis of legitimacy discussed in earlier chapters. Since Canadian bureaucracies have little inherent legitimacy and derive public acceptance from carrying out policies laid down by Parliament and Cabinet, the deterioration of that acceptance made the crisis of legitimacy particularly acute for most agencies. They consequently sought alternative points of legitimation within the public at large. These efforts included fostering the elaboration of policy communities.

The development of policy communities capable of generating public support for agency policies has transformed participating interest groups from useful adjuncts of agencies into vitally important allies. Not surprisingly, this transformation has occurred at the agencies' cost. The tutelary relationship common in earlier stages of the development of the policy process had to give way to one approximating partnership. A dependency relationship has become much more fully an exchange relationship. In effect, the nature of bureaucratic politics has changed in Canada. No longer conducted within the hierarchy and the discreet, tight-knit circle of interest representatives privy to departmental secrets and strategies, it must now from time to time engage public support.

The price of public support is a more open, more dynamic policy system.

Pressure group involvement in the policy process cannot be encouraged without elevating the status of such groups. Once groups have outgrown agency tutelage, it must be expected that to some extent they will act independently to promote their own immediate interests, as well as those of the agency and the policy community at large. The diffusion of power has accentuated the tendency for policy to be developed by specialized policy communities. It has led to the more precise definition of those communities, and has led them to act more openly and vigorously in the general political system as they strive to maintain the control of their key agencies over the policy field. All this promotes a more open and dynamic policy system.

In fostering the development of policy communities, agencies and their allies have generated mechanisms reminiscent of those remarked by students of corporatism: a concern for representativeness and, as one sees in the interest associations of the chemical industry, a tendency to avoid overlap between groups.[62] Such arrangements enhance legitimating capacity and interest aggregation. As well, there is some attempt to build peak associations. Throughout, a good deal of initiative has been taken by government agencies themselves in the fostering of groups and the definition of their role. Nevertheless this is far from approaching full corporatism. The policy community itself is too open, too free of regulation, and too inclined towards pluralist conceptions of behaviour to be considered corporatist in anything but an embryonic sense. Consequently, I have gone no further than to treat these mechanisms as evidence of a growing tendency on the part of governments and interests to orchestrate their relations on a larger scale, and in a more complex manner, than they did in the years before the Second World War, and even during the period of mandarin influence.

In the field of federal-provincial relations, policy communities can be effective actors. They are weakest when the desires of group members conflict with the fundamental interests of governments themselves. At other times, because they pivot around line agencies, they have been successful in resisting central direction. Policy communities that have succeeded in reaching consensus between interests and government at the agency and ministerial level can be a formidable barrier to the efforts of Ottawa's central agencies to secure desired changes in policy: the mineral industries demonstrated this when they and their provincial allies opposed the tax reform proposals of the first Trudeau government. In fact, we might take Schattschneider's level of conflict theory a step further, and argue that in the Canadian situation, the level of conflict that policy communities strive most carefully to avoid is conflict at the intergovernmental level, particularly at the most senior level of all, the first ministers' conference. Policy conflicts attaining that doubtful eminence are not only subject to modification by central agencies and other actors, but are quite likely to miss any kind of resolution at all, falling victim to confrontation politics and its ensuing tendency to result in deadlock, which has often characterized intergovern-mental relations.

Using the concept of the policy community, earlier chapters explored several notions of how the community functions and how it processes policy information. I also looked briefly at its association with the complex tangle of intergovernmental relations, suggesting that in intergovernmental affairs, policy communities serve functions of protection and issue-organization similar to those they carry out in single jurisdictions. Finally, I looked at the role policy communities play in the diffuse power situation found today in several governments, particularly at the federal level. I suggested that policy communities have, to some extent, been the product of, and have contrib-uted to, the growing inability of governmental centres to control the public service. They act as a source of support for the increased autonomy enjoyed by line agencies in recent years.

All in all, it seems that we can apply a good part of the post-pluralist argument to our interpretation of Canadian experience. The post-pluralist models do not fit precisely; I have had to develop a policy community model instead. But their underlying thrust is similar. The policy community, like the American sub-government: exists because of a systemic need for policy specialization. In both, the leading actors strive to maintain stability within the special public and do so through the processes of consensus management.

If these descriptive and analytical aspects of post-pluralism are relevant in Canada, should we not also be concerned about the normative conclusions the approach suggests? Does this analysis of the role of policy communities indicate that these systems of sectoral representation threaten to supplant the traditional pattern of spatial representation embodied in our legislatures? Do our policy communities, with their predilection for consensus management, systematically exclude many Canadians from an effective part in the policy process?

By developing the policy-community concept, I have softened the impact of Lowi's charge that policy is made by the organized at the expense of the unorganized. I have done this by recognizing that the policy community consists not only of the cohesive and authoritative sub-government, but also of the polyglot attentive public with its opposition elements, whose views must be taken into account to some extent. I have argued that the instability of the attentive public can change the policy preferences of policy communi-ties and that therefore assimilation and adaptation are an essential part of consensus management. Instability within the attentive public is a vehicle for adaptation. It reminds the sub-government that it cannot run the policy community entirely in its own way and that new actors must be taken into account because they may signal challenges to prevailing policy paradigms. From the general public's point of view, this diversity of activity and the instability in policy communities are counterweights to the consensus-seeking behaviour of sub-governments. They introduce new ideas into the policy field, precipitate institutional readjustment, and, in the long run, promote the adaptation of policy to the changing needs of society. They help maintain a dynamic, responsive policy system. The early pluralists saw a similar dynamism safeguarding American democratic institutions.

As critics of the pluralists have argued, however, we cannot entirely trust the spontaneous expression of self-interest to ensure that equity and democracy prevail in policy-making. The adaptive capacity of the policy community is a crucially important quality, but it is not enough. Representation within most policy communities is incomplete and unequal. The communities are dominated by institutionalized actors. Generally agencies and institutionalized groups populate sub-governments and comprise a significant part of the attentive public. Though they may not entirely agree with one another, they understand the importance of consensus management and tend to subscribe to established policy paradigms.

Nascent and fledgling groups, whether they oppose the consensus or simply want relatively minor changes in policy, are puny in comparison to institutionalized power. Their resource base often prohibits continuing, effective participation in the life of the community, even if institutionalized members do not explicitly close ranks against them. If they do incur organized opposition from established members, they confront formidable barriers. Their efforts will be ignored, or given unsympathetic coverage by much of the media. Volunteer help may be unavailable or even discouraged by imputations of radicalism. Public recognition of legitimacy will be denied. Sources of funding will dry up, or the costs of opposition driven to impossible heights by the use of expensive counter-tactics. At worst, the power of the state may be exerted against them, as it was at the time of the 'On-to-Ottawa' trek of the unemployed in the 1930s and at Oka in 1990.[63] All these impediments and many more constrain the majority of groups that consistently challenge the conventional wisdom of the policy community.

In the case of groups attempting to represent the disadvantaged, these problems are compounded. By definition, the weak lack the wherewithal to sustain a presence in policy-making circles. Lack of resources is not their only difficulty. The very act of organizing representation for the weak often results in transforming the messages they wish to send to the government and the public. Church groups, social-service organizations, representatives of the caring professions, and even subsidized groups staffed by the underprivileged are all well-intentioned, but have trouble relating to their constituency and speaking for it. They speak on behalf of their constituents, but do not necessarily speak for them. Neither their legitimacy nor their mandate comes from those they represent. The quality of their representation is therefore in doubt.[64]

I must conclude, then, that although Canadian pressure group politics does much to generate open, public discussion of policy issues, and provides our political system with a mechanism for adaptation, its capacity for equitable representation of interests is inadequate. In the concluding chapter, I will look at ways of rendering pressure-group politics more effective, and will address the fundamental issue of the tension between our sectoral and spatial systems of representation.

CHAPTER 10

Space, Sector, and Legitimacy: Addressing the Dilemmas of Representation

This book began with Robert Stanfield's complaint that pressure groups threaten democratic government — a concern that has crept to the surface again and again as we have examined the many aspects of pressure group politics and their impact on the formation of public policy. When we looked at the historical evolution of groups, we saw how closely tied they have been to — and, at times, how strongly influenced by — bureaucracies. I noted how important it is for pressure group representatives to 'get to decision-makers before the parliamentary stage is reached'. In examining the interior life of groups, I found that many received a large portion of their operating income from governments; that government policies can encourage certain kinds of groups and force others out of politics. In two chapters preceding this, I concluded that corporatism, with its tendency to set aside parliamentary discussion, is not a serious possibility in Canada, but also that policy communities, with their tendency to organize issues out of politics, are very much a part of our policy process.

In addressing the normative issues raised by Canadian pressure group politics, I began with the proposition that the fundamental concerns of modern government have to do with space and sector. The effectiveness of contemporary political systems depends on how well their institutions reconcile the territorial and sectoral needs of their members. I have touched on this problem repeatedly. I have argued that for most of this century it has been difficult for Parliament to address sectoral issues, much less to provide adequate representation of special interests. Until the 1960s, the other institutions of policy-making — Cabinet, bureaucracy, federal-provincial conferences, and pressure groups — met these needs virtually without the participation of Parliament. The effect on Canadian democracy was deleterious. Parliament, the country's pre-eminent legitimating institution, proved less and less competent to cope with the questions that a modern economy places on the public agenda, while the institutions that could effectively deal with those questions gradually came to be seen as lacking the legitimacy that would ensure public acceptance of the policies and programs they had devised. I will argue that it is this fundamental tension in Canadian democracy — not the increasing vigour of pressure group politics — that causes the problems raised by Robert Stanfield. Pressure group politics is a symptom, not the cause. In this concluding chapter I suggest that, though the threat of the special-interest state can by no means be ignored in Canada, our highly visible and active pressure group system is not far from being inherently perverse; it may actually contain the means of overcoming the space-sector tension we described.

THE REPRESENTATION OF SPACE AND SECTOR

Everyone has an attachment to place. In some degree, whether we live in a remote mountain valley or an urban neighbourhood, we are all deeply affected by both the physical and the social context of our surroundings. They are immensely important to us. They are, for us, an integrated, interdependent whole — what we think of when we identify ourselves with a community. Historically, this attachment to physical space has been a cornerstone of political organization. Medieval kingdoms were built on the idea that at each level of the social hierarchy men and women were willing to defend specific pieces of territory. Early parliaments were organized around this same attachment. It is not surprising, then, that a concept of representative government built on the principle that each member of the legislature represents the electors living in a spatially defined area was used by western countries to adapt their institutions of government to the exigencies of the industrial revolution. Nor that the single-member constituency, the institutional device embodying that principle, is still with us today.

We take these arrangements for granted — so much so that it comes as a surprise when we are reminded that representative government might have been based on a different principle: the representation of sectors of social and economic activity rather than those of space. Yet many city states were governed in much this way through the guild system. The British have based their parliamentary institutions on the spatial concept, but from an early date they recognized the significance of sectoral concerns. The Woolsack, upon which English chief justices sit (rather uncomfortably) on state occasions, is a tangible relic of one such interest: the wool trade. In the nineteenth century a group of French philosophers, led by Saint-Simon and Auguste Comte, put forward proposals for reforming the system of representation along sectoral lines, proposals that found an echo in the corporatism of Fascist Europe.[1] Though discredited by their association with Fascist dictatorships, these proposals expressed valid doubts that spatially-based representative institutions were meeting the demands of modern society. They also addressed two aspects of a significant issue: (1) that for most of us a concern for what we do is nearly as compelling as, and often in conflict with, intense attachment to the place we live in; and (2) that at times we must give political expression to demands that emanate from what we do. How and why have this tension between our identification with both space and sector, and the need to find a legitimate method representing sectoral concerns, become significant issues?

Modern economies depend on the specialization of function. They operate on the assumption that work can be divided and that each element in any series of tasks can and should be performed by those who can do it most cheaply and expeditiously — in other words, most efficiently. The concept of the division of function can be applied not only on the production line, but in large-scale organizations, and even between geographic regions.

In Canada — which tends to be seen in the international market-place as a source of primary products — certain regions are considered to be the best producers of some products, others of others. From a political point of view, economic specialization has been a mixed blessing. Certainly it has made possible a vast increase in the quality of goods available and has brought prosperity to many centres and regions. But it has also greatly reduced the economic self-sufficiency of countries, regions, and — particularly — individual communities. It has also gone hand in hand with growing concentration of economic power and with the centralization of business decision-making. Not only have whole communities become vulnerable to sudden and unexpected changes in markets and in corporate policy, but they have also experienced a frightening sense of powerlessness.[2] Invariably the dark side of modern economics is reflected in political movements — regional alienation, protest movements, and so on — while even the bright side forces government to take a large part in general economic management, at the risk of upsetting important economic and political groups whose well-being is adversely affected by government intervention. Thus economic development brings with it a long list of political perils for government. In this list, few problems loom as large as the one created by the great pressure the modern economy has placed on the representative institutions of government. It is not an exaggeration to say that in several industrialized democracies, Canada included, this pressure has threatened to undermine the legitimacy of governmental institutions.

The reasons for this are deceptively simple. They relate to the fact that the pre-eminent legitimating institutions in these political systems have been built on the principle of spatial representation and have not successfully adapted to the specialized, or sectoral, demands of the modern economy. This explanation is deceiving in its simplicity because it glosses over the fact that it is not at all easy for governmental institutions to combine representation of both aspects of modern life. In the early years of modern economic development — which were also the first years of our present system of representative government — members of legislatures and the political parties they developed were able to combine both types of representation; but as the economy has grown more specialized and at the same time more interdependent, it has become increasingly difficult for legislators and parties to achieve this combination. The emergence of interest groups provided an outlet for the presentation of sectoral demands, but at the cost of dissociating those demands from the needs of communities.

The Canadian representative system has not adapted to the representation of special interests. Rather, local and regional identity has always been more than usually prominent in our political institutions.* Thus in Parliament members give a very high priority to constituency and regional concerns. When they break party ranks it is more likely to register solidarity with their constituents than to proclaim a difference in principle. The defection of Liberal and Conservative members to form the Bloc Québécois is the most striking instance of this, but by no means the first. In 1983, members of the Quebec caucus announced that they would not support a government bill introducing changes in the Crow's Nest Pass freight rate. The government modified its proposal to meet some of the demands of Quebec farmers, even though doing so aroused bitter complaint in the West.[3] MPs from other regions have broken ranks over issues such as the imposition of the Goods and Services Tax, an issue of principle that was tied to regional alienation. But the strength of constituency ties is not solely registered in such extreme gestures. It is seen in the electoral process itself, in the resistance to the system of 'parachuting' widely practised in European politics. In Canada, it is highly unusual for a constituency to elect a representative who has no ties at all with the area.[4] At a broader level, the strength of regional ties has led to the institutionalization of regional caucuses. The Saskatchewan caucus of the NDP broke ranks with the party over constitutional reform, for example.[5] The Quebec Liberal caucus has been the 'single most important influence in maintaining the Quebec textile industry [through persuading the government to maintain tariff barriers], despite the government's policy of opening up trade with the Third World'.[6] Among members from the Atlantic provinces regional affinities create an especially strong bond — so much so that the Atlantic Provinces Economic Council has organized from time to time meetings of all Members of Parliament from the region, regardless of party label, and claims to have been successful in urging them to forget party differences in promoting policies favourable to the region.[7]

If territorial or spatial concerns are highly institutionalized in Parliament,

---

*For example, W.E. Lyons remarks that 'the impact of space in Canadian legislative representation is especially prominent in the early debates over the principles and formulae to be used in reapportionment, particularly in the concern of the Maritimes provinces that they would lose representation as the population of the rest of the country increased. This became an important issue between 1892 and 1914 when the region did lose representation' (*One Man – One Vote* [Toronto, 1970] 3). I would argue that the impact of space is still fundamental to Canadian politics.

sectoral concerns are by contrast hardly represented at all. In Europe members of legislatures are often associated more closely in the public mind with specific interests than with the constituencies they happen to represent. They are the acknowledged parliamentary representatives for those interests, expected to lead debate on issues that concern them and to lobby for them on committees and behind the scenes. In fact, so pronounced is this type of representation that it is sometimes blamed for the loss of public regard for legislative institutions.[8] Not so in Canada. Here, if a representative for a particular interest emerges in the House of Commons, it is more by chance than by design.

The reasons for this absence of sectoral representation in our legislatures are numerous and beyond the scope of this discussion, but some at least should be mentioned briefly. We can in part attribute it to the territorialism just referred to. Constituencies that resist parachuting by parties are equally likely to turn a cold shoulder to sectoral interests anxious to place a representative in the legislature, unless a single industry dominates the riding in question, as the fishing industry dominates certain constituencies in Atlantic Canada; the textile industry several in Quebec; the automobile industry, Oshawa and Windsor; the public service, the Ottawa area; and mining, agriculture, and the forest industries a number of constituencies across the country. In such constituencies, members either know a great deal or become knowledgeable about the dominant industry. But in the majority of ridings, no one industry is preponderant and the member has neither the time nor the incentive to become expertly informed about the many different types of economic activity — much less non-economic activities — to be found in his or her riding.

Thus the electoral system militates against interest representation in the House of Commons. In the Senate, with its different basis of appointment, a greater emphasis on interest representation can be expected, and in fact the Senate has been called 'a lobby from within'.[9] However, as a lobby it is far more representative of highly institutionalized wealth than of the diversified interests of Canadians. Furthermore, the functions and status of the Senate do not lend themselves to the kind of interest representation that is involved in vigorously and publicly opposing, or promoting, specific kinds of policy, though Senate review of legislation often goes beyond merely correcting technical problems and improving drafting.[10]

Only recently has parliamentary procedure and internal organization encouraged either effective interest representation before the House or the attainment of expertise by members. For example, until the reforms of 1968-69, the committee system was quite incapable of generating among members a thorough understanding of the fields they were asked to legislate for. It is hardly surprising that very few interest groups or their representatives troubled to appear before them. In the House itself, the lack of

informed spokesmen made it difficult for House leaders to organize credita-
ble debate. In the era of the mandarins in particular, *Hansard* presented daily
testimony to the poverty of Parliament's role in the policy process. Even
more important, the timing of Parliament's involvement in the policy
process worked against its ability to consider constructively sectoral concerns. For the most part, such concerns could be addressed either in question
period or through consideration of specific pieces of legislation. The former
is a monitoring device or an opportunity to draw attention to urgent
problems and contributes little to the development of long-term policy,
which is important to most institutionalized interests. In fact, because
question period is a time of rapid, short exchanges, which are highly
publicized, it could actually distort government and interest group positions
or otherwise damage their relationships. Consideration of legislation does
allow more scope for discussion of long-term policy, but here parliamentarians and pressure group representatives were for many years deterred by the
conventions of the policy system. By the time legislation was presented to
the House, it had usually been subject to considerable discussion between
officials, interest group representatives, and finally Cabinet. Even without
the government's customary insistence that each piece of legislation be
treated as a government bill and have the unwavering support of all its
members, most of those involved in drafting and presenting legislation
would have been reluctant to reopen clauses that had been the product of
much research, consultation, and negotiation. In short, Parliament's involvement in the policy process was mistimed and therefore usually ineffectual.[11]

The strength of territorial feeling, the workings of the electoral system,
and the inadequacy of the institution of Parliament itself explain in part why
sectoral interests have until recently virtually ignored the legislature and
have devoted their attention to the political and administrative executive and
to the bureaucracy at large. Other factors have had to do with the greater ease
with which sectorally oriented interest groups have been able to organize
themselves to communicate with administrative agencies—which are
themselves structured around a functional division of labour. Together the
inadequacies of parliamentary representation and the compatibility of sectorally organized interests and agencies militated against the presentation of
special-interest demands through Parliament and encouraged their expression through other channels. Initially, special interests cultivated the political executive itself and in so doing imposed the first great check on
legislative involvement in policy-making. They also greatly weakened the
policy role of party organizations at large. As the tasks of government
became more complex, and as the need for communication with government
became more pervasive and more technical, interests turned their attention
to the administrative branch, reserving contact with the executive to symbolic occasions or to cases where agreement could not be reached at lower

levels. In many respects, contacts between interests and agencies related to, and were conducted by, individuals; but there were numerous occasions when concerted pressure had to be applied by interests combined, or when government sought the collective views of those affected by policies. On these occasions, the benefits of interest group formation were increasingly apparent. Thus pressure groups became the accepted channel for interest representation and the administrative branch became both the object of, and the forum for, communication.

The effect on parliamentary institutions was devastating. Gradually the administrative arm of government assumed powers that earlier had been exercised by the legislature and the political executive. This was part of a world-wide trend that was usually explained in terms of the growing complexity of government activity. Governments, so the argument goes, were so deeply involved in so many highly technical aspects of social and economic life that politicians, overwhelmed by the extent and complexity of these responsibilities, abdicated decision-making authority. More often than not, they felt compelled by the complexity of the issues to follow the advice of their experts.

Canada's experience was similar to that of other countries. Federal and provincial statutes increasingly provided that officials would 'work out the details' by preparing regulations, which would be approved by ministers and Cabinets and, through the passage of orders-in-council, acquired the force of law. This delegated legislation seldom received close scrutiny from politicians. Its volume was, and is, considerable; it is often technical; it rarely catches the public eye, and in any case it has usually been cleared with the affected parties—that is, with those identified, by themselves and by officials, as being interested in the legislation.[12]

The net result of this long progression—it took three-quarters of a century for the effects of delegation to reach these proportions—was to transfer a substantial degree of political power from the political executive to the administrative arm. Just as at the end of the nineteenth century the evolution of the modern economy forced the locus of power from the legislature to the executive, so by the middle of the present century the invocation of administrative competence had effected a further substantial shift of power from the political executive to the bureaucracy. The size and power of the bureaucracy, warned a policy document prepared by the Progressive Conservatives in 1977, 'offer a constant challenge to the moral and actual authority of the House of Commons'.[13] When the Conservatives reached power two years later, they found that the challenge at the executive level was equally great. Gillies and Pigott sum up a widely accepted view of the situation:

It is well known that the process by which organizations put forth their views tends to bypass Parliament. Skilled lobbyists always begin well down in the system so that they will always have a place to which they can appeal if they lose in their first efforts. Thus when legislation is being prepared the first efforts of interest groups are directed at the department involved, their goal being to exclude from the all-important memorandum to Cabinet recommendations which would adversely affect their interests. They generally recognize that once a position has been taken in that document, it can be changed only with difficulty. If, however, a special interest group does fail in its first efforts, it may meet with senior members of the department; perhaps the deputy minister and then even the minister. If these efforts are unsuccessful and legislation is proposed to which it is opposed, the group may then decide to lobby members of Parliament and eventually appear at the hearings on the bill before a committee of the House of Commons. Parliament, in other words, is the last line of defence.[14]

J. Iain Gow makes a similar point when he speaks of policy-making in Quebec, arguing that 'les groupes organisés préfèrent exercer leur pressions à Québec, soit auprès des hommes politiques, le Premier ministre et les ministres, soit auprès de la haute fonction publique' rather than through individual members of the National Assembly.[15] The latter, overwhelmed by the complexity of modern administration, find their own resources and those of their parties and the legislature insufficient. In the words of a British commentator, A.H. Hanson, contemplating the decline of parliamentary institutions in that country, 'we are stuck with a form of government in which bureaucrats and pressure groups play leading roles and in which the legislature can hardly expect to be restored to its former glories'.[16]

The same commentator, however, adds an important qualification to his gloomy view. The decline of Parliament, he maintains, does not imply, 'as the extremer critics have suggested, that Parliament is now no more than a dignified or ornamental institution. Even in the absence of further reform it remains the one institution whose demise would involve the virtual disappearance of everything characteristically democratic about our way of life'.[17] I will argue that Hanson's crucial qualification is at the heart of recent developments in pressure group politics — in Canada at least.

PRESSURE GROUPS AND THE REVIVAL OF PARLIAMENT

In pressure group politics, access is the key to influence. The key to access varies from system to system and from time to time within single systems. The latter variation seems to have occurred recently in Canada. A system of pressure group politics in which access sprang from the ability to provide specialized information has been changed into one in which legitimation is equally important in opening the door to the policy process. From the Parliamentary perspective, this change is significant: a system of pressure group politics in which specialized communication obtains access tends to shun Parliament, whereas one in which legitimation is the wherewithal for participation cultivates Parliament. The reasons for this spring from the capacities and functions of Parliament itself.

A system of pressure group politics that emphasizes the search for legitimation enhances the role of Parliament, for the simple reason that of all the political institutions in Canada, Parliament — the House of Commons in particular — is, after the constitution itself, the pre-eminent legitimating institution. I have explored this point in Chapter 3, pointing out that Canada gives unusual prominence to Parliament as a legitimating institution.[18] Conversely, an information-oriented system of pressure group politics shuns Parliament because, while Parliament is the nation's forum, it is not a reliable source of information. Parliament deals in large ideas and sweeping visions, dreadful wrongs and great calamities. Exaggeration is its stock in trade; information is simply the raw material used to spin candy floss for journalists. Of course, there are other sides to Parliament's handling of information: committees deal with tedious quantities of technical detail and may substantially affect specific policies. But even in committee, partisanship or constituency concerns are forces to be reckoned with. In short, the language of Parliament — the language of politics — is not the language of policy formulation.* It may be used to promote policy, to support policy, or to attack it, but it lacks the precision needed for the analysis of situations, the delineation of alternatives, or the formulation of policy responses.

To say that Parliament is not well adapted to policy formulation is not to say that those who have an interest in specific policies automatically steer clear of it. Quite the contrary, as I will argue shortly. However, in a situation such as we knew in Canada during the mandarin years, where the policy process is both highly bureaucratic and considered to be thoroughly legitimate, interaction with Parliament becomes for most groups dysfunctional. It might raise the level of conflict surrounding specific issues; it might encourage criticism of government actions or intentions; it could lead to the foreclosing of policy options, or put both groups and bureaucrats to a great deal of extra effort to justify, elaborate, and explain policy. For representatives of established, or institutionalized, pressure groups, anxious to maintain good long-term relations with bureaucratic policy-makers, these are situations to be avoided. The simplest way to avoid them is to avoid Parliament.

However, this condition holds only as long as a policy process dominated

---

*We see policy formulation as part of the culminating stage of policy determination. It involves the bringing about of compromises between rival interests and the ultimate selection of alternatives. Both of these are functions that engage the political responsibility of the executive and so properly belong to the Prime Minister and the Cabinet. Policy formulation also involves the precise delineation of policy, a task that is best left to the bureaucracy, duly supervised by the executive.

by the bureaucracy is considered legitimate. In a country such as France, where the legitimacy of the public service derives both from the legitimacy of the president and the executive, and from a deeply rooted public conception of the state, such a condition may last for a very long time indeed. In a country like Canada, where the concept of the state has only limited meaning and where the public service has virtually no independent legitimacy, it is unlikely that such a condition will long outlast the public's realization that the political executive had lost control of the bureaucracy. It is the political executive that has legitimacy and confers that legitimacy on those who serve it. Once it becomes dissociated from the political executive, the bureaucracy forfeits its claim to legitimacy.

The public became convinced during the 1970s that the federal Cabinet had lost control of the machinery of government. This conviction diminished both the political executive and the public service. A Cabinet that cannot work the public service loses public respect and eventually its own aura of legitimacy. A public service that is believed to be 'out of control' comes to be seen as merely self-serving and is treated accordingly. I argued in Chapter 3 that Parliament has, if anything, benefited from the decline of Cabinet and bureaucracy; that the recent evolution of policy processes has placed a premium on Parliament's legitimacy capacity and has thus assured it of an enhanced role. The decline of Cabinet enhances the status of Parliament, for the stability of the political system requires the maintenance of legitimating institutions, and when one such institution is in eclipse we can expect others to become more prominent — particularly those that have been endowed traditionally with legitimating status. Parliament's legitimating capacity, in conjunction with its ability to focus public debate, now makes interaction with the legislature highly desirable in the eyes of many groups and a necessity in the eyes of others. Even John Bulloch, who has a low regard for Parliament's policy-making capacity, admits that 'if . . . you want . . . to put pressure on the system, there is nothing more effective than going to your Member of Parliament' and focusing public attention through caucus and question period.[19] Simply by giving them a hearing, parliamentary committees confer legitimacy on challenging interests and enable them to claim national attention. Furthermore, their participation galvanizes other groups interested in moulding public attitudes and promoting new policies. In the increasingly competitive environment of pressure group politics, the leaders of established groups have to anticipate these challenges, or at least respond to them.

A need to defend their interests in public is only one of the factors encouraging established groups to pay more attention to Parliament. Their behaviour also reflects the changed relations between groups and agencies that we have discussed. On the one hand, institutionalized groups clearly act with more freedom than they did in the past. On the other, it is equally clear that their newly kindled interest is encouraged by government agencies, which, faced with the diminished legitimacy we have pointed out, see the cultivation of friends in Parliament as a means of developing alternative bases of support.* In part, agencies achieve this through direct interaction between parliamentarians and departmental representatives. The reform of the committee system and the tendency for a core at least of MPs to affiliate themselves with specific committees has encouraged more independent and detailed study of issues and policies and the development of a better understanding of agency goals in the House and has increased public service interaction with Parliament.[20] Public servants appear before parliamentary committees to an unprecedented extent. But public servants are prevented by their constitutional role as subordinate advisers from engaging vigorously and independently in advocating and defending the policies they prefer. In consequence, I argued, they have looked to their closest associates in their policy communities — the institutionalized groups — to act as proxies, explaining policy, defending it, and promoting it. Self-interest has thus encouraged government agencies and established groups to engage in public discussion of policy and to accept an expanded role for Parliament and people in policy formulation.

The significance of the legitimating role obliges us to take issue with those who have argued that the complexity of modern government reduces to the purely symbolic Parliament's role in the policy process. Nearly thirty years ago, A.H. Hanson, in an article that will be treated here as reasonably representative of the literature,[21] contrasted the then widely accepted Schumpeterian view of Parliament's role with that enunciated a century earlier by Bagehot. The former confined Parliament to (1) sanctioning the formation of a type of government that the electorate, through its vote, may be considered to have approved of; (2) subjecting that government to criticism of a general kind, thereby acting as a forum for the 'competitive struggle for the people's vote'; and (3) securing where possible the redress of specific grievances. In other words, Parliament was performing its role adequately as long as it acted as an electoral college, as a critic, and as an ombudsman, but its policy role was decidedly limited. While we would not exclude these functions, we would wish to cite as well the more distinctly policy-oriented functions perceived by Bagehot, and are more inclined to

---

*As our earlier comments have implied, the bureaucracy's search for legitimating support by no means focused exclusively on Parliament. Massive public-relations campaigns directed at the public at large; experimentation with representative bureaucracy; efforts to reconstitute traditional patterns of accountability; and a greater part of the work undertaken to create and/or enlarge policy communities impinge on Parliament's role but appear to have been designed to influence public opinion in general. Some of these ventures, in fact, may eventually challenge Parliament. Corporatist arrangements or even policy communities fully representative of policy sectors could fall into that category.

agree with him that the function of Parliament is to 'express the mind of the people'; 'to teach the nation what it does not know'; and to make us 'hear what otherwise we should not'. I have attributed this somewhat restored role to the loosening of the policy system. Because its capacity to legitimate consequently plays a greater part in the competition over policy, and because its talent for focusing public attention is much sought after, Parliament in Canada seems definitely to be playing a more significant role than it did twenty years ago.

The key questions, of course, are how significant is that role and how far can it be extended? How precisely does Parliament express the will of the nation? If very precisely, then Parliament is playing a major role in policy formation. If only very broadly — to the extent, perhaps, of registering the popularity or unpopularity of the government — then Parliament has not progressed beyond the Schumpeterian definition of its functions. The answer seems to lie somewhere between these extremes. The pessimists suggest that the policy role is minimal and is likely to remain so. The optimists claim that caucus has always played a larger part than most critics will admit; that the present more dynamic system has already enhanced Parliament's policy role; and that the recent experiment with parliamentary enquiries into specific policy issues is a portent for the future.[22] Neither side suggests that Parliament can or should actually initiate or formulate policy. But Parliament is playing a larger part in the early stages of policy development, carrying out general discussions with the public, hearing expert opinion, providing an initial reading of the public mind on issues, and contributing to the further development of public opinion. The growth of this kind of activity has been fostered by the reforms of the last twenty-five years, notably in the creation of Opposition Days, in the experiments with policy papers of various hues, and most recently in the widening of committee powers of investigation, in the buttressing of research support, and in their reduction in size. In terms of contributing to long-term policy, the reforms of the committee system seem the most promising because they avoid the temptation to focus on current issues (question period and Opposition Days provide adequately for this) and yet they enable parliamentarians to do more than simply react to White Papers and other preliminary documents when they are tabled. Though care must be taken in selecting topics for investigation by parliamentary committees, experience has shown that Parliament can help express the mind of the people and can perform an educational function. A comment made to the Bar Association committee enquiring into legislative reform illustrates the point:

Most people's general concern is that the place doesn't work and that it is irrelevant to most people on the street and most MPs. If I hadn't got involved in a special committee the frustrations that other MPs feel would have been mine as well. In the committee you get out there and talk to people. You have investigative powers ... you really got into the subject. The proof that you can be effective is that the government has implemented over half of our recommendations.[23]

Parliamentary intervention at this middle stage of policy formation optimizes its legitimacy capacity while avoiding confrontation with the government's need to command the confidence of the House. By encouraging the general public — groups and individuals — to express their views, it legitimizes those views to a degree, thus pre-empting the tendency of the public service to set the parameters for discussion early in the policy process. At the same time, because the exploratory nature of the investigation is widely understood, this approach neither threatens government's ability to make the final determination of policy nor excites the more destructive aspects of partisanship. In short, to make the best use of the ability its legitimating capacity gives it to contribute to the policy process, Parliament should follow a long-standing dictum of Canadian pressure group politics: to influence the shape of legislation, you must present your case before Cabinet has decided its position.[24] It has been amply demonstrated that Parliament is not a suitable vehicle for initiating policy or for formulating policy, but the logic of its position in a diffused power system suggests that it can make a major contribution to the pre-Cabinet stages of policy formation.

We assume that party politics will also benefit from Parliament's revival. If parliamentarians are seen to play a meaningful role in policy formation, the party should attract strong candidates, and community leaders should once again wish to be associated with party organizations. To capitalize on these trends, however, Canada's political parties will have to transform their grass-roots organizations from electoral machines chugging away on the fuel of minor patronage into bodies with a genuine capacity to assist in policy formation. It is probably significant that the Liberals and Conservatives are being challenged by parties — the New Democrats, the Parti Québécois, and Reform — that have institutionalized grass-roots participation in policy-making. If parties succeed in restoring a policy capability to the grass roots, there is reason to hope that the competition of parties and pressure groups will turn into something more productive, not only for the organizations themselves, but for the general public.

Our discussion has linked several phenomena that have been separately observed in Canada: the diffusion of power within the executive-administrative branch, the proliferation and expanded role of pressure groups, and the increased attention Parliament has been receiving from interest organizations. Suggesting that this last may reflect fundamental changes in the policy system as a whole, we argued that the enhanced role of Parliament and the proliferation of interest groups can be partially attributed to the diffusion of power within the executive and administrative branches; that a tendency towards bureaucratic pluralism has led agencies to develop extragovernmental support at the interest group level; and that both interest groups and agencies, finding it useful to exploit the legitimating and publicizing capacities of Parliament, have contributed to the enhancement of Parliament's role in the policy process.

Because I see the proliferation and the growing prominence of pressure groups as part and parcel of the movement that led to this improvement of Parliament's policy role, I do not share Robert Stanfield's concern that an abundance of special-interest organizations threatens democratic government in Canada. Because our pressure groups are less willing, or able, to shelter in the half-light of politics, the public is now more aware than it has been for many years of the debates that lie behind public policy decisions, and our Parliaments are much better informed than were their predecessors of twenty years ago. Recent changes in pressure group behaviour are the product of, and have themselves fostered, a more open and dynamic policy process. Parliament may at last be creating an institutional structure that could effectively reconcile the spatial and sectoral needs of Canadians.

TOWARDS EQUALITY IN REPRESENTATION

Enhanced legislative influence in the policy process ameliorates the tension between our spatial and sectoral systems of representation, but it does little to ensure that all interests in Canadian society have an equal opportunity to contribute to public decision-making. To a degree it promotes inequity, because it imposes on all participants an increasingly complex and expensive procedure that only established and relatively affluent groups can afford.

The problem of equality is second only to that created by the rivalry of spatial and sectoral systems of representation. It has two aspects: first, inequity in group representation lessens public regard for the policies that emerge from the process. A sense of inefficacy breeds alienation. An alienated public will, at best, turn a passive face to public authorities, and at worst will come to see the regime as illegitimate and violently oppose it. Unrest among aboriginal peoples, in particular, but survey reports in general indicating surprisingly high levels of inefficacy for a country that prides itself on its democratic qualities,[25] suggest a need for efforts to maintain and improve the opportunities for all interests to contribute to the policy process. Complete equality in representation will always be an ideal, but that is no reason to ignore it or to think that efforts to achieve it will not strengthen public regard for policy.

Equality of access also enhances the quality of public policy. On the one hand, policy-makers derive breadth of opinion from it. On the other, the free flow of information that generally accompanies equal and open participation raises the level of public understanding and promotes consensus. This, of course, slows down the formation and implementation of public policy; but as long as due process is not allowed to serve as a vehicle for indecision, the time and effort spent on developing policies and programs are probably compensated for by their general acceptance and ease of implementation.

On grounds, then, of ensuring the legitimacy of the policy process and of enhancing its quality, every encouragement should be given to promoting greater equality between groups. The means of achieving that are numerous, though imperfect and far from reliable. They entail modifications in the regulation of organized lobbying; in the provision of resources for interest groups; and in the processes of public-policy formation.

Regulation

One of the first public reactions to the intrusion of pressure groups into the policy process is to call for their regulation. The pleading, often behind the scenes, for special interests arouses the deepest distrust in a democratic society. It is only to be expected that calls for the registration, even for the limitation, of pressure group activity should be heard once their involvement becomes obtrusive, as it has in recent years in this country. As early as 1969, NDP MP Barry Mather presented a private member's bill to Parliament to regulate lobbyists, and a succession of nearly identical proposals was put forward by Liberal, Conservative, and New Democrat members between then and September 1985, when Prime Minister Mulroney announced that the government would introduce legislation to establish a system of registration for lobbyists.[26]

Registration — the minimal first step to regulation — typifies the dilemma faced by public authorities when they try to take the measure of lobbying and limit its harmful side-effects. On the surface, registration seems innocuous and uncomplicated. Examination shows it to be neither, though it may still be desirable. This becomes evident as soon as the legislative drafters attempt to specify who should be required to register. Most frequently, lobbyists are defined as individuals who, for a fee, attempt to influence public policy on behalf of a third party.[27] This definition respects the right of individuals to represent their own interests to policy-makers and it excludes those who altruistically lobby on behalf of others. It applies only to independent lobbyists, lobbying firms, and the paid representatives of interest groups.

By itself, such a definition does not meet the needs of legislators. The impetus behind the government's call for registration was the desire of parliamentarians and officials to know the affiliation of the lobbyists who approach them.[28] They believed that this information would help them assess the motivations behind lobbying efforts and the reasons for the positions taken by lobbyists and interest groups, and so aid negotiation. It might even lead to direct negotiation between officials and interests, and so eliminate intermediaries. Finally, officials wanted this information because they had a duty to know who is attempting to influence public policy. They do not want to be deceived into putting forward policies that are not genuinely supported by the public at large or by affected special publics. Similarly, the public at large expects a registration system to provide it with more information than it now has about the interests competing for concessions from policy-makers.

To meet these needs, registration must entail more than simply recording the name of an individual lobbyist in some central registry. It means providing information about those the lobbyist represents. How much information? Should the organization behind the lobbyist be required simply to file a brief prospectus stating its aims, officers, and address? Such a system could be easily abused. Policy-makers would derive some benefit from the information provided about bona fide groups, but groups fronting for interests unwilling to make their activities known would find it easy to contrive innocuous credentials. The registration procedure would consequently create paperwork for legitimate groups, but do nothing to illuminate the interests behind less legitimate organizations.

An alternative approach would require the lobbyist to file much more information about those he or she represents, including statements of lobbying expenses, sources of financial support, and, in the case of interest groups, copies of their constitutions and membership lists. Provision of such details of interest group aims, structure, and resources would meet many information requirements of policy-makers and of the public at large, but it would entail substantial costs. The least of these would be administrative, although no effective registration service — with the means to exact, verify, or disseminate information — is cheap. Administrative charges, though, deserve less attention than the possible costs to free and open public discussion. Superficially, an information requirement conforms with the ideal of democratic government. It is certainly important for the public to know who is influencing public policy.

Unfortunately, information can lead not only to clarification but to intimidation. Individuals willing to give unobtrusive support to unpopular causes may be loath to do so if their allegiance is to be made public. There are communities, including policy communities, that will not tolerate the alternative views expressed by some interest groups. It takes considerable courage to oppose sealing in St Anthony's, Newfoundland. Vancouver-based opponents of wolf-pack culling were physically as well as verbally attacked when they ventured into the trapping and hunting communities of the British Columbia interior.[29]

Usually Canadians apply fewer physical sanctions against those who challenge the conventional wisdom, but those sanctions can be compelling. Many are reluctant to join groups whose aims might conflict with those of their employers. Environmental groups, for example, threaten many concerns, large and small. Loss of employment is a real possibility for anyone supporting a group whose activities might lead to higher costs for the company. Similarly, corporate support for such groups is hard to come by. Environmentally aware managers and owners of firms are not necessarily free agents — they depend on other companies for supplies and sales. They find it safe to support symphony orchestras, hospitals, and even universities, but until recently they hesitated to overtly support groups campaigning for clean air, clean water, and an attractive landscape. Non-economic sanctions are readily available. On returning to St John's after being away from Newfoundland for some time, Walter Davis, a former president of the city's Rotary Club, found that his application for membership was deferred. He claimed that his work as a peace activist was the cause.[30]

Social ostracism, discrimination, harassment — including vandalism and hate mail — can all be used to discipline errant members of the community, and are not easy to prohibit. Nor is the state always an impartial refuge for those who hold unconventional opinions. Many supporters of the peace movement are convinced that their activities are monitored, recorded, and occasionally used as the basis for harassment. Their fears may be exaggerated, but from time to time actions of security agencies lend them credibility.[31] For these reasons, democracy may be imperilled as much as promoted by the full disclosure of interest group information.

There are other costs to registration. If registration is to be a necessary preliminary to lobbying, how can our political system sustain its spontaneity? The impulse to establish a new group can be undermined if a long process of registration prevents its participation in an immediate and pressing debate. A system of registration that prohibits lobbying until groups have filed considerable documentation, or imposes fixed fees to recover the costs of the registration service, would impede group formation and participation even further.

Perhaps these problems with registration led the Minister of Consumer and Corporate Affairs to propose a system that requires only the registration of the lobbyist, the name of the client, and the subject of lobbying activity. The Lobbyists Registration Act excludes lobbyists gathering policy intelligence, advising clients on strategy, and those arranging appointments between officials and clients.[32] It assumes that the objectives of corporations and formal interest groups can easily be discovered. This is mistaken. Many corporations and major interest groups are multifaceted organizations with diverse interests. If the goal of open government is to be achieved, they should be required to identify for the benefit of other affected interests the undertakings they are engaged in. Furthermore, it is unsound to assume that the purposes and backgrounds of interest groups are transparent and can be easily investigated by the public. Under the system, an unscrupulous interest could quite easily establish an organizational front that would be immune to the disclosure rules applied to others.

Although the creators of registration procedures must take into account the problems that accompany different systems of registration, such an approach is too cautious. None of the objections to registration refutes the argument that democratic politics requires interests to be frank about their reasons for supporting or opposing policy options. The public has a right to know who wants what, and why. The policy-maker has a duty to know. Furthermore, secrecy can discredit the policy process, rendering its output illegitimate. It is in the interests of all bona fide groups that their efforts to influence public policy not be considered clandestine. Disclosure is a necessity.

How can we secure disclosure without precipitating intimidation or fostering the fear of intimidation? A partial solution can be derived from our experience with electoral law, where the debate over secrecy versus openness is also significant. For the individual voter, we have guaranteed the secrecy of the ballot. Similarly, we can respect the privacy of group membership, and we can do so without jeopardizing our efforts to know what interests are actually mounting lobbying campaigns. The mechanism for pursuing this information is also applied in Canadian electoral law, and is found in the requirement that all financial contributions to parties above a certain minimum be recorded and publicly available. In similar fashion, groups could record individual donations over $500 and corporate donations over $5,000.

Under a regime such as that suggested here, all lobbyists — independent professionals, company executives, interest group representatives, and so on — would be required to provide a statement outlining the purposes of the organization represented, naming its officers, and indicating the number of paid-up members. Registration on behalf of organizations would also require a list of the individuals authorized to represent the organization; an audited financial statement of lobbying expenditures; and, if the organization were an interest group, a list of all individual members contributing over $500 and all corporate contributions of more than $5,000. Such a procedure, though not foolproof, would go a long way to ensuring privacy to citizens while identifying major interests.

Similarly, lobbyists should be required to report lobbying campaigns rather than 'meetings'. The object of the campaign should be specified at the outset and followed up with quarterly reports that identify actual interactions with the government and indicate any major changes in the undertaking. Such a procedure could be administered quite simply and would have the advantage of providing essential information in a digestible package to the public. This approach could also be used to address the need for information about the cost of lobbying campaigns. Lobbying campaigns are frequently budgeted for as such. Consequently lobbyists should be able to generate global costs of campaigns quite easily and without divulging hourly charges. Other improvements — like 'sunshine' legislation that would require governments to divulge the names of lobbyists who have made representations concerning specific legislation — have been suggested.

Flexibility in regulatory arrangements, along with their impartial administration, would also help overcome the dangers of fossilizing the group process through a regulatory system. While it is desirable that a minimum of information be available concerning all lobbyists and all groups, it is not necessary to put emergent groups through the same hoops that must be applied to established organizations. Initial registration for new groups should be simple, routine, and totally cost-free, in terms of fees or professional assistance. As organizations establish themselves, registration requirements should be more probing. Groups with budgets above certain levels and with some experience in the policy process should be expected to disclose their resources and interests.

The measures suggested here would go far towards installing pressure group politics legitimately and usefully in our policy process. The data collected would not only help policy-makers and the public assess rival demands, but might also serve to categorize impartially organizations that lack pocketbooks to match their concern for the public interest, and are in genuine need of public assistance. In short, registration — with the regulation it implies — is a dangerous but necessary instrument. Poorly defined and badly constructed, registration can exacerbate the problems now posed by pressure group politics. Sensitively created and implemented, it can be used to make pressure group politics an effective and useful part of our policy process.

Resources

Any regulatory regime has to be the product of a broad philosophical framework for incorporating group activities in the policy process. One such as that described above is naturally based on assumptions — I have articulated some of them — about the need for openness in public discussion and the corresponding need to protect the privacy of those whose views render them vulnerable. But such a regulatory regime would not make fully operational the philosophy behind the concerns I have raised throughout this study. It would help identify the participants in public debate and work against illicit lobbying, but it would do nothing to overcome imbalances created by unequal resource bases. A group with the resources to throw impressive 'power parties', to capture media attention, to maintain full-time representatives in the nation's capitals, and to pay for the elaborate briefs that are part of any sustained policy discussion has the staying power, the authority, and the 'policy capacit'.[33] to outlast most of its rivals, particularly if they happen to be public-interest groups. Yet the rival policy objectives may be no less valid — they may even be more representative of the public's wishes. Therefore an important underlying assumption of a democratic philosophy of pressure group involvement in public-policy formation is that every effort should be made to compensate for extreme differentials in the resource bases of competing groups.

A policy incorporating this philosophy is not easy to arrive at. State provision of resources, as I argued in Chapter 8, can have a deleterious effect on recipient groups and on the dynamism of the policy process. It can lead group organizations to lose touch with their members; it can encourage undertakings that cannot be sustained by the groups' real resources, rendering them ultimately dependent on government rather than on their own members. Not only does dependency encourage sycophancy and destroy free public debate, but a dependent group may occupy a position in the policy community to the exclusion of alternative organizations, thus fostering inertia in the policy system. Finally the state must avoid creating an environment in which pressure group development becomes a cottage industry. Neither its procedures to ensure a fair hearing for all interests nor its resource assistance should encourage entrepreneurs to build organizations — ostensibly representing a particular interest — that actually exist, through government grants, to support a small staff of professional lobbyists whose chief effects will be to consume public funds and to prolong and complicate the resolution of the public business. In this welter of conflicting goals, two imperatives stand out: the need to promote equality and the need to avoid dependence.

Equality can be promoted in a variety of ways, some of which were described in Chapter 8. The resources of groups can be supplemented directly through grants; through the provision of facilities such as space, office equipment, and access to communications tools; and even through the secondment of government personnel to groups. Indirect assistance can be offered through the purchase of group services, such as research or administrative services. Positional policies, such as those that place group representatives on influential advisory boards, also give indirect support because they encourage members to believe that they are tapped into the flow of vital information.

Crucial to equality are not so much the forms assistance takes, but the criteria used to allocate it, and who decides which group should receive what. In 1977, a study commissioned by the Secretary of State reported that though a number of federal agencies supported voluntary groups, each had 'its own unique set of priorities in this area, not to mention its own unique way of reporting on its activities'.[34] The study group was appalled at the lack of consistency it discovered and the unwillingness of agencies to provide information — much less uniform policies — on their support for voluntary groups.[35] Where direct grants and contributions are concerned, impartiality of the allocative process is essential.* A case might be made for removing such decisions entirely from the purview of agencies that have a vested interest in recipient groups' policy field, but in practice this would be counter-productive. Agencies in the policy community, particularly the lead agency, will be reluctant to work with groups they consider to be antagonistic, and will exclude them from the flow of information and use positional politics to render them ineffectual. A more practical approach would vest agencies with authority to make grants to groups, as they now do, but insist that the granting procedure follow government-wide standards and submit to evaluation by an independent body every five years. While this would not entirely eliminate the problems of dependence, it would assure new groups of a more impartial process of grant allocation than currently exists. To discourage groups from becoming dependent on any one agency, the granting process might tie assistance to the development of alternative sources of support.

Indirect assistance offers groups the opportunity to broaden their base of financial support. Here, too, some measure of reform is necessary. Agencies should not be in a position to exploit the groups in their policy community — insisting, for example, on excluding overhead costs from contract calculations. Procedures for awarding contracts to groups should be standardized in a fashion like that used for awarding contracts to private firms, and should be characterized by impartiality. Furthermore, administrative agencies need not be the only beneficiaries of the research capacities of groups: Parliament's revived role in the policy process could be sustained through extended research support, including enlarging the budgets available to parliamentary committees and task forces for commissioning research by groups and consultants.

As we saw in Chapter 8, because the costs of intervening in the regulatory process are often formidable, some regulatory agencies and commissions of

---

*The 1977 study noted with approval the criteria for awarding five-year sustaining grants established by the Department of National Health and Welfare (ibid., 179-84). They called for the development of five-year plans by recipient organizations, including evaluation procedures; they required that the organizations be national in scope and possess a network of affiliated agencies at the provincial and municipal levels; they insisted that target populations be represented in group governing bodies except where physical and mental handicaps made that impracticable. The study recommendation that similar criteria be adopted by the federal government in general appears to have gone unheeded.

inquiry have established procedures for granting to less affluent groups the funds they need to hire expert assistance. As a result, such groups have been able to present briefs and arguments that are as effective as those prepared by wealthy interests. Similar procedures warrant adoption in all regulatory situations and could be supported in part — as they are in some American jurisdictions[36] — through charges levied on those who would benefit materially from the changes they have requested in regulations or through permission to develop public resources. The principle of 'who benefits, pays' could be extended to other settings. In our cities, for example, neighbourhood groups are often unable to sustain the cost of representing their interests against the proposals of developers who wish to secure major changes in existing plans. Such costs should be recoverable from those who will profit from change.

Similar problems are found in litigation. The experience of the few groups that have attempted to obtain their objectives through court action discourages others, often at the expense of the public interest. Unless the legal system is to be abandoned entirely to the wealthy, some means must be found whereby groups concerned with matters of genuine public interest may pursue their concerns without undue hardship.[37] It should be possible for the state to establish funds to help sustain litigation deemed by the courts to raise issues of genuine public concern. A procedure that would both discourage frivolous litigation and aid the resolution of public-interest questions should be feasible and would secure a measure of equality in a field of public-policy formation that is becoming increasingly important.

Thus far we have been unable to escape from the tendency, long evident in Canada, to look to the public purse to support pressure group activity, particularly the activity of public-interest groups. Even though, as I have argued, dependence on government, and particularly on specific agencies, is deleterious, both for the dependent groups and for public debate, the fact is that Canadians — according to a consensus among pressure group activists — are reluctant to give financial support to groups. Though voluntarism is strongly established in this country, private benefaction is not.[38] Pressure groups are forced to rely on direct and indirect government support. The procedures put forward here take this reality into account and attempt to offset the side-effects of dependence by providing for clear criteria to govern both the awarding of support and impartiality in its administration.

It is possible that private benefaction can be encouraged. The Mulroney government's decision to permit registered charities to lobby in a non-partisan fashion removes some of the uncertainty beclouding the application of donated funds to lobbying activities. Governments could go further, however. In particular they could permit individuals and corporations to claim tax credits for such donations — similar to the tax credits allowed for donations to political parties. Tax expenditures of this sort have fallen out of favour in Ottawa. But there is merit in a policy that promises over the long haul to wean interest groups from dependence on the munificence of officials and to return to taxpayers in general the responsibility and authority for determining which groups should exist and which should not.

Finances are generally foremost among the issues relating to the resource bases of groups. But other aspects of the resource base could be addressed by a public concerned about equality between public-interest groups and material-benefit groups. On one level, resource issues can be addressed attitudinally. Voluntarism, for example, can be encouraged still further.[39] So can acceptance and encouragement of group activity, even when it runs counter to the conventional perceptions of the public. Governments and corporations can offer groups assistance in kind; for example, in some communities surplus buildings are made available to groups at a minimal rent. Some governments encourage their middle and senior executives to enter executive interchange programs with the private sector; interchanges with some pressure groups might prove equally challenging and rewarding. These and similar strategies to buttress the role of groups in our political system would help them contribute to public debate. Some of these strategies would enhance government understanding not only of the role of groups but of the communications they transmit.

The problems of dependence and inequality would not be eradicated, even if these measures and many others reinforcing them were put in place. The natural advantages many organizations derive from their place in the economy and their value to policy-makers render unlikely their chances of ever being seriously challenged by public-interest groups. Even so, as Canada moves inexorably into an era when, on the one hand, the state is more pervasive and, on the other, diffusion of power makes the policy process more complex, policies that consciously address the issues of dependence and inequality will not only benefit lesser groups and public-interest groups, but will ultimately contribute to a higher quality of public debate and more effective public policy.

Processes

Ultimately, successful integration of sectoral and spatial systems of representation and amelioration of problems of inequality depend on the maintenance of policy processes that give groups and legislators their due, while reducing the barriers to equal representation of interests. Under cabinet-parliamentary government, legislatures cannot effectively contribute to public-policy formation if they are unable to discuss options before the Cabinet accepts one alternative over others. Even affluent and established groups cannot make an impression on policy if they are denied access to the flow of information and if they are granted no opportunity to present their case. Assistance to the legislature, development of regulations to guide pressure group involvement in the policy process, even development of groups' resource bases can have little effect unless the process itself recognizes their claim to participation and accords them a meaningful role.

Over the last two decades there has been considerable expansion of opportunities for the public to influence policy decisions. The diffusion of power has helped Parliament elicit opinion from various sectors of the community. Agencies, increasingly aware of the legitimating capacity of interest groups, have paid more attention to public hearings and to advance consultation with interests prior to formulating new policies and revising regulations. Some regulatory tribunals have been receptive to the intervention of public-interest groups. In the field of local government, citizen participation in the policy process has been significantly encouraged.

All this brings us a little closer to realizing the potential of group representation in the policy process. There are many shortcomings, however, and some progress from earlier years is being eroded by the tide of 1980s conservatism. Consultation too often depends on the goodwill of officials and influential members of policy communities. Regulatory bodies, sometimes assisted by changes in legislation, have shown a tendency to define more narrowly the interests who may make representations to them.* A restricted economic climate is frequently used to discourage interventions in development investment decisions or to ignore demands for corporations and governments to observe existing social and environmental regulations. It is clear that uncertainty and constraint will increasingly limit the opportunities for group policy participation unless steps are taken to anchor consultation in the processes of policy formation.

The methods of achieving this are numerous. For example, it should be automatic that major revision of regulations be subjected to an open review process and that all the delegated legislation be subjected periodically to formal scrutiny both through agency hearings and Parliament. The public consultation that evolved to meet the requirements of environmental impact assessment during the 1970s should be extended and translated to other levels of government. It should be a matter of course for a process of public consultation to occur whenever a major change in public policy is contemplated. Such consultation might be conducted variously in the public service, through the legislature, or through the services of *ad hoc*

---

*In May 1985, for example, the Nova Scotia Municipal Board delivered an interpretation of revisions to the provincial Planning Act that greatly distressed local citizens' groups. The Board concluded that the revisions barred individuals who were not immediately affected from appealing re-zoning decisions of municipal authorities. Citizens' groups had argued that such an interpretation would inhibit attempts to bring a broader public interest to bear on such decisions. (See Halifax *Chronicle-Herald*, 23 May 1985.)

commissions and task forces, as the exigencies of the public agenda and the importance of the issues determine. Their significance would derive from their taking place at a point in policy formation where the views of the public might influence ultimate decisions. Finally, procedures for consultation should accommodate the public's need to influence both the implementation of policy and its preparation. Despite the fact that consultation has improved at the early stages of decision-making in recent years, very little has been done to admit the public to the periodic reviews of programs that have been called for by critics of public-sector management and that have to some extent been implemented.[40]

The dangers inherent in institutionalizing consultation with groups are that the process of consultation consumes vast amounts of energy and that it frequently delays the implementation of change until its impetus has dissipated and the resources accumulated to achieve it are dispersed. But these problems can be addressed by encouraging simplicity, flexibility, and openness in the decision process, and by imposing reasonable but fixed terms to it. They cannot be evaded by ignoring the necessity for consultation, which is a consequence of social complexity and has an imperative of its own. Consultation can be ignored for the short-run benefit of specific interests, but in the long run the public interest dictates that the processes of policy-making must formally engage the views of citizens and the groups they have created to represent them. This hard lesson was learned at the constitutional level in the debate over the Meech Lake Accord. Perhaps that experience will lead to a more general climate of openness and consultation.

GROUP POLITICS AND PUBLIC POLICY

Group politics has become a vital force in Canada. In this study, I have examined its origins as well as its current place in the policy process. I have applied a number of analytical tools to understand it better, seeking to establish how groups in this country exercise their unique talents for mobilizing opinion and influencing public authorities.

One of the most important of these tools is the concept of the policy community. I have striven to show how policy specialization accords to a relatively small public a dominant say in the creation and implementation of policy. I have analysed the structure of those special publics and suggested the dynamics that govern them. This analysis brought out both the conservative and dynamic tendencies inherent in the relationships generated within the community. I have argued that though the policy community dominates its policy field and is itself dominated by its sub-government, it is by no means impervious to change but experiences constant internal tension as competing groups — particularly those in the active public — challenge established policy paradigms. At the same time, I have suggested that this dynamism is only partially spontaneous, and that a lively, dynamic, attentive public must be fertilized and encouraged through a supportive regulatory regime combined with adequate consultative processes and sensitive resource support.

Through the window of the policy-community concept I have looked at the normative issues pressing upon Canadian understanding of pressure group politics. I concluded that policy communities have developed in part from the diffusion of power in this country and have contributed to it, and that Parliament has been an important beneficiary of the same process. I can in consequence express some optimism that spatial representation through our legislatures is beginning to recapture an importance that it lost through most of this century. Again, this process is not entirely self-asserting. It is encouraged by the diffusion of power and particularly by the needs of sectoral influences — within and outside the bureaucracy — for legitimation; but it can be assured only if Parliament, and to a lesser extent party processes, are so structured and placed that they have a genuine influence on policy. Gregory Pyrcz reaches a similar conclusion:

[R]eform in the Canadian practice of pressure group politics would require . . . a systematic opening of the Canadian legislative system — at the cost of legislative tardiness and perhaps even impotence — and a further development of noninstitutionalized, weaker pressure groups through state-sponsorship — at the cost of decreased autonomy. Neither of these trade-offs would seem warranted if we were certain that some pressure groups in Canada were not now unjustifiably dominating public policy and that the other institutions of Canadian politics and governments, such as political parties, the media, parliaments, federalism, and public opinion were otherwise sufficient to deliver us a liberal democracy. Even if warranted, they seem, on the surface, not quite up to the task.[41]

Viewing interest group politics from the perspective of policy communities draws us inexorably to a set of fundamental questions. Does the assignment of specialized policy responsibility to specific publics preclude the articulation and enforcement of a general will? Is the public interest superseded by special interests? Are group politics the politics of fragmentation?

Alan Cairns, in a succession of observations on the effects of province-building, the extension of the state, and the development of a rights-oriented society, has concluded that specialization in political life has simultaneously extended the involvement of the state into every part of social life while reducing its capacity to influence society as a whole.[42] At the level of the individual, it has politicized our drive for personal advantage and reduced our capacity to activate our civic selves. There are mitigating pressures to be found in the creation of cross-cutting influences through the multiple demands of individuals, but the overwhelming conclusion left by Cairns's profound analysis is that the corrosive effects of specialization are driving the politics of fragmentation in Canada today.

Group politics are not solely, nor even fundamentally, responsible for this. The forces at work in modern Canada are global forces, emanating from the way in which we organize ourselves for work. They find expression in bureaucratic forms of organization and they precipitate opposing impulses in the form of movements for regional independence. Group politics are an adaptation to specialization and symptomatic of it. The drive to fragmentation will not be reversed or even slowed by trying to reduce the influence of group politics. Indeed, as Cairns points out, we must 'rethink the meaning of societal integration and community',[43] and it may be that group politics will help us to do that. After all, some groups — particularly in the women's and the environmental movements — self-consciously strive to oppose the thrust of specialization by articulating and trying to operationalize holistic concepts. More frequently, the multiple concerns of individuals find, as Cairns suggests, new, cross-cutting forms of expression in public interest groups. By encouraging groups with collectivist goals and by directing their energies to reinforcing the integrating institutions in the community — as they have done, for example, in the revival of Parliament — we may be able to assert with Charles Taylor a conviction that 'modern history is not unilinear, not an inexorable progress or decline, or a progress which entails decline. Rather it is made of movements and counter-movements, in which typically modern dangers have bred typically modern defenses'.[44]

Notes

CHAPTER 1. GROUPS AND POLITICS

[1]R. McGregor Dawson, *The Government of Canada* (Toronto, 1946).

[2]Robert L. Stanfield, 'The Fifth George C. Nowlan Lecture', Acadia University, 7 Feb. 1977 (mimeo.).

[3]Jeffrey Simpson, *Globe and Mail*, 5 Sept. 1990.

[4]John Meisel, 'Recent Changes in Canadian Parties' in Hugh G. Thorburn (ed.), *Party Politics in Canada* (Scarborough: Prentice-Hall, 1967), 33-54.

[5]David Kwavnick, *Organized Labour and Pressure Politics: The Canadian Labour Congress, 1956-1968* (Montreal, 1972); Robert Presthus, *Elite Accommodation in Canadian Politics* (Toronto, 1973) and *Elites in the Policy Process* (Toronto, 1974); Ronald W. Lang, *The Politics of Drugs: The British and Canadian Pharmaceutical Industries and Governments* (Lexington, MA, 1974); W.T. Stanbury, *Business Interests and the Reform of Canadian Competition Policy, 1971-75* (Toronto, 1977); and A. Paul Pross (ed.), *Pressure Group Behaviour in Canadian Politics* (Scarborough, 1975). Another major work published in this period was Léon Dion's two-volume *Société et Politique: La vie des groupes* (Québec, 1971). It is notable, however, as a monumental statement of pluralist theory, not as a study of Canadian pressure group politics, which are only occasionally mentioned. A bibliography of Canadian pressure group studies to 1974 is included in Pross, *Pressure Group Behaviour in Canadian Politics*.

[6]'The Lobbyists Registration Act', *Statutes of Canada* 35-36-37 Eliz.II.c.53. See A. Paul Pross, 'The Rise of the Lobbying Issue in Canada: "The Business Card Bill"' in Grant Jordan, *Commercial Lobbyists: Politics for Profit in Britain* (Aberdeen: Aberdeen University Press, 1991).

[7]See Kenneth Kernaghan, 'Codes of Ethics and Administrative Responsibility', *Canadian Public Administration* 17 (1974) 4, 527-41, and Canadian Study of Parliament Group, *Interest Groups and Parliament* (Ottawa, 1989). For journalistic accounts of the impact of lobbying on Ottawa see Doris Shackleton, *Power Town: Democracy Discarded* (Toronto, 1977) and John Sawatsky, *The Insiders: Government, Business and the Lobbyists* (Toronto: McClelland and Stewart, 1987).

[8]J. Alex Corry, 'Sovereign People or Sovereign Governments', in H.V. Kroeker (ed.), *Sovereign People or Sovereign Governments: Proceedings of a Conference Sponsored by the Institute for Research on Public Policy and the Government Studies Program, Dalhousie University, April, 1979* (Montreal, 1981), 3-13, 5.

[9]Jennifer Smith, 'Representation and constitutional reform in Canada', in John Courtney, Peter MacKinnon, and David E. Smith (eds), *After Meech Lake: Lessons for the Future* (Saskatoon, 1991).

[10]Alan C. Cairns, 'The Embedded State: State society relations in Canada', in Keith Banting (ed.), *State and Society: Canada in Comparative Perspective* (Toronto, 1986), 53-8, and 'Citizens (outsiders) and governments (insiders) in constitution-making: The case of Meech Lake', *Canadian Public Policy* XIV (1988), 121-45.

[11]On the definition of a movement see Frances Fox Piven and Richard A. Cloward, *Poor People's Movements* (N.Y., 1979), 4-5, and Bert Klandermans and Sidney Tarrow, 'Mobiliza-

tion into social movements: Synthesizing European and American approaches', in *International Social Movement Research* 1 (1988), 1-38. For Canadian experience see the introduction ('The nature of social movements') to S.D. Clark, J.P. Grayson, and L.M. Grayson, *Prophecy and Protest: Social Movements in Twentieth-Century Canada* (Toronto, 1975), 1-39.

[12]For a stimulating discussion of the relationship between parties and interest groups see Vaughan Lyon, 'The Future of Parties — Inevitable . . . or Obsolete?', *Journal of Canadian Studies* 18 (1983-84) 4, 108-31, particularly 110-12. A good case study of the tension and dependence between parties and interest groups is found in Raymond Hudon, 'Polarization and Depolarization of Quebec Political Parties', in Alain G. Gagnon, *Quebec: State and Society* (Toronto, 1984) 314-30. E.R. Forbes' *Maritime Rights: The Maritime Rights Movement* (Montreal, 1979) vividly describes the difficulties the Maritimes had in expressing regional concerns through the medium of political parties and the region's consequent resort to sectoral interest groups.

[13]Peter Aucoin, *Public Accountability in the Governing of Professions: A Report on the Self-Governing Professions of Accounting, Architecture, Engineering and Law in Ontario* (The Professional Organizations Committee. Working Paper #4. 1978), 5-6. For an example of the state's ability to alter the terms under which such groups exercise power see D.W. Emerson, 'Legislation for Professionals in Quebec: Government moves for tighter controls', *Chemistry in Canada* (December, 1972), 28-9.

[14]An extensive discussion of these categories is found in Mildred C. Schwartz, *The Environment of Policy-Making in Canada and the United States* (Montreal, 1981), 14.

[15]Ibid.

[16]See J.S. Frideres, *Canada's Indians: Contemporary Conflicts* (Scarborough, 1974); Sally M. Weaver, *Making Canadian Indian Policy* (Toronto, 1981); Boyce Richardson (ed.), *Drum Beat: Anger and Renewal in Indian Country* (Toronto, 1990); and J. Anthony Long, 'Political revitalization in Canadian native Indian societies', *Canadian Journal of Political Science* XXIII (1990) 4, 751-774. An interesting case study is found in Tord Larsen, 'Negotiating Identity: the Micmac of Nova Scotia', in Adrian Tanner (ed.), *The Politics of Indianness* (St John's, 1983), 37-136.

[17]R. Manzer, *Canada: A Socio-Political Report* (Toronto, 1974), quoting the *Report* of the Royal Commission on Bilingualism and Biculturalism, 140.

[18]Philip Lowe and Jane Goyder review this tendency in *Environmental Groups and Politics* (London, 1983), 15-18.

[19]*Maclean's*, 20 Sept. 1976, 8; *Time*, 20 Oct. 1975, 13-15; *The 4th Estate*, 21 and 28 Jan. 1976; *Globe and Mail*, 25 Sept. 1976; and *Financial Post*, 9 Oct. 1976, 11.

[20]Sheila McLeod Arnopoulos and Dominique Clift, *The English Fact in Quebec* (Montreal, 1984), ch. 13 'Survival Strategy'.

[21]Ann Pappert, 'A New Life on Lease', *Financial Post Magazine*, June 1985, 28-34; Lars Hjörne, 'Aims and Forms of Tenant Influence: Some Preliminary Considerations', *Acta Sociologica* 24 (1981) 4, 251-79; G. Granatstein, *Marlborough Marathon: One Street Against a Developer* (Toronto, 1971).

[22]For a discussion of the role of legitimation and mandate in pressure group politics see David C. Kwavnick, *Organized Labour and Pressure Politics: The Canadian Labour Congress, 1956-1968* (Montreal, 1972).

[23]I am grateful to William Coleman and Greg Pyrcz for their views on this point.

[24]A.F. Bentley, (ed. P. Odegard), *The Process of Government*, (Cambridge, MA, 1967) and David B. Truman, *The Governmental Process: Political Interests and Public Opinion* (N.Y.,1964).

[25]Grant Jordan, 'Group Approaches to the Study of Politics', in D. Engelfield and G. Drewry (eds), *Politics and Political Science: A Survey Worldwide* (London, 1984).

[26]Frederick C. Engelmann and Mildred C. Schwartz, *Political Parties and the Canadian Social Structure* (Scarborough, 1967), 96.

[27]Ibid.

[28]Presthus, *Elite Accommodation in Canadian Politics* and *Elites in the Policy Process*.

[29]A. Paul Pross (ed.), *Pressure Group Behaviour in Canadian Politics* (Toronto, 1975).

[30]See *inter alia* William Coleman and Henry J. Jacek, 'The Roles and Activities of Business Interest Associations in Canada', *Canadian Journal of Political Science* XVI (1983) 2, 257-80; Coleman, *Business and Politics* (Montreal, 1988), and M. Atkinson and Coleman, *The State, Business and Industrial Change* (Toronto, 1989).

[31]See, for example, the criticisms of conventional pressure group studies voiced by Mancur Olson in *The Logic of Collective Action* (Cambridge, MA, 1971) and Terry M. Moe in *The Organization of Interests* (Chicago, 1980).

CHAPTER 2. BEGINNINGS: SPACE VERSUS SECTOR

[1]André Holleaux, 'Le phénomène associatif', *Revue française d'administration publique* 8 (1978), 683-727; p. 683 refers to very early groups in France. J.M. Beck, *The Government of Nova Scotia* (Toronto, 1957) and Gerald M. Craig, *Upper Canada: The Formative Years, 1784-1841* (Toronto, 1963) give several examples of colonial groups attempting to influence Westminster.

[2]H.A. Innis, *The Cod Fisheries* (Toronto, 1978), 240, 244-5.

[3]See Douglas Sanders, 'The Indian Lobby', in Keith Banting and Richard Simeon (eds), *And No One Cheered: Federalism, Democracy and the Constitution Act* (Toronto, 1983), 301-32.

[4]S.D. Clark, *The Canadian Manufacturers' Association* (Toronto, 1939) and N.J. Lawrie, *The Canadian Construction Association: An Interest Group and Its Environment* (Unpublished PhD thesis. University of Toronto, 1976).

[5]Norman A. Robertson to L. Robertson, 2 March 1932, quoted in J.L. Granatstein, *A Man of Influence: Norman A. Robertson and Canadian Statecraft, 1929-1968* (Toronto, 1981), 40-1.

[6]Khayyam Z. Paltiel, 'The Changing Environment and Role of Special Interest Groups', *Canadian Public Administration* 25 (1982), 2, 198-210, at 205.

[7]See Chapter 10, below and A. Paul Pross, 'Space, Function and Legitimacy: The Problem of Legitimacy in the Canadian State', in O.P. Dwivedi (ed.), *The Administrative State in Canada* (Toronto, 1982), 107-29.

[8]Robert Presthus, *Elites in the Policy Process* (Toronto, 1974), 8.

[9]Patricia Hollis, 'Pressure from Without: an introduction', in Hollis (ed.), *Pressure From Without in Early Victorian England* (London, 1974), 1-26, 6.

[10]J.M.S. Careless describes one instance of this transfer of ideas in 'The Toronto *Globe* and Agrarian Radicalism', *Canadian Historical Review* XXIX (1948) 1, 14-19, 34-9.

[11]Aileen Dunham, *Political Unrest in Upper Canada, 1815-1836* (Toronto, 1963), 51.

[12]Margaret Angus, 'Health, Emigration and Welfare in Kingston, 1820-1840', in Donald Swainson (ed.), *Oliver Mowat's Ontario* (Toronto, 1972) 120-35, 126. A similar development took place in Saint John, New Brunswick, also a major entry point for immigrants. There Moses Perley, the Emigration Agent for the colony, distressed by the conditions faced by immigrants — particularly the unsanitary and inadequate accommodation for those in quarantine on Partridge Island — engaged the help of the local Mechanics' Institute. In 1847, for example, the Institute raised substantial funds to assist immigrants and in 1843 assisted Perley in setting up the Mechanics' Settlement near Saint John. Allison Mitcham, *Three Remarkable Maritimers* (Hantsport: Lancelot Press, 1985), 43, 44.

[13]Angus, 'Health, Emigration and Welfare in Kingston', 128.

[14]Richard B. Splane, *Social Welfare in Ontario, 1791-1893* (Toronto, 1965), 76, 77.

[15]The following comments are based on two articles appearing in *Recherches sociographiques* XVI (1975) 2: Yves Lamande, 'Le Membership d'une Association du 19ième siècle: Le cas de

Longueuil (1857-1860)', 219-241 and Johanne Ménard, 'L'Institut des Artisans du Comté de Drummond, 1856-1890', 207-19. See also Lamande's *Gens de parole: Conférences publiques, essais et débats à l'Institut canadien de Montréal, 1845-1871* (Montreal, 1990).

[16]Ménard, 'L'Institut des Artisans', 210.

[17]Hereward Senior, 'Orangeism in Ontario Politics, 1872-1896', in Swainson, *Oliver Mowat's Ontario*, 136-53, 137.

[18]Ibid., 150-1.

[19]Splane, *Social Welfare in Ontario*, 176-7.

[20]Quoted ibid., 270.

[21]Douglas McCalla, 'The Commercial Policies of the Toronto Board of Trade, 1850-1860', *The Canadian Historical Review* 50 (1969), 51-67, 55.

[22]Ibid., 54.

[23]Michael Bliss, 'The Protective Impulse: An Approach to the Social History of Oliver Mowat's Ontario', in Swainson, *Oliver Mowat's Ontario*, 174-188, 174-5.

[24]Ibid., 184.

[25]Quoted in P.B. Waite, *The Life and Times of Confederation* (Toronto, 1962), 16-17.

[26]McCalla, 'The Toronto Board of Trade', 52.

[27]McCalla, ibid., 55.

[28]Splane, *Social Welfare in Ontario*, 187.

[29]R.S. Lambert with A. Paul Pross, *Renewing Nature's Wealth* (Toronto, 1967), 178.

[30]Ibid., 181 ff. These responses included the establishment of conservation organizations, government agencies, and educational institutions, both in Canada and the United States.

[31]Although evidence is limited, it seems that in the nineteenth century, pressure groups were the instrument of the middle class, as, in many ways, they still are today. One of the few systematic presentations of data on this point appears in Carol Lee Bacchi's *Liberation Deferred: The Ideas of the English-Canadian Suffragists: 1877-1918* (Toronto, 1983), 6. In an analysis of suffrage leaders she shows that all but a very few were professionals, business people, or independently wealthy. Only one of 37 male leaders with known occupations was a labour representative and only one of 103 female leaders with known occupations was a union organizer, though two were 'agriculturalists'.

[32]See Bacchi, *Liberation Deferred*, passim. An extensive account of Lady Aberdeen's work is contained in Sandra Gwyn, *The Private Capital: Ambition and Love in the Age of Macdonald and Laurier* (Toronto, 1985), ch. 20, 'The Remarkable Ishbel'.

[33]Graeme Decarie, 'Something Old, Something New ... Aspects of Prohibitionism in Ontario in the 1890s', in Swainson, *Oliver Mowat's Ontario*, 154-71. The Women's Christian Temperance Union was established in this country in 1873. Bacchi places its membership in 1900 at 6,000 members in Prince Edward Island, Nova Scotia, New Brunswick, Québec, Ontario, and the Northwest Territories. See *Liberation Deferred*, 17. Presumably these are dues-paying members and Decarie is referring to supporters. Bacchi's study of the links between the womens' suffrage groups, the temperance movement, and other reform groups is particularly useful, as are her discussions of the ties between these groups and their counterparts in Britain and the United States.

[34]Judith Fingard, *Jack in Port: Sailor Towns of Eastern Canada* (Toronto, 1982), 220.

[35]See Lambert and Pross, *Renewing Nature's Wealth*, chs. 9, 10, and Pross, *The Development of a Forest Policy* (Toronto: University of Toronto. Unpublished PhD thesis, 1967), ch. 2.

[36]See annual *Reports* of the Commissioners of Crown Lands and the Departments of Agriculture for these provinces as well as the *Reports* of the Canadian Commission of Conservation.

[37]Splane, *Social Welfare in Ontario*, 176-7.

[38]J.I. Gow, 'L'Histoire de l'administration publique québécoise', *Recherches sociographiques* XVI (1975), 3, 385-412, esp. 389, 392, and 406-7.

[39]The argument in this and the following paragraphs is a shortened version of a thesis presented by the writer in 'Space, Function and Legitimacy'.

[40]Norman Ward, 'The Formative Years of the House of Commons, 1867-1891', *The Canadian Journal of Economics and Political Science* 18 (1952) 4, 431-51. In other words, the member had to juggle the pressures emanating from his riding against those initiated by the executive. At the provincial level, member independence appears to have lasted longer. Doyle, in *Front Benches and Back Rooms* (p. 17) records its persistence in New Brunswick until the turn of the century and Martin Robin, in *The Rush for Spoils: The Company Province, 1871-1933* (Toronto, 1972), some years later in British Columbia.

[41]J.M. Beck, *The Government of Nova Scotia* (Toronto, 1957), 155-62.

[42]Quoted in Robin, *The Company Province*, 74.

[43]Christopher Armstrong, 'The Mowat Heritage in Federal-Provincial Relations', in Swainson, *Oliver Mowat's Ontario*, 93-119 at 97.

[44]Doyle, *Front Benches and Back Rooms*, 80.

[45]In the Maritimes these influences were felt acutely. Control of financial institutions slipped away first, to be followed by the selling-out of local manufacturing firms and resource enterprises to competitors and speculators in distant centres. In the latters' hands physical plant and equipment deteriorated and concerns were milked of their assets. By the First World War the region was fighting a desperate and losing rearguard action to retain control of the last element of its economic core, the railway system. The journal *Acadiensis* has published a number of articles dealing with the evolution of the regional economy during this period. See particularly T.W. Acheson, 'The National Policy and the Industrialization of the Maritimes, 1880-1910', *Acadiensis* I (1971) 2, 3-28; L.D. McCann, 'The Mercantile-Industrial Transition in the Metal Towns of Pictou County, 1857-1931', *Acadiensis* X (1981) 2, 29-64; and David Frank, 'The Cape Breton Coal Industry and the Rise and Fall of the British Empire Steel Corporation', *Acadiensis* VII (1977), 3-34. Ernest R. Forbes has documented the transition in *Maritime Rights: The Maritime Rights Movement, 1919-1927* (Montreal, 1979). Tom Naylor's two-volume *The History of Canadian Business, 1867-1914* (Toronto, 1975) is useful as a general discussion of the period.

[46]Christopher Armstrong and H.V. Nelles offer an illustration of these processes in their study of the campaign of E.A. Roberts and his associates to control Halifax's electrical monopoly ('Getting Your Way in Nova Scotia: Tweaking Halifax, 1909-1917', *Acadiensis* V (1976) 2, 105-131). They conclude:

> ...they were men who knew a great deal about getting their own way.... [L]ike promoters in other Canadian cities, [they] were not satisfied simply with operating profits; they wanted the vastly greater speculative returns offered by a merger and a recapitalization. Thus they had first to deal with rival entrepreneurs, then to oust the management from the control of the street railway, while all the time pressing their case with the city and the province. That they attained their objectives was less a measure of their business acumen than of their ability to command political influence. Sir Frederick Borden's presence in the syndicate was symbolic of this: he could be relied upon to deliver the necessary Liberal votes. The 'grab' for Halifax succeeded only through the acquiescence of Premier Murray. While idealists might argue that he acted out of ideological hostility to public ownership in encouraging Robert's schemes, it is difficult to see why he should have alienated his own followers from Halifax as well as local politicians, when he could have thrown his weight behind the plan to have an independent concern, like the Halifax Development Company, generate hydroelectricity and transmit it to the city for sale to the street railway and to other light and power users. Political influence, perhaps cemented by financial generosity, seems the most plausible explanation for his behaviour, and it was this that enabled Robert to outflank irate citizens and municipal officials (p. 130).

Nelles' *The Politics of Development: Forest, Mines and Electric Power in Ontario, 1911-1941* (Toronto, 1974) is replete with similar illustrations. First-hand accounts of these practices can be found in the proceedings of the numerous inquiries commissioned by newly elected governments into the affairs of their predecessors (e.g. The Ontario Royal Commission to investigate Crown Timber returns — the Latchford-Riddell Commission — whose proceedings are lodged at the Ontario Archives and whose *Report* was published in 1921-22 by the Ontario King's Printer) and in the often doubtful reminiscences of political veterans (e.g. Doyle, *Front Benches and Back Rooms*).

[47]M.G. Lofquist to F.H. Keefer, 9 Feb. 1926, Ferguson Papers, Ontario Archives.

[48]See Kenneth M. Gibbons and Donald C. Rowat, *Political Corruption in Canada: Cases, Causes and Cures* (Ottawa: Carleton, 1976). An incident in the life of the Conservative party in 1935 illustrated the pressures political leaders were under. At that time the interests controlling the Canadian Pacific Railway, lobbying for railroad unification, contributed $50,000 to the party's election fund and sought to control the Manion leadership. See J.L. Granatstein, *The Politics of Survival* (Toronto, 1967), 13, 16, 17, 20, 43-5.

[49]Wallace Clements, using 1972 data, reports that 51.1% of the Canadian corporate élite belongs to the six most important clubs. While this is a respectable percentage it is considerably less than one might expect of social institutions that are as important as Clements (*The Canadian Corporate Elite* [Toronto, 1975] 247-9) and John Porter (*The Vertical Mosaic* [Toronto, 1965] 304-5) suggest. Furthermore, it appears that these member-ships do not include the international élite that controls many of Canada's most powerful corporations. (See Clements, *The Canadian Corporate Elite*, 117.) In other words, even the six most important clubs in the country must enjoy the support of far fewer key economic decisions-makers than Clement's own figures indicate. Finally, it should be noted that the six clubs considered to be watering-holes for the economic élite are located in Ottawa, Toronto, and Montreal, a fact that reinforces the claim made here that clubs in regional centres no longer perform a significant socio-economic and political function.

[50]See, for example, Escott Reid, 'The Saskatchewan Liberal Machine Before 1929', *Canadian Journal of Economics and Political Science* 11 (1936) 27; Herbert Quinn, *The Union Nationale* (Toronto, 1963); Ernest Watkins, *R.B. Bennett* (London, 1963); Neil McKenty, *Mitch Hepburn* (Toronto, 1967); and Ramsay Cook (ed.), *Politics of Discontent* (Toronto, 1967).

[51]R.M. Dawson and N. Ward, *The Government of Canada* 5th ed. (Toronto, 1970), 473. Leon Epstein notes Dawson reporting as early as 1922 that 'few Canadian members of parliament have shown their independence of party'. Leon D. Epstein, 'A Comparative Study of Canadian Parties', *American Political Science Review* 58 (1964), 46-59. For an account of the role of constituency organizations in patronage politics see Norman Ward, 'The Bristol Papers: A Note of Patronage', *Canadian Journal of Economics and Political Science* 12 (1946), 1, 78-86. The local organization was concerned almost exclusively with civil service appointments and minor contracts. However, a letter from W.C. Cain, deputy minister of the Ontario Department of Lands and Forests, to several provincial MLAs illustrates both the effects of centralization and the efforts that were made to maintain the illusion of local influence: 'We are considering ... making certain additions to our Provincial Forests and creating an occasional new one, and inasmuch as a part of a suggested Provincial Forest lies within your constituency I am writing to you in order that you may understand it and take whatever credit is necessary for the addition if and when the occasion arises.' Cain to W.L. Miller, 9 Jan. 1939, Ontario Department of Lands and Forests, Central Files, #119191 — Provincial Forests.

[52]See S.D. Clark, *The Canadian Manufacturers' Association* (Toronto, 1939) and Forbes, *Maritime Rights*. O. Mary Hill credits the CMA with bringing about the creation of the Department of Trade and Commerce, a sure sign of sectoral influence. *Canada's Salesman to the World* (Montreal, 1977), 2.

[53]Forbes, *The Maritime Rights Movement*, 116, and Clark, *The Canadian Manufacturers' Association, passim*.

[54]Ibid., 39.

[55]Ibid., 15.

[56]J.M. Beck, 'The Party System in Nova Scotia: Tradition and Conservatism', in Martin Robin (ed.), *Canadian Provincial Politics* (Scarborough, 1972), 168-98, 175.

[57]See P.G. Johnson, 'The Nova Scotia Union of Municipalities as a Pressure Group'. Paper. Canadian Political Science Association, 1970, p. 21.

[58]See J.E. Hodgetts, *The Canadian Public Service: A Physiology of Government, 1867-1970* (Toronto, 1973), particularly Part I, and Dwivedi, *The Administrative State in Canada* (Toronto, 1982), 61.

[59]J.L. Granatstein, *The Ottawa Men: The Civil Service Mandarins, 1935-57* (Toronto, 1982), ch. 2, 'The Early Civil Service' and ch. 3, 'The Founders'.

[60]See, for example, the complaint of Flora MacDonald in 'The Minister and the Mandarins', *Policy Options* (Sept./Oct. 1980), 29-32. It is our contention, however, that this fear is misplaced; that a great deal of power has indeed escaped the hands of the political executive, just as in an earlier period it escaped the legislature, but that rather than falling into the hands of a small group of mandarins it has been diffused throughout the administrative apparatus of government. The consequences of this are just as problematic as a shift of power to senior officials, but they are quite different.

[61]See, for example, the effort involved in organizing the 1925 pilgrimage of some 600 Maritimers to Ottawa to protest the neglect of the region's interests in transportation policy. Forbes, *Maritime Rights*, 112-15. The size of the delegation and its members' resentment of federal policy did much to give legitimacy to a cause the nation had chosen to ignore.

[62]See Hodgetts, *The Canadian Public Service*, 108-9, and Dennis Guest, *The Emergence of Social Security in Canada* (Vancouver, 1980).

[63]H.H. Hannam, 'The Interest Group and its Activities', Institute of Public Administration of Canada, *Proceedings of the Fifth Annual Conference* (1953), 173.

[64]In many cases such organizations were sponsored and encouraged not by government but by the railways, which were anxious to sell off their vacant western lands. See David C. Corbett, *Canada's Immigration Policy* (Toronto, 1957), 11-15. Religious organizations were also active. See John H. Redekop, 'Mennonites and Politics in Canada and the United States', *Journal of Mennonite Studies* I (1983), 1.

[65]A. Holleaux, 'Le phénomène associatif', *Revue française d'administration publique* 8 (1978), 683-787, 689, and Vincent Lemieux, 'Administration et publics: leur problème de communication', *Recherches sociographiques* XVI (1973) 3, 299-307, 304.

[66]S.D. Clark, *Canadian Manufacturers' Association*, 72.

[67]Hill, *Canada's Salesman to the World*, 254 .

[68]N.J. Lawrie, *The Canadian Construction Association: An Interest Group Organization and its Environment* (PhD thesis. University of Toronto, 1976), 219.

[69]The origins of the Consumers' Association are reported in Helen Jones Dawson, 'The Consumers' Association of Canada', *Canadian Public Administration* 6 (1963), 92. Examples of the encouragement of citizen participation by those responsible for programs in regional economic expansion include the Prince Edward Island Development Plan, which contained several provisions for citizen participation. See *Agricultural Rehabilitation and Development Act: Federal-Provincial Rural Development Agreement* (Ottawa, 1965) parts IV, VI, and VIII; J.D. McNiven, 'Bureaucracy and Participation in Prince Edward Island'. Paper. Canadian Political Science Association, Annual Meeting, 1976; and a feasibility study for a combined high school and community centre at Port Hawkesbury, Nova Scotia, which was funded by DREE on condition that there be extensive citizen consultation. (See Graham, Napier, Hebert and Associates, Ltd, *Project 3.9: Junior-Senior High School and Associated Community Facilities, Port Hawkesbury, Nova Scotia, Report 2*, (n.d.) vol. 1. The Ministry of State for Urban Affairs was seen by many citizens' groups as a source of material and moral support. It is not clear, however, whether very many were given significant support by the Ministry. The experience of the Movement for Citizens' Voice and Action (MOVE), a Halifax umbrella group, may have been typical. In March, 1971, MOVE asked for a little less

than $5,000 to support its efforts to co-ordinate some thirty citizens' groups interested in participating in the work of the Metro Area Planning Committee, a tri-level project supported by the Province of Nova Scotia and MSUA. By April 1972, after much correspondence and many telephone calls, neither the Province nor MSUA had approved the grant. (MOVE, 'Planning Meeting', 12 Feb. 1973.)

[70]Lunenburg *Progress-Enterprise*, 5 April 1978, 16.

CHAPTER 3. 'TO HAVE A SAY YOU NEED A VOICE'

[1]See Robert L. Heilbroner with Aaron Singer, *The Economic Transformation of America* (N.Y., 1977); J.K. Galbraith, *The New Industrial State* (N.Y., 1971) and *Economics and the Public Purpose* (Boston, 1973).

[2]See J.W.B. Sisam, *Forestry Education at Toronto* (Toronto, 1961); R.S. Lambert with A. Paul Pross, *Renewing Nature's Wealth* (Toronto, 1967), 178; and H.V. Nelles, *The Politics of Development: Forest, Mines and Electric Power in Ontario, 1911-1941* (Toronto, 1974).

[3]A point amply documented in Michael M. Atkinson and William D. Coleman, *The State, Business and Industrial Change in Canada* (Toronto, 1989).

[4]See, for example, William MacLeod, *Water Management in the Canadian North* (Ottawa, 1977); Thomas R. Berger, *Northern Frontier, Northern Homeland: Report of the Mackenzie Valley Pipeline Inquiry* (Ottawa, 1977); and Federal Environmental Assessment Review Office, *Beaufort Sea Hydrocarbon Production and Transportation* (Ottawa, 1984).

[5]This type of debate pervades the report and background studies of the Royal Commission on the Economic Union and Development Prospects for Canada (Ottawa: 1985).

[6]Galbraith, *The New Industrial State*.

[7]Gerard Timsit and Celine Wiener, 'Adminstration et Politique', *Revue française de science politique* 30 (1980) 3, 506-33. For a review of bureaucratic influence in a number of countries, see Ezra N. Suleiman, *Bureaucrats and Policy Making* (N.Y.: Holmes, 1984).

[8]The role of language in determining the power relations of policy actors is often commented on. See, for example, Guy Benveniste, *The Politics of Expertise* (Berkeley, CA, 1972); Dorothy Smith, 'The social construction of documentary reality', *Sociological Inquiry* 44 (1974) 4, 257-68 and 'Textually Mediated Organizations', *International Social Science Quarterly* 36 (1984) 1, 59-75.

[9]The spread of forestry concepts into forest policy can be reviewed in Sisam, *Forestry Education at Toronto*; Lambert and Pross, *Renewing Nature's Wealth*; and Pross, 'The Development of Professions in the Public Service: The Foresters in Ontario', *Canadian Public Administration* x (1967) 3, 376-404.

[10]Jacques de Guise, 'Le colloque: une réflexion sur la relation Etat-citoyen', *Recherches sociographiques* XVI (1975) 3, 321-37.

[11]David Hoffman, 'Liaison Officers and Ombudsmen: Canadian MPs and the Relations with the Federal Bureaucracy and Executive', in Thomas A. Hockin, *Apex of Power: The Prime Minister and Political Leadership in Canada* (Scarborough, 1971), 146-62. Paul Thomas 'Unfinished Reform', *Policy Options*, September 1984, 28-31, 31.

[12]Kenneth M. Gibbons and Donald C. Rowat, *Political Corruption in Canada: Cases, Causes and Cures* (Ottawa, 1976), and Jeffrey Simpson, *Spoils of Power: The Politics of Patronage* (Toronto, 1988).

[13]J.E. Hodgetts *et al.*, *Biography of an Institution* (Montreal, 1972), and V. Seymour Wilson, 'The Relationship between Scientific Management and Personnel Policy in North American Administrative Systems', *Public Administration Review* (London, 1973), 193-205.

[14]J.E. Hodgetts and O.P. Dwivedi, *Provincial Governments as Employers: A Survey of Public Personnel Administration in Canada* (Montreal, 1974).

[15]For the impact of professional development on forest policy see Sisam, *Forestry Education at Toronto*; K.G. Fensom, *Expanding Forestry Horizons: A History of the Canadian Institute of Forestry-Institut Forestier du Canada, 1908-1969* (MacDonald College, P.Q.: CIF, 1972); Pross, 'The Development of Professions' and 'Input versus Withinput: Pressure Group Demands and Administrative Survival', in Pross (ed.), *Pressure Group Behaviour in Canada Politics* (Toronto, 1975), 148-72. The contribution of the Professional Institute of the Public Service of Canada to civil service reform is reported in John Swettenham and David Kealy, *Serving the State: A History of the Professional Institute of the Public Service of Canada, 1920-1970* (Ottawa, 1970).

[16]H.H. Hannam, 'The Interest Group and its Activities', Institute of Public Administration of Canada. *Proceedings of the Fifth Annual Conference*, (Toronto, 1953), 173.

[17]S.D. Clark, *The Canadian Manufacturers' Association* (Toronto, 1939), 71-2.

[18]Robert Presthus, 'Interest Groups and the Canadian Parliament', *Canadian Journal of Political Science* IV (1971), 444-60, 445-6. See also Léon Dion, *Société et Politique* (Québec, 1971), vol. I, 290-303. Dion shows that public suspicion of pressure group influence is common, though less prevalent in Germany and Italy than in France, for example.

[19]See Grant McConnell, *Private Power and American Democracy* (N.Y., 1966), and Gibbons and Rowat, *Political Corruption in Canada* (Ottawa, 1976).

[20]J.M. Beck, *The Evolution of Municipal Government in Nova Scotia, 1749 to 1973* (Halifax, 1973), 30, quoting the Halifax *Morning Chronicle*, 15 March 1911.

[21]Dawson, 'The Consumers' Association of Canada', *Canadian Public Administration* VI (1963), 92-118, 100, 102, 103. See also Jonah Goldstein, 'Public Interest Groups and Public Policy: The Case of the Consumers' Association of Canada', *Canadian Journal of Political Science* XII (1979) 1, 137-56, especially 142-6.

[22]David Kwavnick, *Organized Labour and Pressure Politics: The Canadian Labour Congress, 1956-1968* (Montreal, 1972).

[23]See Stephen Clarkson, 'The Defeat of the Government; the Decline of the Liberal Party, and the (Temporary) Fall of Pierre Trudeau', in Howard R. Penneman (ed.), *Canada at the Polls* (Washington, 1981), 152-89.

[24]John Porter, *The Vertical Mosaic* (Toronto, 1965), 425-6. On the mandarins see J.L. Granatstein, *A Man of Influence: Norman A. Robertson and Canadian Statecraft, 1929-1968* (Toronto, 1981) and *The Ottawa Men: The Civil Service Mandarins, 1935-57* (Toronto, 1982); and V. Seymour Wilson, 'Mandarins and kibitzers: men in and around the trenches of power in Ottawa', *Canadian Public Administration* 26 (1983) 3, 446-61.

[25]In the provinces the civil service was slower to achieve a position of influence. In Quebec, for example, Jean Meynaud, writing in the fifties, argued that the extreme weakness of the provincial civil service gave major interests a bargaining advantage (Jean Meynaud, 'Groupes de pression et politique gouvernementale au Québec', in André Bernard [ed.], *Réflexions sur la Politiques au Québec* [Montreal, 1968], 69-96, 83). Until the Quiet Revolution was well established, the political executive continued to be the focal point of lobbying activity. By the 1970s, however, civil service influence was well established. J. Iain Gow commented in 1975 that the growing specialized expertise of public servants gave them a decided advantage over their political masters. Deputy ministers and assistant deputy ministers had even come to think of themselves as policy and program innovators, rather than as functionaries carrying out the wishes of the government of the day (J. Iain Gow, 'L'histoire de l'administration public québécoise', *Recherches sociographiques* XVI [1975] 3, 385-413, 404-5). There is little doubt that senior federal servants had reached this stage by the end of the Second World War.

[26]A.H. Cameron, Administrative Assistant (Health) B.C. Department of Health and Welfare, IPAC *Proceedings*, 1953, 204.

[27]Wilfrid Eggleston, 'The Cabinet and Pressure Groups', ibid., 157-67, at 160. McIlraith

defined lobbying as 'interference or pressure by an organized group to influence government to serve the special interests of the group as opposed to the general interest'.

[28]Ibid., 205.

[29]See particularly the proceedings of the 1953 and 1957 IPAC meetings. Properly representative advisory committees were seen by some as appropriate vehicles for presenting interest group demands. They would, in effect, act as buffers between the administrator and pressure groups. In J.A. Corry's words they were 'the democratic answer to the challenge of the corporate state'. (Quoted by T.K. Shoyama, 'Advisory Committees in Administration', IPAC, *Proceedings*, 1957, 145-153, at 147.) See also D.C. Corbett, 'The Pressure Group and the Public Interest', IPAC, *Proceedings*, 1953, 185-95 and IPAC, *Proceedings*, 1957, where the utility of advisory committees is questioned.

[30]See J.E. Hodgetts, 'The Civil Service and Policy Formation', *Canadian Journal of Economics and Political Science* 23 (1957) 4, 467-78, at 476.

[31]G.W. Stead, Assistant Secretary to the Treasury Board, Ottawa, commented, for example, that 'when the bureaucrats in a department dream up some scheme for expanding their empire they use the advisory committee as a means of obtaining popular support.' IPAC, *Proceedings*, 1957, 156.

[32]IPAC, *Proceedings*, 1953, 205.

[33]'Relations between Farm Organizations and the Civil Service', *Canadian Public Administration* X (1967) 4, 450-71, 454.

[34]Quoted in Clive Baxter, 'Lobbying — Ottawa's Fastest Growing Business', in Paul Fox (ed.), *Politics: Canada* (Toronto, 1966), 206-10.

[35]See Donald Barry's comments on the hesitation displayed by established Church groups in the debate over the Biafra issue. 'Interest Groups and the Foreign Policy Process: The Case of Biafra', in Pross, *Pressure Group Behaviour...* , 115-48, 125 and 132. See also Kwavnick, *Organized Labour and Pressure Politics*, ch. 7.

[36]W.T. Stanbury, *Business-Government Relations in Canada* (Toronto, 1986).

[37]Pross, 'Pressure Groups: Adaptive Instruments of Political Communication', in Pross (ed.), *Pressure Group Behaviour...* , 1-27, 19-20.

[38]Robert Presthus, 'Interest Groups and the Canadian Parliament: Activities, Interaction, Legitimacy, and Influence', *Canadian Journal of Political Science* IV (1971) 4, 444-460. His parliamentary respondents reported encountering group representatives primarily at Committee hearings (41%), at informal meetings arranged by groups (33%), and only rarely at social functions (20%). See also Bruce MacNaughton and Allan Gregg, 'Interest Group Influence in the Canadian Parliament'. Paper. CPSA, June 1977.

[39]James Gillies and Jean Pigott, 'Participation in the Legislative Process', *Canadian Public Administration* 25 (1982) 2, 254-65, 256.

[40]Dawson, 'National Pressure Groups and the Federal Government', in Pross, *Pressure Group Behaviour...* , 29-58, 39-45, *passim*.

[41]Dawson, 'National Pressure Groups', 41.

[42]J.E. Anderson, 'Pressure Groups and Canadian Bureaucracy', in W.D.K. Kernaghan and A.M. Willms (eds), *Public Administration in Canada: Selected Readings* (Toronto, 1970), 370-9. See also the remarks of Eric Hehner, a lobbyist in Ottawa since the 1940s, in Canadian Study of Parliament Group, *Interest Groups and Parliament* (Ottawa, 1989), 11-12.

[43]*Canadian Almanac and Directory* and Brian Land, *Directory of Associations in Canada* (Toronto). Discrepancies between listings are due to different policies for listing associations. Land, for example, excluded regional and local groups after 1973. William D. Coleman, *Business and Politics: A Study of Collective Action* (Montreal: McGill-Queen's University Press, 1988), 18. Coleman's figures are presented in tabular form as follows:

The evidence cited is reinforced by other indicators. Between 1900 and 1970, 1,502 associations were incorporated under federal regulations. Between 1965 and 1970, 522 were

Period of Founding of Existing Associations Representing Business

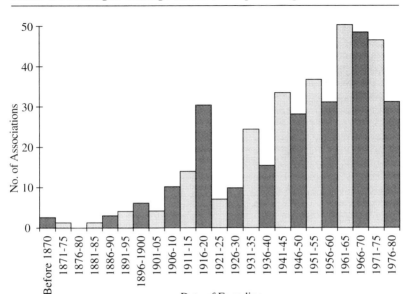

Date of Founding

Source: Royal Commission on the Economic Union and Development Prospects for Canada
    (Macdonald Commission) *Report* (Ottawa, 1985), vol.III, 58-9.

incorporated; 16% of all these groups were incorporated in the last year of the period. (H. Perry and M. de Soto, 'The proposed new law for federally incorporating associations', *Canadian Association Executive*, Feb.-March 1975, 12-25.) Aggregate figures for provincial group formation in the period are not available and we also lack any means for estimating the number of groups that have ceased to function.

[44]Hugh G. Thorburn, for example, draws attention to the increased number of interest group briefs (897) presented to the recent Royal Commission on the Economic Union and Development Prospects for Canada (Macdonald Commission), in comparison to the 331 presented to the 1937 Royal Commission on Dominion-Provincial Relations (Rowell-Sirois Commission) and the 297 presented to the 1957 Royal Commission on Canada's Economic Prospects (the Gordon Commission). *Interest Groups in the Canadian Federal System* (Toronto, 1985), 83-4.

[45]Hugh G. Thorburn, 'Pressure Groups in Canadian Politics: Recent Revisions of the Anti-Combines Legislation', *Canadian Journal of Economics and Political Science* XXX (1964) 2, 157-74.

[46]J. Hugh Faulkner, 'Pressuring the Executive', *Canadian Public Administration* 25 (1982) 2, 240-53, 251.

[47]The 1980-81 figures are presented in Faulkner, 'Pressuring the Executive', 251; those for 1966-67 in M. Rush, 'The Development of the Committee System in the Canadian House of Commons — Reassessment and Reform', *The Parliamentarian*, LV (1974) 3, 149-59, 153. The number of public interventions in the abortion bill hearings are reported in Canada

House of Commons *Minutes of Proceedings and Evidence of the Legislative Committee on Bill C-43. An Act Respecting Abortion* (2nd Session. 34th Parliament) (Ottawa, 1989-90) 22:30.

[48]See Robert Bothwell, Ian Drummond, and John English, *Canada Since 1945: Power, Politics and Provincialism* (Toronto, 1981).

[49]Ibid.

[50]*Financial Post*, 24 July 1976.

[51]CAUT *Bulletin*, February 1975.

[52]David B. Truman, *The Governmental Process* (N.Y., 1951), 66-108. A Canadian instance was the institutionalization of Native and new-Canadian interest groups precipitated by the federal government's move toward a policy on bilingualism and biculturalism, cited in ch. 1.

[53]*Globe and Mail*, 14 June 1974.

[54]*Montreal Star*, 18 July 1970, and W.T. Stanbury, *Business Interests and the Reform of Canadian Competition Policy, 1971-1975* (Toronto, 1977).

[55]*Financial Post*, 1 July 1976.

[56]Halifax *Chronicle-Herald*, 21 Dec. 1972, and R. John Arseneau, 'The Government-Small Business Relationship', Dalhousie University. Student Paper, 1984.

[57]See *Financial Post*, 16 Dec. 1972 and 9 June 1973.

[58]*Financial Post*, 16 Dec. 1972

[59]CAUT *Bulletin*, June 1974 and subsequent issues.

[60]See G. David Garson, *Group Theories of Politics* (Beverly Hills, CA, 1978), ch. 4.

[61]Faulkner, 'Pressuring the Executive', 248-9; Khayyam Z. Paltiel, 'The Changing Environment and Role of Special Interest Groups', *Canadian Public Administration* 25 (1982) 2, 198-211, 205-6, and Susan D. Phillips, 'How Ottawa Blends: Shifting Government Relationships With Interest Groups', in Frances Abele (ed.), *How Ottawa Spends 1991-92: The Politics of Fragmentation* (Ottawa, 1991), 183-213.

[62]Even after the reforms discussed below, this remained a problem, as it has elsewhere. Radwanski, for example, describes Prime Minister Trudeau's practice of paying little attention to policy fields to which he attached a low priority. G. Radwanski, *Trudeau* (Toronto: Macmillan, 1978), 179.

[63]Described in G. Bruce Doern and Peter Aucoin (eds), *Public Policy in Canada* (Toronto: Macmillan, 1979); R. French, *How Ottawa Decides* (Ottawa, 1980); and Colin Campbell and George J. Szablowski, *The Superbureaucrats: Structure and Behaviour in Central Agencies* (Toronto, 1979).

[64]See French, *How Ottawa Decides*; James Gillies, *Where Business Fails: Business-Government Relations at the Federal Level in Canada* (Montreal, 1981); Colin Campbell, *Governments Under Stress: Political Executives and Key Bureaucrats in Washington, London and Ottawa* (Toronto, 1983); and Richard J. van Loon, 'Stop the music: the current policy and expenditure management system in Ottawa', *Canadian Public Administration* 24 (1981), 175-200.

[65]See French, *How Ottawa Decides*.

[66]On these points see particularly French, *How Ottawa Decides*; Gillies, *Where Business Fails*; Pross, 'Summary of Discussions — Fourteenth National Seminar, 1981', *Canadian Public Administration* 25 (1982) 2, 170-83; Richard J. Schultz, *Federalism and the Regulatory Process* (Montreal, 1979).

[67]Gillies, *Where Business Fails*.

[68]'Comment', in Neilson and MacPherson (eds), *The Legislative Process in Canada*, 214. Roman reports being told 'on more than one occasion by someone at the "private" level that they were amazed or frightened at the ease with which their policy proposals (often in important areas in which they had no specialized knowledge or expertise, had only a time to prepare, and did very superficial research) sailed through to the Cabinet level virtually unaltered' (215).

[69]Quoted in a review of J. Bruce-Gardyne and N. Lawson, *The Policy Game* (London: Macmillan, 1976).

[70]Confidential interview.

[71]Freda Hawkins, *Canada and Immigration: Public Policy and Public Concern* (Montreal, 1972), 312-13.

[72]Fensom, *Expanding Forestry Horizons*, 230-1.

[73]Canada. Department of the Environment. *Submission to the Management Committee: A Regularized Operational Program for Public Participation* (Mimeo. n.d. *c*.1975).

[74]By policy communities we mean the clustering of interest groups, associated agencies, and interested and/or informed individuals around the agencies generally considered to be the key policy actors in a specific field of government activity. The concept is discussed in ch. 5.

[75]R.D.S. Macdonald, 'Inshore Fishing Interests on the Atlantic Coast: Their Response to Extended Jurisdiction by Canada', *Marine Policy* (July 1979), 171-89.

[76]Faulkner, 'Pressuring the Executive', 248.

[77]See, for example, Marc Lalonde, Minister of National Health and Welfare, House of Commons, *Debates* (20 June 1975), 6954 (daily edition).

[78]Phillips, 'How Ottawa Blends'.

[79]Thus the federal government required that local groups be accorded participation in regional development planning. See *Agricultural Rehabilitation and Development Act: Federal-Provincial Rural Development Agreement* (Ottawa, 1965), pt IV, VI, and VIII.

[80]Macdonald, 'Inshore Fishing Interests . . .'; *The Policy for Canada's Atlantic Fisheries in the 1980s: A Discussion Paper* (Ottawa, 1981) took direct aim at the individualism of fishermen: 'Fishermen must continue the movement away from their historic pattern of individual voices to make their views known more effectively as a group. Greater unity has to come before fishermen can talk with any confidence about the future' (8-9).

[81]Brian Chapman remarks that 'it is . . . interesting to view the development of the Canadian police system as an exercise in the gradual emergence of new and continually changing administrative coalitions.' 'The Canadian Police: A Survey', *Government and Opposition* 12 (1977) 4, 496-516.

[82]See Kwavnick, *Organized Labour and Pressure Politics*.

[83]So, for example, Parks Canada maintains regular contact with conservation associations, various outdoor leisure groups, biologists, and geographers. The Canadian Forestry Service policy community includes members of the forestry profession and their associations, forest industry groups, and so on.

[84]See Pross, 'Pressure Groups Adaptive Instruments'.

[85]Confidential letter.

[86]This point, a major theme in Gillies, *Where Business Fails* is illustrated in Sally M. Weaver, *Making Canadian Indian Policy* (Toronto: University of Toronto Press, 1981). We should bear in mind, however, Schultz's argument (*Federalism and the Regulatory Process*) that by virtue of their responsibility for defining detailed regulation and interpreting policy issues to the centre, line departments retain considerable influence.

[87]Faulkner, 'Pressuring the Executive', 252-3.

[88]Quoted in Pross, 'Summary', 180.

[89]The term 'legitimacy' as used in the following paragraphs refers to the extent to which the community at large acknowledges and supports the work of a particular institution. The terms 'legitimation' and 'legitimating capacity' refer to the ability of an institution to confer legitimacy on some other institution or on some claim or argument.

[90]Some of the evidence supporting this position is referred to below and in the Gillies and French works cited above. For more detailed and fully documented discussions the reader is referred to the literature on accountability, particularly the *Reports* of the Auditor General of Canada during the mid-1970s, which repeatedly warned that government was not in control of the budgetary expenditure system, and the *Report* of the Royal Commission on Financial

Management and Accountability (Ottawa: 1979) (Lambert Commission), which tended to confirm the Auditor General's criticism.

[91]'I felt that the five years of minority government that we went through were a kind of situation where we weren't able to plan our legislation, we weren't able to bring in all the necessary reforms . . . and I was quite concerned about the machinery of government. . . . One of the reasons why I wanted this job, when I was told that it might be there, is because I felt it very important to have a strong central government, build up the executive, build up the Prime Minister's Office, strengthen Parliament.' Pierre Elliott Trudeau. Interview with J. Walz, *New York Times*, 22 Nov. 1968. PMO Transcript. Quoted in George Radwanski, *Trudeau* (Toronto, 1978), 146.

[92]Sandra Gwyn, 'Ottawa's incredible bureaucratic explosion', *Saturday Night*, Aug. 1975.

[93]Auditor General of Canada, *Report*, (Ottawa, 1976).

[94]See S.L. Sutherland, 'The evolution of ideas in Canada: Does Parliament benefit from Estimates reform?', 33 *Canadian Public Administration* (1990) 2, 133-64 and 'Responsible Government and Ministerial Responsibility: Every Reform Is Its Own Problem', *Canadian Journal of Political Science* XXIV (1991) 1, 91-120.

[95]Flora MacDonald, 'The Minister and the Mandarins', *Policy Options*, Sept./Oct. 1980.

[96]Public regard for civil servants is difficult to document. Decima polls indicate that 'net ratings' (calculated by subtracting the percentage of respondents having 'hardly any confidence' in those running institutions from those having 'a great deal of confidence') of the civil service fluctuated considerably in the 1980s. On a scale of -50 to 50, ratings peaked at 18 in late 1981 before dropping to -18 two years later and descending still further to -21 in 1986 before rising to 11 in 1989 (Alan Gregg and Michael Posner, *The Big Picture* [Toronto, 1990]). Respondents to *The Gallup Report*'s annual question: 'Speaking of our future, which do you think will be the biggest threat to Canada in years to come — big business, big labour or big government?' have, since 1981, nearly always seen big government as the larger threat.

[97]As I have suggested, apart from the legitimacy they derive from subordination to the Cabinet, Canadian federal agencies have very limited standing and credibility. Like their American counterparts, they cannot avail themselves of the status of the state itself. Furthermore, despite their professional competence, public servants are not held in high esteem by the general public, which tends to look askance at experts and to applaud such sophisms as 'civil servants should be on tap, not on top'. This is not a topic discussed at length in the literature, though some useful insight is to be gained from the 1969 report of the Task Force on Government Information, *To Know and Be Known* (Ottawa, 1979), especially ch. 4, 'National Opinion Survey', vol. 2, 47-89, and David Zussman, 'The Image of the Public Service in Canada', *Canadian Public Administration* 25 (1982) I, 63-80.

[98]See Royal Commission on Government Organization, (Glassco Commission) *Report* (Ottawa, 1962) I, *Management of the Public Service*.

[99]See Royal Commission on Bilingualism and Biculturalism, *Report* Book III, *The Work World*, vol. 3A, pt. 2 'The Federal Administration' (Ottawa, 1969).

[100]It is interesting to note in a content analysis of the *Winnipeg Free Press* that during the 1970s the paper shifted editorial concern from Cabinet and Parliament to the bureaucracy. See Allan Kornberg and Judith D. Wolfe, 'Parliament, the Media and the Polls', in Clarke *et al.*, *Parliament, Policy and Representation*, 35-58, at 46; *Globe and Mail*, 15 July 1982, 1; Marci MacDonald, *et al.*, 'The Money Wasters', *Maclean's*, 15 December 1975; Douglas Hartle, 'Refugees from Ottawa: five public servants and why they left', *Saturday Night*, March 1976; Gordon W. Stead, 'The Federal Bureaucracy and Canadian Disunity', in Elliot J. Feldman and Neil Nevitte (eds), *The Future of North America: Canada, the United States and Quebec Nationalism* (Cambridge/Montreal: Harvard Center for International Affairs and Institute for Research on Public Policy, 1979), 213-35; and MacDonald, 'The Minister and the Mandarins'.

[101]V. Seymour Wilson, 'Representative Bureaucracy: linguistic/ethnic aspects in Canadian public policy', *Canadian Public Administration* 21 (1978) 4, 513-38.

[102]See Rush, 'The Development of the Committee System . . .', 154. See C.E.S. Franks, *The Parliament of Canada* (Toronto, 1987).

[103]John F. Bulloch, 'A View from a Special Interest Group', in Daniel L. Bon, *Lobbying: A Right? A Necessity? A Danger?* (Ottawa, 1981), 12.

[104]'The Committee Track Record: A Limited Pay-off', *Parliamentary Government*, 3 (1983) 4, 7-10,9.

[105]Herb Breau, quoted in 'Commons Committee Witnesses: A Process of Enlightenment', *Parliamentary Government*, 3 (1982) 4, 3-6, 6.

[106]See ibid.

[107]According to R.A. Weir, 'From 1965 to 1967, the period of intensive public debate over the medicaid [*sic*] programme, national officials of the CMA met physician-MPs informally only once and did not meet any larger group of MPs at all.' 'Federalism, Interest Groups and Parliamentary Government: The Canadian Medical Association', *Journal of Comparative Political Studies*, XI (1973) 2, 159-75, at 165.

[108]'The Committee Track Record', 10.

[109]Ernest Steele, president of the Canadian Association of Broadcasters. Ibid.

[110]'A View from a Special Interest Group', 13.

[111]Canadian Bar Association, *Report of the Canadian Bar Association Committee on the Reform of Parliament* (Parliament as Lawmaker) (Ottawa, 1982) vii.

[112]On the other hand, respondents were much less complimentary in their assessment of the work of parliamentarians, leading Kornberg *et al.* to conclude that the institution of Parliament rather than its then current membership and accomplishments had very broad public support. See Allan Kornberg, Harold D. Clarke, and Arthur Goddard, 'Parliament and the Representational Process in Contemporary Canada', in D. Clarke *et al.*, *Parliament, Policy and Representation*, xxvi-25, at 9-10.

Out of a sample of 2,095 individuals over 18 interviewed in 1979 for the Canadian Gallup Polls, only 38% reported that they had 'a great deal of respect' or 'quite a lot of respect' for the House of Commons. Thirty-six per cent had 'some' respect; 15% very little, and 11% had no opinion. Even so the House ranked fourth in a list of eight social institutions, behind the Church or organized religion, the Supreme Court, and public schools but ahead of newspapers, large corporations, political parties, and labour unions. F. Kielty, *et al.*, *Canadians Speak Out: The Canadian Gallup Polls, 1980* (Toronto, 1980).

[113]A. H. Hanson, 'The Purpose of Parliament', *Parliamentary Affairs* XVII (1964) 3, 279-96, 295.

[114]Audrey Doerr, 'Public Administration: federalism and intergovernmental relations', *Canadian Public Administration* 25 (1982) 4, 564-79, 575

[115]See Audrey Doerr, 'Parliamentary Accountability and Legislative Potential', in Clarke *et al.*, *Parliament, Policy and Representation*, 144-60.

[116]Douglas C. Nord, 'MPs and Senators as Middlemen: The special Joint Committee on Immigration Policy', in Clarke *et al.*, *Parliament, Policy and Representation*, 181-94.

[117]Rush, 'The Development of the Committee System' and 'Committees in the Canadian House of Commons'.

[118]Nord, 'MPs and Senators as Middlemen', 185.

[119]Letter, John McDonough, Project Officer, Research Branch, Library of Parliament, to Dr P. Smith, 22 Feb. 1980, quoted in G.W.C. Hunter, *The Role of the Member of Parliament and the Standing Committees of the House of Commons*, MA thesis, Acadia University (1982), 82.

[120]See ibid.; Butler, 'The Adequacy of Committee Consideration of Legislation', and M. MacGuigan, 'The Role of the Standing Committee on Justice and Legal Affairs of the Canadian House of Commons: 1968-78', in J. Menezes (ed.), *Decade of Adjustment — Legal Perspectives on Contemporary Social Issues* (Toronto, 1980). For the 1976 debate over gun control see MacGuigan, and for the 1990-1 debates, see the *Proceedings* of the Committee.

[121]Canada. House of Commons, *Status of Bills and Motions: At Prorogation May 12, 1991* (2nd

Session, 34th Parliament) (Ottawa, 1991). See also Stanbury, *Business Interests and the Reform of Canadian Competition Policy*; MacGuigan, 'The Role of the Standing Committee on Justice and Legal Affairs'; Butler, 'The Adequacy of Committee Consideration of Legislation'; Friedland, 'Pressure Groups and the Development of the Criminal Law'; and Grace Skogstad, 'Interest Groups, Representation and Conflict Management in the Standing Committees of House of Commons', *Canadian Journal of Political Science* XVIII (1985) 4, 739-78.

[122]M. Rush, 'Committees in the Canadian House of Commons', at 230 quoting Hockin, CPA (1970), 201.

CHAPTER 4. TYPES OF GROUPS

[1]*Interest Groups and the Bureaucracy: The Politics of Energy* (Stanford, CA, 1983), 21.

[2]The level of analysis problems can be observed frequently in corporatist writings where it is common to drift between the analysis of specific groups and of group systems. See, for example, W.D. Coleman, *Business and Politics* (Montreal, 1988), 55.

[3]This lesson was, however, learned slowly. As late as the 1950s David Truman underestimated the significance of organization in interest group politics, considering it 'merely a stage or degree of interaction'. David B. Truman, *The Government Process* (N.Y.: Knopf, 1951), 36.

[4]Francis G. Castles, *Pressure Groups and Political Culture* (London: Routledge & Kegan Paul, 1967), 2.

[5]Jeffrey R. Berry, *Lobbying for the People* (Princeton, N.J.: Princeton University Press, 1977). See also Andrew S. McFarland, *Public Interest Lobbies* (Washington: American Enterprise Institute, 1976).

[6]William Stanbury's case study 'The CFIB and the November 1981, Budget' in *Business-Government Relations in Canada* (Toronto, 1986, 378-85) illustrates the use of confrontational techniques by one business group and draws out the arguments for and against the approach.

[7]John E. Chubb develops a dichotomized classification scheme based on the assumption that some groups are cost-bearers and others are beneficiaries of policy. The approach yields insight into the strategies of both groups and agencies in specific cases, but has limited broader application because the burden of costs and benefits varies across cases and affects group strategy and behaviour accordingly. See *Interest Groups and Bureaucracy* (Stanford, CA: Stanford University Press, 1983).

[8]Berry, *Lobbying for the People*, 45-55, 226-30; Peter H. Schuck, 'Public Interest Groups and the Policy Process', *Public Administration Review* (1977), 132-40.

[9]Although Ontario's experimental *Intervenor Funding Act*, S.O. 1988, c. 71 is an interesting exception. See Michael I. Jeffrey, 'Ontario's Intervenor Funding Project Act', *Canadian Journal of Administrative Law and Practice* 3 (1989) 1, 69-80.

[10]Philippe C. Schmitter, *Trends Toward Corporatist Intermediation* (London, 1979); Coleman, *Business and Politics*; Michael M. Atkinson and William D. Coleman, *The State, Business and Industrial Change in Canada* (Toronto, 1989); and L. Harmon Ziegler, *Pluralism, Corporatism and Confucianism: political association and conflict regulation in the United States, Europe, and Taiwan* (Philadelphia: Temple University Press, 1988).

[11]See, for example, Ursula Franklin, 'Voices of Women: Feminist Leadership', *Edges* 2 (1989) 4, 14-17; Sandra Burt, 'Canadian Women's Groups in the 1980s: Organizational Development and Policy Influence', *Canadian Public Policy* XVI (1990) 1, 17-28; and Frances Fox Piven and Richard A. Cloward, *Poor Peoples Movements: Why They Succeed, How They Fail* (N.Y.: Vintage, 1977).

[12]Or, as David Easton has put it, public policy is the 'authoritative allocation through the

political process of values to groups or individuals in the society'. *The Political Process* (N.Y.: Knopf, 1953), 129.

[13]In this vein, a coalition organized to persuade the government to moderate CBC budget cuts emphasized in its publicity the fact that it comprised 27 groups with national standing and a combined membership of 2.5 million. *Globe and Mail*, 6 Feb. 1991.

[14]The present discussion builds on my earlier attempts to develop a taxonomy of groups (see, for example, the first edition of this book) and on the critique of that taxonomy by Burt, 'Canadian Women's Groups in the 1980s', (see also Pross, 'Typologies, Claims, Institutions and the Capacity for Discourse: A Reply', *Canadian Public Policy* XVI (1990) 2, 209-13; and Burt, 'Women's Groups and the Pross Continuum: The Need for More Discourse', *Canadian Public Policy* XVI (1990) 3, 339-340); Trevor Matthews, ' "Vitally important allies?" The role of interest groups in government decision-making: A review essay', *Australian Journal of Public Administration* XLVII (1988) 2, 147-63. It also draws on the corporatist concept of 'organizational development' put forward by P. Schmitter and W. Streeck in 'The organization of business interests' (Berlin: International Institute of Management. Labour Market Discussion Paper. 1981).

[15]Burt, 'Canadian Women's Groups in the 1980s'.

[16]Theodore Lowi, *The Politics of Disorder* (N.Y.: Basic Books, 1971), 11. Canadian studies of the agricultural field demonstrate similar patterns. See J.D. Forbes, *Institutions and Influence Groups in Canadian Farm and Food Policy* (Toronto, 1985); Grace Skogstad, *The Politics of Agricultural Policy-Making in Canada* (Toronto: University of Toronto Press, 1987); and Barry K. Wilson, *Farming the System: How Politics and Farmers Shape Agricultural Policy* (Saskatoon, SK.: Western Producer Prairie Books, 1990).

[17]Alan Cawson, 'Varieties of corporatism: the importance of the meso-level of interest intermediation', in Cawson (ed.), *Organized interests and the state: studies in meso-corporatism* (London: Sage, 1985); Coleman, *Business and Politics*; William Coleman and Wyn Grant, 'Business Associations and Public Policy: a Comparison of Organizational Development in Britain and Canada', *Journal of Public Policy* 4 (1984) 3, 209-35.

[18]Examples. Schmitter and Streeck associate organizational development with 'the more safely [groups'] supply of strategic resources is institutionalized.' (Schmitter and Streeck, 'The organization of business interests', quoted in Coleman and Grant, 'Business Associations and Public Policy', 212.) Gamson found that 17% of the social protest groups that he investigated practised 'institutionaled secrecy' in conducting their challenges of public policy. (William Gamson, *The Strategy of Social Protest* [Homewood, IL, 1975] 179.)

[20]Phillip Selznick, *Leadership in Administration* (N.Y., 1957), 21, 5, 139.

[21]Talcott Parsons and Neil Smelser, *Economy and Society* (Glencoe, IL: Free Press, 1956), 102, in Robert R. Alford and Roger Friedland, *Powers of Theory* (Cambridge University Press, 1985), 38.

[22]J. Anthony Long, 'Political revitalization in Canadian native Indian societies', *Canadian Journal of Political Science* XXIII (1990) 4, 751-74, 754.

[23]Selznick, *Leadership in Administration*, 20.

[24]See, for example, Burt's comments on the changing community and status of women's issues at the federal level in 'Organized Women's Groups and the State', in William D. Coleman and Grace Skogstad (eds), *Policy Communities and Public Policy in Canada* (Toronto, 1990), 191-215, 24.

[25]Witness the many studies of national pressure group systems such as A.G. Jordan and J.J. Richardson, *Government and Pressure Groups in Britain* (Oxford, 1987); Coleman, *Business and Politics*; Atkinson and Coleman, *The State, Business and Industrial Change in Canada*; Stanbury, *Business-Government Relations in Canada*; and Wootten, *Interest Groups: Policy and Politics in America*.

[26]Lowi, *The Politics of Disorder*, 34.

[27]Forbes, *Institutions and Influence Groups in Canadian Farm and Food Policy*, 118.

[28]For an illuminating discussion of this process see Lowi, *Politics of Disorder*, 43-51.

[29]Following Schmitter and Streecks' scheme as outlined in their paper 'The organization of business interests', as reported in Coleman, *Business and Politics*, 50-2; Coleman and Grant, 'Business associations and public policy', 213.

[30]House of Commons. Standing Committee on Elections Privileges and Procedure. *Minutes of Proceedings and Evidence*, 2/33. 1986-7, 14: 9.

[31]See A.M.C. Waterman, 'The Catholic Bishops and Canadian Public Policy', *Canadian Public Policy* IX (1983) 3, 374-82; B.W. Wilkinson, 'The Catholic Bishops and Canadian Public Policy: A Comment', *Canadian Public Policy* X (1981) 1, 88-92; and Waterman, 'The Catholic Bishops and Canadian Public Policy: A Reply', *Canadian Public Policy* X (1984) 3, 338-9.

[32]Coleman and Grant, 'Business Associations and Public Policy', 228-30.

[33]Lowi, *The Politics of Disorder*, 43-51.

[34]See Mayer N. Zald and Michael A. Berger, 'Social movements in organizations: coup d'état, insurgency, and mass movements', *American Journal of Sociology* 83 (1978) 4, 823-61 at 829 for a discussion of the impact of infrastructure on the development of collective action.

[35]See C.G. Gifford, *Canada's Fighting Seniors* (Toronto, 1990), 19-20.

[36]Interview. James W. McClatchie, Executive Director, John Howard Society, 3 Jan. 1991.

[37]Coleman, *Business and Politics*, 58.

[38]Burt, 'Canadian Women's Groups in the 1980s'; Gifford, *Canada's Fighting Seniors*; Gamson, *The Strategy of Social Protest*, 92-3. Gamson excluded hierarchy from his definition of bureaucracy, which, for him, comprised 'formality of procedures, record keeping, and some complexity of role differentiation'.

[39]This is, in fact, the pattern discovered by Jeffrey Berry among Washington-based public interest groups. See *Lobbying for the People*.

[40]Freda Hawkins' description of voluntary groups working in the immigration field could be applied to many nascent and fledgling groups. They 'do not have an office, never keep records, and simply respond to the needs of the moment. Their program, objectives, and performance may change totally from year to year. Only a very few officials and experienced community workers in a particular city, who have been working with these agencies, committees and groups for some time can really assess the quality and usefulness of the work they do.' Freda Hawkins, *Canada and Immigration: Public Policy and Public Concern* (Montreal, 1972), 294.

[41]See Coleman and Grant, 'Business Associations and Public Policy', 217.

[42]For example, 'The Pharmaceutical Manufacturers' Association of Canada participates in the design and implementation of policy for regulating the safety and efficacy of drugs and for ensuring proper advertising of drugs through a series of joint committees with the Health Protection Branch of the Department of Health and Welfare. The Proprietary Association of Canada enjoys somewhat regularized access to policy formulation in the Health Protection Branch and the Canadian Agricultural Chemicals Association the same in the Department of Agriculture.' Coleman and Grant, 'Business Associations and Public Policy', 213, 217-18, 227.

[43]Coleman and Grant, 'Business Associations and Public Policy', 213.

[44]See, for example, Roxana Ng, *The Politics of Community Services: Immigrant Women, Class and State* (Toronto: Garamond, 1988), 26-7, 32-3.

CHAPTER 5. CONTEXT: POLICY COMMUNITIES AND GROUP FUNCTIONS

[1]See, for example, L.C. Bacchi, *Liberation Deferred: The Ideas of the English-Canadian*

Suffragists, 1877-1918 (Toronto, 1983), and Ramsay Cook, *The Regenerators: Social criticism in late Victorian English Canada* (Toronto, 1985).

²As in the consolidation of the Boards of Trade in the Maritimes as a result of the dispute with the federal government over Maritime Freight Rates. By the 1930s this consolidation had led to the establishment of an affiliate research centre, the Atlantic Provinces Transportation Commission, which was assigned a permanent head: a good illustration of the development of policy capacity. See E.R. Forbes, *Maritime Rights: The Maritime Rights Movement* (Montreal, 1979), 189-92.

³See, for example, J.D. Forbes' discussion of the role of producers' interests in the policy community concerned with food production and distribution in *Institutions and Influence Groups in Canadian Farm and Food Policy* (Toronto, 1985), chs 3 and 7.

⁴The following paragraph draws on a large body of literature. See particularly Robert K. Merton, *Social Theory and Social Structure* (N.Y.: Free Press, 1968), chs 8, 9, and 19.

⁵Forbes, *Institutions and Influence Groups in Canadian Farm and Food Policy*, ch. 3.

⁶Theodore Lowi, *The Politics of Disorder* (N.Y.: Basic Books, 1971), ch. 2.

⁷For a review of this nomenclature see Grant Jordan, 'Iron Triangles, Woolly Corporatism and Elastic Nets: Images of the Policy Process', *Journal of Public Policy* 1 (1981) pt 1: 95-123; 'Sub-governments, policy communities and networks: Refilling old bottles?', *Journal of Theoretical Politics* 2 (1990) 3, 319-38; and 'Policy community realism versus "new" institutionalist ambiguity', *Political Studies* XXXVIII (1990), 470-84.

⁸Of a number of other definitions some of the most interesting are presented in a series of articles on policy communities in different countries which appeared in *Governance* 2 (1989) 1, under the editorship of Jack L. Walker. R. Rhodes sees policy communities as networks, 'characterised by stability of relationships, continuity of restricted membership, vertical interdependence based on shared service delivery responsibilities, and insulation from other networks and invariably to the general public (including Parliament).' ('Power-dependence, policy communities and intergovernmental networks', *Public Administration Bulletin* 49, Dec. 1985, 4-31, 12, 15. See also his *Beyond Westminster and Whitehall* [London, 1988]). Stephen Wilks and Maurice Wright define the policy community as 'actors or potential actors with a direct or indirect interest in a policy area or function who share a common "policy focus", and who, with varying degrees of influence shape policy outcomes over the long run.' ('Conclusion: Comparing Government-Industry Relations: States, Sectors, and Networks' in Wilks and Wright [eds], *Comparative Government-Industry Relations* [Oxford, 1987].) Our definition shares with those of Rhodes and Wilks, Wright an emphasis on the long-term influence of the community; its stability and the presence of 'asymmetrical' power relations within it. However, it differs in drawing attention to the tendency of the state to permit the community to occupy and dominate a policy field and it sets the boundaries of the community beyond what is frequently called the sub-government (described below). Here the sub-government is seen as the community's central core, but the attentive public is believed to play a dynamic role in linking the community to the community at large.

⁹William D. Coleman and Grace Skogstad (eds), 'Policy Communities and Policy Networks: A Structural Approach', in Coleman and Skogstad, *Policy Communities and Public Policy in Canada* (Toronto, 1990), 14-33, at 23-4.

¹⁰For example, in chapter 4 of *The State, Business and Industrial Change in Canada* (Toronto, 1989), William D. Coleman and Michael M. Atkinson define networks in terms very similar to those used both here and in Coleman and Skogstad's 'Policy Communities and Policy Networks' to describe policy communities. They speak, for example, of associational systems and bureaucratic agencies as forming the 'core' of policy networks (p. 77).

¹¹Sally M. Weaver, *Making Canadian Indian Policy* (Toronto, 1981).

¹²Compare Theodore Lowi's perception of a less constructive tension between the 'decadence' of the highly institutionalized groups that dominate sectoral policy-making and the dynamism of nascent groups (*The Politics of Disorder* [New York, 1971], 47-53).

[13]See William D. Coleman and Henry J. Jacek, 'The Political Organization of the Chemical Industry in Canada'. Paper. Canadian Political Science Association, 1981: 22.

[14]Denis Stairs, 'Publics and Policy-Makers: The Domestic Environment of Canada's Foreign Policy Community', *International Journal* (1970-1), 221-48.

[15]Coleman and Jacek, 'The Political Organization of the Chemical Industry in Canada': 32, 36, 58; and Coleman and Wyn Grant, 'Business Associations and Public Policy: a Comparison of Organisational Development in Britain and Canada', *Journal of Public Policy* 4 (1984) 3: 209-35.

[16]See, for example, Chris Parke, 'The Setting of Minimum Wage Policy in the Maritimes' (Halifax: Dalhousie Institute of Public Affairs, 1980).

[17]J.B. Falls, 'Douglas H. Pimlott — Lessons for Action', *Nature Canada* 8 (April-June 1979), 18-23.

[18]Committee documents. SSFC (then SSHRCC) Bulletin for the period.

[19]This paragraph reflects the approach developed in E.E. Schattschneider, *The Semi-Sovereign People: A Realist's View of Democracy in America* (N.Y.: Holt, Rinehart & Winston, 1960). The approach is examined more closely in chapter 10.

[20]M.L. Friedland comments that policy-making in the field of criminal law takes place in a more public forum than policy-making in many other fields, is more subject to intervention by nascent groups, and is more likely to be characterized by heated debate. He suggests that this is due to the fact that public policy in the field is declared in law rather than regulation; that political parties prefer not to take a party line but rather to invite public debate. ('Pressure Groups and the Development of the Criminal Law,' in P.R. Glazebrook (ed.), *Reshaping the Criminal Law: Essays in Honour of Glanville Williams* [London, 1978], 205). The argument that policy processes vary between sectors is currently receiving considerable academic attention, particularly from the corporatists whose interest in 'meso-corporatism' has prompted numerous sector studies. See Alan Cawson, *Organized Interests and the State: Studies in meso-corporatism* (London: Sage, 1985); Atkinson and Coleman, *The State, Business and Industrial Change in Canada*; and Coleman and Skogstad, *Policy Communities and Public Policy in Canada*.

[21]See Roderick Byers, 'Canadian Foreign Policy and Selective Attentive Publics' (Ottawa: Department of External Affairs, mimeo, 1967) and Trevor Price, 'The Rise and Demise of the Ministry of State for Urban Affairs'. Paper. Canadian Political Science Association, 1981.

[22]The following account is condensed from A. Paul Pross, 'Mobilizing Regional Concern: freight rates and political learning in the Canadian Maritimes', in William D. Coleman and Henry J. Jacek, *Regionalism, Business Interests and Public Policy* (London, 1989), 173-200. A more extensive treatment of the Maritime Rights Movement and the subsidy issue will be found in E.R. Forbes, *Maritime Rights: The Maritime Rights Movement* (Montreal, 1979). Since the formulation of the policy community presented here was first generally circulated (in Pross, 'Duality and Public Policy: A conceptual framework for analyzing the policy system of Atlantic Canada' [Dalhousie Institute of Pubic Affairs, 1980]) it has been applied in several analyses, notably: Forbes, *Institutions and Influence Groups in Canadian Farm and Food Policy*; Jeremy Wilson, 'Wilderness Politics in B.C.: The Business Dominated State and the Containment of Environmentalism', in Coleman and Skogstad, *Policy Communities and Public Policy in Canada*, 141-69; Skogstad, 'The Farm Policy Community', ibid., 59-90; Leslie C. Carrothers, 'Telecommunications policy and the Manitoba New Democratic Party: party politics and the policy community'(University of Manitoba. MA Thesis, 1987); and in Pross and McCorquodale, *Economic Resurgence and the Constitutional Agenda* (Kingston, Ont., 1987).

[23]See Henry W. Ehrmann (ed.), *Interest Groups on Four Continents* (Pittsburgh, 1958); Robert Presthus, *Elites in the Policy Process* (Toronto: Macmillan, 1974); Graham K. Wilson, *Special Interests and Policy Making* (London, 1977) and *Business and Politics: A comparative introduction* (London, 1985); Suzanne D. Berger (ed.), *Organizing Interests in Western Europe: Pluralism, corporatism, and the transformation of politics* (Cambridge, 1981); Alan

Cawson, *Organized Interests and the State: Studies in meso-corporatism* (London: Sage, 1985); Alan R. Ball and Frances Millard, *Pressure politics in industrial societies: a comparative introduction* (London, 1986); and Clive Thomas (ed.), *Interest Groups in Post Industrial Democracies* (Westport, forthcoming).

[24]Robert Presthus, 'Interest Groups and the Canadian Parliament: Activities, Interaction, Legitimacy and Influence', *Canadian Journal of Political Science* IV (1971) 4, 446-60, at 446.

[25]*Financial Post*, 10 Jan. 1972.

[26]Peter G. Johnson, 'The Union of Nova Scotia Municipalities as a Pressure Group'. *Proceedings*, Canadian Political Science Association. Winnipeg: June 1970, 2, 5.

[27]C.E. Dalphond, 'L'information administrative: une analyse politique préliminaire', *Recherches sociographiques* XVI (1975) 3, 307-21, 311.

[28]Martin Robin, *The Rush for Spoils: The Company Province, 1871-1933* (Toronto, 1972), 55-6.

[29]See the APEC *Newsletter* and the organization's *Annual Reports*.

[30]See Donald C. Savage, 'Freedom of Information Legislation and the University Community', CAUT *Bulletin*, Feb. 1983, 5-6.

[31]Bacchi, *Liberation Deferred*.

[32]Ottawa *Citizen*, 24 June 1982.

[33]Hon. Romeo Leblanc, *Speech*, Rotary Club of Yarmouth, N.S., 28 Nov. 1977.

[34]This discussion is based on research reported in A. Paul Pross and Susan McCorquodale, *Economic Resurgence and the Constitutional Agenda: The case of the East Coast fisheries* (Kingston, Ont., 1987), and 'The state, interests and policy making in the East Coast fishery', in William D. Coleman and Grace Skogstad (eds), *Policy Communities and Public Policies: a structural approach* (Toronto, 1990). Wallace Clement has explored the problems of fishermen's organization at length in *The Struggle to Organize: Resistance in Canada's Fishery* (Toronto, 1986).

[35]Kingston *Whig-Standard*, 21 June 1983.

[36]The classic exploration of the 'capture thesis' is Marver Bernstein's *Regulating Business by Independent Commission* (Princeton, 1955). Doern and Toner present a Canadian illustration in their discussion of Canadian energy policy. During the 1960s, they argue that the major oil companies, through their control of technical, geological, economic, and financial information, were able to manipulate federal and Alberta energy policy in their own interests. See G. Bruce Doern and Glen Toner, *The Politics of Energy* (Toronto, 1985), 131 ff. Canadian critiques of the thesis are found in W.H.N. Hull, 'Captive or victim: The Board of Broadcast Governors and Bernstein's Law, 1958-68', *Canadian Public Administration* 26 (1983), 560, and in John C. Strick, *The Economics of Government Regulation: Theory and Canadian Practice* (Toronto, 1990), 20-2.

[37]Kenneth Woodside, 'The Political Economy of Policy Instruments: Tax Expenditures and Subsidies in Canada', in M. Atkinson and Marsha Chandler, *The Politics of Canadian Public Policy* (Toronto, 1983) 173-99, 190-1.

[38]See Joan Boase.

[39]See Henry J. Jacek, 'Business Interest Associations as Private Interest Governments', in Wyn Grant (ed.), *Business Interests, Organizational Development and Private Interest Government* (Berlin, 1987), 34-62.

[40]The work of voluntary groups in providing and agitating for social services is a recurrent theme in Allan Moscovitch and Jim Albert, *The Benevolent State: The growth of welfare in Canada* (Toronto, 1987). The general role of voluntary organizations is discussed in the *Report* of the National Advisory Council on Voluntary Action entitled *People in Action* (Ottawa, 1977). See also Novia Carter, *Trends in Voluntary Support for Non-governmental Social Service Agencies* (Ottawa, 1974). A specific illustration of the practice of contracting services out to voluntary groups is found in Roxanna Ng, *The Politics of Community Services: Immigrant women, class and state* (Toronto, 1988).

[41]Freda Hawkins, *Canada and Immigration: Public Policy and Public Concern* (Montreal, 1972), 301.

[42]See National Council of Welfare, *In the Best Interests of the Child: A Report by the National Council of Welfare on the Child Welfare System in Canada* (Ottawa: The Council, 1979), and L.F. Hurl, 'Privatized Social Service Systems: Lessons from Ontario Children's Services', *Canadian Public Policy* x (1984), 395-406.

[43]Reported in *Le Devoir*, 22 Sept. 1982.

[44]See, for example, John Kearney, 'The Transformation of the Bay of Fundy Herring Fisheries, 1976-78: An Experiment in Fishermen-Government Co-Management', in Cynthia Lamson and Arthur J. Hanson (eds), *Atlantic Fisheries and Coastal Communities: Fisheries Decision-Making Case Studies* (Halifax, 1984), 165-204.

[45]Leslie Bella, *Parks for Profit* (Montreal, 1987) 154.

[46]World University Service of Canada, for example, prior to its bankruptcy in December 1990 had received $20 million per year from the federal government to administer development projects and student assistance. *Globe and Mail*, 4 Dec. 1990.

[47]J.G. Nelson, 'Public participation in comprehensive resource and environmental management', *Science and Public Policy*, Oct. 1982, 204-50, 247.

[48]William D. Coleman, 'Canadian Business and the State', in Keith Banting (Research Coordinator), *The State and Economic Interests* (Toronto, 1985).

CHAPTER 6. GROUPS IN ACTION

[1]*Globe and Mail*, 13, 14 March 1991.

[2]Frustration has been most recently expressed in these ways by aboriginal groups (see Boyce Richardson [ed.], *Drumbeat: Anger and Renewal in Indian Country* [Toronto, 1990]) and environmentalists (for example, 'Styrofoam cups latest anti-logging weapon', *Globe and Mail*, 29 Dec. 1990, and Dave Foreman and Bill Haywood [eds], *Ecodefense: A Field Guide to Monkeywrenching* [Tucson, Ariz.: 1987]). Historically the unrest of the Depression years (see Michiel Horn, *The Dirty Thirties* [Toronto, 1971]) and the rise of the FLQ (see Louis Fournier, *F.L.Q.: The Anatomy of an Underground Movement* [Toronto, 1984] tr. by E. Baxter) are but two of the best remembered of many clashes between the frustrated and authority. An overview is found in Judy M. Torrance, *Public Violence in Canada, 1867-1982* (Montreal, 1986).

[3]See Kenneth M. Gibbons and Donald C. Rowat, *Political Corruption in Canada: Cases, Causes and Cures* (Ottawa: Carleton University Press, 1976). A recent discussion of patronage is Jeffrey Simpson's *Spoils of Power* (Toronto, 1988). John Sawatsky's *The Insiders: Government, Business and the Lobbyists* (Toronto, 1987) is a survey of some of the more glamorous lobbyists in Ottawa.

[4]Charlotte Gray, 'Friendly Persuasion', *Saturday Night*, March 1983, 11-14, 11-12.

[5]J. Hugh Faulkner, 'Pressuring the Executive', *Canadian Public Administration* 25 (1982) 2, 241.

[6]Ibid., 240-1.

[7]See James Gillies, *Where Business Fails: Business-Government Relations at the Federal Level in Canada* (Montreal, 1981), and H.L. Laframboise, 'Conscience and Conformity: The Uncomfortable Bedfellows of Accountability', *Canadian Public Administration* 26 (1983) 3, 325-44.

[8]As early as 1968 between $1,500 and $4,000 a month (Sawatsky, *The Insiders*, 45) and in 1980 up to $6,500 a month (Julianne La Breche, 'The Quiet Persuaders of Parliament Hill', *Financial Post Magazine*, 29 Nov. 1980). The firm's executive was headed for some years by Bill Lee, for several periods associated with Liberal cabinet ministers, and Bill Neville of the

Conservatives; more recently by Sam Hughes, for ten years president of the Canadian Chambers of Commerce. *Financial Post*, 2 Feb. 1985.

[9]David Kwavnick, *Organized Labour and Pressure Politics: The Canadian Labour Congress, 1956-1968* (Montreal, 1972), ch. 7.

[10]Helen Jones Dawson, 'National Pressure Groups and the Federal Government', in A. Paul Pross (ed.), *Pressure Group Behaviour in Canadian Politics* (Toronto, 1975), 35-9.

[11]Forbes, 'Institutions and Interest Groups in the Canadian Food System Policy Process'. *Report*. Ottawa, 1982, 90-1.

[12]Faulkner, 'Pressuring the Executive', 241-2.

[13]*Social Sciences in Canada*, 13 (1985) 1, iii.

[14]See Richard Schultz, *Federalism, Bureaucracy and Public Policy: The Politics of Highway Transport Regulation* (Montreal, 1980), and Harold Kaplan, *Policy and Rationality: The Regulation of Canadian Trucking* (Toronto, 1989), ch. 4.

[15]Quoted in Hyman Solomon, 'Business got its feet wet in public policy', *Financial Post*, 5 Dec. 1988. Harold Kaplan presents a fascinating account of the play of organizational cultures in the relations between the Canadian Trucking Association and federal and provincial bureaucracies in *Policy and Rationality: The Regulation of Canadian Trucking* (Toronto, 1989).

[16]A. Paul Pross, 'Pressure Groups: Adaptive Instruments of Political Communication', in Pross (ed.), *Pressure Group Behaviour in Canadian Politics* (Toronto, 1975), 19.

[17]Larry Smith, 'Getting Your Way With a Bureaucrat', *Canadian Business* Sept. 1980, 104.

[18]Ibid., 104.

[19]This and the following quotations are taken from ibid., 107.

[20]'In order to influence legislation and budgetary matters you must get into the system almost a year in advance, before the politicians begin thinking seriously about options. That is the time it takes the bureaucracy to study your proposal.' John Bulloch, 'A view from a special interest group', in Daniel L. Bon, *Lobbying: A Right? A Necessity? A Danger?* (Ottawa, 1981), 13.

[21]Jim Lotz, 'A citizen's guide to effective community action', *The Southender*, Dec. 1984.

[22]Lotz, 'A citizen's guide'.

[23]*Social Sciences in Canada*, chs 4, 7.

[24]La Breche, 'The Quiet Persuaders of Parliament Hill', 40.

[25]Canadian Nuclear Association. Public Information Program, *1987-1988 Business Plan* (mimeo).

[26]La Breche, 'The Quiet Persuaders of Parliament Hill', 40.

[27]John Cowan, 'Academic lobby aims to halt erosion of research funds', *CAUT Bulletin*, Feb. 1981, 5.

[28]Cowan, 'Academic lobby'.

[29]David Kwavnick, *Organized Labour and Pressure Politics*, 15-25, and Peter Aucoin, 'Pressure Groups and Recent Changes in the Policy-Making Process', in A. Paul Pross (ed.), *Pressure Group Behaviour in Canadian Politics* (Toronto, 1975), 172-93, 188-9.

[30]Forbes, 'The Canadian Food System Policy Process', 97-104, 36, and Grace Skogstad, 'The Farm Policy Community and Public Policy in Ontario and Quebec', in William D. Coleman and Grace Skogstad (eds), *Policy Comunities and Public Policy in Canada* (Toronto, 1990), 59-91. For a more sceptical view of the strength of NFU's main rival, the Canadian Federation of Agriculture, see Barry K. Wilson, *Farming the System* (Saskatoon, 1990), ch. 7.

[31]Coleman, *Business and Politics*, ch. 9; Leslie T. MacDonald, 'Taxing Comprehensive Income: Power and Participation in Canadian Politics, 1962-1972' , PhD thesis (Ottawa: Carleton 1985); R. John Arseneau, 'The Government-Small Business Relationship' Dalhousie University. Student Paper, 1984, 21; Charlotte Gray, 'Friendly Persuasion', *Saturday Night*, March 1983 and *Maclean's*, 14 May 1984.

[32]In the words of one group leader, 'pressure groups have to resist government pressure to participate.' Quoted in A. Paul Pross, 'Governing Under Pressure: Summary of Discussions', *Canadian Public Administration* 25 (1982) 2, 170-83, at 178.

[33]E.E. Schattschneider, *The Semi-Sovereign People* (N.Y.: Holt, Rinehart and Winston, 1960), 71.

[34]David Kwavnick, *Organized Labour and Pressure Politics*, 16.

[35]L.C. Bacchi, *Liberation Deferred: The Ideas of the English-Canadian Suffragists, 1877-1918* (Toronto, 1983), 73-85.

[36]Bacchi, *Liberation Deferred*, 85.

[37]Ibid.

[38]David Kwavnick, *Organized Labour and Pressure Politics*, 16.

[39]Ibid., 18.

[40]David Neave of Wildlife Habitat Canada quoted speaking to an audience of forest industry executives. *Globe and Mail*, 27 March 1991.

[41]Ron Arnold, 'The Politics of Environmentalism', *Notes on Agriculture*, Oct. 1981, 25-9, 25; and 'Anti-pesticide organizations and future trends', Speech. Atlantic Vegetation Management Association, Halifax, Oct. 1984, 16.

[42]*Globe and Mail*, 30 Aug. 1988.

[43]Memo. I. Mumford to R. Veilleux. Atomic Energy of Canada Ltd, 12 Jan. 1988, and database.

[44]See Christopher Majka, 'Anti-environmentalism: Ideology on the front lines', *New Maritimes*, June 1986, 12-13.

[45]As many labour, arts, academic, nationalist, and public interest groups supported the CBC in its fight against the 1990-91 budget cuts. *Globe and Mail*, 12 Dec. 1991, and Michael Valpy, 'Culture shock', *Globe and Mail*, 8 April 1991.

[46]For example, the Council of Canadians' Maud Barlow vigorously attacks the Mulroney government's economic policies in *A Parcel of Rogues: How Free Trade is Ruining Canada* (Toronto, 1990).

[47]*The Institute*, Sept.-Oct. 1983, and Hyman Solomon, 'Cars can't be divorced from politics', *Financial Post* 15 Oct. 1983. I am also grateful to Gil Winham for his recollections of the conference.

[48]The most important of which are noted and summarized in *The Network*, the newsletter of the Network on the Constitution, which is based at the University of Ottawa.

[49]Donald Savage, 'Freedom of Information Legislation and the University Community', *CAUT Bulletin*, Feb. 1983, 5-6, 5.

[50]Ibid.

CHAPTER 7. BEYOND THE POLICY COMMUNITY

[1]Isaiah Litvak, 'The Lobbying Strategies of Business Interest Groups', in James D. Fleck and Isaiah A. Litvak (eds), *Business Can Succeed! Understanding the Political Environment* (Toronto, 1984), 65-75, 70. See also W.T. Stanbury, *Business-Government Relations in Canada* (Toronto, 1986), ch. 12.

[2]Litvak, 'Lobbying Strategies of Business Interest Groups', 70.

[3]Goldfarb Associates, 'A Public Education and Communications Strategy for the Nuclear Industry in Canada' (mimeo, Aug. 1987), 3, 11.

[4]Canadian Nuclear Association, 'Public Information Program. 1987-1988 Business Plan' (mimeo, n.d.), 8.

[5]*Globe and Mail*, 21 March 1991.

[6]See Donald Barry.

[7]See, for example, *Globe and Mail*, 9 Feb. 1991.

[8]*Globe and Mail*, 8, 9 April 1991.

[9]As a lobbyist put it during the campaign to ensure continuation of freight subsidies in the

Maritimes: 'Politicians respond to what the media reveals.' Moncton *Times Transcript*, 3 June 1983.

[10]*Financial Post*, 10 Dec. 1983. Thorburn attributes the paucity of these briefs to business conviction that the Trudeau government was unfriendly to business and uninterested in following its advice. Aware of the growing likelihood of a Liberal defeat in the next election, business preferred to direct its attention to influencing the likely winners. Hugh G. Thorburn, *Interest Groups in the Canadian Federal System* (Toronto, 1985), 114.

[11]James Gillies and Jean Pigott, 'Participation in the Legislative Process', and J. Hugh Faulkner, 'Pressuring the Executive', *Canadian Public Administration* 25 (1982) 2, 254-64 and 240-54.

[12]The Atlantic Provinces Economic Council first sponsored a meeting with Atlantic area MPs in 1975 (Halifax *Chronicle-Herald*, 7 March 1975); Faulkner credits the Quebec caucus with particular influence during the Trudeau years. (See 'Pressuring the Executive', 244.) Forbes reports a particularly close liaison between the Canadian Dairy Commission and the Liberal caucus, (J.D. Forbes, 'Institutions and Interest Groups in the Canadian Food System Policy Process' [Ottawa, 1982], 63).

[13]See J. Pigott and G. Drewry, 'Parliament and hanging: further episodes in an undying saga', *Parliamentary Affairs* 27 (1974) 3, 251-61.

[14]J.D. Stewart, *British Pressure Groups: Their Role in Relation to the House of Commons* (Oxford, 1958), 152-204.

[15]'. . . the Senate has had considerable impact upon the Investment Companies Act, the Income Tax Act, and the Foreign Investments Act. . . . Salter Hayden, Chairman of the Senate's Banking and Commerce Committee, gives . . . a very simple explanation of how senators successfully perform business review. These tactics comprise the essential components of lobbying from within. First, senators hear grievances from the business community members who feel that civil servants and Cabinet Ministers have ignored them. Then, senators astutely wield their corporate reputations through the powerful Banking Committee to persuade the department in charge of a bill that certain "technical" changes must be made within it. If the department's Minister finds the case convincing, he will arrange for the government to sponsor amendments that would accommodate the senators' concerns. Cumulatively "technical" changes often water down such bills, and this result is the aim of lobbying from within.' Colin Campbell, *The Canadian Senate: A Lobby from Within* (Toronto, 1978), 69.

[16]However, it is quite common for MPs to present the views of particular groups to the House. See, for example, the presentation of the case of the Canadian Aviation Fellowship during the dispute of bilingual air traffic control. *Hansard*, 12 July 1977, 7613.

[17]*Financial Post*, 8 October 1983. The Canadian House at times actively discourages 'lobbying' by members. In 1983, it was reported that 'an outspoken group of antinuclear MPs and Senators' had been removed from the list of parliamentary associations eligible for travel and study funds. The chair, a Conservative, and a Liberal member of the Canadian Parliamentarians for World Order, charged that the government was punishing the group for taking 'unpopular stands with the government'. The Speaker, Madame Sauvé, would not allow the matter to be raised in the House, and a spokesperson for the Parliamentary Relations Secretariat told the press that a Commons-Senate committee had decided to withdraw funding because the association 'too strongly resembled a lobby group'. Kingston *Whig-Standard*, 16 March 1983.

[18]*Globe and Mail*, 30 Aug. 1984.

[19]R. Lewis, 'The hidden persuaders', *Maclean's* 13 June 1977, quoted in David MacDonald, 'The Art of the State: Resisting Pressure Group Demands in Canada'. Dalhousie University. Student Paper, 1984. The influence of the gun lobby again became an issue in 1991 when the Minister of Justice, Kim Campbell, proposed gun control legislation that critics considered inadequate. See *Globe and Mail* 31 May and 1 June 1991.

[20]Kristian S. Palda, 'The Election Act and Voter Information', *Canadian Public Policy* XI

(1985) 3, 533-43, and Janet Hiebert, 'Fair Elections and Freedom of Expression Under the Charter', *Journal of Canadian Studies* 24 (1989-90) 4, 72-86. In footnote 10 Hiebert lists several abuses.

[21] *Globe and Mail* 17 July 1984. See also Hiebert, 'Fair Elections and Freedom of Expression'.

[22] Ibid.

[23] *Globe and Mail*, 27 June 1984, and *Maclean's*, 9 July 1984.

[24] *Maclean's*, 9 July 1984.

[25] National Citizens' Coalition Inc. and Brown v. A-G of Canada, *Western Weekly Reports* (1984) 5, 436, at 453.

[26] The *Globe and Mail* (28 June 1984) felt the government would be foolish to enforce the Act: 'The coming general election should be fought by all interested parties and not artificially restricted to the registered parties, the candidates and those voices which meet with their gracious approval.' Other press comment is cited by Hiebert.

[27] Halifax *Mail-Star*, 19 July 1984.

[28] Theodore J. Eismeier and Philip H. Pollock III, *Business, Money, and the Rise of Corporate PACs in American Elections* (N.Y., 1988), ch. 5.

[29] 'Political Action Committees', *Maclean's*, 14 May 1984. Academic accounts are found in M. Margaret Conway, 'PACs, the New Politics and Congressional Campaigns', in Allan J. Cigler and Burdett A. Loomis (eds), *Interest Group Politics* (Washington, 1983), 126-45; Graham Wootton, *Interest Groups: Policy and Politics in America* (Englewood Cliffs, N.J., 1985); and Eismeier and Pollock, *Business, Money, and the Rise of Corporate PACs*.

[30] Hiebert, 'Fair Elections and Freedom of Expression', 81. The Commissioner's position lends support to the critics of the amendment who have argued that a constraint on advertising for or against a party also constrains debate over issues.

[31] Eismeier and Pollock, *Business, Money, and the Rise of Corporate PACs*, 103.

[32] Richard Simeon, *Federal-Provincial Diplomacy: The Making of Recent Policy in Canada* (Toronto, 1973), 144-5, 280-3. Simeon argues that the processes of intergovernmental negotiations limit the number and scope of participants. Other studies offer evidence that interest groups can influence federal-provincial diplomacy. We have already discussed the success Maritime business interest groups have had in using provincial governments to lobby on their behalf for transportation subsidies. Similar cases are found in the evolution of the Crow Rate.(See Roger Gibbins, *Prairie Politics and Society: Regionalism in Decline* [Toronto, 1980], 84-91; and Barry Wilson, *Beyond the Harvest: Canadian Grain at the Crossroads* [Saskatoon, 1981] and *Farming the System* [Saskatoon, 1990], ch. 11.) Bucovetsky shows that by persuading key provinces that their economies would suffer if tax reforms proposed by the Trudeau government were adopted, the mining industry, particularly the oil lobby, brought about major revisions in the proposals. (Bucovetsky, 'The Mining Industry and the Great Tax Reform Debate'.) Other examples of the oil lobby's exploitation of differences between Ottawa and the provinces are well documented (Peter Foster, *The Blue-Eyed Sheiks: The Canadian Oil Establishment* [Don Mills, Ontario, 1979] and *The Sorcerer's Apprentice* [Toronto, 1982]; G. Bruce Doern and Glen Toner, *The Politics of Energy: The Development and Implementation of the NEP* [Toronto, 1985].)

[33] Hugh G. Thorburn, *Interest Groups in the Canadian Federal System* (Toronto, 1985), 60-8, 118, 119.

[34] Ibid., 53-4, 116.

[35] Coleman, *Business and Politics*, 245, 248, and Coleman and Henry J. Jacek, 'Capitalists, Collective Action and Regionalism', in Coleman and Jacek (eds), *Regionalism, Business Interests and Public Policy* (London, 1989), 1-13, 9.

[36] Thorburn, *Interest Groups in the Canadian Federal System*, 116.

[37] 'A Perspective on Canadian Mining: Interview with C. George Miller', *CRS Perspectives*, March 1985. In 1970, according to Gordon Robertson, there were nine meetings of the federal government and all the provinces that permitted or involved the attendance of outside groups. See 'The Changing Role of the Privy Council Office', *Canadian Public*

Administration XIV (1971), 487-508, at 497. See also D.V. Smiley, *Canada in Question: Federalism in the Seventies* (Toronto, 1976) 58.

[38]*Globe and Mail*, 4 April 1991.

[39]David Lies and James Lawrence, 'Red Tape and Fine Cheddar', *Harrowsmith* 3 (1978) 3.

[40]Coleman, *Business and Politics*, 260.

[41]See Faulkner, 'Pressuring the Executive', 243-4; Pross, 'Governing Under Pressure: Summary of Discussions,' 175-6; Aucoin, 'Pressure Groups and Recent Changes in the Policy-Making Process', 175-7, 183, 185.

[42]Thorburn, *Interest Groups in the Canadian Federal System*, 119.

[43]Alan C. Cairns, 'The Governments and Societies of Canadian Federalism', *Canadian Journal of Political Science* X (1977) 4, 695-725, 706.

[44]See A. Paul Pross and Susan MacCorquodale, *Economic Resurgence and the Constitutional Agenda: The Case of the East Coast Fisheries* (Kingston, Ontario, 1987).

[45]The Council sponsored a major study of the constitutional problems under the direction of Ronald L. Watts and used it as the focal point of an influential symposium held in January, 1991. See The Council, 'Symposium on Canada's Constitutional Options', 16 Jan. 1991.The symposium papers were later edited by Ronald L. Watts and Douglas M. Brown and published under the title *Options for a New Canada* (Toronto, 1991).

[46]See J. Stefan Dupre, 'Canadian constitutionalism and the sequel to the Meech Lake/Langevin accord', in D.P. Shugarman and R. Whitaker (eds), *Federalism and Political Community* (Peterborough, 1989); Alan C. Cairns, 'Citizens (outsiders) and governments (insiders) in constitution-making: The case of Meech Lake', *Canadian Public Policy* XIV (1988); and Jennifer Smith, 'Representation and constitutional reform in Canada', in David E. Smith and John C. Courtney (eds), *After Meech Lake* (Saskatoon, 1991), 69-82.

[47]For a succinct overview of Canadian groups active regularly in the foreign policy field, see Elizabeth Riddell-Dixon, *The Domestic Mosaic: Domestic Groups and Canadian Foreign Policy* (Toronto, 1985).

[48]An analysis of registrations under the US Foreign Agents Registration Act shows that between 1981 and 1986 US lobbyists who had been senior government officials registered 24 separate undertakings on behalf of Canadian interests. On 12 occasions the concerned interests were corporations; on 4, a pressure group; on 5, the Government of Canada; on 2, the Government of Manitoba and on 1, the Government of Ontario. The issues tackled ranged from corporate concerns to major tariff disputes, such as the soft-wood lumber dispute, to acid rain (US General Accounting Office. *Briefing Report to Representative Marcy Kaptur, Representative Howard Wolpe: Foreign Representation — Former High-Level Officials Representing Foreign Interests* [Washington, July 1986]). Since these figures refer only to lobbying activities of former senior officials — such as Thomas Donnelly and Michael Deaver — they represent only a few of the lobbying undertakings conducted by Canadian interests in Washington during the period.

[49]*Globe and Mail*, 12 Feb. 1991.

[50]For example, in October 1982 the President of the Canadian Export Association, warning that 'we are no longer living in a world of boy scouts', urged Canadian negotiators to follow closely the needs of exporters in order to take advantage of those opportunities that are available elsewhere. *Le Devoir*, 20 October 1982.

[51]See Riddell-Dixon, *The Domestic Mosaic*, 45-47; and Jorgen Dahlie and Tissa Fernando (eds), *Ethnicity, Power and Politics in Canada* (Toronto, 1981).

[52]*Globe and Mail*, 19 Feb. 1991. An account of the work of the Canadian Coalition on Acid Rain is to be found the House of Commons. Standing Committee on Elections Privileges and Procedure. *Minutes of Proceedings*, 27 May 1986. (Ottawa, 1986), 12:3-30. See also Jurgen Schmandt, Roderick Hilliard, and Judith Clarkson (eds), *Acid Rain and Friendly Neighbours: The Policy Dispute Between Canada and the United States* (Durham, N.C., 1988), which in ch. 9 ('Supporting Structures for Resolving Environmental Disputes among Friendly Neighbors' by Andrew Morriss) discusses at length the difficulties faced by foreign

interest groups in lobbying in Canada. Countervailing pressure was attempted by American interests when they sought an alliance with Canadian industry to oppose Canada's position. At least one business group, the Canadian Chamber of Commerce, rejected the proposal. Kingston *Whig-Standard* 14, 15 Feb. 1983.

[53]*Financial Post*, 3 December 1983. See also Alan Herscovici, *Second Nature: The Animal Rights Controversy* (Toronto, 1985).

[54]*Globe and Mail*, 27 Feb. 1988 and 17 Oct. 1990.

[55]Halifax *Mail-Star*, 30 Dec. 1983.

[56]See *Globe and Mail*, 24 July and 22 Nov. 1990.

[57]For example, a major Halifax dispute over the destruction of an older building and modification of the city plan to permit construction of a high-rise condominium. See 'Halifax Condo Battle Heads for the Courts', *Globe and Mail*, 8 May 1984; and 'NS Court Ruling Bolsters Opponents of Halifax Project' *Globe and Mail*, 8 Oct. 1984; and 'To Build or Not to Build? High Rise Splits Citizens', *Globe and Mail*, 27 July 1985.

[58]John Swaigen, *How to Fight for What's Right: The Citizen's Guide to Public Interest Law* (Toronto, 1981), 131-2.

[59]See Peter Cumming, *Nova Scotia's Herbicide Case: A Court Diary* (Gabarus, N.S., 1983); *Between the Issues: The Newsletter of the Ecology Action Centre*, various issues, 1983; the Halifax *Chronicle-Herald*, 16 Sept. 1983, 3 Oct. 1983, 8 Oct. 1983, 10 Dec. 1983; and the *Globe and Mail*, 17 Sept. 1983. A film of the case, *Herbicide Trials*, has been issued by the National Film Board.

[60]A. Anne McLellan, 'Legal implications of the "persons" case', *Constitutional Forum* 1 (1989) 1, 11-14, 13. On the other hand government officials have at times assisted concerned citizens in undertaking private prosecution. See Kernaghan Webb, 'Taking matters into their own hands: The role of the citizen in Canadian pollution control enforcement', *McGill Law Journal* 36 (1991).

[61]Swaigen, *How to Fight for What's Right*, 3.

[62]Ibid., 12-17.

[63]Stephen Bindman, 'Door opens: Supreme Court lets groups intervene in cases', Ottawa *Citizen,* 9 March 1991. Bindman lists some 24 groups intervening in recent Supreme Court cases.

[64]H. Patrick Glenn, 'Class Actions in Ontario and Quebec', *Canadian Bar Review* 62 (1984) 3, 247-77, 277.

[65]Swaigen, *How to Fight for What's Right*, 133.

CHAPTER 8. THE INTERIOR LIFE OF GROUPS

[1]David Truman, *The Process of Government* (N.Y., 1964) *passim*, but particularly 56-62.

[2]V.O. Key, *Parties, Pressure Groups and Politics* (N.Y., 1958).

[3]Mancur Olson, *The Logic of Collective Action* (Cambridge, MA, 1971), 132-41.

[4]Olson, *The Logic of Collective Action*, 133.

[5]Terry M. Moe, *The Organization of Interests* (Chicago, 1980), 28.

[6]W.D. Coleman and H.J. Jacek, 'The Political Organization of the Chemical Industry in Canada'. Paper. CPSA. 1981, 62. It is interesting to note that the Canadian Manufacturers' Association was offering additional incentives to members in the 1920s and 1930s. See S.D. Clark, *The Canadian Manufacturers' Association* (Toronto, 1939), 40-63.

[7]Olson, *The Logic of Collective Action*, 133.

[8]Olson, *The Logic of Collective Action*, ch. 1 and 133-4.

[9]Helen Jones Dawson, 'The Consumers' Association of Canada', *Canadian Public Administration* VI (1963) 1, 92-118, 96.

[10]See, for example, Jonah Goldstein, 'Public Interest Groups and Public Policy: The Case of the Consumers' Association of Canada', *Canadian Journal of Political Science* 12 (1979) 1, 137-55.

[11]See *TransAction*, Transport 2000's quarterly publication.

[12]See Moe, *The Organization of Interests*, 16-19, 30-4 (on the effect of imperfect information), and 119-21 (on non-economic incentives to participate).

[13]Moe, *The Organization of Interests*, 32.

[14]Or, as James Q. Wilson suggests, individuals are moved by guilt to join certain types of organizations. *Political Organizations* (N.Y., 1973), 25.

[15]This view is supported by James N. Rosenau's survey of some 4,600 members of Americans for Democratic Action and reported in *Citizenship Between Elections* (N.Y.: 1974).

[16]J.A. Corry, remarks to a conference on 'Citizen Involvement in Government: The Art of the Possible', sponsored by the Institute for Research on Public Policy and the Government Studies Programme, Dalhousie University, 1979. The remarks are elaborated in the published version of Dr Corry's talk, entitled 'Sovereign People or Sovereign Governments', in H.V. Kroeker (ed.) *Sovereign People or Sovereign Governments* (Montreal, 1981), 3-13, especially 10-13.

[17]Léon Dion, 'Participating in the Political Process', *Queen's Quarterly* LXXV (1968) 3, 433.

[18]A. Holleaux, 'Le phénomène associatif', *Revue française d'administration publique* 8 (1978), 683-727, 701-2.

[19]J. Meynaud, *Nouvelles études sur les groupes de pression en France* (Paris, 1962), 24-6.

[20]For a fascinating discussion of the use of substantive and process knowledge see Guy Benveniste, *The Politics of Expertise* (Berkeley, CA, 1972).

[21]Ian Helliwell, 'The National Energy Board's 1974-75 Natural Gas Supply Hearings', *Canadian Public Policy* 1 (1973) 2, 415-25.

[22]Coleman and Jacek, 'Chemical Industry in Canada', 37.

[23]Larry Smith, 'Getting Your Way With a Bureaucrat', *Canadian Business*, Sept. 1980, 104.

[24]John F. Bulloch, 'A View From a Special Interest Group' in Daniel L. Bon, *Lobbying: A Right? A Necessity? A Danger?* (Ottawa: Conference Board of Canada, 1981), 8.

[25]Bulloch, 'A View From a Special Interest Group', 12.

[26]Smith, 'Getting Your Way . . .'

[27]Bulloch, 'A View From a Special Interest Group', 13.

[28]D.A. Chant, 'Pollution Probe: Fighting Polluters With Their Own Weapons', in A.P. Pross, *Pressure Group Behaviour in Canadian Politics* (Toronto, 1975), 61-8.

[29]Chant, 'Pollution Probe', 64.

[30]David Hoffman, 'Interacting With Government: The General Public and Interest Groups', in Donald MacDonald (ed.), *Politics in Ontario* (Toronto, 1975) 275-92, at 288-9.

[31]Quoted in A.P. Pross, 'Governing Under Pressure: The Special Interest Groups — Summary of Discussion', in Pross (ed.), *Governing Under Pressure: The Special Interest Groups — 14th National Seminar, Institute of Public Administration of Canada* (Toronto: The Institute, 1982), 171-83, at 180.

[32]Coleman and Jacek, 'The Chemical Industry in Canada . . .', 27, 31, and 37.

[33]Ibid.

[34]For an excellent discussion of the two concepts as they relate to pressure groups, see D. Kwavnick, *Organized Labour and Pressure Politics* (Montreal, 1972), 3-25.

[35]David Kwavnick, 'Pressure Group Demands and the Struggle for Organizational Status: The Case of Organized Labour in Canada', *Canadian Journal of Political Science*, III (1970) 1, 56-72, 58.

[36]Sally M. Weaver, 'The Joint Cabinet Committee/National Indian Brotherhood Committee: A

Unique Experiment in Pressure Group Relations', *Canadian Public Administration* 25 (1982) 2, 211-39, at 227-9.

[37]Kwavnick, *Organized Labour and Pressure Politics*, 73-4.

[38]Kell Antoft, 'The Role of Non-Governmental Agencies in the Provincial-Municipal Relationship in Nova Scotia', Typescript. n.d.

[39]W.T. Stanbury, *Business-Government Relations in Canada* (Toronto, 1986), 569-79.

[40]Memo. I. Mumford to R. Veilleux. Atomic Energy of Canada Ltd, 12 Jan. 1988, and data base.

[41]See Donald Barry, 'Interest Groups in the Foreign Policy Process', in Pross, *Pressure Group Behaviour...* , 117-47, at 125-32.

[42]See Cathy Munroe and Jim Stewart, *Fishermen's Organizations in Nova Scotia: The Potential for Unification* (Halifax, 1981), 131.

[43]Holleaux, 'Le phénomène associatif', 696; *Le Monde*, 28 Jan. and 12 Dec. 1982.

[44]For a review of non-financial support provided to groups by government, see National Advisory Council on Voluntary Action, *People in Action: Report to the Government of Canada* (Ottawa, 1977), 156-9 and 253-72.

[45] In Peter Finkle, Kernaghan Webb, William T. Stanbury, and A. Paul Pross, *Federal Government Relations with Interest Groups: A Reconsideration* (Ottawa: forthcoming), 129, 131.

[46]Consumer and Corporate Affairs, *Applicant's Guide — Grants and Contributions Program 1991-92* (Ottawa, 1990).

[47]Philip L. Bryden, 'Public Interest Intervention in the Courts', *Canadian Bar Review* 60 (1987), 3, 390-528. Ontario has in recent years been particularly supportive of interventions by public interest groups. The Ontario Intervenor Funding Project Act, 1988 S.O. 199, c. 71 provides support for groups wishing to intervene in hearings of regulatory boards on matters of general public interest. (See J. Jeffery, 'Ontario's Intervenor Funding Project Act', *Canadian Journal of Administrative Law and Practice* 3 [1990], 69-80.) In the environmental field the Ontario Environmental Assessment Board in 1990 directed Ontario Hydro to provide $21.5 million in funding to 28 groups and one person to support the preparation of briefs commenting on the corporation's 25-year plan to spend $85 billion on expansion of its generating capacity. *Globe and Mail*, 26 Dec. 1990.

[48]Finkle *et al.*, *Federal Government Relations with Interest Groups*, Table 7-3, 132. Categories of groups, the amount allocated to each category, and the estimated number of recipient groups were: bilingualism-related, $1,631,000 (6); consumer interests, $1,724,000 (6); environmental, $2,112,000 (16); health, $5,654,000 (46); legal/human relations, $4,505,000 (23); parliamentary associations, $1,157,000 (17); and unity, $6,171,000.

[49]In 1983, for example, the Executive Director of the Social Science and Humanities Research Council of Canada noted that Council had supported the two principal learned societies in the humanities (Canadian Federation for the Humanities) and the social sciences (Social Science Federation of Canada) at a rate varying between 62.7% and 80.9% of budget. (*Council Update*, Summer 1983, 8). SSHRCC support for learned societies reached $1.8 million in 1983-84, but declined to $1.5 million in 1984-85. (*Five-year Plan for Financing Research in the Social Sciences and the Humanities, 1985-1990* [Ottawa: The Council, 1985], 10.)

[50]Coleman and Jacek, 'The Chemical Industry in Canada...', 42.

[51]See especially the *Report* of the Auditor General for 1990, ch. 10: 'Charities, Non-Profit Organizations and the Income Tax Act', and the House of Commons Standing Committee on the Public Accounts, *Minutes of Proceedings and Evidence* (Ottawa, 1990), 25 April 1990.

[52]As in the cuts to grants and contributions announced in the 1991 budget speech. See *Toronto Star*, 27 Feb. 1991.

[53]For the reaction of one affected group, the National Action Committee on the Status of Women, see 'Budget Victims Fight Back', *Winnipeg Free Press* 26 March 1991. See also Finkle *et al.*, *Federal Government Relations with Interest Groups*, 140-9. See also Michele Landsberg, 'Tory Hit List Has Groups Fearing Fate', *Toronto Star*, 27 April 1991.

[54]*People in Action*; and Program Evaluation Directorate, Secretary of State, *A Framework for*

Cross-Sectoral Evaluation of Core Funding in the Secretary of State (Ottawa, 1986) cited in Phillips, 'How Ottawa Blends: Shifting Government Relationships with Interest Groups', in Frances Abele (ed.) *How Ottawa Spends 1991-92: The Politics of Fragmentation* (Ottawa, 1991), 183-213.

[55] National Advisory Council on Voluntary Action, *People in Action*, 97.

[56] Ibid.

[57] Donald V. Smiley, 'The Managed Mosaic', in V. Nelles and A. Rotstein, *Nationalism or Local Control* (Toronto, 1973), 73.

[58] Munroe and Stewart, *Fishermen's Organizations in Nova Scotia*, 81-92.

[59] 'L'Etat et les groupes d'intérêts', *Canadian Public Administration* 25 (1982) 2, 265-77, 268.

[60] Quoted in Bon, *Lobbying: A Right?* ... , 14.

[61] Phillips, 'How Ottawa Blends'.

[62] See Jennifer Smith, 'Representation and constitutional reform in Canada', in John Courtney, Peter MacKinnon and David E. Smith (eds), *After Meech Lake: Lessons for the Future* (Saskatoon, 1991).

[63] *People in Action*, 161.

[64] Phillips, 'How Ottawa Blends', 201, and Sylvia Bashevkin, 'Free Trade and Canadian Feminism: The Case of the National Action Committee on the Status of Women', *Canadian Public Policy* xv (1989) 4, 363-75.

[65] Phillips, 'How Ottawa Blends', 203.

[66] This is a conundrum to which there is no solution. Even very broadly representative groups must themselves be represented by a few leaders who in turn must often express views and take positions without having sought full discussion in and endorsement of the membership at large. For a discussion of this point, see Liora Salter and Debra Slaco, *Public Inquiries in Canada* (Ottawa: Science Council of Canada, 1981), 184.

[67] The Canadian Library Association, for example, derives approximately half of its revenue from the sale of publications. (Canadian Library Association. *The 1979-80 Revised Members' Handbook and Directory* [Ottawa: CLA, 1979], 11.)

[68] Dawson, 'The Consumers' Association of Canada', 99.

[69] N.J. Lawrie, *The Canadian Construction Association* (Toronto: University of Toronto. PhD Thesis, 1976), 165. A similar problem of distance between the Canadian Federation of Agriculture and its individual members led to the creation of the National Farmers' Union in the 1930s. See Helen Jones Dawson, 'An Interest Group: The Canadian Federation of Agriculture', *Canadian Public Administration* iii (1960) 2, 134-49 and 'Relations Between Farm Organizations and the Civil Service in Canada and Great Britain', *Canadian Public Administration* x (1967) 4, 450-71.

[70] A. Paul Pross, 'Mobilizing Regional Concern: freight rates and political learning in the Canadian Maritimes', in William D. Coleman and Henry J. Jacek, *Regionalism, Business Interests and Public Policy* (London, 1989), 173-200.

[71] The Canadian Library Association *1986 Revised Members Handbook and Directory* (Ottawa, 1986) lists standing committees, co-ordinating groups, and special interest groups concerned with matters as diverse as the promotion of literacy, the law of copyright, association publications, professional education, and the bringing of library services to special groups.

[72] William D. Coleman, *Business and Politics* (Montreal, 1988), ch. 8.

[73] See, for example, 'The Nuts and Bolts of Association Management', in *Canadian Associations*, March 1985, 19-34; Moe's discussion of the influence of staff on group goals, *The Organization of Interests*, 98-9; and Jeffrey M. Berry's observations of the role of staff in American public interest groups: *Lobbying for the People: The Political Behaviour of Public Interest Groups* (Princeton, 1977).

[74] See, for example, David Kwavnick, 'Pressure Group Demands and Organizational Objectives: The CNTU, the Lapalme Affair, and National Bargaining Units', *Canadian Journal of Political Science* vi (1973) 4, 582-601.

[75] Brian Land (ed.), *Directory of Associations In Canada* (Toronto, 1991).

CHAPTER 9. MODELS OF INTEREST REPRESENTATION: CORPORATISM, PLURALISM, AND POST-PLURALISM

[1]The Maritime Rights debate discussed in Chapter 5 illustrates the fact that interest groups, even sub-government members, are not always the first to organize issues out of politics; they are often forced out of politics by party leaders. At the turn of the century the Prairies and the Maritimes were equally concerned about the effects of federal transportation policy on their regional economies. Unfortunately the remedies they proposed and the claims they made on the policy system brought the two regions into conflict with one another, so much so that the fledgling Progressive Party was unable to hold Maritime support. The Conservatives and Liberals were no more effective in dealing with the conflict internally. They, however, could count on the inertia of the traditional vote. Certain that ultimately Maritimers would remain loyal to the established parties, the Liberals, in particular, set aside demands from that region in favour of appeasing the more volatile West and eliminating the rival Progressives. Maritimers found themselves in a paradoxical situation. Unable to articulate their demands through the party system, they turned to interest groups and successfully established several that were effective in bringing the issue to national attention.

[2]J. Hugh Faulkner, 'Pressuring the Executive', *Canadian Public Administration* 25 (1982) 2, 240-54.

[3]See Law Reform Commission, *Parliament and Administrative Agencies* (Ottawa: The Commission. Administrative Law Series, 1982); and Paul G. Thomas, 'Administrative law reform: legal versus political controls on administrative discretion', *Canadian Public Administration* 27 (1984) 1, 120-8; Law Reform Commission, 'Working Paper on Independent Administrative Agencies' (Ottawa, 1980 Working Paper No. 25); and Philip Anisman, *A Catalogue of Discretionary Powers in the Revised Statutes of Canada, 1970* (Ottawa, 1975), 33-4.

[4]See, for example, Leslie T. Macdonald, 'Taxing Comprehensive Income: Power and Participation in Canadian Politics, 1962-1972', PhD thesis (Carleton University, 1985); and Rianne Mahon, 'Canadian Public Policy: The Unequal Structure of Representation', in Leo Panitch (ed.), *The Canadian State: Political Economy and Political Power* (Toronto, 1977), 164-98, and *The Politics of Industrial Restructuring: Canadian Textiles* (Toronto, 1984).

[5]For example, J. Cheverny, 'Le mode autoritaire de l'anarchie', *Esprit*, janvier 1970; F. Bloch-Lainie, 'Les associations comme contre-pouvoirs', *Pouvoirs* 7 (1978), 65.

[6]As in Dominique Clift, 'L'Etat et les groupes d'intérêts: perspectives d'avenir', *Canadian Public Administration* 25 (1982) 2, 265-78. The programs of privatization, de-regulation, and austerity in public services followed by most Canadian governments during the late 1980s should be seen as attempts to stifle *dirigisme*, as well as attempts to address the problems caused by high government spending deficits.

[7]See Linn A. Hammergran, 'Corporatism in Latin American Politics: A Re-examination of the Unique Tradition', *Comparative Politics* 9 (1977) 4, 443-63; Les Metcalfe and Will McQuillan, 'Corporatism or Industrial Democracy?', *Political Studies* XXVII (1979) 2, 266-82; and Leo Panitch, 'Corporatism in Canada?', in Richard Schultz, Orest M. Kruhlak, and John C. Terry, *The Canadian Political Process* (Toronto, 1979), 53-72; Leo Panitch, 'Recent Theorizations of Corporatism', *British Journal of Sociology* XXXI (1980) 2, 159-88; Jordan, 'Pluralistic Corporatisms and Corporate Pluralism'; Philippe C. Schmitter and Gerhard Lehmbruch (eds), *Trends Toward Corporatist Intermediation* (Beverly Hills, 1979); G. David Garson, *Group Theories of Politics* (Beverly Hills, 1978); and John R. Freeman, *Democracy and Markets: The Politics of Mixed Economies* (Ithaca, N.Y., 1989).

[8]Philippe C. Schmitter, 'Still the Century of Corporatism?', in Schmitter and Lehmbruch (eds), *Trends Toward Corporatist Intermediation*, 7-52, 13.

[9]Philippe C. Schmitter, 'Interest intermediation and regime governability', in S. Berger (ed.), *Organizing Interests in Western Europe* (Cambridge, 1981), 287-331, at 292.

[10]Léon Dion, *Société et Politique* (Québec, 1971) vol. 1, 198. See also Garson, *Group Theories*

of Politics, ch. 2, 'Pluralist, Statist and Corporatist Elements in the Emergence of Group Theories'.

[11]Schmitter, 'Interest intermediation and regime governability', 213, 292.

[12]Quoted in Leo Panitch, 'Corporatism in Canada?' in Richard Schultz, Orest M. Kruhlak, and John C. Terry, *The Canadian Political Process* (Toronto, 1979), 53-72, 55.

[13]Panitch, 'Corporatism in Canada?', 55.

[14]Ibid.

[15]See also J.I. Gow, 'L'histoire de l'administration publique québécoise', *Recherches sociographiques* XVI (1975) 3, 385. Gow points out that these unions soon moved away from church domination and presumably from the concepts associated with church sponsorship.

[16]Panitch, 'Corporatism in Canada?', 57.

[17]It might also be argued that on attaining power the proponents of corporatism found that they could achieve their ends by creating (informal) limited arrangements that were not explicitly corporatist. Thus Duplessis was able to co-opt union leaders by appointing them to boards, commissions, and so on. See Herbert F. Quinn, 'Quebec: Corruption under Duplessis', in K. M. Gibbon and D. C. Rowat, *Political Corruption in Canada* (Ottawa, 1976), 67-81.

[18]Panitch, 'Corporatism in Canada?', 63-4.

[19]Ibid., 64.

[20]Ibid.

[21]William D. Coleman and Henry J. Jacek, 'The Political Organization of the Chemical Industry in Canada'. Paper. Canadian Political Science Association, 1981, 60.

[22]Panitch, 'Corporatism in Canada', 61.

[23]Douglas Brown, Julia Eastman with Ian Robinson, *The Limits of Consultation: A Debate Among Ottawa, the Provinces and the Private Sector on an Industrial Strategy* (Kingston and Ottawa, 1981), 176.

[24]Brown *et al.*, *The Limits of Consultation*, 176.

[25]Ibid.

[26]Ibid., 178.

[27]Ibid., 179.

[28]*Le Devoir*, 22 Oct. 1982.

[29]Brown *et al.*, *The Limits of Consultation*, 178.

[30]William D. Coleman, *Business and Politics* (Montreal, 1988), 234-7.

[31]Brown *et al.*, *The Limits of Consultation*, 188; 'Bad News, Bad Marks: Tory Summit', Vancouver *Sun* 22 March 1985; 'Conference on Economy Called Waste', *Globe and Mail*, 22 March 1985; 'Deep Rift Between Business and Labour Revealed as Economic Talks Begin', *Globe and Mail* 23 March 1985; 'Agreement Eludes Ottawa', *Winnipeg Free Press*, 24 March 1985.

[32]M.M. Atkinson and William D. Coleman, *The State, Business and Industrial Change in Canada* (Toronto, 1989), 185-96.

[33]Each of these institutional changes is documented in a variety of articles, reports, and book-length studies. Perhaps the two most useful places in which to find a broad perspective on them are the annual reviews of *How Ottawa Spends* (published by the School of Public Administration at Carleton University) and the journal *Canadian Public Administration*. The argument that the central policy structures had promoted the 1970s interest in corporatism is presented in the first edition of *Group Politics and Public Policy*, 220-4.

[34]See William D. Coleman and Grace Skogstad, *Policy Communities and Public Policy in Canada* (Toronto, 1990), and Atkinson and Coleman, *The State, Business and Industrial Change* (Toronto, 1989).

[35]This view is most clearly expressed in Earl Latham, *The Group Basis of Politics* (N.Y., 1965), but see also David B. Truman, *The Governmental Process: Political Interests and Public Opinion* (N.Y., 1951). G. David Garson, *Group Theories of Politics* (Beverly Hills, 1978) presents a useful guide to the pluralist debate.

[36]R.M. MacIver, *The Web of Government* (N.Y., 1947), 220-1.

[37]Mancur Olson, *The Logic of Collective Action* (Cambridge, MA: Harvard University Press, 1971), 14.

[38]M. Crenson, 'Non-issues in City Politics: The case of air pollution', in M. Surkin and A. Wolfe, *An End to Political Science* (N.Y., 1970), 144-66, 149.

[39]Theodore Lowi, *The End of Liberalism* (N.Y., 1969).

[40]Robert H. Salisbury, 'An Exchange Theory of Interest Groups', in Salisbury (ed.), *Interest Group Politics in America* (N.Y., 1970), 32-6. In a more recent publication, however, Salisbury notes that a new understanding of American interest groups will 'systematically distinguish institution-based interest activity from that deriving support from individual citizens, and it will note the former's greater staying power and long-term effectiveness in Washington'. ('Interest Groups: Toward a New Understanding', in Allan J. Cigler and Burdett A. Loomis [eds], *Interest Group Politics* [Washington, 1983], 354-69, 365.)

[41]See Olson's *The Logic of Collective Action*.

[42]Salisbury, 'An Exchange Theory of Interest Groups', 33-4.

[43]Eric A. Nordlinger, *On the Autonomy of the State* (Cambridge, MA, 1981), and Peter B. Evans, Dietrich Rueschemeyer, and Theda Skocpol (eds), *Bringing the State Back In* (Cambridge, 1985).

[44]Schattschneider, *The Semi-Sovereign People* (N.Y., 1960), 70.

[45]Ibid., 68.

[46]Schattschneider, *Party Government* (N.Y., 1962), 33.

[47]Schattschneider, *The Semi-Sovereign People*, 31. See also Salisbury, *An Exchange Theory*; Crenson, *Non-issues in City Politics*; and Olson, *The Logic of Collective Action*.

[48]Thus an effort is made to ensure that conflict remains 'private'. It is 'taken into the public arena precisely because someone wants to make certain that the power ratio among the private interest most immediately involved shall not prevail'. (Schattschneider, *The Semi-Sovereign People*, 38.) In other words, the resort to politics is a resort to extreme measures.

[49]Garson, *Group Theories of Politics*, 126-7. See also P. Bachrach and M. Baratz, 'Two Faces of Power', *American Political Science Review* 56 (1962) 4, 947-52, and 'Decisions and Non-decisions: An analytical framework' *American Political Science Review* 57 (1963) 3, 632-42. David Kwavnick, after presenting several striking Canadian illustrations, concludes that 'once the views of the interest groups are known the proverbial timidity inherent in bureaucratic organization is their most trustworthy ally. The anticipated representation is among the most powerful tools available to interest groups in influencing the policy advice that a minister will receive from his officials.' *Organized Labour and Pressure Politics* (Montreal, 1972), 182.

[50]Randall B. Ripley, and Grace A. Franklin, *Congress, the Bureaucracy and Public Policy* (Homewood, IL, 1976), 5-6.

[51]Ibid.

[52]Schattschneider, *The Semi-Sovereign People*.

[53]J.J. Richardson and Grant Jordan, *Governing Under Pressure* (Oxford, 1979), 190-1. See also Richardson (ed.), *Policy Styles in Western Europe* (London, 1982); the corporatist literature referred to earlier; and Harmon Zeigler, *Pluralism, Corporatism and Confucianism: Political Association and Conflict Resolution in the United States, Europe and Taiwan* (Philadelphia, 1988), 42; Robert E. Goodin, 'Banana Time in British Politics', *Political Studies* xxx (1982) 1, 42-58.

[54]Richardson and Jordan, *Governing Under Pressure* (Oxford, 1979), 191; Goodin, 'Banana Time in British Politics', *Political Studies* xxx (1982) 1, 42-58.

[55]See the first edition of *Group Politics and Public Policy*, 236; Grant Jordan, 'Iron Triangles, Woolly Corporatism and Elastic Nets: Images of the Policy Process', *Journal of Public Policy*, 1 (1981), 1.

[56]William D. Coleman, 'Canadian Business and the State', in Keith Banting (ed.), *The State and Economic Interests* (Toronto, 1986), 245-90, 275.

[57]Ibid., 276.

[58]Pierre Fournier, 'Consensus Building in Canada: Case Studies and Prospects', in Banting, *The State and Economic Interests*, 291-336, 327; William Coleman and Wyn Grant, 'Business associations and public policy: a comparison of organizational development in Britain and Canada', *Journal of Public Policy* 4 (1984) 3, 209-35; and Michael M. Atkinson and William D. Coleman, *The State, Business and Industrial Change in Canada* (Toronto, 1989), 184-96.

[59]A policy community approach is not explicit in Canadian pressure group studies. However, there are close parallels between it and the sectoral approach adopted by Julien Bauer in 'Administration consultatif: La commission du textile et du vêtement' (Montréal: Note de recherche No. 11. Departement de science politique. Université de Québec à Montréal, 1978). See also J.D. Forbes, 'Institutions and Interest Groups in the Canadian Food System Policy Process', *Report* (Ottawa: Economic Council of Canada. Regulation Reference. 1982), and A. Paul Pross and Susan McCorquodale, *Economic Resurgence and the Constitutional Debate: The Case of the East Coast Fishing Industry* (Kingston, Ont., 1987).

[60]An illustration is found in timber-cutting policy applied in Ontario parks. In the late 1960s conventional wisdom endorsed the traditional practice of cutting in the parks; by then, however, environmentalists concerned with preserving wilderness areas had begun to bitterly attack the practice. Ontario parks policy has been suspect ever since. See 'National concern over fate of Algonquin Park', *Canadian Audubon* 30. (Nov.-Dec. 1968) 153, and D.H. Pimlott, 'Struggle to Save a Park', *Canadian Audubon* 31 (May-June 1969), 72-81.

[61]The Applebaum-Hébert Committee noted, for example, that the non-departmental agencies administering cultural policy found in the late 1970s that their traditional arm's-length relationship with ministers was increasingly being called into question and that they, and their policy communities, were having to adapt to more direct ministerial involvement in policy formation and in their internal affairs. (Canada. Department of Communications. *Report of the Federal Cultural Policy Review Committee* [Ottawa, 1982] 20-26.)

[62]William Coleman and Henry J. Jacek, 'The Political Organization of the Chemical Industry in Canada', Paper. Canadian Political Science Association. Halifax, 1981, 41.

[63]On the 'On-to-Ottawa' trek, see Walter D. Young, *Democracy and Discontent: Progressivism, Socialism and Social Credit in the Canadian West* (Toronto: McGraw-Hill, 1978), and Michiel Horn (ed.), *The Dirty Thirties* (Toronto: Copp Clark, 1972).

[64] 'The poor', declared Marjorie Hartling, when executive director of the National Anti-Poverty Organization, 'are out. They're out of everything.' (Quoted in H. V. Kroeker [ed.], *Sovereign People or Sovereign Government* [Montreal, 1981], 91.) See also the remarks of Havi Echenberg, a successor to Ms Hartling, to the Canadian Study of Parliament Group seminar on *Interest Groups and Parliament* (Ottawa, 1989), 3-4; more extensively, Rodney Haddow, 'The Poverty Policy Community in Canada's Liberal Welfare State', in William D. Coleman and Grace Skogstad, *Policy Communities and Public Policy in Canada: A Structural Approach* (Toronto, 1990), 212-37, and Frances Fox Piven and Richard A. Cloward, *Poor People's Movements* (N.Y., 1979).

CHAPTER 10. SPACE, SECTOR, AND LEGITIMACY: ADDRESSING THE DILEMMAS OF REPRESENTATION

[1]A particularly comprehensive review of European ideas about parliamentary forms of sectoral representation is found in J.-P. Parrot, *La représentation des intérêts dans le mouvement des idées politiques* (Paris, 1974).

[2]See, for example, the experience of residents of Port Hawkesbury reported in Raymond Foote, *The Case of Port Hawkesbury: Rapid Industrialization and Local Unrest in a Nova*

Scotia Community (Toronto, 1979) and A. Paul Pross, *Planning and Development: A Case of Two Nova Scotia Communities* (Halifax, 1975).

³See Kingston *Whig-Standard*, 16-25 May 1983, *Globe and Mail*, 29 July 1983, and 15 Nov. 1983.

⁴R. MacGregor Dawson and Norman Ward, *The Government of Canada* 4th ed. (Toronto, 1963), 361.

⁵Roy Romanow, John White, and Howard Lesson, *Canada . . . Notwithstanding: The Making of the Constitution, 1976-82* (Toronto, 1984), 108-11 and 'Four Western NDP MPs Break Ranks on Patriation', *Globe and Mail*, 19 Feb. 1981.

⁶Confidential interview.

⁷Halifax *Chronicle Herald*, 7 March 1975.

⁸J. Meynaud, *Nouvelles études sur les groupes de pression en France* (Paris, 1962), 251. See also Philippe Schmitter, 'Interest intermediation and regime governability', in Suzanne D. Berger (ed.), *Organizing Interests in Western Europe* (Cambridge, 1981), 287-331.

⁹Colin Campbell, *The Canadian Senate: A Lobby from Within* (Toronto, 1978).

¹⁰Ibid., 69.

¹¹Helen Jones Dawson, 'National Pressure Groups and the Federal Government', in A. Paul Pross (ed.), *Pressure Group Behaviour in Canadian Politics* (Toronto, 1975).

¹²See the Law Reform Commission reports cited in footnote 3, ch. 9.

¹³W.D. Baker (MP) and G.W. Baldwin (MP), 'Government Institutions' Position Paper. PC Annual Meeting, 4-6 November 1977.

¹⁴James Gillies and Jean Pigott, 'Participation in the Legislative Process', *Canadian Public Administration* 25 (1982) 2, 254-65, 256.

¹⁵J.I. Gow, 'L'histoire de l'administration publique québécoise', *Recherches sociographiques* XVI (1975) 3, 385-413.

¹⁶A.H. Hanson, 'The Purpose of Parliament', *Parliamentary Affairs* XVIII (1964) 3, 279-96, 295.

¹⁷Ibid.

¹⁸See Chapter 3.

¹⁹John F. Bulloch, 'A View from a Special Interest Group', in Daniel L. Bon, *Lobbying: A Right? A Necessity? A Danger?* (Ottawa, 1981), 13.

²⁰See C.E.S. Franks, *The Parliament of Canada* (Toronto, 1987), chs 9, 10, and 12.

²¹A.H. Hanson, 'The Purpose of Parliament'.

²²See, for example, Gillies and Pigott, 'Participation in the Legislative Process'; Faulkner, 'Pressuring the Executive'; Kathryn Randle, 'Committees at the Crossroads: Will Innovation Lead to Reform?', *Parliamentary Government* 2 (1981) 3, 3; and Franks, *The Parliament of Canada*, 176-85.

²³The Canadian Bar Association, *Report of the Canadian Bar Association Committee on the Reform of Parliament (Parliament as Lawmaker)* (Ottawa, 1982), 29-30.

²⁴This is consistent with John Stewart's observation that further reform of the committee system would not see the committees make more decisions, but rather would provide that 'the governors and members would meet on the issues of the times and do so before the governors had decided what they, under the full weight of their responsibility, must recommend to the House'. *The Canadian House of Commons* (Montreal, 1977), 283.

²⁵See, for example, R. Manzer, *Canada: A Social and Political Report* (Toronto, 1974), 321; and Mildred A. Schwartz, *Politics and Territory: The Sociology of Regional Persistence in Canada* (Montreal, 1974), ch. 9.

²⁶For a fuller account and analysis of the development of the *Lobbyists Registration Act* see A. Paul Pross, 'The Rise of the Lobbying Issue in Canada: "The Business Card Bill"', in Grant Jordan, *Commercial Lobbyists: Politics for Profit in Britain* (Aberdeen, 1991).

²⁷There is less agreement about what activities lobbying regulation should cover. The US Federal Regulation of Lobbying Act, for example, seems to be concerned only with lobbying directed at influencing the passage of legislation. (Title III. Legislative Reorganization Act of

1946. Public Law 601, 79th Congress. 2d. Session. 2 USC 261-270). Efforts to influence the bureaucratic interpretation of legislation or its implementation do not appear to be covered. Most Canadian bills have taken a broader approach, seeking to regulate those who work to influence the introduction and passage of legislation and who work to affect policy decisions at the ministerial and bureacratic level.

28Julianne La Breche, 'The Quiet Persuaders of Parliament Hill', *Financial Post Magazine*, 29 Nov. 1980.

29'Environmentalists Await Airlift to Wolf Hunt Area', Vancouver *Sun*, 29 Feb. 1984.

30'Activist No Longer Welcome in Rotary', Halifax *Chronicle- Herald*, 24 Sept. 1985.

31See, for example, the reports of the McCruer, MacDonald, and Keable commissions. Respectively: Ontario. Royal Commission into Civil Rights *Report* (Toronto, 1968); Canada. Privy Council Office. Commission of Inquiry Concerning Certain Acts of the Royal Canadian Mounted Police *Report* (Ottawa, 1981); and Québec. Commission d'enquête sur des opérations policières en territoires québécois. *Rapport* (Québec, 1981). See also, *Globe and Mail* 24 Nov. 1989 (editorial on police surveillance) and accounts of a series of burglaries at the offices of environmental groups (*Globe and Mail*, 17 Mar. and 21 Apr. 1989, and *Maclean's* 15 May 1989).

32See *Statutes of Canada* 1988, c. 53. In addition to requiring insufficient information, the act imposes sanctions against violation that are inappropriate and attaches its administration to a government agency rather than to Parliament itself. The Act imposes fines whereas a prohibition on lobbying activity might be more effective. A reporting relationship to Parliament would ensure the openness and transparency sought by early proponents of the legislation.

33'Policy capacity' is defined in Chapter 4, page102.

34Secretary of State, *People in Action: Report of the National Advisory Council on Voluntary Action to the Government of Canada* (Ottawa, 1977), 162.

35Ibid., 165. The problem remains. See Peter Finkle, Kernaghan Webb, William T. Stanbury, and A. Paul Pross, *Federal Government Relations with Interest Groups: A Reconsideration* (Ottawa, forthcoming).

36See Peter H. Schuck, 'Public Interest Groups and the Policy Process', *Public Administration Review* 37 (1977) 2, 132-40.

37For a discussion of American approaches to litigation by groups see Stephen L. Wasby, 'Interest Groups in Court: Race Relations Litigation', in Allan J. Cigler and Burdett A. Loomis (eds), *Interest Group Politics* (Washington, 1983). See also ch. 7, above.

38See Samuel A. Martin, *An Essential Grace: Funding Canada's Health Care, Education, Welfare, Religion and Culture* (Toronto, 1985), particularly chs 7 and 10.

39See Secretary of State, *People in Action*.

40J.C. Nelson, 'Public participation in comprehensive resource and environmental management', *Science and Public Policy* Oct. 1982, 240-50.

41Gregory Pyrcz, 'Pressure Groups', in T.C. Pocklington (ed.), *Liberal Democracy in Canada and the United States* (Toronto, 1985), 340-73, 372.

42See particularly Cairns, 'The Embedded State: State-Society Relations in Canada', in Keith Banting (ed.), *State and Society: Canada in Comparative Perspective* (Toronto, 1986), 53-86; but also the two collections of his essays recently edited by Douglas E. Williams and entitled *Constitution, Government and Society in Canada* (Toronto, 1988) and *Disruptions: Constitutional Struggles, from the Charter to Meech Lake* (Toronto, 1991).

43Cairns, 'The Embedded State', 55.

44'Alternative Futures: Legitimacy, Identity and Alienation in Late Twentieth Century Canada', in Alan C. Cairns and Cynthia Williams (eds), *Constitutionalism, Citizenship and Society in Canada* (Toronto, 1985), 183-230, 223.

A Select Bibliography
ON CANADIAN PRESSURE GROUPS

Anderson, J.E. 'Pressure Groups and Canadian Bureaucracy' in W.D.K. Kernaghan and A.M. Willms, eds, *Public Administration in Canada: Selected Readings*. Toronto: Methuen, 1970 (370-9).

Andrew, Caroline. 'Women and the Welfare State', *Canadian Journal of Political Science* XVII:4, 1984 (667-83).

Angus, Margaret. 'Health, Emigration and Welfare in Kingston, 1820-1840' in Donald Swainson, ed., *Oliver Mowat's Ontario*. Toronto: Macmillan, 1972 (120-35).

Archbold, William D. 'Business Council on National Issues: A New Factor in Business Communication', *Canadian Business Review* 4:2, 1977 (13-15).

Archibald, Clinton. 'Corporatist Tendencies in Quebec' in Alain G. Gagnon, *Quebec: State and Society*. Toronto: Methuen, 1984 (353-64).

_____ and Kayyam Z. Paltiel. 'Du passage des corps intermédiaires aux groupes de pression: la transformation d'une idée illustrée par le mouvement coopératif Desjardins', *Recherches sociographiques* 18:1, 1977 (59-91).

Armstrong, Christopher and H.V. Nelles. 'Getting Your Way in Nova Scotia: Tweaking Halifax, 1909-1917', *Acadiensis* V:2, 1976 (105-31).

Armstrong, R. 'Pressure Group Activity and Policy Formation: Collective Bargaining in the Federal Public Service' in W.D.K. Kernaghan, ed., *Bureaucracy in Canadian Government*. Toronto: Methuen, 1969 (120-8).

Arnold, Ron. 'The Politics of Environmentalism', *Notes on Agriculture*, Oct. 1981 (25-9).

Arnopoulos, Sheila McLeod and Dominique Clift. *The English Fact in Quebec*. Montreal: McGill-Queen's, 1984.

Atkinson, M.M. and William D. Coleman. 'Bureaucrats and Politicians in Canada: An Examination of the Political Administrative Model', *Comparative Political Studies* 18:1, 1985 (66).

_____ . 'Corporatism and Industrial Policy' in Alan Cawson, ed., *Organized Interests and the State: Studies in Meso Corporatism*. London: Sage, 1985.

_____ . *The State, Business and Industrial Change in Canada*. Toronto: University of Toronto Press, 1989.

_____ . 'Strong States and Weak States: Sectoral Policy Networks in Advanced Capitalist Economies', *British Journal of Political Science* 19, 1989 (47-66).

_____ . 'Is there a crisis in business-government relations?', *Canadian Journal of Administrative Science* 4:4, 1987 (321-40).

Aucoin, Peter. 'Pressure Groups and Recent Changes in the Policy-Making Process' in A. Paul Pross, ed., *Pressure Group Behaviour in Canadian Politics*. Toronto: McGraw-Hill, 1975 (172-93).

_____. *Public Accountability in the Governing of Professions: A Report on the Self-Governing Professions of Accounting, Architecture, Engineering and Law in Ontario*. Toronto: The Professional Organizations Committee, 1978.

Ba, Tran Quang. 'Les études canadiennes sur les groupes de pression: un travail pré-théorique à faire?', *Communications*. Montreal: Société canadienne de Science politique, 1976.

Bacchi, L.C. *Liberation Deferred: The Ideas of the English-Canadian Suffragists, 1877-1918*. Toronto: University of Toronto Press, 1983.

Badgley, R.F. and Samuel Wolfe. *Doctors' Strike: Medical Care and Conflict in Saskatchewan*. Toronto: Macmillan, 1967.

Baetz, Mark. 'Sector Strategy', *Policy Options*, January, 1985 (14-16).

Bakvis, Herman. 'Alternative Models of Governance: Federalism, Consociationalism and Corporatism', in H. Bakvis and W. Chandler, eds, *Federalism and the Role of the State*. Toronto: University of Toronto Press, 1987.

Banting, Keith (Research Coordinator). *The State and Economic Interests*. Toronto: University of Toronto Press. The Collected Research Studies/ Royal Commission on Economic Union and Development Prospects for Canada. No. 32, 1986.

Barry, Donald. 'Interest Groups and the Canadian Foreign Policy Formulation Process: The Case of Biafra'. Halifax: Dalhousie University, MA thesis, 1971.

_____. 'Interest Groups and the Foreign Policy Process: The Case of Biafra' in A. Paul Pross, ed., *Pressure Group Behaviour in Canadian Politics*. Toronto: McGraw-Hill, 1975 (115-48).

Bartha, Peter F. 'Organizational Competence in Business-Government Relations: A Managerial Perspective', *Canadian Public Administration* 28:2, 1985 (202-20).

_____. 'Managing Corporate External Issues: An Analytical Framework' in James D. Fleck and Isaiah A. Litvak, eds, *Business Can Succeed! Understanding the Political Environment*. Toronto: Gage, 1984 (9-27).

Bashevkin, S. 'Free Trade and Canadian Feminism: The Case of the National Action Committee on the Status of Women', *Canadian Public Policy* XV:4, 1989 (363-75).

Bauer, Julien. 'Administration consultatif: La Commission du Textile et du Vêtement'. Montréal: Département de Science politique. Université de Québec à Montréal. Note de recherche no. 11, 1978.

_____. 'Patrons et patronat au Québec', *Canadian Journal of Political Science*, IX, 1976 (473-91).

Baureiss, Gunter. 'Toward a Theory of Ethnic Organizations', *Canadian Ethnic Studies* XIV:2, 1982 (21-42).

Baxter, Clive. 'Lobbying — Ottawa's Fastest Growing Business' in Paul Fox, ed., *Politics Canada*. Toronto: McGraw-Hill, 1966 (206-10).

Beattie, Margaret Eileen. 'Pressure Group Politics: The Case of the Student Christian Movement of Canada'. Edmonton: University of Alberta PhD dissertation, 1972.

Beckman, M. Dale. 'The Problem of Communicating Public Policy Effectively: Bill C-256 and Winnipeg Business', *Canadian Journal of Political Science* VIII:1, 1975 (138-43).

Belanger, M. 'L'Association volontaire: le cas des Chambres de Commerce'. Québec: Laval University PhD dissertation, 1969.

Bennett, Scott. 'Some Relationships between Changes in the Number of Interest Group Organizations and Changes in Other Political System Organizations'. Toronto: York University PhD dissertation, 1982.

Bercuson, David J. 'Western Labour Radicalism and the One Big Union: Myths and Realities' in S. Trofimenkoff, ed., *The Twenties in Western Canada.* Ottawa: National Museum of Man, 1972 (32-49).

Berger, Thomas R. *Fragile Freedoms: Human Rights and Dissent in Canada.* Toronto: Clark, Irwin, 1981.

Berry, Glyn R. 'Bureaucratic Politics and Canadian Economic Policies Affecting the Developing Countries — the Case of the "Strategy for International Development Cooperation" 1975-1980'. Halifax: Dalhousie University PhD dissertation, 1981.

_____. 'The Oil Lobby and the Energy Crisis', *Canadian Public Administration* 17:4, 1974 (600-35).

Blais, André, Philippe Faucher, and Robert Young. 'La dynamique de l'aide financière directe du gouvernement fédéral à l'industrie manufacturière au Canada', *Canadian Journal of Political Science* xix:1, 1986 (29-52).

Bliss, Michael. 'The Protective Impulse: An Approach to the Social History of Oliver Mowat's Ontario' in Donald Swainson, ed., *Oliver Mowat's Ontario.* Toronto: Macmillan, 1972 (174-88, 174-5).

Boase, Joan. 'Public Policy and the Regulation of the Health Disciplines: An Historical and Comparative Perspective'. Toronto: York University PhD dissertation, 1986.

_____. 'Regulation and the Para-medical Professions: An Interest Group Study', *Canadian Public Administration* 25:3, 1982 (332-53).

_____. *Shifting Sands: Government-Group Relationships in the Health Care Field* (forthcoming).

Boivin, Dominique. *Le Lobbying.* Montreal: Meridien, 1984.

Bon, Daniel L. *Lobbying: A Right? A Necessity? A Danger?.* Ottawa: The Conference Board of Canada, 1981.

Bonepath, Ellen, ed. *Women, Power and Policy.* Toronto: Pergamon, 1982.

Braden, George. 'The Emergence of Interest Groups in the Northwest Territories'. Halifax: Dalhousie University MA thesis, 1976.

Brown, Douglas and Julia Eastman with Ian Robinson. *The Limits of Consultation: A Debate Among Ottawa, the Provinces and the Private Sector on an Industrial Strategy.* Kingston and Ottawa: Queen's University Institute of Intergovernmental Relations and the Science Council of Canada, 1981 (176).

Brown-John, Lloyd. 'Comprehensive regulatory consultation in Canada's food processing industry', *Canadian Public Administration* 28:1, 1985 (70-98).

Bruce, Harry, ed. *'You've got ten minutes to get that flag down . . .': Proceedings of the Halifax Conference — A national forum on Canadian cultural policy.* Halifax: Nova Scotia Coalition on Arts and Culture, 1986.

Bryden, Philip L. 'Public Interest Intervention in the Courts', *Canadian Bar Review* 60:3, 1987 (490-528).

Brynaert, Kenneth. 'Marketing Approach' (to development of Canadian Wildlife Federation), *Canadian Associations* April 1986 (11-13).

Bucovetsky, M.W. 'The Mining Industry and the Great Tax Reform Debate' in A. Paul Pross, ed., *Pressure Group Behaviour in Canadian Politics.* Toronto: McGraw-Hill, 1975 (87-115).

Burke, Mike, Harold D. Clarke, Lawrence LeDuc. 'Federal and Provincial Political Participation in Canada: Some Methodological and Substantive Considerations', *Canadian Review of Sociology and Anthropology* 15:1, 1978 (61-75).

Burt, Sandra D. 'Canadian Women's Groups in the 1980s: Organizational Development and Policy Influence', *Canadian Public Policy* XVI:1, 1990 (17-28).

——. 'The Charter of Rights and the Ad Hoc Lobby: The Limits of the Success', *Atlantis* 14:1, 1988 (74-81).

——. 'Legislators, Women and Public Policy' in Sandra Burt et al., eds, *Changing Patterns*. Toronto: McClelland and Stewart, 1988.

——. 'Organized Women's Groups and the State' in William D. Coleman and Grace Skogstad, eds, *Policy Communities and Public Policy in Canada: A Structural Approach*. Toronto: Copp Clark Pitman, 1990 (191-211).

——. 'Women's Groups and the Pross Continuum: The Need for More Discourse', *Canadian Public Policy* XVI:3, 1990 (339-40).

——. 'Women's Issues and the Women's Movement in Canada' in Alan Cairns and Cynthia Williams, eds, *The Politics of Gender, Ethnicity and Language in Canada*. Toronto: University of Toronto Press, 1986.

Byers, Roddick, 'Executive Leadership and Influence: Parliamentary Perceptions of Canadian Defence Policy' in Thomas A. Hockin, ed., *Apex of Power*. Scarborough: Prentice-Hall, 1971.

Bulloch, John F. 'A View from a Special Interest Group' in Daniel L. Bon, *Lobbying: A Right? A Necessity? A Danger?*. Ottawa: Conference Board, 1981 (12).

Cairns, Alan C. 'Citizens (outsiders) and governments (insiders) in constitution-making: The case of Meech Lake', *Canadian Public Policy* XIV, 1988 (121-45).

——. 'The embedded state: State society relations in Canada' in Keith Banting, ed., *State and Society: Canada in Comparative Perspective*. Toronto: University of Toronto Press, 1986 (53-8).

——. 'The Governments and Societies of Canadian Federalism', *Canadian Journal of Political Science* X:4, 1977 (695-725).

—— and Cynthia Williams. 'Constitutionalism, Citizenship and Society in Canada: An Overview' in Alan C. Cairns and Cynthia Williams, eds, *Constitutionalism, Citizenship and Society in Canada*. Toronto: University of Toronto Press, 1985 (1-50).

——, eds. *Constitutionalism, Citizenship and Society in Canada*. Toronto: University of Toronto Press, 1985.

——, eds. *The Politics of Gender, Ethnicity and Language in Canada*. Toronto: University of Toronto Press, 1986.

Cairns, Alan C. (Douglas E. Williams, ed.). *Constitution, Government and Society in Canada*. Toronto: University of Toronto Press, 1988.

——. *Disruption: Constitutional Struggles from the Charter to Meech Lake*. Toronto: University of Toronto Press, 1991.

Campbell, Colin. *The Canadian Senate: A Lobby from Within*. Toronto: Macmillan, 1978.

Canada. Auditor General. *Report*. Ottawa: Office of the Auditor General, 1990.

——, Consumer and Corporate Affairs. *Lobbying and the Registration of Paid Lobbyists: A Discussion Paper*. Ottawa: Consumer and Corporate Affairs, 1985.

——, Environment Canada. *Environmentally Interested Citizen's Groups in Canada*. Ottawa: Canada DOE Information Branch, 1974.

_____, Library of Parliament. Research Branch. 'Pressure Groups in Canada', *The Parliamentarian* LI:1, 1970 (11-20).

_____. Bibliography and Compilations Section. Information and Technical Services Branch. *Select Bibliography No. 54: Pressure Groups*. Ottawa: The Library of Parliament, 1988.

_____, National Council of Welfare. *Poor People's Groups: A Report of the National Council of Welfare Seminar on Self-Help Problem Solving by Low-Income Communities*. Ottawa: The Council, 1973.

_____. *Organizing for Social Action: The Canadian Experiences*. Ottawa: The Council, 1975.

_____, Privy Council Office. *The Way Ahead: A Framework for Discussion*, Ottawa: Privy Council Office, 1976.

_____, Revenue Canada. Taxation. 'Registered charities — ancillary and incidental political activities', *Information Circular No. 87-1*. Ottawa: Revenue Canada, Taxation, 25 Feb. 1987.

_____. *Better Tax Administration in Support of Charities*. Ottawa: The Department, 1990.

_____, Secretary of State. *A Framework for Cross-Sectoral Evaluation of Core Funding in the Secretary of State*. Ottawa: Secretary of State, 1986.

_____. *Sources of Government of Canada Support to Voluntary Organizations, 1986-87*. Ottawa: Voluntary Action Directorate, 1986.

Canadian Associations (Journal of the Institute of Association Executives) June/July 1982- (Formerly: *Canadian Association Executive* Apr./May 1973-Apr./May 1982.)

Canadian Manufacturers' Association. *Inside Government*. Toronto: The Association, 1981.

Canadian Study of Parliament Group. *Interest Groups and Parliament*. Ottawa: 1989.

Carrothers, Leslie C. 'Telecommunications Policy and the Manitoba New Democratic Party: Party Politics and the Policy Community' Winnipeg: University of Manitoba MPA thesis, 1987.

Carter, Novia. *Trends in Voluntary Support for Non-Governmental Social Service Agencies*. Ottawa: The Canadian Council on Social Development, 1974.

Chant, D.A. 'Pollution Probe: Fighting Polluters with Their Own Weapons' in A. Paul Pross, ed., *Pressure Group Behaviour in Canadian Politics*. Toronto: McGraw-Hill, 1975 (59-68).

Clague, Michael. 'Citizen Participation in the Legislative Process' in James A. Draper, ed., *Citizen Participation: Canada*. Toronto: New Press, 1971 (30-44).

Clancy, Peter. 'Working on the Railway: A Case Study in Capital-State Relations', *Canadian Public Administration* 30:3, 1987 (450-71).

Clark, S.D. 'The Canadian Manufacturers' Association: A Political Pressure Group', *Canadian Journal of Economics and Political Science* v:4, 1938.

_____. *The Canadian Manufacturers' Association*. Toronto: University of Toronto Press, 1939.

_____, J. Paul Grayson, and Linda M. Grayson, eds. *Prophecy and Protest: Social Movements in Twentieth-Century Canada*. Toronto: Gage, 1975.

Cleverdon, Catherine. *The Woman Suffrage Movement in Canada*. Toronto: University of Toronto Press, 1974.

Clift, Dominique. 'L'Etat et les groupes d'intérêts: perspectives d'avenir', *Canadian Public Administration* 25:2, 1982 (265-78).

Cohen, Andrew. 'Who makes the rules?', *Canadian Associations*, June 1984 (10-12).

Coleman, William D. 'Agricultural Policy and the Associations of the Food Processing Industry' in Wyn Grant, ed., *Business Interests, Organizational Development and Private Interest Government*. Berlin: Walter de Gruyter, 1987.

_____. 'Analysing the associative action of business: policy advocacy and policy participation', *Canadian Public Administration* 28:3, 1985 (413-33).

_____. 'The Banking Policy Community and Financial Change' in William D. Coleman and Grace Skogstad, eds, *Policy Communities and Public Policy in Canada: A Structural Approach*. Toronto: Copp Clark Pitman, 1990 (91-117).

_____. *Business and Politics: A study of collective action*. Montreal: McGill-Queen's, 1988.

_____. 'Interest groups and democracy in Canada', *Canadian Public Administration* 30:4, 1987 (610-22).

_____. 'Canadian Business and the State' in Keith Banting (Research Coordinator), *The State and Economic Interests*. Toronto: University of Toronto Press. The Collected Research Studies/ Royal Commission on the Economic Union and Development Prospects for Canada. No. 32, 1986 (245-90).

_____. 'Federalism and Interest Group Organization' in H. Bakvis and W. Chandler, eds, *Federalism and the Role of the State*. Toronto: University of Toronto Press, 1987 (171-87).

_____. 'From Bill 22 to Bill 101: The Politics of Language under the Parti Quebecois', *Canadian Journal of Political Science* xiv:3, 1981 (459-86).

_____. 'State Traditions and Comprehensive Business Associations: A Comparative Structural Analysis', *Political Studies* 38, 1990 (231-52).

_____. *The Independence Movement in Quebec, 1945-1980*. Toronto: University of Toronto Press, 1984.

_____ and Wyn P. Grant. 'Business Associations and Public Policy: a Comparison of Organizational Development in Britain and Canada', *Journal of Public Policy* 4:3, 1985 (209-33).

_____. 'Regional Differentiation of Business Interest Associations: A Comparison of Canada and the United Kingdom', *Canadian Journal of Political Science* xviii:1, 1985 (3-30).

_____ and Henry J. Jacek. 'Capitalists, Collective Action and Regionalism' in Coleman and Jacek, eds. *Regionalism, Business Interests and Public Policy*. London: Sage, 1989 (1-13).

_____, eds. *Regionalism, Business Interests and Public Policy*. London: Sage, 1989.

_____ and H.J. Jacek. 'The Roles and Activities of Business Interest Associations in Canada', *Canadian Journal of Political Science* xvi:2, 1983 (257-80).

_____ and Grace Skogstad. 'Policy communities and policy networks: A structural approach' in Coleman and Skogstad, eds, *Policy Communities and Public Policy in Canada*. Toronto: Copp Clark Pitman, 1990 (14-33).

_____, eds. *Policy Communities and Public Policy in Canada*. Toronto: Copp Clark Pitman, 1990.

Cook, Ramsay. *The Regenerators: Social criticism in late Victorian English Canada*. Toronto: University of Toronto Press, 1985.

Corbett, D.C. 'The Pressure Group and the Public Interest' in J.E. Hodgetts and D.C. Corbett, *Canadian Public Administration*. Toronto: Macmillan, 1960 (452-62).

Corry, J.A. 'Sovereign People or Sovereign Governments' in H.V. Kroeker, ed., *Sovereign People or Sovereign Governments*. Montreal: Institute for Research on Public Policy, 1981 (3-12).

Cumming, Peter. *Nova Scotia's Herbicide Case. A Court Diary*. Garbarus, Nova Scotia: Herbicide Fund Society, 1983.

Cummings, Milton C. and Richard S. Katz. 'Government and the Arts in the Modern World: Trends and Portents' in Milton C. Cummings and Richard S. Katz, *The Patron State: Government and the Arts in Europe, North America and Japan*. N.Y.: Oxford University Press, 1987 (350-68).

Cunningham, Frank, Sue Findlay, Marlene Kadar, Alan Lennon, and Ed Silva. *Social Movements/Social Change: The Politics and Practice of Organizing*. Toronto: Between the Lines, 1988.

Curtis, James. 'Voluntary Association Joining: A Cross-National Comparative Note', *American Sociological Review* 36, 1971 (872-80).

Dahlie, Jorgen and Tissa Fernando, eds. *Ethnicity, Power and Politics in Canada*. Toronto: Methuen, 1981.

Dalhousie Institute of Public Affairs and Richard H. Leach. *Interprovincial Relations in the Maritime Provinces*. Fredericton: Maritime Union Study, 1970 (81).

Dawson, Helen Jones. 'Agricultural Interest Groups in Canada and Great Britain'. Oxford University, thesis, 1966.

————. 'The Consumers Association of Canada', *Canadian Public Administration* VI:1, 1963 (92-188).

————. 'An Interest Group: The Canadian Federation of Agriculture', *Canadian Public Administration* III:2, 1960 (134-49).

————. 'Relations Between Farm Organizations and the Civil Service in Canada and Great Britain', *Canadian Public Administration* X:4, 1967 (450-71).

————. 'National Pressure Groups and the Federal Government' in A. Paul Pross, ed., *Pressure Group Behaviour in Canadian Politics*. Toronto: McGraw-Hill, 1975 (27-58).

Decarie, Graeme. 'Something Old, Something New ... Aspects of Prohibitionism in Ontario in the 1890's' in Donald Swainson, ed., *Oliver Mowat's Ontario*. Toronto: Macmillan, 1972 (154-71).

Delbridge, Pat. 'David vs. Goliath: Voluntary Sector Interest Groups in Canada Today' in James D. Fleck and Isaiah Litvak, eds, *Business Can Succeed! Understanding the Political Environment*. Toronto: Gage, 1984 (46-64).

————. 'The 10 Commandments of Public Affairs Management', *Canadian Associations* Apr. 1987 (14-15).

Deveaux, Bert and Kaye. 'The Enemies Within Community Development' in James A. Draper, ed., *Citizen Participation: Canada*. Toronto: New Press, 1971 (93-105).

Dion, Leon. 'Anti-politics and marginals', *Government and Opposition* 9:1, 1974 (28-41).

————. *Le bill 60 et la société québécoise*. Montreal: Editions HMH, 1967.

————. 'Participation in the Political Process', *Queen's Quarterly* 75:3, 1968.

————. 'Politique consultative et système politique', *Canadian Journal of Political Science* II:2, 1969 (226-44).

————. 'Quebec: Interest Groups and the Search for an Alternative Political System', *The Annals of the American Academy of Political and Social Science* 413, 1974 (124-44).

————. 'A la recherche d'une méthode d'analyse des partis et des groups d'intérêt', *Canadian Journal of Political Science* II:1, 1969 (45-63).

————. *Société et Politique: la vie des groupes*. Quebec: Laval, 1971.

Dobell, A.R. and S.H. Mansbridge. *The Social Policy Process in Canada*. Montreal: Institute for Research on Public Policy, 1986.

Doern, G. Bruce. 'The National Research Council: The Causes of Goal Displacement', *Canadian Public Administration* XIII:2, 1970 (140-85).

————. 'Pressure Groups and the Canadian Bureaucracy: Scientists and Science Policy Machinery' in W.D.K. Kernaghan, ed., *Bureaucracy in Canadian Government*. Toronto: Methuen, 1969 (112-19).

————. *Science and Politics in Canada*. Montreal: McGill-Queen's University Press, 1972.

———— and M.J. Prince. 'The Political Administration of School Closures: Administrators, Trustees and Community Groups', *Canadian Public Policy* XV:4, 1989 (450-69).

———— and Glen Toner. *The Politics of Energy: The Development and Implementation of the NEP*. Toronto: Methuen, 1985.

Donovan, S.J. and R.B. Winmill. 'The Beauharnois Power Scandal' in Kenneth M. Gibbons and Donald C. Rowat, *Political Corruption in Canada: Cases, Causes and Cures*. Ottawa: Carleton, 1976 (57-66).

Draper, Dianne. 'Environmental Interest Groups and Institutional Arrangements in British Columbia Water Management Issues' in Bruce Mitchell, ed., *Institutional Arrangements for Water Management: Canadian Experiences*. Waterloo, Ontario: University of Waterloo, 1975 (119-70).

Duchesne, Pierre and Russell Ducasse. 'Must Lobbying be Regulated?', *Canadian Parliamentary Review* 7:4, 1984-5 (82-7).

Dupre, Stefan. 'Canadian Constitutionalism and the Sequel to the Meech Lake/Langevin Accord' in D. P. Shugarman and R. Whitaker, eds, *Federalism and Political Community*. Peterborough: Broadview Press, 1989.

Dussault, René. 'L'Evolution du professionalisme au Québec', *Canadian Public Administration* 20:2, 1977 (275-91).

Edwards, Gordon. 'Nuclear Power: A New Dimension in Politics', *Alternatives* 5:2, 1976 (26-32).

Eggerton, Bill. 'A Proven Technique for Reaching and Influencing Public Officials', *Canadian Associations* Mar./Apr. 1983 (19-21).

Eggleston, Wilfrid. 'The Cabinet and Pressure Groups', *Proceedings of the Fifth Annual Conference*, The Institute of Public Administration of Canada. Toronto: IPAC, 1953 (156-7).

Emmerson, D.W. 'Legislation for Professionals in Quebec — Government Moves for Tighter Controls', *Chemistry in Canada* Dec. 1972 (28-9).

Engelmann, F.C. and Mildred A. Schwartz. *Canadian Political Parties: Origin, Character, Impact*. Scarborough: Prentice-Hall, 1975.

Epstein, Leon D. 'A comparative study of Canadian parties', *American Political Science Review* 58, 1964 (46-59).

Fairley, Bryant, Colin Leys, and James Sacouman, eds. *Restructuring and Resistance: Perspectives from Atlantic Canada*. Toronto: Garamond, 1990.

Faulkner, J. Hugh. 'The business-government relationship in Canada'. *Optimum* 7:1, 1976 (5-16).

_____. 'Pressuring the Executive', *Canadian Public Administration* 25:2, 1982 (240-54).

Fazio, Charles R. and Jack R. Alsip. 'The art and science of successful association fund raising', *Canadian Associations* Mar. 1985 (19-23).

Fensom, K.G. *Expanding Forestry Horizons: A History of the Canadian Institute of Forestry-Institut Forestier du Canada, 1908-1969*. Macdonald College, P.Q.: CIF, 1972.

Findlay, Sue. 'Facing the State: The Politics of the Women's Movement Reconsidered' in *Feminism and Political Economy*. Toronto: Methuen, 1987.

Finkle, Peter, Kernaghan Webb, William T. Stanbury, and A. Paul Pross. *Federal Government Relations with Interest Groups: A Reconsideration*. Ottawa: Consumer and Corporate Affairs Canada. Occasional Paper, 1991.

Finlay, John J. 'How the Taxman Dunned One Non-Profit Organization', *Canadian Associations* Feb. 1984 (20-2).

Fleck, James D. and Isaiah A. Litvak, eds. *Business Can Succeed! Understanding the Political Environment*. Toronto: Gage, 1984.

Forbes, E.R. *Maritime Rights: The Maritime Rights Movement*. Montreal: McGill-Queen's University Press, 1979.

Forbes J.D. *Institutions and Influence Groups in Canadian Farm and Food Policy*. Toronto: Institute of Public Administration of Canada. Monographs on *Canadian Public Administration*. No. 10, 1985.

_____. 'Institutions and Interest Groups in the Canadian Food System Policy Process', *Report*. Ottawa: Economic Council of Canada. Regulation Reference, 1982.

Forster, Ben. *A Conjunction of Interests: Business, Politics, and Tariffs 1825-1879*. Toronto: University of Toronto Press, 1986.

Foster, Peter. *The Blue-Eyed Sheiks: The Canadian Oil Establishment*. Don Mills, Ontario: Collins, 1979.

_____. *The Sorcerer's Apprentice*. Toronto: Collins, 1982.

Fournier, Louis (tr. E. Baxter). *F.L.Q.: The Anatomy of an Underground Movement*. Toronto: NC Press, 1984.

Fournier, Pierre. 'Consensus Building in Canada: Cases Studies and Prospects' in Keith Banting (Research Coordinator), *The State and Economic Interests*. Toronto: University of Toronto Press. The Collected Research Studies/ Royal Commission on the Economic Union and Development Prospects for Canada. No. 32, 1986 (291-336).

Fox, David. *Public Participation in the Administrative Process*. Ottawa: Law Reform Commission. Administrative Law Series, 1979.

Frank, J.A. 'La dynamique des manifestations violentes', *Canadian Journal of Political Science* XVII:2, 1984 (324-49).

Franklin, Ursula. 'Voices of Women: Feminist Leadership', *Edges* 2:4, 1989 (14-17).

Franks, C.E.S. *The Parliament of Canada*. Toronto: University of Toronto Press, 1987.

Frechette, W.D.H. 'The CMA — Spokesman for Industry' in Paul Fox, ed., *Politics Canada*. Toronto: McGraw-Hill, 1970 (172-5).

Frideres, J.S. *Canada's Indians: Contemporary Conflicts*. Scarborough: Prentice-Hall, 1974.

Friedland, M.L. 'Pressure Groups and the Development of the Criminal Law' in P.R. Glazebrook, ed., *Reshaping the Criminal Law: Essays in Honour of Glanville Williams*. London: Stevens and Sons, 1978.

Friedman, Kenneth Michael. 'Cigarette Smoking and Public Policy: A Comparative Study of Government and Interest Group Response'. East Lansing: Michigan State University, PhD dissertation, 1973.

Fulton, M. Jane and W.T. Stanbury. 'Comparative lobbying strategies in influencing health care policy', *Canadian Public Administration* 28:2, 1985 (269-300).

Fulford, Robert. 'Blaming the Yanks', *Saturday Night* Mar. 1986 (7-9).

Gibbons, Kenneth M. and Donald C. Rowat. *Political Corruption in Canada: Cases, Causes and Cures*. Ottawa: Carleton, 1976.

Gifford, C.G. 'Grey is Strong', *Policy Options* Oct. 1985 (16-17).

————. *Canada's Fighting Seniors*. Toronto: James Lorimer, 1990.

Gillies, James. *Where Business Fails: Business-Government Relations at the Federal Level in Canada*. Montreal: Institute for Research on Public Policy, 1981.

———— and Jean Pigott. 'Participation in the Legislative Process', *Canadian Public Administration* 25:2, 1982 (254-64).

Glenn, H. Patrick. 'Class Actions in Ontario and Quebec', *Canadian Bar Review* 62:3, 1984 (247-77).

Goldstein, Jonah. 'Public Interest Groups and Public Policy: The Case of the Consumers' Association of Canada', *Canadian Journal of Political Science* 16:1, 1979.

Granatstein, G. *Marlborough Marathon: One Street Against a Developer*. Toronto: James Lewis and Samuel, 1971.

Grant, Wyn P. 'Forestry and Forest Products' in William D. Coleman and Grace Skogstad, eds, *Policy Communities and Public Policy in Canada: A Structural Approach*. Toronto: Copp Clark Pitman, 1990 (118-40).

Gray, Charlotte. 'Friendly Persuasion', *Saturday Night* Mar. 1983.

————. 'How to be a Lobbyist', *Chatelaine* Nov. 1985 (104-6).

Grayson, L.M. and J. Paul Grayson. 'Interest Aggregation and Canadian Politics: The Case of the Central Bank', *Canadian Public Administration* 16:4, 1973 (557-72).

Greene, Stephen and Thomas Keating. 'Domestic Factors and Canada-United States Fisheries Relations', *Canadian Journal of Political Science* 13:4, 1980 (731-50).

Groulx, L.H.J. 'L'action communautaire: diversité et ambiguité', *Canadian Journal of Political Science* VIII, 1975 (510-19).

Guindon, Hubert. 'Social Unrest, Social Class and Quebec's Bureaucratic Revolution', *Queen's Quarterly* 71:2, 1964 (150-62).

de Guise, Jacques. 'Le colloque: une réflexion sur la relation Etat-citoyen', *Recherches sociographiques* XVI:3, 1975 (321-37).

Gunther, Peter E. 'The Atlantic Provinces Economic Council: Structure and Prospects', *Canadian Business Review* 4:4, 1977 (17-19).

Gutzke, David William. *The Brewing Industry as a Pressure Group, 1875-1914*. University of Toronto PhD dissertation, 1982.

Haddow, Rodney. 'The Poverty Policy Community in Canada's Liberal Welfare State' in William D. Coleman and Grace Skogstad, eds, *Policy Communities and Public Policy in Canada: A Structural Approach*. Toronto: Copp Clark Pitman, 1990 (212-37).

Hagy, James William. 'Quebec Separatists: The First Twelve Years' in W.E. Mann, ed., *Social and Cultural Change in Canada*. Toronto: Copp Clark, 1970 (288-95).

Hamilton, Ian. *The Children's Crusade: The Story of the Company of Young Canadians*. Toronto: Peter Martin Associates, 1970.

Hamel, Pierre, Jean-François Leonard, Françine Senecal. *Bibliographie sur les mobilisations populaires à Montréal (1960-1978)* Montreal: Université du Québec à Montréal. Departement de science politique. Note de recherche no. 17, 1979.

Hannam, H.H. 'The Interest Group and its Activities', *Proceedings of the Fifth Annual Conference, the Institute of Public Administration of Canada*. Toronto: IPAC, 1953 (171-81).

Hawkins, Freda. *Canada and Immigration: Public Policy and Public Concern*. Montreal: McGill-Queen's University Press, 1972.

Heibert, Janet. 'Fair Elections and Freedom of Expression Under the Charter', *Journal of Canadian Studies* 24:4, 1989-90 (72-98).

Himes, Mel. 'Interest Groups and Foreign Policy: The Case of Bangladesh'. Montreal: McGill University PhD dissertation, 1978.

Henke, Janice Scott. *Seal Wars: An American Perspective*. St John's: Breakwater, 1985.

Herscovici, Alan. *Second Nature: The Animal Rights Controversy*. Montreal: CBC Enterprises, 1985.

Hodgetts, J.E. 'Bureaucratic Initiative, Citizen Involvement and Administrative Accountability', *Transactions of the Royal Society of Canada Series* IV, vol. XII, 1974 (227-36).

_____. 'The Civil Service and Policy Formation', *Canadian Journal of Economics and Political Science* XXIII:4, 1957 (467-79).

Hoffman, David. 'Interacting With Government: The General Public and Interest Groups', in Donald MacDonald, ed., *Politics in Ontario*. Toronto: Macmillan, 1975 (275-92).

Hoberg, George, Jr. 'Risk, Science and Politics: Alachlor Regulation in Canada and the United States', *Canadian Journal of Political Science* 23:2, 1990 (257-77).

Horowitz, Gad. *Canadian Labour in Politics*. Toronto: University of Toronto Press, 1968.

Hosek, Chaviva. 'Women and the Constitutional Process' in Keith Banting and Richard Simeon, *And No One Cheered: Federalism, Democracy and the The Constituion Act*. Toronto: Methuen, 1983 (280-300).

House, J.D. *The Last of the Free Enterprisers: The Oilmen of Calgary*. Toronto: Macmillan, 1979.

Hudon, Raymond. 'Polarization and Depolarization of Quebec Political Parties' in Alain G. Gagnon, *Quebec: State and Society*. Toronto: Methuen, 1984 (314-30).

_____. 'La poursuite des fins organisationnelles par un groupe de pression: la

CSN et les unités nationales de négociation dans l'affaire Lapalme (deux versions contradictoires)', *Canadian Journal of Political Science* VII:2, 1974 (328-33).

Hurl, L.F. 'Privatized Social Service Systems: Lessons from Ontario Children's Services', *Canadian Public Policy* X, 1984 (395-406).

Hyde, Peter and Andre Dulude. 'How associations are taxed', *Canadian Associations* 12-13 April 1987.

Ilgen, Thomas L. 'Between Europe and America, Ottawa and the Provinces: Regulating Toxic Substances in Canada', *Canadian Public Policy* XI:3, 1985 (578-90).

Isbister, Fraser. 'The CNTU Comes of Age' in W.E. Mann, ed., *Social and Cultural Change in Canada*. Toronto: Copp Clark, 1970 (261-74).

Islam, Nasir and Sadrudin A. Ahmed. 'Business influence on government: a comparison of public and private sector perceptions', *Canadian Public Administration* 27:1, 1984 (87-102).

Jacek, Henry J. 'Business Interest Associations as Private Interest Governments' in Wyn Grant, ed., *Business Interests, Organizational Development and Private Interest Government*. Berlin, N.Y: de Gruyter, 1987 (34-62).

Jacobs, Dorene E. 'The Annex Ratepayers' Association: Citizens' Efforts to Exercise Social Choice in Their Urban Environment' in James A. Draper, ed., *Citizen Participation: Canada*. Toronto: Copp Clark, 1970 (261-74).

Jeffrey, Michael I. 'Ontario's Intervenor Funding Project Act', *Canadian Journal of Administrative Law and Practice* 3:1 1989 (69-80).

Johnson, James Donald. *Interest Groups and the Legislative Process in Canada: A Case Study in Anti-Combines Legislation*. East Lansing: Michigan State University PhD dissertation, 1973.

Johnson, P.G. 'The Union of Nova Scotia Municipalities'. Halifax: Dalhousie University MA thesis, 1969.

————. 'The Union of Nova Scotia Municipalities', *Proceedings* Canadian Political Science Association, Winnipeg. June 1970.

Kaplan, Harold. *Policy and Rationality: The Regulation of Canadian Trucking*. Toronto: University of Toronto Press, 1989.

Kealey, Linda, ed. *A Not Unreasonable Claim*. Toronto: The Women's Press, 1979.

Kearney, John. 'The Transformation of the Bay of Fundy Herring Fisheries, 1976-78: An Experiment in Fishermen-Government Co-Management' in Cynthia Lamson and Arthur J. Hanson, eds, *Atlantic Fisheries and Coastal Communities: Fisheries Decision-Making Case Studies*. Halifax: Dalhousie Ocean Studies Programme, 1984.

Keating, Donald R. 'Power to Make it Happen', *Urban Forum* 1:1, 1975 (16-22).

Keeping, Janet. 'Practice Notes: Intervenors' Costs', *Canadian Journal of Administrative Law and Practice* 3:1 1989 (81-90).

Knopff, Rainer and F.L. Morton. 'Nation-Building and the Canadian Charter of Rights' in Alan C. Cairns and Cynthia Williams, eds, *Constitutionalism, Citizenship and Society in Canada*. Toronto: University of Toronto Press, 1985 (133-82).

Kome, Penney. *Women of Influence: Canadian Women and Politics*. Toronto: Doubleday, 1985.

Kreutzwiser, Reid D. 'Ontario Cottager Associations and Shoreline Management', *Coastal Zone Management Journal* 14:1/2, 1986 (93-111).

Kroeker, H.V., ed. *Sovereign People or Sovereign Governments*. Montreal: Institute for Research on Public Policy, 1981.

Kwavnick, David. 'Interest Group Demands and the Federal Political System: Two Canadian Case Studies' in A. Paul Pross, ed., *Pressure Group Behaviour in Canadian Politics*. Toronto: McGraw-Hill, 1975 (69-86).

_____. *Organized Labour and Pressure Politics: The Canadian Labour Congress, 1956-1968*. Montreal: McGill-Queen's University Press, 1972.

_____. 'Pressure Group Demands and Organizational Objectives: The CNTU, the Lapalme Affair, and National Bargaining Units', *Canadian Journal of Political Science* VI:4, 1973 (582-601).

_____. 'Pressure Group Demands and the Struggle for Organizational Status: The Case of Organized Labour in Canada', *Canadian Journal of Political Science* III:1, 1970 (56-72).

Kyba, Patrick. 'Ballots and Burning Crosses: The Election of 1929' in Norman Ward and Duff Spafford, *Politics in Saskatchewan*. Don Mills: Longmans, 1968 (105-24).

La Breche, Julianne. 'The Quiet Persuaders of Parliament Hill', *Financial Post Magazine* 29 Nov. 1980.

Lamande, Yvan. 'Le Membership d'une Association du 19ième siècle: Le cas de Longueuil (1857-1860)', *Recherches sociographiques* XVI:2, 1975 (219-41).

_____. *Gens de Parole: Conférences publiques, essais et debats à l'Institut Canadien de Montréal, 1845-1871*. Montréal: Boréal, 1990.

Lamport, Anthony. *Common Ground: Twenty-five Years of Voluntary Planning in Nova Scotia*. Halifax: Nova Scotia Department of Small Business Development, 1988.

Lamson, Cynthia. *'Bloody Decks and a Bumper Crop': The Rhetoric of Sealing Counter-Protest*. St John's: Memorial University of Newfoundland, Institute for Social and Economic Research, 1979.

Land, Brian. *Directory of Associations in Canada*. Toronto: University of Toronto Press.

Landry, Réjean. 'Biases in the Supply of Public Policies to Organized Interests: Some Empirical Evidence' in William D. Coleman and Grace Skogstad, eds, *Policy Communities and Public Policy in Canada: A Structural Approach*. Toronto: Copp Clark Pitman, 1990 (291-312).

Lang, Ronald W. *The Politics of Drugs: The British and Canadian pharmaceutical industries and governments—A comparative study*. Farnborough: Saxon House, 1974.

Larson, J. and A.J. Baumgart. 'Overview: Use of the Political Process' in A.J. Baumgart and J. Larson, eds, *Canadian Nursing Faces the Future*. Toronto: C. Mosky, 1988.

Larson, Tord. 'Negotiating Identity: the Micmac of Nova Scotia' in Adrian Tanner, ed., *The Politics of Indianness*. St John's: Memorial University of Newfoundland, Institute for Social and Economic Research, 1983 (37-136).

Lawrie, N.J. 'The Canadian Construction Association: An Interest Group and its Environment'. Toronto: University of Toronto PhD dissertation, 1976.

Leclerc, Wilbrod. 'Negotiating Subsidies Away', *Policy Options* 8:7, 1987 (36-7).

Lemieux, F. 'Lobbying Plus... The CMA' in Paul Fox, ed., *Politics: Canada*. Toronto: McGraw-Hill, 1970.

Lemieux, V. 'Administration et publics: leur problème de communication', *Recherches sociographiques* XVI:3, 1973 (299-307).

Lenoski, J. Gerard. 'Interest Groups and the Canadian Legislative Process: A Case Study of the Canada Water Act'. Ottawa: Carleton University MA thesis, 1972.

Lies, David and James Lawrence. 'Red Tape and Fine Cheddar', *Harrowsmith* 3, 1978.

Lipsig-Mumme, Carla. 'The Web of Dependence: Quebec Unions in Politics Before 1976' in Alain G. Gagnon, *Quebec: State and Society*. Toronto: Methuen, 1984 (286-313).

Litvak, Isaiah. 'The Lobbying Strategies of Business Interest Groups' in James D. Fleck and Isaiah A. Litvak, eds, *Business Can Succeed! Understanding the Political Environment*. Toronto: Gage, 1984 (65-75).

————— and Christopher J. Maule. 'Interest-Group Tactics and the Politics of Foreign Investment: The Time-Reader's Digest Case Study', *Canadian Journal of Political Science* VII:4, 1974 (616-29).

The Lobby Digest: A Monthly Review of Lobbying Issues. Ottawa: Advocacy Research Centre Inc., 1989- .

The Lobby Monitor. Ottawa: Advocacy Research Associates. Bi-weekly, 1990- .

Logan, Robert K., ed. *The Way Ahead for Canada: A Paperback Referendum*. Toronto: Lester and Orpen, 1977.

Loney, Martin. 'A political economy of citizen participation' in Leo Panitch, ed., *The Canadian State: Political Economy and Political Power*. Toronto: University of Toronto Press, 1977 (446-72).

Long, J. Anthony. 'Political revitalization in Canadian native Indian societies', *Canadian Journal of Political Science* XXIII:4, 1990 (751-74).

————— and Menno Boldt. 'Conformity Trap', *Policy Options* Sept. 1984 (5-8).

McBride, Stephen. 'Public Policy as a Determinant of Interest Group Behaviour: The Canadian Labour Congress' Corporatist Initiative, 1976-1978', *Canadian Journal of Political Science* 16:4, 1983 (501-17).

McCalla, Douglas. 'The Commercial Policies of the Toronto Board of Trade, 1850-1860', *The Canadian Historical Review* 50, 1969 (51-67, 55).

MacDonald, A.A. *Policy Formation Process: Nova Scotia Dairy Marketing, 1933-1978*. Halifax: Dalhousie University Institute of Public Affairs, 1980.

Macdonald, Leslie T. 'Taxing Comprehensive Income: Power and Participation in Canadian Politics, 1962-1972'. Ottawa: Carleton University PhD dissertation, 1985.

Macdonald, R.D.S. 'Inshore Fishing Interests on the Atlantic Coast: Their Response to Extended Jurisdiction by Canada', *Marine Policy* July 1979 (171-89).

McGillivray, Don. 'Lobbying at Ottawa' in Paul Fox, ed., *Politics: Canada*. Toronto: McGraw-Hill, 1970 (163-72).

McKie, Craig. 'Some Views on Canadian Corporatism' in Christopher Beattie and Stewart Crysdale, eds, *Sociology Canada: Readings*, 2nd ed. Toronto: Butterworths, 1977 (226-40).

MacLeod, Alexandre. *Les commissions parlémentaire et les groupes de pression a l'Assemblée nationale du Québec: évaluation d'une tentative de politique consul-*

tative parlémentaire. Montréal: Université du Québec à Montréal. Departement de science politique. Notes de Recherche: Nos. 6-7, 1977.

McLeod, J.M. 'The Corporatist Strain in Canadian Politics: The Invisible Fist'. Paper. The Conference on Canadian Political Ideas, York University, 1978.

MacNaughton, Bruce and Allan Gregg. 'Interest Group Influence in the Canadian Parliament'. Paper. CPSA, June 1977.

McNiven, J.D. *Evaluation of the Public Participation Programme Embodied in the Prince Edward Island Development Plan*. Halifax: Dalhousie University Institute of Public Affairs, 1974.

McRae, Kenneth D. 'The plural society and the Western political tradition', *Canadian Journal of Political Science* 12:4, 1978 (675-88).

Mahon, Rianne. 'Canadian public policy: the unequal structure of representation' in Leo Panitch, ed., *The Canadian State: Political Economy and Political Power*. Toronto: University of Toronto Press, 1977 (164-98).

_____. *The Politics of Industrial Restructuring: Canadian Textiles*. Toronto: University of Toronto Press, 1984.

Majka, Christopher. 'Anti-environmentalism: Ideology on the Front Lines', *New Maritimes* June 1986 (12-).

Malvern, Paul. *Persuaders: Lobbying, Influence Peddling and Political Corruption in Canada*. Toronto: Methuen, 1985.

Manzer, Ronald. 'Selective Inducements and the Development of Pressure Groups: The Case of Canadian Teachers' Associations', *Canadian Journal of Economics and Political Science* II:1, 1969 (103-18).

Maroney, Heather Jon and Meg Luxton, eds. *Feminism and Political Economy*. Toronto: Methuen, 1987.

Martin, Andrew. 'The Politics of Employment and Welfare: National Policies and International Interdependence' in Keith Banting (Research Coordinator), *The State and Economic Interests*. Toronto: University of Toronto Press. The Collected Research Studies/ Royal Commission on Economic Union and Development Prospects for Canada. No. 32, 1986 (157-241).

Martin, Samuel A. *An Essential Grace: Funding Canada's Health Care, Education, Welfare, Religion and Culture*. Toronto: McClelland and Stewart, 1985.

May, Elizabeth. 'Canada's Moth War: Cape Breton Islanders Break a Multi-National', *New Ecologist*, July-Aug. 1978 (115-20).

_____. *Budworm Battles*. Halifax: Four East Publications, 1982.

Meen, Sharon Patricia. 'The Battle for the Sabbath: The Sabbatarian Lobby in Canada, 1890-1912'. Vancouver: University of British Columbia PhD dissertation, 1979.

Meisel, John. 'Cultivating the Bushgarden: Cultural Policy in Canada' in Milton C. Cummings, Jr and Richard S. Katz, eds, *The Patron State: Government and the Arts in Europe, North America and Japan*. N.Y.: Oxford University Press, 1987 (276-310).

_____. 'Recent Changes in Canadian Parties' in Hugh G. Thorburn, ed., *Party Politics in Canada*. Scarborough: Prentice-Hall, 1967 (33-54).

Ménard, Johanne. 'L'Institut des Artisans du Comté de Drummond, 1856-1890', *Recherches sociographiques* XVI:2, 1975 (207-19).

Menzies, June. 'Votes for Saskatchewan's Women' in Duff Spafford and Norman Ward, eds, *Politics in Saskatchewan*. Toronto: Longmans, 1968 (78-92).

Meynaud, Jean. 'Groupes de pression et politique gouvernementale au Québec' in André Bernard, ed., *Réflexions sur la politique au Québec*. Montreal: Sainte Marie, 1968 (69-96).

Milligan, Frank. 'The Canada Council as a public body', *Canadian Public Administration* 22:2, 1979 (269-89).

Milner, Henry. 'Quebec Educational Reform and the Protestant School Establishment' in Alain G. Gagnon, *Quebec: State and Society*. Toronto: Methuen, 1984 (410-26).

Mooney, George S. 'The Canadian Federation of Mayors and Municipalities: Its Role and Function', *Canadian Public Administration* 3, 1960 (82-92).

Mowat, Farley. *Rescue the Earth! Conversations with the Green Crusaders*. Toronto: McClelland and Stewart, 1991.

Munroe, Cathy and Jim Stewart. *Fishermen's Organizations in Nova Scotia — the Potential for Unification*. Halifax: School of Public Administration, 1981.

Munton, Don. *Groups and Governments in Canadian Foreign Policy*. Proceedings of a Conference. Ottawa, 1982. Toronto: Canadian Institute for International Affairs, 1985.

National Advisory Council on Voluntary Action. *People in Action: The report of the National Advisory Council on Voluntary Action to the Government of Canada*. Ottawa: Secretary of State, 1977.

Naylor, C. David. *Private Practice, Public Payment: Canadian Medicine and the Politics of Health Insurance, 1911-1986*. Montreal: McGill-Queen's University Press, 1986.

Nelson, J.G. 'Public participation in comprehensive resource and environmental management', *Science and Public Policy* Oct. 1982 (240-50).

Ng, Roxana. *The Politics of Community Services: Immigrant Women, Class and State*. Toronto: Garamond, 1988.

Niosi, Jorge. *Canadian Capitalism: A Study of Power in the Canadian Business Establishment*. Toronto: James Lorimer, 1981.

Nord, Douglas C. 'MPs and Senators as Middlemen: The special Joint Committee on Immigration Policy' in Clarke et al., *Parliament, Policy and Representation*. Toronto: Methuen, 1980 (181-94).

Olley, Robert E. 'The Canadian Consumer Movement: Basis and Objectives', *Canadian Business Review* 4:4, 1977 (26-29).

O'Neill, T.J. *Educator, Advocate and Critic: APEC's 25 Years*. Halifax: Atlantic Provinces Economic Council, 1979.

Ouellet, F. *Histoire de la Chambre de Commerce de Québec, 1809-1959*. Québec: Université Laval, 1959.

Ouellet, Lionel. *Sommaire vers un développement de la concertation et de la consultation au Québec*. Montréal: Les Cahiers de l'ENAP, 1 juin 1981 (5-31).

Pal, Leslie A. 'Official Language Minorities and the State: Dual Dynamics in a Single Policy Network' in Coleman and Skogstad, eds, *Policy Communities and Public Policy in Canada*. Toronto: Copp Clark Pitman, 1990 (170-90).

————. 'Relative Autonomy Revisited: The Origins of Canadian Unemployment Insurance', *Canadian Journal of Political Science* 19:1, 1986 (71-92).

_____. *State, Class, and Bureaucracy: Canadian Unemployment Insurance and Public Policy*. Montreal: McGill-Queen's University Press, 1988.

Palda, Kristian S. 'Does Canada's Election Act Impede Voters' Access to Information?', *Canadian Public Policy* XI:3, 1985 (533-42).

Paltiel, Khayyam Z. 'The changing environment and role of special interest groups', *Canadian Public Administration* 25:3, 1982 (198-210).

Panitch, Leo. 'The Development of Corporatism in Liberal Democracies', *Comparative Political Studies* XI:1, 1977 (61-90).

_____. 'Corporatism in Canada?' in Richard Schultz, Orest M. Kruhlak, John C. Terry, *The Canadian Political Process*. Toronto: Holt, Rinehart and Winston, 1979 (53-72).

_____. 'Corporatism: A Growth Industry Reaches the Monopoly Stage', *Canadian Journal of Political Science* 21:4, 1988 (813-18).

_____. 'Recent Theorizations of Corporatism', *British Journal of Sociology* XXXI:2, 1980 (159-88).

_____. 'The Tripartite Experience' in Keith Banting (Research Coordinator), *The State and Economic Interests*. Toronto: University of Toronto Press. The Collected Research Studies/ Royal Commission on Economic Union and Development Prospects for Canada. No. 32, 1986 (35-120).

Pappert, Anne. 'A New Life on Lease: The Tenant Fight for Rental Rights is Paying Off', *Financial Post Magazine* June 1985 (25).

Parke, Chris. 'The Setting of Minimum Wage Policy in the Maritimes'. Halifax: Dalhousie Institute of Public Affairs, 1980.

Parliamentary Government. 'Committees, MPs and Witnesses', *Parliamentary Government* 3, 1982 (4).

_____.'The Committee Track Record: A Limited Pay-off', *Parliamentary Government* 3, 1983 (4).

Phillips, Susan D. 'How Ottawa Blends: Shifting Government Relationships With Interest Groups' in Frances Abele, ed., *How Ottawa Spends 1991-91: The Politics of Fragmentation*. Ottawa: 1991 (183-213).

Pigott, Jean and G. Drewry. 'Parliament and hanging: further episodes in an undying saga', *Parliamentary Affairs* 27:3, 1974, (251-61).

Pinard, Yolande and Marie Lavigne, eds. *Travailleuse et féministes*. Montréal: Boréal Express, 1983.

Ponting, J.R. and R. Gibbins. *Out of Irrelevance: A Socio-political Introduction to Indian Affairs in Canada*. Toronto: Butterworths, 1980.

Pouyez, Christian M. 'A Canadian Social Science Lobby: Conditions and Prospects' in Baha Abu-Laban and Brendan Gail Rule, eds, *The Human Sciences: Their Contribution to Society and Future Research Needs*. Edmonton: University of Alberta Press, 1988 (257-63).

Presthus, Robert. *Elite Accommodations in Canadian Politics*. Toronto: Macmillan, 1973.

_____. *Elites in the Policy Process*. Toronto: Macmillan, 1974.

_____. 'Interest Groups and the Canadian Parliament: Activities, Interaction, Legitimacy, and Influence', *Canadian Journal of Political Science* IV:4, 1971 (444-60).

_____. 'Interest Groups and Lobbying: Canada and the United States', *The*

Annals of the American Academy of Political and Social Science 413, 1974 (44-57).

Pross, A. Paul. 'Canadian Pressure Groups in the 1970s: Their Role and their Relationship with the Public Service', *Canadian Public Administration* 18:1, 1975 (121-35).

_____. 'Comments on the Proposed *Lobbyists Registration Act*'. Canada. Parliament. House of Commons. Legislative Committee on Bill C-82. *Minutes of Proceedings and Evidence*. Ottawa: 19 April 1988.

_____. 'The Development of Professions in the Public Service: The Foresters in Ontario', *Canadian Public Administration* x:3, 1967 (376-404).

_____. 'Governing Under Pressure: Summary of Discussions', *Canadian Public Administration* 25:2, 1982 (170-83).

_____. 'Input Versus Withinput: Pressure Group Demands and Administrative Survival' in A. Paul Pross, ed., *Pressure Group Behaviour in Canadian Politics*. Toronto: McGraw-Hill, 1975 (148-72).

_____. 'Mobilizing Regional Concern: freight rates and political learning in the Canadian Maritimes' in Coleman and Jacek, eds, *Regionalism, Business Interests and Public Policy*. London: Sage, 1989 (173-200).

_____. 'Parliamentary Influence and the Diffusion of Power', *Canadian Journal of Political Science* xviii:2, 1985 (235-66).

_____, ed. *Pressure Group Behaviour in Canadian Politics*. Toronto: McGraw-Hill, 1975.

_____. 'Pressure Groups: Talking Chameleons' in Michael S. Whittington and Glen Williams, *Canadian Politics in the 1980s*. Toronto: Methuen, 1984 (287-311).

_____. 'The Rise of the Lobbying Issue in Canada: "The Business Card Bill" ' in Grant Jordan, *Commercial Lobbyists: Politics for Profit in Britain*. Aberdeen: Aberdeen University Press, 1991 (76-95).

_____. 'Space, Function and Interest: The Problem of Legitimacy in the Canadian State' in O.P. Dwivedi, ed., *The Administrative State in Canada*. Toronto: University of Toronto Press, 1982 (107-29).

_____. 'From System to Serendipity: The Practice and Study of Public Policy in the Trudeau Years', *Canadian Public Administration* 25:4, 1982 (520-44).

_____ and Susan MacCorquodale. *Economic Resurgence and the Constitutional Agenda: The Case of the East Coast Fisheries*. Kingston, Ontario: Queen's University Institute of Intergovernmental Relations, 1987.

_____. 'The State, Interests and Policy-Making in the East Coast Fishery' in Coleman and Skogstad, eds, *Policy Communities and Public Policy in Canada*. Toronto: Copp Clark Pitman, 1990 (34-58).

Public Interest Advocacy Centre. *PIAC: The First Ten Years, 1977-1987*. Ottawa: PIAC, 1988.

Pyrcz, Greg. 'Pressure Groups' in T.C. Pocklington, *Liberal Democracy in Canada and the United States: An Introduction to Politics and Government*. Toronto: Holt, Rinehart, 1985.

Québec. *La conférence au sommet Québec, 1982*, Rapport. Québec: Editeur officiel de Québec, 1982.

Radecki, Henry. 'Ethnic Voluntary Organizational Dynamics in Canada: A Report', *International Journal of Comparative Sociology* xvii:3/4, 1976 (275-84).

Rayner, Jeremy and David Perla. 'The Spruce Budworm Spray Controversy in Canada: Foresters' Perceptions of Power and Conflict in the Policy Process' in Marc L. Miller, Richard P. Gale, and Perry J. Brown, eds, *Social Science in Natural Resource Management Systems*. Boulder, CO.: Westview Press, 1987 (213-31).

Razack, Sherene. *Canadian Feminism and the Law: The Women's Legal Education Fund and the Pursuit of Equity*. Toronto: Second Story, 1991.

Redekop, John H. 'Mennonites and Politics in Canada and the United States', *Journal of Mennonite Studies* I:1, 1983.

Richardson, Boyce, ed. *Drum Beat: Anger and Renewal in Indian Country*. Toronto: Summerhill Press and Assembly of First Nations, 1990.

Riddell-Dixon, Elizabeth. *The Domestic Mosaic: Domestic Groups and Canadian Foreign Policy*. Toronto: Canadian Institute of International Affairs, 1985.

_____. 'State Autonomy and Canadian Foreign Policy; The Case of Canadian Deep Seabed Mining', *Canadian Journal of Political Science* 21:2, 1988 (297-317).

Robichaud, Jean-Bernard. *Voluntary Action: Provincial Policies and Practices*. Ottawa: Canadian Council on Social Development, 1985.

Ross, Arthur Larry. 'National Development and Sectional Politics: Social Conflict and the Rise of a Protest Movement'. Toronto: University of Toronto PhD dissertation, 1979.

Salter, Liora. 'Observations on the Politics of Assessment: The Captan Case', *Canadian Public Policy* XI:1, 1985 (64-76).

Sanders, Douglas. 'The Indian Lobby' in Keith Banting and Richard Simeon, *And No One Cheered: Federalism, Democracy and the Constitution Act*. Toronto: Methuen, 1983 (301-33).

Sawatsky, John. *The Insiders: Government, Business and the Lobbyists*. Toronto: McClelland and Stewart, 1987.

Savage, Donald C. 'Freedom of Information Legislation and the University Community', *CAUT Bulletin* (Canadian Association of University Teachers) Feb. 1985 (5-6).

Schmand, Jurgen, Roderick Hilliard, and Judith Clarkson, eds. *Acid Rain and Friendly Neighbours: The Policy Dispute Between Canada and the United States*. Durham, N.C.: Duke University Press, 1988.

Schwartz, Mildred A. *The Environment for Policy-Making in Canada and the United States*. Montreal: C.D. Howe Institute, 1981.

_____. 'Politics and Moral Causes in Canada and the United States', *Comparative Social Research* 4, 1981 (65-90).

_____. 'Group Basis of Politics' in John H. Redekop, ed., *Approaches to Canadian Politics*. Scarborough: Prentice-Hall, 1978.

Senior, Hereward. 'Orangeism in Ontario Politics, 1872-1896' in Donald Swainson, ed., *Oliver Mowat's Ontario*. Toronto: Macmillan, 1972 (136-53).

Sewell, John. *Up Against City Hall*. Toronto: James Lewis and Samuel, 1972.

Shackleton, Doris. *Power Town: Democracy Discarded*. Toronto: McClelland and Stewart, 1977.

Sharp, P.F. *Agrarian Revolt in Western Canada*. Minneapolis: University of Minnesota Press, 1948.

Sharpkaya, S. *Lobbying in Canada: Ways and Means*. Toronto: CCH, 1988.

Sheeha, Nancy M. 'National Pressure Groups and the Provincial Curriculum Policy: Temperance in Nova Scotia Schools, 1880-1930', *Canadian Journal of Education* 9:1, 1984 (73-88).

Simeon, Richard. *Federal-Provincial Diplomacy: The Making of Recent Policy in Canada*. Toronto: University of Toronto Press, 1973.

Simpson, Jeffrey. *Spoils of Power: The Politics of Patronage*. Toronto: Collins, 1988.

Sinclair, John Earl. 'Legislation and Lobbyists in Canada and the United States', Buffalo: State University of New York, PhD dissertation, 1973.

Skogstad, Grace. 'The Farm Policy Community and Public Policy in Ontario and Quebec' in William D. Coleman and Grace Skogstad, eds, *Policy Communities and Public Policy in Canada: A Structural Approach*. Toronto, Copp Clark Pitman, 1990 (59-90).

————. 'Interest Groups, Representation and Conflict Management in the Standing Committees of the House of Commons', *Canadian Journal of Political Science* XVIII:4, 1985 (739-73).

————. *The Politics of Agricultural Policy-Making in Canada*. Toronto: University of Toronto Press, 1987.

————. 'State Autonomy and Provincial Policy-Making: Potato Marketing in New Brunswick and Prince Edward Island', *Canadian Journal of Political Science* XX:3, 1987 (501-25).

Slayton, M. and Michael Trebilcock. *The Professions and Public Policy*. Toronto: University of Toronto Press, 1978.

Smiley, Donald V. 'The Managed Mosaic' in V. Nelles and A. Rotstein, eds, *Nationalism or Local Control*. Toronto: New Press, 1973 (69-78).

Smith, Larry. 'Getting Your Way With a Bureaucrat', *Canadian Business* Sept. 1980.

Smith, Jennifer. 'Representation and constitutional reform in Canada' in John Courtney, Peter MacKinnon, and David E. Smith, eds, *After Meech Lake: Lessons for the Future*. Saskatoon: Fifth House, 1991 (69-82).

Splane, Richard B. *Social Welfare in Ontario, 1791-1893*. Toronto: University of Toronto Press, 1965.

Sproule-Jones, Mark and Patricia L. Richards. 'Toward a Theory of the Regulated Environment', *Canadian Public Policy* X:3, 1984 (305-16).

Stairs, Denis. 'Public and Policy-Makers: The Domestic Environment of Canada's Foreign Policy Community', *International Journal* 1970-1 (221-48).

Stanbury, W.T. *Business-Government Relations in Canada*. Toronto: Methuen, 1986.

————. *Business Interests and the Reform of Canadian Competition Policy, 1971-75*. Toronto: Methuen, 1977.

————. 'Lobbying and Interest Group Representation in the Legislative Process', in W.A.W. Neilson and J.C. Macpherson, eds., *The Legislative Process in Canada*. Montreal: Institute for Research in Public Policy, 1978 (167-226).

————. 'Regulation and the Redistribution of Wealth', *Canadian Public Administration* 26:3, 1983 (378-401).

Stanfield, Robert L. 'The Fifth George C. Nowlan Lecture', Acadia University, 7 Feb. 1977 (mimeo).

Stasiulis, Daiva K. 'The Political Restructuring of Ethnic Community Action: A Reformulation', *Canadian Ethnic Studies* XII:3, 1980 (19-40).

Stelter, Gilbert A. and Alan F.J. Artibise, eds. *Power and Place: Canadian Urban Development in the North American Context*. Vancouver: University of British Columbia Press, 1986.

Strong-Boag, V. *The Parliament of Women: The National Council of Women of Canada, 1893-1929*. Ottawa: National Museum of Canada, 1976.

Swettenham, John and David Kealy. *Serving the State: A History of the Professional Institute of the Public Service of Canada, 1920-1970*. Ottawa: The Institute, 1970.

Switzer, K.B. 'Baron de Hirsch, the Jewish Colonization Association and Canada, 1891-1914'. PhD dissertation, University of London, 1982.

Tanguay, Brian. 'Concerted Action in Quebec, 1976-1983: Dialogue of the Deaf' in Alain G. Gagnon, *Quebec: State and Society*. Toronto: Methuen, 1984 (365-86).

Tanner, Adrian, ed. *The Politics of Indianness: Case Studies of Native Ethnopolitics in Canada*. St John's: Memorial University of Newfoundland, Institute of Social and Economic Research, 1983.

Taylor, Charles. 'Alternative Futures: Legitimacy, Identity and Alienation in Late Twentieth Century Canada' in Alan C. Cairns and Cynthia Williams, eds, *Constitutionalism, Citizenship and Society in Canada*. Toronto: University of Toronto Press, 1985 (183-230).

Taylor, D. Wayne. *Business and Government Relations: Partners in the 1990s*. Toronto: Gage, 1991.

_____ and Victor V. Murray. 'An Interpretive Understanding of the Non-fulfillment of Business-Government Relations', *Canadian Public Administration* 30:3, 1987 (421-32).

Taylor, Malcolm G. 'Quebec medicare: policy formulation in conflict and crisis', *Canadian Public Administration* 15:2, 1972 (211-50).

_____. 'The Role of the Medical Profession in the Formulation of Public Policy', *Canadian Journal of Economics and Political Science* XXVI:1, 1960 (108-27).

Teeter, Michael G. 'Check Your Anonymity at the Door: Times are Changing in the Lobbying Business', *Canadian Associations* Dec. 1985 (15-16).

Teichman, Judith. 'Businessmen and Politics in the Process of Economic Development: Argentina and Canada', *Canadian Journal of Political Science* XV:1, 1982 (47-66).

Therien, Jean-Philippe. 'Les organisations non-gouvernementales et la politique canadienne d'aide au développement', *Canadian Public Policy* XVII:1, 1991 (37-51).

Thompson, Fred and W.T. Stanbury. 'Looking Out for No.1: Incumbency and Interest Group Politics', *Canadian Public Policy* X:2, 1984 (239-45).

_____. *The Political Economy of Interest Groups in the Legislative Process in Canada*. Montreal: Institute for Research on Public Policy, 1979.

Thorburn, Hugh G. *Interest Groups and the Canadian Federal System*. Toronto: University of Toronto Press. Collected Research Studies/ Royal Commission on the Economic Union and Development Prospects for Canada. No. 69, 1985.

_____. *Planning and the Economy: Building Federal-Provincial Consensus*. Ottawa: Canadian Institute for Economic Policy, 1984.

_____. 'Pressure Groups in Canadian Politics: Recent Revisions of the Anti-Combines Legislation', *Canadian Journal of Economics and Political Science* XXX:2, 1964 (157-74).

Timms, Arthur M. 'The complementary interplay of charitable organizations and governments', *Canadian Associations* March 1986 (32-3).

Tollefson, Edwin A. 'The Medicare Dispute' in Duff Spafford and Norman Ward, eds, *Politics in Saskatchewan*. Toronto: Longmans, 1968 (238-79).

Toner, Glen and G. Bruce Doern. 'The Two Energy Crises and Canadian Oil and Gas Interest Groups: A Re-examination of Berry's Proposition', *Canadian Journal of Political Science* XIX:3, 1986 (467-95).

Torrance, Judy. 'The Response of Canadian Governments to Violence', *Canadian Journal of Political Science* X:3, 1977 (473-96).

————, *Public Violence in Canada, 1867-1982*. Montreal: McGill-Queen's University Press, 1986.

Trebilcock, M.J., R.S. Pritchard, D.G. Hartle, and D.N. Dewees. *The Choice of Governing Instrument*. Ottawa: Economic Council of Canada, 1982.

Townson, Frank W. 'The Labour Federations as Pressure Groups' in Donald C. Rowat, ed., *Provincial Government and Politics: Comparative Essays*. Ottawa: Department of Political Science, 1972 (495-520).

Trofimenkoff, Susan Mann and Alison Prentice, eds. *The Neglected Majority*. Toronto: McClelland and Stewart, 1977.

Tuohy, Carolyn. 'Institutions and Interests in the Occupational Health Arena: The Case of Quebec' in William D. Coleman and Grace Skogstad, eds, *Policy Communities and Public Policy in Canada: A Structural Approach*. Toronto: Copp Clark Pitman, 1990 (238-65).

Tuohy, Carolyn J. 'Pluralism and Corporatism in Ontario Medical Politics' in K.J. Rea and J.T. McLeod, eds, *Business and Government in Canada: Selected Readings* 2nd ed. Toronto: Methuen, 1976 (395-413).

————. 'Private Government, Property and Professionalism', *Canadian Journal of Political Science* IX:4, 1976 (668-81).

Verney, Douglas V. 'The Role of the Private Social Research Council of Canada in the Formation of Public Science Policy, 1968-1974', *Canadian Public Policy* I:1, 1975.

Versteeg, H. 'Practice Notes: Intervenor Funding — The Alachlor Review Board Experience', *Canadian Journal of Administrative Law and Practice* 3:1, 1989 (91-101).

Waterman, A.M.C. 'The Catholic Bishops and Canadian Public Policy', *Canadian Public Policy* IX:3, 1983 (374-82).

————. 'The Catholic Bishops and Canadian Public Policy: A Reply', *Canadian Public Policy* X:3, 1984 (338-9).

Weaver, Sally M. 'The Joint Cabinet/National Indian Brotherhood Committee: a unique experiment in pressure group relations', *Canadian Public Administration* 25:2, 1982 (211-39).

————. *Making Canadian Indian Policy*. Toronto: University of Toronto Press, 1981.

————. 'Federal Policy-Making for Métis and Non-status Indians in the Context of Native Policy', *Canadian Ethnic Studies* XVII:2, 1985 (80-102).

————. 'Political Representivity: Indigenous Minorities in Canada and Australia' in N. Dyck, ed., *Indigenous Peoples and the Nation State*. St John's: Memorial University Institute for Social and Economic Research, 1985 (113-50).

Weir, R.A. 'Federalism, Interest Groups and Parliamentary Government: The Canadian Medical Association', *Journal of Comparative Political Studies* XI:2, 1973 (159-75).

Weiss, Gilliam. 'As Women and as Citizens: Clubwomen in Vancouver, 1910-1918'. Vancouver: University of British Columbia PhD dissertation, 1983.

Welch, Susan. 'Dimensions of Political Participation in a Canadian Sample', *Canadian Journal of Political Science* VIII:4, 1975 (553-9).

West, James V. *Public Interest Groups and the Judicial Process in Canada: The Need for a More Realistic Jurisprudence*. Ottawa: Carleton University, Department of Political Science. Occasional Papers. No. 5, 1979.

White, Terrence H. 'Canadian Labour and International Unions in the Seventies' in S.D. Clark, J. Paul Grayson, and Linda M. Grayson, eds, *Prophecy and Protest: Social Movements in Twentieth-Century Canada*. Toronto: Gage, 1975 (288-305).

Wilkinson, B.W. 'The Catholic Bishops and Canadian Public Policy: A Comment', *Canadian Public Policy* X:1, 1981 (88-92).

Wilkinson, Paul Frank. 'Public Participation and Environmental Management: The Role of Public Participation and Public Interest Groups in Environmental Quality Management'. Toronto: University of Toronto PhD dissertation, 1974.

Williams, Cynthia. 'The Changing Nature of Citizen Rights' in Alan C. Cairns and Cynthia Williams, eds, *Constitutionalism, Citizenship and Society in Canada*. Toronto: University of Toronto Press, 1985 (99-132).

Williams, W. Blair. 'The Canadian Federation of Agriculture: The Problems of a General Political Interest Group'. Ottawa: Carleton University PhD dissertation, 1974.

Wilson, Barry. *Beyond the Harvest: Canadian Grain at the Crossroads*. Saskatoon: Western Producer Prairie Books, 1981.

————. *Farming the System: How Politicians and Producers Shape Canadian Agricultural Policy*. Saskatoon: Western Producer Prairie Books, 1990.

Wilson, Jeremy. 'Wilderness Politics in BC: The Business Dominated State and the Containment of Environmentalism' in William D. Coleman and Grace Skogstad, eds, *Policy Communities and Public Policy in Canada: A Structural Approach*. Toronto: Copp Clark Pitman, 1990 (141-69).

Wilson, Hon. Michael, Minister of Finance. *Technical notes to a bill amending the Income Tax Act and related statutes*. Ottawa: Department of Finance, Nov. 1985.

Winham, Gilbert R. 'Bureaucratic Politics and Canadian Trade Negotiation', *International Journal* 34:1, 1978-9 (64-89).

Yates, Charlotte. 'Labor and Lobbying: A Political Economy Approach' in William D. Coleman and Grace Skogstad, eds, *Policy Communities and Public Policy in Canada: A Structural Approach*. Toronto: Copp Clark Pitman, 1990 (266-90).

Young, Brian J. 'C. George McCullagh and the Leadership League', in Ramsay Cook, ed., *The Politics of Discontent*. Toronto: University of Toronto Press, 1967.

Young, R.A. 'Planning for Power: The New Brunswick Electric Power Commission in the 1950's', *Acadiensis* XII:1, 1982 (73-100).

Yudelman, David. *Canadian Mineral Policy Formulation: A Case Study of the Adversarial Process*. Kingston, Ontario: Queen's University, Centre for Resource Studies. Working Paper No. 30, 1984.

Index

Aberdeen, Lady, 31

Aboriginal groups, 2, 3, 7, 8, 66, 71, 92, 121, 125, 166, 179, 179n, 201, 206, 208; and Expo '86 protest, 3; and Haida land claims, 3; and Indian Act, 181; and lobbying of British Parliament concerning constitution, 181; and Northern Quebec Cree and James Bay projects, 181; and Oka confrontation, 181, 242

ACCESS ('A Citizens' Committee' for the Right to Public Information'), 133, 163

Action Canada Network, *see* Pro-Canada Network

Agriculture, Department of, 59, 69, 209

Alberta: and Environmental Trust, 138; and Leduc discovery, 125; *see also* Provincial governments

American Association for the Advancement of Women, 31

American Forestry Congress, 31

Amnesty International, 181

Anti-Corn Law League, 25

Arnold, Ron, 159

Assembly of First Nations, 7

Association of B.C. Professional Foresters, 110n

Atkinson, M.M., 229

Atlantic Provinces Chambers of Commerce (APCC), 128, 129, 173

Atlantic Provinces Economic Council (APEC), 128, 133, 247

Atlantic Provinces Transportation Commission (APTC), 128, 129

Atomic Energy of Canada Limited, 159, 204

Austria, 221

Automotive Parts Manufacturers' Association of Canada, 161-2

Bachrach, P., 233

Bagehot, Walter, 254-5

Baldwin, Ged, 163

Bank of Canada, 43, 55

Baratz, M., 233

B.C. Power, 50

Beck, J.M., 40, 56

Bennett, R.B., 21, 38, 180

Bentley, Arthur, 13, 230; *The Process of Government*, 13, 230

Berry, Jeffrey, 90, 91; survey of public interest groups, 83, 91

Bloc Québécois, 219, 247

Boards of Trade, 28, 29, 30, 38; Toronto Board of Trade, 28-9, 30; Vancouver Board of Trade, 35

Britain: decline of parliamentary institutions in, 251; and influence on Canadian interests, 25, 28, 29, 180; and influence on Canadian policy, 181; interest groups in, 25, 28, 29, 60, 163; and pluralist approaches to government, 221; and post-pluralist approaches to government, 235, 236; and spatial vs sectoral concerns, 245; and sub-governments, 237

British Columbia Employers' Council, 228

British National Union of Women's Suffrage Societies, 31

Brown, Douglas, 227

Bryce, R.B., 58

Bulloch, John F., 67, 77, 196, 197, 253

Bureaucracy: decline of legitimacy of, 76-77, 253, 254n; decline of public regard for, 74; and discipline in civil service, 59; and expansion of bureaucratic influence, 48, 54-5, 115; and 'mandarins', 41, 57-9, 64, 75, 115; and merit system in civil service, 76; and 'neutral competence', 51, 53, 58; and representativeness of civil service, 76; role of in policy development, 1, 3, 21, 24, 40-7, 83; and sponsorship of interest groups, 45-6; and structure and mores of civil service, 57-60; and value of interest groups to, 42-7, 142-3

LeBlanc, Romeo, 46, 135
Leman, Christopher, 36
Lemieux, Vincent, 44
Liberal Party of Canada, 57, 163, 225, 247, 256, 258
Litvak, Isaiah, 166
Lobbyists Registration Act, 260-1
Lobbying: costs of, 203-4; techniques of, 142, 150-3, 196-7
Lortie, Pierre, 174
Lowi, Theodore, 94, 99, 99n, 231, 232, 241; *The End of Liberalism*, 231; *The Politics of Disorder*, 99n
Lyons, W.E., 247n

McClure, Dr George, 129
McCullagh, George, 115n
Macdonald, Angus L., 44
MacDonald, Flora, 75
Machinery and Equipment Manufacturers' Association of Canada, 138
McIlraith, George, 58
McInness, Thomas R., 35
MacIver, R.M., 230
Mackenzie Valley Pipeline issue, 91, 166; and assistance to intervening groups, 91
Mackintosh, W.A., 41, 58, 58n
MacLean, A.K., 45
Manzer, Ronald, 7
Maritime Boards of Trade, 128
Maritime Fishermen's Union, 208
Maritime Lumber Bureau, 129
Maritime Rights Movement, 128
Mather, Barry, 258
Mechanics' Institutes, 29; Drummond County Mechanics' Institute and Library Association, 26-7
Medhurst, Justice Donald, 173-4
Media Foundation, 167
Meech Lake Accord, 175, 179, 268
Meisel, John, 1
Members of Parliament: elected as legislative advocates, 171-2; importance of to interest groups, 34-5, 36, 60-4 (tables 3-1, 3-2), 77-8, 146-7, 171-2
Meynaud, J., 193
Mines and Technical Surveys, Department of, 198
Moe, Terry M., 191, 192; survey of associations and inducements for joining, 192; theory of selective inducements and group goals, 191

Monroe, Denis, 131-2
Morrison, Ian, 210n
Mount Royal Club (Montreal), 38
Mowat, Farley, 168n
Mowat, Sir Oliver, 35
Mulroney, Brian, government of, 2, 79, 172, 179n, 228, 229, 258, 265

National Action Committee on the Status of Women, 209
National Cancer Institute, 138
National Citizens' Coalition, 173, 182
National Club (Toronto), 38
National Coalition of Voluntary Organizations, 210n
National Council of Women, 31
National Defence, Department of, 127
National Economic Conference (1985), 228-9
National Energy Board, 195
National Farmers' Union, 117, 118, 154, 209
National Indian Brotherhood, 7, 201
National Trust (Britain), 138
Native groups, *see* Aboriginal groups
Networks, 119-20, 128; defined, 119; distinguished from policy communities, 119-29
Neville, Bill, 101
New Brunswick, 30n; and fishing industry, 131; and forest industry, 49, 50; interest groups in, 33; *see also* Provincial governments
New Democratic Party (NDP), 40, 172, 247, 256, 258
Newfoundland: and fishing industry, 131; and Hibernia oil field, 125
Nord, Douglas C., 79, 80
Nova Scotia, and forest industry, 49-50, 129; interest groups in, 33, 40, 56; merchants' lobby, 20, 29; and Voluntary Planning Board, 128; *see also* Provincial governments
Nova Scotia Fishermen's Association (NSFA), 208
Nova Scotia Municipal Board, 267n

Oberle, Frank, 167
Oil Producers' Association of Canada, 195
Olson, Mancur, 188, 231; *The Logic of Collective Action*, 188; theory of collective and selective benefits, 188-91, 192
Ontario: and environmental movement, 138; and forest industry, 32-3, 36-7, 49, 50, 125;

Trudeau, Pierre Elliott, 58n, 75, 210n, 226, 227; Trudeau government, 3, 45, 64, 124, 144, 172, 226, 229, 240
Truman, David B., 13, 67, 187; *The Governmental Process*, 13

Union of Nova Scotia Municipalities, 56, 132, 202
United Farmers of Alberta, 225
United Nations Human Rights Committee, 181
United States: and access of pressure groups to policy process, 91; and difference in party system, 174-5; and funding for pressure groups, 265; and influence on Canadian interests, 180; and influence on Canadian policy, 124, 181; and lobbying, 56, 166, 171, 180; and pluralist approaches to government, 221, 224, 231-2; and Political Action Committees (PACs), 174; and post-pluralism, 236; pressure groups

in, 16, 28, 29, 33, 57, 60, 62, 167; and sub-governments, 233-4; and technostructure, 53; and use of courts, 184
Urban Affairs, Ministry of State for, 45, 127

Veterans' Affairs, Department of, 59

Ward, Norman, 35n
Wertheimer, Fred, 174
Whitaker, R., 224
Wiener, Celine, 51
Wilson, Michael, 136
Women's Christian Temperance Union (WCTU), 32
Women's Educational Legal Education and Action Fund (LEAF), 184
Women's movement, 2, 8, 31, 66, 67, 90, 92, 94, 96-7, 106, 171, 179, 182, 206, 208; and suffrage movement, 31, 156-7

York Club (Toronto), 38